coding

The Handbook for Information Technology

coding

The Handbook for Information Technology

Written by

Knute Axelson, Mary Bellino, Dave Harper, Dave Iffland, Dan Ignat, Greg Kick, Paul Landes, Paul Millar, Sonny Mounicou, Greg Munger, Travis Pettijohn, Mike Shelton, Murli Subramany, Mike VanDeWoestyne, Srinivasa Yeramati

Blue Line Press – Chicago

blpress.com

Coding: The Handbook for Information Technology

by Knute Axelson, Mary Bellino, Dave Harper, Dave Iffland, Dan Ignat, Greg Kick, Paul Landes, Paul Millar, Sonny Mounicou, Greg Munger, Travis Pettijohn, Mike Shelton, Murli Subramany, Mike VanDeWoestyne, Srinivasa Yeramati

Printed in the United States of America

Published by Blue Line Press, Inc., 2127 W. Homer St, Chicago, IL 60647

http://www.blpress.com

ISBN: 0-9766279-0-6

green press INITIATIVE

Blue Line Press has elected to print this title on 50% postconsumer recycled paper. As a result we have saved the following resources:

5.7 trees
270 lbs of solid waste
2,447 gallons of water
530 lbs of net greenhouse gases
984 kW hours of electricity

Blue Line Press is a member of the Green Press Initiative, a nonprofit program dedicated to supporting publishers in their efforts to reduce their use of fiber sourced from endangered forests. For more, visit www.greenpressinitiative.org.

Contents

About the Authors

Knute Axelson is an independent Java contractor currently working in the Chicago area. He received his BS from the University of Illinois, and lives in Northbrook, IL with his wife and son. Knute also runs a small real estate brokerage, Axelson Realty. Knute is the author of the Java chapter, and the technical editor of the XML chapter. You can contact him at kaxelson@blpress.com.

Mary Bellino is a Senior Technical Team Lead at SBC in Hoffman Estates, IL. She received her Bachelor of Music degree in Vocal Performance from Nazareth College in Rochester, NY in 1993. She has been working in IT since 1997 as a programmer/consultant with an interest in SQL and efficient database design. Mary enjoys traveling, music, gardening, home improvement projects and reading. She lives in Carol Stream, IL with her son, Matthew. Mary is the author of the DB2 chapter, and she can be reached at mbellino@blpress.com.

Dave Harper is currently working as a technical architect for SBC designing modifications to the billing system. He started his career as an electrical engineer designing systems for spacecraft, but in 1993 he found software to be a more responsive canvas for artistic creation. Dave currently lives in Lake in the Hills, IL. His hobbies pretty much center around having two small children these days. Not as glamorous as the old days, but infinitely more rewarding! Dave is the author of the Unix chapter, as well as the technical editor of the C++ chapter, and can be reached at dharper@blpress.com.

David Iffland is a Research Programmer at the University of Illinois at Urbana-Champaign where he founded a custom software development team specializing in .NET. He received his BS in Computer Engineering from the University of Illinois in 1999. David has recently started a custom home theater installation business at www.avindigo.com. He is single for now living in Savoy, IL with his dog Emma. David is the author of the VB.NET chapter, and can be contacted at diffland@blpress.com.

Dan Ignat was born in Bucharest, Romania, and grew up in New York City. He received his BA in Computer Science and Mathematics from the University of Virginia, and his MS in Computer Science from the University of Pennsylvania. Dan is currently an independent contractor working on J2EE projects in Chicago, where he will live with his wife after their wedding in Greece. His interests include adrenaline and the arts. Dan is the author of the JavaServer Pages chapter, and may be contacted at dignat@blpress.com.

Greg Kick is a Computer Science major at UCLA. He has worked as an assistant instructor in Java and C++ and is working for Accenture. Greg is the author of the Mac OS X chapter, and can be reached at gkick@blpress.com.

Paul Landes is the president of Zenos Solutions (http://zenos-solutions.com), a company that specializes in EAI software architecture and development. Zenos Solutions also provides open systems consulting, more specifically, Java open source projects, GNU software, and GNU/Linux operating systems. He currently lives in Chicago with his wife and son. He received a Bachelor of Science from the University of North Texas. Paul is the author of the Linux and Perl chapters, and he can be contacted at plandes@blpress.com.

Paul Millar is an independent consultant in Chicago specializing in Java and EAI solutions. He has a BS in Electrical Engineering from the University of Illinois, and he lives with his wife in Chicago. Paul is the author of the SQL Server chapter as well as the technical editor of the Oracle chapter. He can be reached at pmillar@blpress.com.

Sonny Mounicou is a Sr. Oracle DBA in Memphis, Tennessee. He currently works at Accredo Health Inc. Sonny received his BBA from the University of Mississippi. He lives with his wife Jennifer in Olive Branch, Mississippi. He enjoys programming, performance tuning large databases, and lately, photography. Sonny is the author of the Oracle chapter, and he can be reached at smounicou@blpress.com.

Greg Munger has BFA from Eastern Michigan University, and an MS in computer science from the University of Michigan. He enjoys programming in Java, and painting semi-abstract paintings in oil. Greg has worked at a number of companies, from very large (IBM) to very small (now out of business). He is currently a developer at TransUnion in Chicago. Greg is the author of the XML chapter. He lives in Chesterton, Indiana, and can be reached at gmunger@blpress.com.

Travis Pettijohn received his BS in Computer Engineering from the University of Illinois at Urbana-Champaign. He has done .NET Development for Departmental Services at the University, and is currently a consultant at Avanade. Travis enjoys the outdoors, running and music, as well as a good book or movie. He lives in Chicago, and his personal website and blog may be found at www.pettijohn.com. Travis is the author of the C#, ASP.NET, and PHP chapters, and he can be reached at tpettijohn@blpress.com.

Mike Shelton is an IT administrator at International Paper in Memphis, TN. He received his BA in History from the Christian Brothers University in Memphis. He lives in Arlington, TN with his wife Lauren and his cats. Mike is the author of the Windows and HTML chapters, and can be reached at mshelton@blpress.com.

Murli Subramany is a Senior Consultant for Deloitte Consulting. Over the past ten years, he has worked in several technical areas with projects in India, Switzerland, Germany and the United Arab Emirates. He currently focuses on Enterprise Business Integration. He received his Bachelor's degree from Bombay University in Computer Engineering. Murli works out of Alexandria, Virginia, where he lives with his wife, Aarti. He is the author of the C++ chapter, and can be reached at msubramany@blpress.com.

Mike VanDeWoestyne completed his undergraduate studies at the University of Illinois in Champaign-Urbana and post graduate studies at DePaul University. He works in the telecommunications industry doing mainframe development and most recently doing web development for the industry's video on demand via fiber project. Mike enjoys dining and traveling with his wife, spending time with family and friends, sports, and the outdoors. Mike is the author of the COBOL chapter. Reach him at mvandewoestyne@blpress.com.

Srinivasa Yeramati is a software professional with over 10 years of IT experience. His expertise includes e-commerce technologies, Java, Microsoft technologies as well as Oracle. He earned his Masters of Engineering at M.S.University, India. He works in Chicago area as a development lead managing a team of software developers. Srini lives in Carpentersville, IL, with his wife, Srilatha and sons Sivaram and SatyaDev. Srini is the author of the VBScript and JavaScript chapters. Reach him at syeramati@blpress.com.

Tech Editors

Matthew Keane is a Technical Lead for WhittmanHart Inc. located in Chicago. He has experience with DB2 programming, as a Senior Oracle DBA, and more recently Java and PHP/MySQL programming. Matt is the technical editor for the DB2 chapter, and you can reach him at mkeane@blpress.com.

John Loesel is a software developer for the Hartford Technology Services Company. He has a BA degree in Economics and Computer Analysis from Valparaiso and a Master of Music degree from Depaul University. John is the technical editor of the Java chapter. Reach him at jloesel@blpress.com.

Jack Minster is a web applications developer at Playboy Enterprises, Inc. in Chicago working with ColdFusion MX 7, Flex 1.5, Oracle 10g, and other Macromedia products. Jack is the technical editor of the HTML and JavaScript chapters. Reach him at jminster@blpress.com.

Scot Mitchell is a freelance writer, trainer, and consultant with ASP.NET expertise. His most recent book is Create Your Own Website (Using What You Already Know) (Sams). Scott is the technical editor of the C#, VB.NET, and ASP.NET chapters. You can reach him at smitchell@blpress.com.

Daniel Read is a software developer/architect and also editor and publisher of the web-based publication developer.* Magazine (DeveloperDotStar.com), winner of the Software Development Productivity Award. Dan is the technical editor of the VBScript chapter, and can be reached at dread@blpress.com.

Ray Rankins is a database designer, administrator, and president of Gotham Consulting Services (gothamconsulting.com). His most recent books include Microsoft SQL Server 2000 Unleashed (Sams). Ray is the technical editor of the SQL Server chapter. He can be reached at rrankins@blpress.com.

Debra Riemersma is a recent MBA graduate of the Tepper School of Business at Carnegie Mellon University in Pittsburgh, PA. She is an associate at a management consulting firm in New York City. Debbie is the technical editor of the Windows chapter, and you can reach her at driemersma@blpress.com.

David Sklar is an independent software development and strategic technology consultant in New York. His has authored several PHP books, including his most recent, Learning PHP 5 (O'Reilly). He is the technical editor ofthe PHP chapter, and you can reach him at dsklar@blpress.com.

Ron Smith consults for clients developing J2EE-based enterprise applications. He develops software products within his company, RPS Technologies (www.rpstechnologies.net), and is launching topico.com. Ron is the technical editor of the Perl chapter, and you can contact at rsmith@blpress.com.

Tim Tagge is a project leader at JP Morgan Chase in Chicago. His expertise is in Java and JSPs, and J2EE applications using Struts technology. His software company is Weave The People (weavethepeople.com). Tim is the technical editor of the JSP chapter, and you can reach him at ttagge@blpress.com.

Padma Vemulakonda is a Sr. Systems Analyst in Northbrook, IL, working on Oracle Apps and Optio. She got her M.S (CS) from NIU and her expertise includes client server and web based technologies. Padma is the technical editor of the COBOL chapter. Contact her at pvemulakonda@blpress.com.

Matt Verratti is a one man IT department for Impact Productions, a graphic design and digital pre-press company in IL. He is currently developing software for Microsoft's .NET framework in his spare time. Matt is the technical editor of the MAC OS X chapter, and can be reached at mverratti@blpress.com.

Brian Ward is a consultant and instructor in San Francisco. He is the author of the Linux Kernel-HOWTO, though he has since stopped updating it. His most recent book is How Linux Works (No Starch Press). Brian lives in San Francisco and is the technical editor of the Linux chapter.

Wie Yang has over ten years of experience in software development. He has developed client/server and real-time multi-threaded software in C++/C under Unix, Windows and RTOS for Tellabs and SBC. Wei is the technical editor of the Unix chapter, and you can reach him at wyang@blpress.com.

Production Editors

Kendra Pohl is the publications editor for the State Universities Retirement System of Illinois, where she is responsible for member guides, newsletters, Web site content, forms, and more. She received her BA in English with a minor in writing from Illinois State University. Kendra currently resides in Savoy, Illinois, and is the copyeditor for this book. She can be reached at kpohl@blpress.com.

Dani Schooley is a supply chain manager at Abbott Laboratories in Lake Bluff, IL. She recently moved to the Andersonville neighborhood of Chicago, after living in Amsterdam for two years. Dani enjoys correcting other people's punctuation and grammar mistakes in her spare time. You can reach her at dschooley@blpress.com.

Introduction

Consider the following situation: You're at the airport ready to board your plane when you get a phone call – a production process is failing. There is a shell script that needs to be modified. The suspect line needs to be commented out so that no further damage is done until the morning. Somebody on the other end of the phone has access to the file, but hasn't the slightest idea of what to do, and you're not a UNIX expert. So what do you do?

You relax, reach into your bag, pull out your Handbook, turn to the UNIX chapter, and relay to your counterpart on the phone the following commands:

1. $vi processOrders.sh
2. Press Escape to enter Command mode, navigate to the start of the failing line.
3. Press i to enter Edit mode, and type a # to comment that line out.
4. Press Escape again, then :wq to save and quit.

Crisis averted…until tomorrow at least. Maybe you are already familiar with these vi commands. But suppose instead of a shell script, you needed to edit a C# or Java file and quickly recompile? Or suppose the problem was a failing trigger in an Oracle database, and you needed to disable that trigger? Now suppose it was a DB2 database trigger? Or maybe it was a C++ file, or a JavaScript error, or a PHP page that was failing to display? What if it was a COBOL program?

Technology is evolving faster today than ever before, and in the IT field you need to be on top of a broad range of technologies. The technology you are most familiar with no longer exists in a vacuum. If you're a Java programmer, you more than likely have a pretty good handle on the Java language. You might need help, however, when your program needs to access a database; or when you're working with XML and Web Services; or when you need to port an existing C++ program to Java; or Java to C#.

There is a lot to learn out there in the IT world, besides your bread-and-butter technology. This book was written to help you keep it all straight.

Fifteen bright IT professionals got together and each wrote a chapter or two summarizing the technologies they specialize in. We added fourteen additional specialists to edit the content technically, making sure the most important aspects were covered, and the less important verbiage was left out. The result, we feel, is a book you can use every day, regardless of what technology you define yourself by.

How to Use This Book

There are several ways to get the most value out of this book. When you have a question about a topic, flip to the chapter of the book dedicated to that topic – there is a good chance it's in here. If you're looking at a JavaScript program and need to modify it to return only the first 3 letters of a city instead of the entire city name, flip to the Built-In Objects section of the JavaScript chapter, and find that there is a substring() function on the String object. You can also use the index and find out very quickly that the Built-In Objects section begins on page 311.

You may find it useful to read a chapter, start to finish. You may be a web developer and a PERL programmer, but perhaps you never got around to learning COBOL. You can flip to the COBOL chapter, read through the sample program, the definitions and explanations of terms, and in 30 minutes you'll be comfortable navigating a real COBOL program.

You can apply this same concept to every chapter in the book that you are not familiar with, and in a short time, you'll become familiar. This is ideal for managers or someone looking for a quick overview of a technology.

Organization

Each chapter begins with a few paragraphs discussing the background of the technology, followed by a page of bullet points. Here you'll find quick answers to common questions, so it's a great place to start looking for answers. Every chapter starts with the basics of the technology and progresses into more advanced topics, packed with useful examples. The last section of each chapter looks at the future of the technology, and may recommend resources for further information.

The first six chapters of the book cover programming languages, and the next seven chapters review web and scripting technologies. The third group of chapters is dedicated to operating systems, and the last section of chapters covers popular database technologies.

Chapter 1

Java

Java is a class-based, object-oriented programming language. Designed with portability in mind, its slogan is "write once, run anywhere." Java is a strongly typed language featuring automatic garbage collection and support for threading.

The language, owned and maintained by Sun Microsystems, has quickly become one of the most widely used programming languages for business and Internet applications. Originated by a small group of developers at Sun in the early 1990s, it became available for download in May of 1995. With the release of version 1.2, Sun's Java platform became known as the Java 2 platform.

There are three "flavors" of Java currently available. These are known as Java 2 Micro Edition (J2ME), Java 2 Standard Edition (J2SE), and Java 2 Enterprise Edition (J2EE). Java 2 Micro Edition is intended for low memory or embedded applications commonly found in small handheld devices such as PDAs or cell phones. Certain features of the standard Java language are either absent or limited in J2ME. Java 2 Standard Edition is the full-featured, core Java language. J2SE is used for Java application development on most platforms. Java 2 Enterprise Edition builds on top of J2SE and provides a framework and server specification for developing Java Internet applications.

Though much of this chapter will apply to all Java editions, the main focus will be on J2SE as it represents the core Java language from which the other editions are derived. A software development kit (SDK) for J2SE is available as a free download from Sun and is highly recommended if you plan on learning Java or doing any Java development. To obtain the SDK, go to http://java.sun.com.

Fast Facts

- Java is case sensitive. For example, myClass is different from MyClass.
- A Java source file must end with the .java extension. The compiled version of this file will have the same name, but will end with the .class extension.
- A Java program is made up of classes and interfaces, which are often grouped together into packages.
- Comments can appear either between /* and */ (for comments that may span multiple lines), between /** and */ (for javadoc comments), or after // (for single-line comments).
- Each statement must end with a semicolon (;).
- All Java statements, with the exception of package and import statements, must occur within the context of a class or interface.
- There may be only one top-level (not contained in another class), public class or interface in a file, and the name of that class or interface must be the same as the name of the file in which it is contained, not including the .java extension. That class may contain a main() method having the following signature:

  ```
  public static void main(String args[])
  ```
- Garbage collection occurs automatically in Java.
- Use System.out.println("your string here") to print to the console.
- Using the Java Development Kit (JDK), a class is compiled with the Java compiler (javac). A class is executed with the Java application launcher (java).
- To execute a class that is part of a package from the command line, you must specify the fully-qualified class name (i.e. the package name followed by the class name). For example, to execute a class named MyClass that is part of a package com.myjava.programs, use this command:

  ```
  java com.myjava.programs.MyClass
  ```
- When *compiling* a Java program, all classes and interfaces directly referenced by a given class must reside at a location specified in the classpath. When *running* a Java program, all classes and interfaces directly or indirectly referenced by a given class must reside at a location specified in the classpath.

Sample Java Program

The text below represents a single class file. A complete Java application may actually contain many interrelated and supporting classes. The following program is a working example. Running this program with no arguments will produce a single line of output containing the text: "Hello, World!"

```
// package declaration
package sample;

// import statements
import java.util.ArrayList;
import java.util.Arrays;
import java.util.Iterator;
import java.util.List;

// class declaration
public class HelloWorldSample extends Sample {
  // constructor
  public HelloWorldSample() {
    super(new String[] {"Hello, World!"});
  }

  // a public method
  public String getListAsString() {
    String s = new String();
    for (Iterator i = getStringList().iterator(); i.hasNext(); ) {
      s += (String)i.next() + getDelimiter(i);
    }
    return s;
  }

  // a private method
  private String getDelimiter(Iterator i) {
    return i.hasNext() ? "," : "";
  }

  // main method
  public static void main(String[] args) {
    HelloWorldSample sample = new HelloWorldSample();
```

```
      System.out.println(sample.getListAsString());
    }
  }

  // class declaration
  class Sample {
    // field
    private List stringList;

    // constructor
    public Sample(String[] stringArray) {
      stringList = new ArrayList();
      stringList.addAll(Arrays.asList(stringArray));
    }

    // a public method
    public List getStringList() {
      return stringList;
    }
  }
```

Main Components of a Java Program

Java is an object-oriented language. If you have not worked with object-oriented languages in the past, you may discover that your idea of what a program is must change. A Java program consists of a set of classes and interfaces that work together to perform a desired set of operations. These classes and interfaces will usually be spread out over many source files. In fact, it is often the case that you will have a separate file for each class or interface.

At least one of the classes included in your program must contain a method with the following signature: `public static void main(String[])`. A method having this signature is an *entry point* into your Java program. In other words, when a Java program is run, processing must begin with the invocation of a method having this signature.

Package Declarations

The `package` declaration is not required. If present, the class becomes part of the specified package, and if not present, the class becomes part of the default package. The package name must correspond to the directory subtree in which your source code is stored.

For example, a class file that belongs to the package com.myhome.mycouch will be stored in the following directory subtree: com/myhome/mycouch. The root of this directory subtree can be anywhere in the file system. Sun Java coding conventions dictate that package names should be all lowercase, though this is not a requirement of the language. It is also common practice to use the domain name of your company or organization in reverse order as a prefix for package names. Thus, if you were working for a company called Cool Widgets, Inc., with a domain name of coolwidgets.com, you would prefix your package names with com.coolwidgets.

Import Statements

Import statements are also not required. They allow classes that belong to other packages to be referenced in the current class file without having to be fully qualified. Import statements can end with a wildcard (*) character to indicate that all classes and interfaces contained in the specified package should be imported. When an import statement for a particular class is not included, that class can still be referenced through its fully qualified name. For example, com.coolwidgets.Widget is the fully qualified representation of the Widget class in the com.coolwidgets package. If the class com.coolwidgets.Widget were included at the top of the class file, the com.coolwidgets.Widget class could be referenced simply as Widget rather than by its fully qualified name. Please note that if you import two classes with the same name that reside in different packages, the compiler will require you to fully qualify all references for at least one of the classes to avoid ambiguity.

Classes

A class declaration is required. Any number of classes may be declared within a given source file; however, only one top-level class (a class not contained with another class) may be declared to be public. The name of the source file must be the name of the file's public class followed by the .java extension. For example, a Java source file containing a public class called RequestProcessor must be named RequestProcessor.java. A class may inherit from a single parent class using the extends keyword or implement one or more interfaces using the implements keyword. Each class is made up of fields, methods, and, in some cases, other classes.

Fields

A field is a variable declared at the class level (as opposed to a variable declared inside a method). Any number of fields may be declared inside a class. A field may be referenced by all methods of the class, and may, depending on the access modifiers with which it is declared, also be referenced by clients or subclasses of the class.

Constructors

A constructor is a special method having the same name as the class to which it belongs. No return value is declared for a constructor. A constructor is used to initialize a new instance of a class. A class may define any number of overloaded constructors, each having a unique ordered list of argument types. If a constructor is not specified, a default constructor is provided by the compiler. The default constructor takes no arguments and calls the constructor of the parent class.

Methods

The work of a program is done in its methods. A method may take arguments and may return a value. If a method does not return a value, it must be declared to return void. Multiple overloaded methods with the same name may exist, as long as each has a unique ordered list of argument types. Please note that overloaded methods are not distinguished based on return type alone.

Basics of Java

There are three main steps to utilizing the Java language and platform. First, source code is written using any text editor and the files saved with a .java extension. Next, the files must be compiled into bytecode using a Java compiler. A Java compiler will output a file with the same name as the source file, but with a .class extension in place of the .java extension. Finally, the compiled code can be executed inside a Java Virtual Machine (JVM). The JVM, which is usually a piece of software, serves to make the compiled bytecode independent of any particular hardware platform. These steps will be elaborated in the sections that follow.

Writing a Java Program

A Java program is comprised of one or more Java source files. A Java source file is a simple text file with the .java extension. Each Java source file must contain exactly one top-level class declared with the public modifier. The name of the Java source file must correlate with the name of the single top-level, public class declared in the source file. The sections that follow describe the various components that can be contained within a Java source file and how to put them together.

Types

Java is a strictly-typed language. All variables must be declared, and variables must be used in ways that conform to specified interfaces and declarations. The following sections explore the built-in types available in Java and how to create your own types.

Primitive Types

The following is a list of the primitive types built into the Java language:

boolean, byte, short, int, long, char, float, double

Each primitive type takes up a predetermined amount of memory, and any variable of one of these types points directly to the memory location where the value is stored. Primitive types may be used for fields and local variables.

Reference Types

Any type that is not a primitive type is a reference type. Any variable declared to be of a reference type points to a location is memory that holds, not the value of the variable, but a reference to another memory location at which the actual value is held. Reference types fall into three categories: arrays, classes, and interfaces.

Arrays

An array in Java can be composed of primitive elements or reference elements (including other arrays). When declaring an array, you must specify its specific type, which is determined by the type of the elements it will hold. That means that the type "array of integers" (i.e. int[]) is a different type than the type "array of Objects" (i.e. Object[]) or "array of floats" (i.e. float[]).

Classes

Classes, which are blueprints for the construction of objects, are what the Java language is all about. Classes (and interfaces) differ from arrays in that, in addition to simply declaring a variable to be of a particular class type, you can also define an entirely new class type. Declaring a variable of a class type is exactly like declaring any other variable. When defining a new class, you must specify the data that will be contained in the class (i.e. the fields or member variables of the class) and the operations of the class (i.e. the methods of the class).

Interfaces

Interfaces bear some similarity to classes. You can define new interfaces and declare variables to be of a particular interface type. Interfaces differ from classes in that interfaces cannot be instantiated. An interface defines a *contract* between Java classes and can also specify static fields. Interfaces specify a set of abstract methods than must be implemented by any implementing class.

Strings

A string in Java is not a primitive data type, but rather an instance of the java.lang.String class. A constant string expression must always be enclosed in double quotes (""). When the compiler encounters a value in quotes, it creates a new String object containing this value. Both of the following statements create new String objects:

```
String myString = new String("hello");
String yourString = "hello";
```

Since strings are actually objects, care must be taken when comparing string values. Using the double equal sign (==), which is used to check for equivalent object references, will not necessarily yield the expected result. When in doubt, use the equals() method, which checks for equivalent object values:

```
myString.equals(yourString)
```

Note that a double quote within a string must be preceded by a backslash (\):

```
String myString = “This is \"my string\"”;
```

Declaring Variables

All Java variables must be declared before they can be used. If you fail to declare a variable, your code will not compile. Whenever a variable is declared, its type must be specified. A variable's type may never change, and only values compatible with a variable's type may be assigned to that variable. Variable declarations follow the following format:

```
[modifiers] variable_type variable_name [= initial_variable_value];
```

Here are some examples of variable declarations:

```
private int numberOfAttempts = 0;
public String[] names;
private static FileInputStream input = new FileInputStream(“myfile.txt”);
private List songs;
```

Java variables fall into four main categories: (1) instance variables, (2) class variables, (3) local variables, and (4) constants.

Instance Variables

Instance variables are fields, which means that they are declared at the class level (i.e. directly enclosed within a class, rather than a method). Instance variables are associated with a particular instance of a class. Each time a new object of a particular class type is instantiated, new copies of all instance variables declared in that class will be created. If an instance variable is not initialized, a default initial value will be provided by the compiler.

Class Variables

Class variables are fields declared with the static modifier. Because class variables are fields, they are declared at the class level, just like instance variables. Class variables, however, are associated directly with a class, rather than being associated with an instance of a class. Every instance of a class having a class variable will share the same copy of that class variable. In a given JVM, there will only be one copy of a particular class variable. If a class variable is not initialized, a default initial value will be provided by the compiler.

Local Variables

Local variables are directly enclosed by a method rather than a class. Each time a thread enters a method or a statement block within a method, new instances of all local variables declared in that method or statement block are created. A local variable ceases to exist once the method or statement block in which it is declared has completed execution. The compiler will not provide default initial values for local variables. They must be initialized before they are used. Attempting to reference an uninitialized local variable will result in a compile error. An argument passed to a method, constructor, or catch clause is equivalent to a local variable declared within that method, constructor, or catch clause.

Constants

Constants are special cases of the three variable types we have discussed. Any variable may be made a constant by specifying the modifier final in the variable declaration. A variable declared with the final modifier cannot be modified once its value has been set. Instance variables and static variables declared as constants must be explicitly initialized.

Access Modifiers for Variables

Access modifiers can be applied to a field declaration to specify the other classes that should be allowed to reference that field. By default, access to a field extends to the entire package in which it is declared. This is known as default access.

Three modifiers can be applied to a field declaration to specify the classes that should be allowed to reference that field. These modifiers are public, protected, and private. A field declared with the public modifier will be available to all other classes. All interface fields are implicitly public. If a field is declared to be protected, it is available to the package in which it is declared and to all subclasses of the class in which it is declared. A field that is declared to be private is accessible only within the class in which it is declared.

Statements

All statements in Java occur within the context of a class or interface. Statements in Java may be simple or compound. A simple statement is terminated by a single semicolon (;). A compound statement, also known as a block, is comprised of one or more simple statements surrounded by curly braces ({}). Each simple statement in a compound statement is terminated by a single semicolon (;). A compound statement can be abruptly terminated using a break statement, a continue statement, a return statement, or a throw statement.

Statements in Java can be labeled. This is accomplished by inserting a name of your choice followed by a colon (:) just before the statement. Labeling of statements is useful in conjunction with the break and continue statements, which will be described in more detail below. Following is a list of the various statement types allowed in Java along with their syntax and examples.

The if Statement

The code following an if statement will be executed only if the *boolean expression* evaluates to true. The else statement will be executed if the *boolean expression* evaluates to false. The else statement is optional.

```
if (boolean expression) {
   //code to execute if boolean expression evaluated to true.
} else {
   //code to execute if boolean expression evaluates to false.
}
```

The switch Statement

A switch statement can be used instead of multiple if statements. The *operand* must be of type byte, short, int, or char. If the *operand* does not equal a value specified in a case clause, the code after the default label executes. If the *operand* equals *case1*, but there is no break statement, execution falls through and *case2* will be compared.

```
switch (operand) {
   case case1:
      //code to execute if operand = case1.
      break;
   case case2:
      //code to execute if operand = case2.
      break;
   default:
      //code to execute if operand does not match any case clause.
}
```

The while Statement

The code following a while statement gets executed until the *boolean expression* is no longer true. The *boolean expression* is evaluated first, so if the condition is not met initially, the loop will not even execute once.

```
while (boolean expression) {
    //code to execute each time boolean expression evaluates to true.
}
```

The do Statement

The code after a do statement gets executed until the while condition is no longer met. Unlike the while statement, statement(s) following do will always be executed at least once because the *boolean expression* is not tested until after the code has executed the first time.

```
do {
    //code to execute each time before evaluating boolean expression to see if we
    //should exit the loop.
} while (boolean expression)
```

The for Statement

A for loop is designed to execute a known number of times. The *initialization statement* is executed once before the loop is started. During each iteration of the loop, the following steps occur: (1) The *boolean expression* is evaluated. If the result of the evaluation is false, the loop terminates. (2) The body of the loop executes. (3) Finally, the *update expression* is executed.

```
for (initialization statement; boolean expression; update expression) {
    //code to execute when boolean expression evaluates to true.
}
```

The break Statement

The break statement causes the currently executing statement block to terminate. A label may be specified as part of the break statement to indicate the enclosing statement from which you are breaking. This feature becomes valuable when your code involves nested statement blocks.

```
break label_name;
```

The continue Statement

The continue statement causes the currently executing statement block to proceed to its next iteration. The continue statement should only be used with a statement block that involves a loop, such as a for, while, or do statement. A label may be specified as part of the continue statement to indicate the enclosing statement which you are continuing. Like the break statement, the continue statement is valuable when your code involves nested statement blocks.

continue *label_name*;

The return Statement

The return statement causes the currently executing method to terminate, pops the call stack, and returns control to the calling method. A return value may be specified as part of the return statement. The type of the return value, if specified, must conform to the return type specified in the method declaration.

return *return_value*;

The throw Statement

The throw statement is used to indicate that an exceptional condition has been encountered. The throw statement causes the currently executing method to terminate and initiates the process of bubbling an exception up the call stack. When using a throw statement, the exception to be thrown must be specified. The exception thrown must conform to the throws clause specified in the method declaration.

throw *exception_object*;

The try Statement

The try statement is used to enclose another statement or statement block that is capable of throwing an exception. A try statement must specify as many catch blocks as are necessary to account for all checked exceptions that can be thrown by the statements contained within the try statement and are neither caught by an enclosing try statement nor declared to be thrown by the enclosing method.

A try statement may specify a finally clause to indicate code that should execute at the end of the statement, regardless of whether or not an exception is thrown by code executed within the try block.

```
try {
   //code that can throw an unchecked exception.
} catch (exception1 e1) {
   //code to handle exception1.
} catch (exception2 e2) {
   //code to handle exception2.
} finally {
   //code to be executed regardless of whether an exception is thrown.
}
```

Expressions

All expressions in Java resolve to one of three things: a variable (or lvalue), a value (or rvalue), or void. Expressions that resolve to variables are used as assignment targets. Expressions that resolve to values can be used on the right hand side of an assignment statement. They can also be combined with other values or modified using operators. A value that results from one of these expressions can be of a primitive type or a reference type. The only expressions that can resolve to void are invocations of methods that are declared to return void. A void expression may not be used in a variable assignment.

Operators

Operators are used to combine or modify expressions that resolve to values. Operators fall into the following groups: arithmetic operators, relational operators, logical operators, unary operators, shift operators, the assignment operator, and the member access operator. The various operators are enumerated in Table 1-1. Unless otherwise specified, each one operates on two operands.

Class Instance Creation

An instance of a class is created using the new keyword:

```
Integer age = new Integer(7)
```

This expression creates a new object of type Integer initialized with a value of 7. The object is assigned to a variable called age.

Array Creation

Arrays are also created using the new keyword:

```
Integer[] ages = new Integer[10]
```

This expression creates a new array of Integers. The array size is set to 10. The 10 elements of the array are initialized to null because the element type is a reference type. If the array elements were of a primitive type, the elements would be initialized to the appropriate default values. The array of Integers is assigned to a variable called ages.

Table 1-1. Java Operators

<table>
<tr><th colspan="2">Arithmetic</th><th colspan="2">Relational</th></tr>
<tr><td>+</td><td>addition or concatenation</td><td>==</td><td>equal to</td></tr>
<tr><td>-</td><td>subtraction</td><td>!=</td><td>not equal to</td></tr>
<tr><td>*</td><td>multiplication</td><td><</td><td>less than</td></tr>
<tr><td>/</td><td>division</td><td><=</td><td>less than or equal to</td></tr>
<tr><td>%</td><td>remainder</td><td>></td><td>greater than</td></tr>
<tr><td></td><td></td><td>>=</td><td>greater than or equal to</td></tr>
<tr><td></td><td></td><td>instanceof</td><td>is an instance of</td></tr>
<tr><th colspan="2">Logical</th><th colspan="2">Unary</th></tr>
<tr><td>&</td><td>bitwise and</td><td>+</td><td>positive</td></tr>
<tr><td>^</td><td>bitwise not</td><td>-</td><td>negative</td></tr>
<tr><td>|</td><td>bitwise or</td><td>~</td><td>bitwise complement</td></tr>
<tr><td>&&</td><td>conditional and</td><td>!</td><td>logical complement</td></tr>
<tr><td>||</td><td>conditional or</td><td>++</td><td>increment</td></tr>
<tr><td>? :</td><td>conditional ternary, 3 opearands</td><td>--</td><td>decrement</td></tr>
<tr><th colspan="2">Shift</th><th colspan="2">Assignment</th></tr>
<tr><td><<</td><td>left shift</td><td>=</td><td>assignment</td></tr>
<tr><td>>></td><td>signed right shift</td><td></td><td></td></tr>
<tr><td>>>></td><td>unsigned right shift</td><td></td><td></td></tr>
<tr><th colspan="2">Member Access</th><th colspan="2"></th></tr>
<tr><td>.</td><td>member access</td><td></td><td></td></tr>
</table>

Accessing Fields

Fields are accessed by using the member access operator described above:

```
String name = user.fullName
```

This expression retrieves the value of the fullName field from the user object and assigns it to a variable called name. For this expression to compile, the class of which user is an instance (or a superclass thereof) must have a field called fullName that is of type String (or a subclass thereof).

Invoking Methods

Methods are also invoked by using the member access operator:

```
String name = user.getName()
```

This expression invokes the getName() method of the user object and assigns the returned value to a variable called name. For this expression to compile, the class of which user is an instance (or a superclass thereof) must have a method with the signature getName() that returns a value of type String (or a subclass thereof).

Accessing Arrays

Array elements are accessed by specifying the index of the desired element in square brackets:

```
Integer age6 = ages[5]
```

This expression retrieves the element of the ages array at index 5 and assigns it to a variable called age6. Arrays in Java are zero-based, which means that the first element of a Java array is at index zero. In the example above, the element at index 5 is, therefore, the sixth element of the array. For this expression to compile, the ages array must be of type Integer[] (or a subclass thereof).

Constant Expressions

Constants can also be used as expressions or in expressions:

```
int count = 15
String name = "John Doe"
```

The first expression above assigns the constant value 15 to a variable called count. The second expression assigns the constant value "John Doe" (without the quotes) to a variable called name.

Classes

A class is a collection of related data fields and methods. Each class begins with a declaration of the following form:

modifiers class *ClassName [*extends *ParentClass] [*implements *InterfaceName(s)]*

The class declaration is followed by the class body, which is enclosed in curly braces ({}). A class body can contain any number of field declarations, constructors, methods, static initializers, and/or member class definitions in any order.

Modifiers for Classes

When declaring a class, there are several modifiers that can be specified. Access control modifiers govern access to the class in much the same way as access control modifiers apply to field declarations. The final modifier can also be applied to a class, though it has a somewhat different meaning than when applied to a variable. In addition, the abstract modifier can be applied. The meanings of these modifiers as they apply to classes will be discussed below.

Access Modifiers for Classes

The only access control modifier that can be specified in a top-level class (a class not contained with another class) is the public modifier. Specifying the public modifier for a top-level class is optional. If it is not specified, the class has default access and is available within the package in which it is declared. If public is specified, the class is globally accessible. Exactly one class within each .java file must be declared to be public.

Member classes are classes nested within other classes. The access control modifiers public, private, and protected may be applied to member classes. If no access control modifier is specified for a member class, that class has default access. These access control modifiers have the same effect as when applied to field declarations.

Final Classes

A class that is declared to be final may not be subclassed.

Abstract Classes

A class that is declared to be abstract cannot be instantiated. In addition, an abstract class may declare methods without providing implementations for those methods, much like an interface. Any method declared in this way must also be declared to be abstract by specifying the abstract modifier in the method declaration. Any non-abstract class that extends an abstract class must provide an implementation for any abstract methods in that abstract class. An abstract class may also contain non-abstract methods.

Inheritance

When a class *extends* another class, the child class inherits all the fields and methods of the parent class. The extends clause is used in a class declaration to indicate that the class should inherit from another class. When a class extends another class, it is said to be a subclass or subtype of the class it is extending.

The access control modifiers used to declare the fields and methods of a parent class will dictate whether a subclass has access to those fields and methods. Fields and methods declared private will be inaccessible to subclasses, while fields and methods declared to be public or protected will be accessible to subclasses. If no access control modifier is specified, access will only be available if the subclass and superclass are members of the same package.

In Java, every class, with the exception of java.lang.Object, extends exactly one superclass. Multiple inheritance is not supported. If you do not include an extends clause in a class declaration, the class extends java.lang.Object by default.

Implementing Interfaces

A class may implement any number of interfaces. If a class is a concrete class (not declared with the abstract keyword), it must provide implementations for all methods defined by all implemented interfaces. A class declared abstract may leave some or all methods of its implemented interfaces unimplemented.

When a class implements a particular interface, it is possible to reference that class by the type of the implemented interface. For example, a class called HomeAddress that implements the Address interface may be assigned to a variable of type Address or a variable of type HomeAddress. Fields and methods defined in HomeAddress, but not declared in Address, are inaccessible using a reference to Address. To access a method declared in HomeAddress, you must *cast* the interface reference back to its implementing class (i.e. ((HomeAddress)address).someHomeAddressMethod();).

Field Declarations

Any number or fields may be declared within a Java class. The specifics or field declarations are discussed in the section on Java types.

Constructors

All Java classes have constructors that are used to initialize a new object of that type. The constructor is called every time an object of that class is created. A constructor has the same name as the class with no return type (an instance of the object is implicitly returned). Typically, instance variable initialization takes place within the constructor.

A constructor can be overloaded to allow for multiple argument combinations, like any method (see *Overloading Methods* earlier). Based on the number and type of arguments that you pass into the constructor, the compiler determines which constructor to use. If a constructor is not specified, a default constructor is provided by the compiler. The default constructor takes no arguments, and calls the no-argument constructor of the parent class. This is equivalent to using the super keyword, which invokes the constructor of the parent class (parameters can also be passed using super(arg1, arg2) if applicable):

```
public MyChildClass() { super();}
```

This is an example of what the compiler implicitly calls when there is no constructor declared for class MyChildClass. If the parent of MyChildClass does not have a no-argument constructor, a compiler error is generated.

Methods

The behavior of an object is implemented by its methods. The method body is enclosed in brackets and follows the method declaration:

modifier returnType methodName(argType argName) [throws *exceptionType*]

Arguments are optional; multiple arguments may be included, separated by a comma. An argument variable may be referenced only within that method. The *modifier* can be any of the method access modifiers listed earlier in Table 1-1. The *returnType* can be any of the data types, as well as any object that is defined in the class of the method.

An instance method is called by applying the member access operator (.) to an object reference, followed by the name of the method to be invoked (e.g. myObject.toString()). If the method is declared with the static keyword, it is referred to as a class method. Each instance of a class does not have its own copy of a class method; rather, the method is shared among all objects of the class. A class method can be invoked by applying the member access operator to the name of the class, followed by the method name (e.g. System.currentTimeMillis()).

main() Methods

The main() method is where execution of a class begins. In every application, the class that is invoked at the command line must have a main() method with the following signature:

public static void main(String *args[]*)

The array of strings that is passed in consists of the parameters entered at the command line. In the following example, the main() method of MyClass is called. The *args[]* array will contain the three elements, firstName, hello, and 12345, as *args[0]*, *args[1]*, and *args[2]*, respectively.

```
java MyClass firstName hello 12345
```

Overloading Methods

Multiple methods can be created with the same name, a process known as overloading the method. That overloaded method can then be called passing different parameters, and the JVM will execute the corresponding method. Most of the time, overloaded methods perform similar functions, but do so with a different parameter set. Each method is required to have a different signature—the arguments must be of different types or in a different order. Simply altering the return type or exception will not result in overloading but rather overriding the method, which may cause a compiler error.

Overriding Methods

Method overriding occurs when a method has the same name, return type, and arguments as a method in a parent class. When this overridden method is called, the new code of the child class is executed, as opposed to the code in the parent class.

Abstract Methods

An abstract method (a method declared with the abstract keyword) consists only of the method signature followed by a semicolon. Any class containing an abstract method must itself be declared abstract, thereby preventing it from being instantiated. A subclass of an abstract class must either provide a method body for every abstract method or must itself be declared abstract. See *Abstract Classes* later in this chapter for more information.

```
access_modifier abstract return_type methodName();
```

Static Initializers

A static initializer is used to specify any code that should be executed when a class is loaded. A static initializer is guaranteed to execute prior to any accesses to class level variables or methods. If any setup is required prior to a class level variable or method access, this is where the setup code should be specified. A class may have any number of static initialization blocks. They will all execute in order based on where they appear in the Java source file. Instance variables and non-static methods of the class containing a static initializer may not be directly referenced within that static initializer.

```
//Class level variable
static long sysTime;
static {
  //init a class level var
  sysTime = System.currentTimeMillis();
}
```

Member Class Definitions

Classes or interfaces may be defined as members of an enclosing class. These classes are called member classes or member interfaces. The fully-qualified name of a member class contains the name of its enclosing class. So, if you have a class org.myorg.ClassA and it has a member class called ClassB, the fully-qualified name of ClassB is org.myorg.ClassA.ClassB.

A member class has access to all of the variables and methods defined in its enclosing class; however, any variable or method declared inside a member class that has the same name or signature as a variable or method in its enclosing class will *shadow* or hide the variable or method of the same name in the enclosing class. The usual access modifiers (public, private, and protected) may be applied to member classes and interfaces. These access modifiers have their usual meanings. Member classes can also be declared to be static. A static member class cannot reference any instance variables or non-static methods of its enclosing class. Member interfaces are static by default.

Interfaces

A Java interface defines a *contract* for interaction with a set of types. Think of two classes as parties to a transaction. If one of the classes implements a particular interface, it is as if that class has signed a contract agreeing to abide by a set of terms. These terms are the method signatures defined in the interface. The other class may access the implementing class according to these specific terms (using the defined method signatures) and be guaranteed that the implementing class will be able to respond. Coding to interfaces rather than classes can help insulate your code from changes to implementing classes.

Because an interface is simply the contract, an interface does not implement the terms it specifies. It is the job of an implementing class to implement these terms. As such, a Java interface is limited to declaring static, final variables and public, abstract methods. Variables and methods declared with any other modifiers will trigger a compile error. If no modifiers are specified, variables will default to static final and methods will default to public abstract. Furthermore, a Java interface is always both public and abstract. These modifiers may be specified, but, if not present, will also be applied by default. The following is an example of an interface definition:

```
interface Address { // the interface is public and abstract even though not specified
    String DEFAULT_COUNTRY = "USA"; // variable is static and final by default
    static final String DEFAULT_STATE = "IL"; // static and final may be specified
    String getAddressLine1(); // public and abstract by default
    public abstract String getAddressLine2()l; // public, abstract may be specified
    private String getCity(); // this will cause a compile error
}
```

The difference between an abstract class and an interface is that each method of an interface must be abstract, whereas an abstract class may implement some or all of its methods. Furthermore, while a class is only allowed to extend one other class, an interface may extend any number of other interfaces.

Exceptions

An exception in Java is an instance of a class that is a subclass of java.lang.Throwable. java.lang.Error and java.lang.Exception are the immediate child classes of Throwable. Subclasses of java.lang.Error usually indicate a fatal error and should not be handled. The exceptions that a programmer is concerned with are instances of a class that is a subclass of java.lang.Exception. A custom exception can be created by writing a class that extends java.lang.Throwable (or a subclass thereof).

Exception Handling

If a statement is capable of generating a particular exception, that statement must be enclosed within a try/catch block, or the method enclosing that statement must declare that it throws that particular exception (or a superclass thereof). The format of a try/catch block is illustrated here:

```
try {
  //code in which an exception may be thrown
} catch (SomeException variable_name) {
  //what to do when SomeException is caught
} catch (SomeOtherException variable_name) {
  //what to do when SomeOtherException is caught
} finally {
  //code that should always be executed
}
```

If an exception is thrown by code executed within the try block, catch blocks are evaluated in the order they appear in a source file until one is encountered that declares that it catches the particular exception thrown or a superclass thereof. Once a matching catch block is found, the code in that catch block is executed. None of the other catch blocks are executed. Because exceptions are caught in the order they are listed in the code, the most general exceptions must be caught last. Code in the finally block will always execute last, whether or not an exception is caught. The finally block is a good place to perform any cleanup on resources that may have been accessed by code within the try or catch blocks (i.e. database connections, files, etc.).

Bubbling Exceptions

An unhandled exception (one that is not caught by a catch block) causes the current method to immediately terminate. The exception is then bubbled up the call stack to the caller of the method throwing the exception. If the caller has defined an appropriate catch block for this exception, this catch block will be executed. If not, the exception will continue to bubble up the call stack until an appropriate catch block is encountered or the current thread of execution is terminated.

Checked Exceptions

Exceptions that are subclasses of java.lang.Throwable, but not subclasses of java.lang.Error or java.lang.RuntimeException, are known as checked exceptions. If a particular checked exception can possibly be generated by a statement that is not enclosed in a try/catch block, the method enclosing that statement must be declared to throw that exception:

```
public void myMthd(argType argOne) throws ChckdException1, ChckdException2
```

Unchecked exceptions do not have to be handled; however, if it is possible that your code will throw an unchecked exception, it is a good idea to account for it somewhere.

Throwing Exceptions

An exception is thrown using the throw keyword:

```
throw new MyException ("This is my exception");
```

Compiling a Java Program

Once you've finished writing your Java program, it's time to compile. Java is compiled into an intermediate format known as bytecode. This, together with the Java Virtual Machine (discussed in the section on running Java programs) is what makes "write once, run anywhere" possible.

The Sun Java Compiler (javac)

Though it is not the only Java compiler, the Sun Java compiler, javac, which comes with the Java Development Kit, is by far the most popular. Once you've gotten your Java source files to the point where you want to compile, you can invoke the Sun Java compiler by executing the command javac:

```
javac [options] [sourcefiles] [@argfiles]
```

Any number of *sourcefiles* can be listed on the command line as arguments to javac. Wildcards (*) can also be used. If you have too many *sourcefiles* to list on the command line, you can list the *sourcefiles* in another text file and specify that text file on the command line preceded by the @ symbol.

```
javac ./com/mypackage/MyClass.java ./com/mypackage/mypackage2/*
javac @mysourcelist.txt
```

When javac is compiling a set of Java source files, it relies on a compile-time classpath to determine the location of classes which you have not written but are referenced by your source code. If your program relies on third-party libraries, you will need to specify the location of those libraries when you invoke the javac command. The -classpath option is used for this.

```
javac –classpath ./lib/classes/*;./lib/somejar.jar @mysourcelist.txt
```

Jar Files

When distributing Java applications, it is usually inconvenient to distribute a large set of .class files. This is where the jar file format and the jar utility come in. A set of class files can be combined into a jar file using the jar utility distributed with the JDK. The jar file format is a specialized version of the zip file format. In fact, a jar file is a zip file. The following is an example use of the jar utility included in the JDK:

```
jar –cvf myjar.jar ./com/*
```

Executing this command will create a file called myjar.jar containing all the files and directories under the com directory, which must be a child of the current directory. The directory structure (including the com directory) is maintained inside the jar file. A default manifest or description file will be created and included within the jar file.

A full description of the capabilities of the jar file format and the jar file utility is beyond the scope of this chapter. Please consult the JDK documentation for more information.

Ant

Ant is short for Another Neat Tool. It is, basically, the Java equivalent of the make utility used to build C/C++ projects. Ant is an open source tool distributed and maintained by the Apache Software Foundation and has become the de facto standard for building Java projects. Ant is an extensible tool that comes with, among other things, the ability to automatically invoke javac and jar. Once you create an Ant script for a project (stored by default in a file called build.xml), you can build the project simply by executing the ant command. A full discussion of Ant is beyond the scope of this chapter. The Ant tool, source code, and documentation are freely available at the Apache Ant website (http://ant.apache.org).

Running a Java Program

Once you've compiled the set of classes and interfaces that comprise your Java program, you can run the program by invoking any of the entry points you have defined. Remember that an entry point to a Java program is simply a method in a public class with the following signature: `public static void main(String[])`. In any given set of classes, there may be as many entry points as there are public classes.

In order to run a Java program, you will need a Java virtual machine (JVM). A JVM is usually a piece of software, but it can be specially designed hardware. A JVM is capable of interpreting the Java bytecode that is output by a Java compiler and correctly executing it on the platform on which the JVM is running. The Java Development Kit (JDK) comes with a JVM which can be invoked using the `java` command. In order to use this JVM to execute a program having an entry point in a class called `com.myclass.Startup`, you would specify, minimally, the following command line:

```
java com.myclass.Startup
```

There are many options that can be specified when invoking the `java` command. Some of the options will be discussed in the sections that follow.

JVM

A JVM is a Java virtual machine. It is capable of interpreting Java bytecode and executing it correctly on the platform on which it is running. When a JVM is invoked, there are two especially important runtime configuration sets that govern the way in which it will behave. These configuration sets are (1) the classpath and (2) the Java system properties. If you have a problem running a Java program and it is not related to a coding error, it may be related to one of these runtime configuration sets.

Classpath

The classpath is a list of jars (`.jar` files) and/or directories on the file system that contain compiled Java classes (`.class` files) and other supporting files such as property files or XML files which may be used for application configuration. When the JVM is invoked, the JVM will search the classpath to find the class that was passed as an argument on the command line. This class must have a `main()` method.

There are three sources used by the java command to build the classpath (other JVMs may have their own ways of building the classpath). These three sources are (1) the lib folder, (2) the system classpath variable, and (3) the classpath specified on the command line when invoking the java command.

The Java Runtime Environment (JRE) that comes with the JDK includes the following directories: .../jre/lib and .../jre/lib/ext. The JVM invoked by the java command will include the lib directory, the standard jars contained in the lib, and all jars contained in the lib/ext directory. If you have written a Java library or have obtained a third-party Java library, and you would like to make the classes contained therein available to all Java programs running on a particular machine, you may add the library's jar to the lib/ext directory. This is the standard Java extension directory.

The second place that classpath information can be specified is in the system classpath variable. Use whatever mechanism is appropriate for your platform to specify a system environment variable having the name "classpath". Set this variable equal to a list of directories and/or jar files you would like the JVM to search whenever it is attempting to find a class.

Finally, a classpath may be specified on the command line when the JVM is invoked. Use the -classpath or -cp switches followed by a list of directories and/or jars that should be added to the system classpath. This list should be delimited using the path delimiter for the platform on which you are running the JVM.

Java System Properties

The second major configuration set governing the behavior of a runtime Java system is the set of Java system properties. Some of these properties are intrinsic to the Java platform, others are used to configure Java libraries, and others are application specific. Execute the following statement to get a listing of the current set of system properties:

```
System.getProperties().list(System.out);
```

Additional Java system properties may be specified on the command line using the -D switch. When using this switch, the -D should be followed immediately (no space) by the property name, followed by an equals sign, followed by the property value:

```
-Ddebug=true
```

Other Configuration Settings

A Java runtime system is a highly configurable environment. We have only touched on the three most common and most important configuration mechanisms. Please refer to the documentation for the version of the JDK you are using for more information on this subject.

Looking Forward

Java technology has grown from youth to maturity and is making a huge impact on the IT world. Java's popularity and acceptance have continued to grow since its introduction in 1995. Sun's goal is to create a new release about every 18 months, and the 5.0 release features many improvements over its predecessor.

Performance is improved again in version 5.0, and hundreds of new classes and interfaces have been added to the standard library. Version 5.0 introduces new features such as generics (templated types), autoboxing (smart type conversions), and metadata annotations (to simplify code generation by pre-processing tools).

Java continues to mature and evolve through the Java Community Process (JCP). Companies such as IBM, Oracle, Borland, and HP have joined Sun in defining new features for the Java platform. The JCP is an open process with the goal of maintaining the stability and compatibility of the Java platform while developing and revising Java technology specifications to meet the needs of developers and technology companies around the world. Anybody can join the JCP, and more information about the JCP can be found at the JCP Web site (http:// www.jcp.org).

The best source for anything related to Java technology is the Java website (http://java.sun.com). In addition to platform downloads, check the Java website for documentation, press releases, tutorials, information about Java certification and training, and just about anything related to Java and its associated technologies.

Chapter 2

C++

C++ is a superset of C in terms of structure and flow, thereby enabling the use of all C constructs while enriching the immensely popular language. This fact aside, it is conceptually very different from its procedural predecessor. First developed by Bjarne Stroustrup in 1979 in cooperation with AT&T Bell Labs (currently AT&T), it saw meteoric acceptance in the 80s and early 90s until the advent of Java slowed its pace.

The current definition of C++ is the ISO C++ Standard (ISO/IEC 14882:1998) and can be downloaded for a fee from the National Committee for Information Technology Standards Electronic Store (http://www.ncits.org/). The Standard is copyrighted by the International Organization for Standardization (ISO), which controls its revisions.

Fast Facts

- C++ is a case sensitive language. "Hello" is not the same as "hello".
- Every statement in C++ must end with a semicolon(;).
- C++ uses a double slash (//) to indicate a single-line comment or /* comment_here */ to mark a comment spanning multiple lines.
- Values are printed to the console using the cout function call. The values to output to the console follow cout using this syntax:

  ```
  cout << myStringOne << " hello ";
  ```
- C++ is a compiled language that produces optimized executable code, resulting in faster execution than interpreted languages.
- C++ is strongly typed, meaning there is significant compile-time type checking, thus ensuring fewer type-mismatch related errors in the compiled code.
- C++ is designed towards object-oriented programming and encourages its use with extensive support of its three tenets - inheritance, polymorphism, and encapsulation.
- The use of abstract base classes enables the definition of *interfaces*, an extremely powerful concept in object-oriented programming.
- C++ is far superior in its support of error handling than its predecessor, C.
- Source code reuse. C++ supports *templates*, a construct unheard of in C.
- The Standard Template Library (STL), earlier a third-party library for common programming constructs, is now part of the language specification and is directly supported by all compilers.
- C++ fully supports pointers, a mainstay of C. It enhances the original concept, making pointers safer and easier to use.
- Memory management functions such as delete are enhanced, safer versions of C equivalents such as free.
- Operator overloading is supported, thereby enhancing code readability. This would otherwise have to be accomplished with the use of functions.
- The ternary if operator provides a convenient alternative to the traditional if statement.

Sample C++ Program

The following is a simple program that will help illustrate basic concepts:

```
1. /*Hello.cpp
2. Hello with C++*/
3. #include <iostream> // Stream declarations
4. using namespace std;
5.
6. int main()
7. {
8. cout << "Hello, World! For the " << 100 << "th time!" << endl;
9. }
```

Main Components of a C++ Program

The above "Hello, World" program is a very simple C++ program that prints text to the console. The above code has to be compiled before it can be executed. There are several good compilers available, many of them including shareware or freeware. It is best to refer to individual compiler documentation for compilation syntax. A good example is the Borland C++ 5.5 compiler, available for free download from http://www.borland.com. The above program can be compiled with the following command line statement:

```
C:\> bcc32 Hello.cpp
```

Comments

Lines 1 and 2 are comments. C++ supports the two different commenting styles. The first style caters to blocks of text and has the following structure /* TEXT */. The "TEXT" represents the code being commented as in Lines 1 and 2. The second style is used to comment a line at a time, as in Line 3.

#include

Line 3 is an #include statement that permits the inclusion of header files. Header files will be discussed later in this book. The # is a pre-processor directive. In this case, the standard C++ IO classes are included. Other pre-processor directives that are commonly used are #define, #ifdef, and #ifndef. The first one is used to define a constant that represents a value or a macro. The last two check for such definitions.

Here's an example:

```
#define FALSE 0
#ifdef FALSE
  #define max(A, B) ((A) > (B) ? (A):(B))
#endif
```

namespace

Line 4 is a means of wrapping the code in this program in a namespace such that it will never conflict with similar identifier and function names in other sections of code that may become a part of this program. std is the default namespace.

main()

Line 6 defines the function main(). Every executable C++ program must include this function. Every time a program is run, initialization code is executed internally and main() is called. main() always has a return type of int. This return value is an error code and indicates success or failure of program execution.

Lines 7 and 9 are the beginning and ending brace, respectively. They define the boundaries of a section of code. Variable scope is determined by these braces. Scope defines the boundaries within which variables and other program constructs have relevance.

Line 8 contains the cout object. It is handed a series of arguments via the << operators and prints out these arguments in left-to-right order. The special iostream function endl outputs the line and a newline.

Basics of C++

Let's begin our voyage into the realm of C++ by first describing the process of writing a C++ program. The source files, or un-compiled program, can be written using any text editor and the file should be saved with a .cpp extension. Often, the class declaration is saved in a separate file of the same name except for an .hpp extension. The extensions of a C++ source file are usually not required to be anything in particular, but this depends on the compiler. It is common practice to use the .cpp and 1ws extensions for C++.

The next step involves turning the source file(s) into language understood by the computer through use of a compiler. The conversion of C++ programs from code to executable comprises two processes – compilation and linking. Compilation results in the generation of object code files, called .obj files from .cpp files. .obj files of a program are then linked together to form an executable image. Compile and link commands are specific to each make of compiler/linker and are best referenced from the product's documentation.

Once compiled, the program can be executed without additional resources. C++ uses two separate areas of memory for program execution. The *stack* is the default memory area where program elements are stored. Function calls always use the stack for passing variable back and forth. Variables created without the use of the new keyword are automatically relegated to the stack. In contrast, variables created with the use of the new keyword are automatically assigned to the *heap*.

One of the primary differences between the two is that variables created on the stack are released when scope termination occurs, whereas heap variables have to be specifically released and are independent of scope. There are several other considerations when it comes to memory management. This information is best obtained from books dedicated for the purpose.

Header Files

A header file is a file containing declarations of classes, global functions, and global variables used with a C++ program. The use of a header file permits the splitting of the *interface* from the *implementation*. The header file (in readable form) can be distributed along with the compiled C++ source file (in object binary form). This makes the declarations of the header file available for inclusion in programs, but secures the source file from being read or modified.

Header files are included with an #include statement, a precompiler directive that results in the physical interspersion of header file contents into the calling program. Header files are usually names with an .h at the end of the filename. Older naming standards used .hxx or .hpp.

There are two ways in which the include statement can be constructed. The first is:

```
#include <headerFile.h>
```

It indicates that the header file is to be found in a standard search path that is defined for the environment. This varies from compiler to compiler. The other way is:

```
#include "headerFile.h"
```

It indicates the file relative to the current directory. A path can also be specified along with the file name. If the file is not found, the include statement is processed as if it had angle brackets instead of quotes.

Data Types

The use of data types defines the amount and type of storage that is allocated and the way is it used. Data types can be either built-in or abstract. The former is native to the compiler, whereas the latter is user-defined through definition of classes or structures.

Basic Data Types

There are four basic built-in data types – char, int, float and double. Since storage details can vary based on environment, the four data types only specify the minimum and maximum values that each one can hold; the implementation is left to the operating system/hardware. The minimum and maximum values that can be stored in the various data types are defined in the system header files limits.h and float.h.

A char is for character storage and uses a minimum of 8 bits (one byte) of storage. An int stores an integral number and uses a minimum of two bytes of storage. The float and double types store floating-point numbers, usually in IEEE floating-point format. Float is for single-precision floating point and double is for double-precision floating point.

Variables can be defined at any point in the program and initialized either at definition or later. Here are some examples:

```
// Variable definition examples
int main(){
  // Definition without initialization
  char aChar;
  int anInt;
  float aFloat;
  double aDouble;

  // Definition and initialization
  char anotherChar = 'C';
  int anotherInt = 50, yetAnotherInt = 250;
  float anotherFloat = 1.4142;

  // Double in exponential form
  double anotherDouble = 12e-3;
}
```

Please note that failure to initialize a variable during definition results in the contents of that variable being *undefined* (contains an unknown value).

Extended Data Types

The extended set of data types goes beyond the set of basic data types. The most important extensions are the bool data type and the set of four specifiers: short, long, signed, and unsigned. bool, along with the constants true and false, is the C++ standard of depicting Boolean behavior.

The set of four specifiers modify the meaning of the basic data types and expand them to a much larger set.

Let's start with bool. It can have two states, either true or false, which are built-in C++ keywords. Several language elements have also been modified to support the bool extension. For example, operators such as > and <, along with conditional expressions such as while, for, do and if convert to bool values.

Next are the specifiers: long and short modify the maximum and minimum values that a data type will hold. The size hierarchy for integral types is: short int, int, long int. All the sizes could conceivably be the same, as long as they satisfy the minimum/maximum value requirements. On a machine with a 64-bit word, for instance, all the data types might be 64 bits. The size hierarchy for floating point numbers is: float, double, and long double. long float is not a legal type. There are no short floating-point numbers.

The signed and unsigned specifiers tell the compiler how to use the sign bit with integral types and characters (floating-point numbers always contain a sign). An unsigned number does not keep track of the sign and thus has an extra bit available so it can store positive numbers twice as large as the positive numbers that can be stored in a signed number. signed is the default and is only necessary with char; char may or may not default to signed. By specifying signed char, the use of the sign bit is forced.

The following example shows the size of the data types in bytes by using the sizeof operator. The sizeof operator provides information about the amount of memory allocated for data items. sizeof can also be used to get the size of a data type:

```
// Specifier examples
#include <iostream>
int main(){
  // char examples
  char c;
  unsigned char cu;

  // short examples
  int i;
  unsigned int iu;
  short int is;
  short iis; // Same as short int
  unsigned short int isu;
  unsigned short iisu;
```

```
    // long examples
    long int il;
    long iil;  // Same as long int
    unsigned long int ilu;
    unsigned long iilu;

    // other examples
    float f;
    double d;
    long double ld;
    cout << "\n char= " << sizeof(c) << "\n unsigned char = " << sizeof(cu) << "\n int
    = " << sizeof(i) << "\n unsigned int = " << sizeof(iu) << "\n short = " << sizeof(is)
    << "\n unsigned short = " << sizeof(isu) << "\n long = " << sizeof(il) << "\n
    unsigned long = " << sizeof(ilu) << "\n float = " << sizeof(f) << "\n double = " <<
    sizeof(d) << "\n long double = " << sizeof(ld) << endl;
}
```

Operators

The type of operators in C++ is not very different from that of other languages. C++ treats operators as a special type of function. Like a function, an operator takes in one or more arguments and produces a value as output.

When a discussion about operators comes up, precedence thoughts soon follow. Similar to other programming languages, multiplication and division occur before addition and subtraction. Also, parentheses have the power to change precedence as in other languages.

A unique feature of C++ syntax is the support of the auto increment (++) and decrement operators (--). As the names suggest, these perform the functions of incrementing and decrementing by one. Functionality varies when they appear before or after a variable. In the former case (prefix), the increment/decrement of the variable occurs first and then the operation is performed. In the latter case (postfix), the increment/decrement of the variable occurs after the operation is performed. The following examples illustrate this:

```
#include <iostream>
int main(){
    int i, j = 0;
    cout << ++i << endl; // Pre-increment
    cout << j++ << endl; // Post-increment
    cout << --i << endl; // Pre-decrement
    cout << j-- << endl; // Post decrement
}
```

Assignment

Assignment is performed with the = operator. It deals with the assignment of the value on the right side of the =, called the *rvalue,* to the variable on the left of the =, called the *lvalue*. An rvalue is any constant, variable, or expression that can produce a value, but an lvalue must be a distinct, named variable.

Mathematical Operators

C++ uses the basic mathematical operators addition (+), subtraction (-), division (/), multiplication (*), and modulus (%). The one shortcut that C++ provides is a combination of an operation and an assignment. This is denoted by an operator followed by an assignment sign. For example, the following statement adds the value 5 to the variable i:

```
i+ = 5;
```

Relational Operators

Relational operators establish a relationship between the values of the operands. They produce a Boolean (specified with the bool keyword in C++) true if the relationship is true, and false if the relationship is false. The relational operators are: less than (<), greater than (>), less than or equal to (<=), greater than or equal to (>=), equivalent (==), and not equivalent (!=).

Logical Operators

The logical operators and (&&) and or (||) produce a true or false based on the logical relationship of its arguments. A statement is true if it has a non-zero value, and false if it has a value of zero.

Bitwise Operators

Bitwise operators perform Boolean algebra on the corresponding bits in the arguments to produce the result. The bitwise operators: bitwise and (&), bitwise or(|), bitwise xor(^), and bitwise not(~) permit the manipulation of individual bits in a number. The bitwise operators work only with integral types: char, int and long.

Shift Operators

The shift operators also manipulate bits. The left-shift operator (<<) produces the operand shifted to the left by the number of bits specified after the operator. The right-shift operator (>>) produces the operand shifted to the right by the number of bits specified after the operator.

Unary Operators

Unary operators take a single argument. The increment(++) and decrement(--) operators discussed earlier are examples. The last unary operators are the address-of (&), dereference (* and ->), and cast operators in C and C++, and new and delete in C++.

Ternary Operators

The ternary if-else operator is unique because it requires three operands. Unlike the standard if-else that requires two parameters, it consists of three expressions: if the first expression (followed by a ?) evaluates to true, the expression following the ? is evaluated and its result becomes the value produced by the operator. If the first expression is false, the third expression (following a :) is executed and its result becomes the value produced by the operator. Here's an example:

```
varA = --varB ? varB : (varB = 100);
```

In the above example, varB is first decremented. The resulting value is then checked to ensure that it is not zero (this is the default behavior, the same statement could be written as --varB != 0). If it is not, the value of varB ends up being assigned to varA. If it is, varB is set to 100 and this is assigned to varA.

Comma Operators

The comma can behave as an operator in separating function argument lists. For instance, in the following example, varA is assigned the value of varD, although all increments take place. The comma is not commonly used in this manner:

```
varA = (++varB, varC++, varD++);
```

Casting Operators

Casting forces the C++ compiler to read the memory space as if the variable were of the cast type. Casting is not required in cases where integral data types are used; a conversion from an int to a float is automatically done by the compiler. To perform a cast, the desired data type (including all modifiers) is put inside parentheses to the left of the value. This value can be a variable, a constant, a value produced by an expression, or a return value of a function. Here's an example:

```
//Casting
int main(){
  int anInt = 100;
  unsigned long aLong = (unsigned long int)anInt;
}
```

Casting, although powerful, is prone to human error, especially when it comes to pointers. For instance, casting a char pointer to an int pointer results in the system using additional space as if it belonged to the variable, thereby potentially overwriting space allocated to other variables.

Operator Overloading

Operator overloading is very similar to the definition of a function except that an operator's default functionality is modified. The only real value addition is in enhancing code readability. The syntax can be quite confusing and is best avoided. This book will not cover this topic in detail. However, here is a basic example:

```
//Operator overloading example
#include <iostream>

class Counter{
    int i;
  public:
    Counter(int ii) : i(ii) {}
    const Counter operator+(const Counter& counterObj) const {
      return Counter(i + counterObj.i);
    }
    Counter& operator+=(const Counter& counterObj){
      i += counterObj.i;
      return *this;
    }
};

int main(){
  Counter count1(1), count2(2), count3(3);
  count1 += count2 + count3;
}
```

The + and += operators are overloaded in this example to perform specific functions for the class Counter. As is apparent from the example, the syntax is quite complex and is prone to human error; the same functionality can be achieved by using a function. However, overriding the =operator or == operator is commonly done because the default functionality is not typically useful if the class contains pointer attributes.

Pointers

Pointers are a very powerful (and error-prone, if not used carefully) feature of C++. In order to understand pointers, it is important to understand how program elements are stored in memory. Every element of a program is allocated a location in memory when a program is run. The size of each of these memory locations is usually eight bytes, but that can vary with machine architecture. The number of locations allocated for each program element depends on the data type of the element.

Each memory location has an *address*. There are two operators in C++ that work with addresses – & and *. The address-of & operator outputs the address of the element specified. For example:

```
int i = 55;
cout << "Address of i = " << &i;
```

The output would be the address where storage in memory for the variable i has been allocated. The default output format is hexadecimal.

A pointer is a special kind of variable that holds addresses of elements. The notation for the definition of a pointer is an * followed by a variable name.

```
int* pi = &i;
```

In the above example, the address of *i*, obtained by the statement &i is stored in a pointer variable, ip. The notation indicates that the variable ip is a pointer to an int. This definition ensures that the system knows that the variable whose address has been stored is of type int. Therefore, when the contents of i are to be obtained using the pointer ip, the system knows how many memory locations to access. The following example depicts this concept:

```
int j = *pi;
```

The statement reads, "copy the contents of the memory location pointed to by ip into the int variable j." This process, called dereferencing, is done by using the * operator, which is read as "contents of the memory location pointed to by the pointer." Another use of the *dereferencing* operator is illustrated below:

```
*pi = 50;
```

In this case, the variable i will now contain 50. It must be noted that j will still contain 55 since j was initialized with the value of the contents pointed to by ip, which was 55.

Also note that the pointer ip, a program element, has its own address. The following statement should help towards clarifying this concept:

```
cout << "Address of 'pi' = " << &pi << " is different from address of the location
pointed to by 'pi' which is = " << pi;
```

Storage Allocation

Storage allocation for variables and other C++ program elements depends on their type. Two of the most important types are static and constant.

Static Variables

Static variables, denoted by the addition of the static qualifier before the variable data type, are a way of maintaining persistence during the life of a program. Storage for a static variable is allocated once during the life of an executing program. Any further references to the variable always refer to the same allocated portion of memory. Here's an example:

```
void updateCounter() {
  static int counter = 0;
  cout << "The new value of counter is" << ++counter << endl;
}
int main() {
  for(int j = 0; j < 10; j++)
    updateCounter();
}
```

In this example, the function updateCounter() serves as a means of updating a counter. Note that although it seems that the initialization of the variable counter would take place with every call to updateCounter(), it is not so. Initialization of a static variable is done only once. With every subsequent call to updateCounter(), the same memory location that stores the value of counter is updated, although it is an independent function call every time from within the loop. If the static specifier were not used, the value of counter would always be 1 on each output line since memory for the variable would be re-allocated every time.

Constants

The const specifier ensures that the value of a variable cannot be modified once it has been initialized. Variables defined in this manner are subject to all rules that regular variables are, except the rule just mentioned. Here's an example:

```
const int constVar = 1;
```

Functions

A function in C++ is a reusable subroutine as it is in other programming languages. The syntax for the definition of a function is as follows:

returnType functionName(inputVariable1 type, inputVariable2 type,...)

The *returnType* placeholder in the above statement describes the data type of the return value of the function. Note that a function can have only one return value; this may be a composite structure. The *functionName* placeholder defines the name of function. This usually has to be unique within the scope in which the function is being defined. The *type* placeholders indicate the data type of the input variables. Note that the number of inputs may be more than one. Also, the input types can be composite. The default input or output value(s) is void, if not explicitly specified.

Variables can be passed by *value* or *reference*. In the former case, the object being passed is copied completely (in the case of a complex object, the class's copy constructor is used, if defined). Variables passed by reference are internally manipulated using pointers so that original copies of the objects are acted upon. The syntax used is the data type or class name followed by an &. e.g. counterClass& would mean that an object of type, counterClass is being passed by reference.

Function Overloading

A function that performs a set of actions can, at times, require different types of inputs. The only way this can be achieved by traditional methods is by the definition of different functions with the appropriate inputs. C++ provides a more convenient way of achieving the same goal by means of function overloading.

With function overloading, several functions with the same name can be defined with each one having a unique combination of inputs/output. For example, there could be two functions as follows:

```
int computeValue(int val1, double val2);
double computeValue(double val1, double val2);
```

Function overloading is a powerful technique that will prove especially useful when dealing with constructors of classes (discussed in later sections). Note that destructors cannot be overloaded.

Inline Functions

Functions, although very successful in promoting reusability of code, have an overhead. The overhead results from execution branching off from the execution path to the function code and back, potentially involving the copying of input variables and bringing back output variables.

This overhead can be avoided by using inline functions. Inline functions are defined as follows in a header file:

```
inline int computeValue(int val1, double val2);
```

The keyword inline tells the compiler to insert the complete function definition at every point where the function is called. This process works well when the function size is reasonably small and when the function is called several times in a program. The inline code does occupy space, but if the function is small, it can actually take less space than the code generated to do an ordinary function call.

Flow constructs

Flow statements are the control mechanisms that help realize conditional and repetitive execution of statements. C++ shares several of its constructs with other programming languages.

Blocks and Scope

Blocks determine scope in C++. A *block* is defined by enclosing a series of statements in curly braces – {}. The scope of program elements is defined within these braces.

Program elements can have either *global* or *local* scope. The following example illustrates these two scopes:

```
1. int varA = 55;
2.
3. int func(int inA){
4.    int varA = mod(inA/10);
5.    varA += inA;
6.    return ((varA) > (::varA) ? (varA) : (::varA));
7. }
```

Two variables called varA are defined, one within the context of a function – func (Line 4), giving it local scope and the other outside the context of any function or class (Line 1), giving it global scope. The former exists only within the function while the latter is available throughout the program.

Line 6 illustrates the scope resolution operator, ::. With the use of this operator, the global varA variable can be accessed.

if-else

This is a conditional construct that enables an action or a series of actions to take place depending on the outcome of a test. The braces enclosing the *do something* and *do something else* statements permit the inclusion of more than one statement in the block. If there is a single statement to be executed, the use of the ternary if is encouraged. If-else statements can also be nested, as follows, thereby permitting the nesting of conditions.

Here's an example:

```
if (condition)
  {do something}
else if (condition)
  {do anything}
else
  {do something else}
```

In the above example, *do anything* is executed if the first condition was false and the second condition was true. If the second condition was also false, then *do something else* block is executed.

while

The while construct facilitates the execution of a statement or a set of statements. This construct is used when the number of resulting iterations is not known and when it is required that the enclosed block be executed only when the determining condition is met.

```
while (condition)
  {do something}
```

The statements in the block execute until the condition evaluates to false. Another common usage of while is in conjunction with break and continue, discussed shortly.

do-while

The do-while construct is very similar to the while construct. It also facilitates the execution of a statement or a set of statements and is used when the number of resulting iterations is not known. The only difference is that the block of statements is executed at least once since the condition evaluation is done at the end of the block:

```
do
  {something}
while (condition)
```

The statements in the block execute until the condition evaluates to false or until the loop is terminated with a break.

for

A for statement is used when the number of iterations are known or can be determined beforehand.

The syntax is as follows:

```
for( initialization;test condition;increment )
  {do something}
```

The *initialization* involves the seeding of a variable that will be used as a counter to control the loop. The test *condition* is used to check the current value of the control variable against a value (fixed or calculated). The *increment* placeholder indicates the point where the counter variable is incremented by a constant value. Here's an example:

```
for(int i = 0; i < 50; i++) {
  cout << "This is loop number << i;
}
```

The for statement can be used in a manner similar to while:

```
for (;;)
  {do something}
```

In this form, break and/or continue can be used to control the loop.

break and continue

The break statement causes execution in a loop to terminate immediately; execution continues with the statement immediately following the boundaries of the loop. The statement is used on its own with no parameters.

The continue statement is used in a loop to skip the all statements of the block immediately after the continue statement. Execution resumes with the first statement of the loop.

switch

A switch statement is used instead of if/else statements when there are several conditions to deal with. This makes code more readable and structured:

```
switch(expression){
case valueOne:
  {do something}
  break;
case valueTwo:
  {do something else}
  break;
default:
  {do anything}
}
```

In the example, depending upon the value resulting from the evaluation of the expression, the first or the second case is chosen. If the resulting value does not correspond to either case values, the statements under the default section are executed. Note that the default section is optional; if it doesn't exist and none of the case statements match up, execution continues after the ending brace of the switch statement. If the break statement were not used, the execution would fall through to the default case even if a case condition had been satisfied earlier.

goto

The goto statement has been inherited from structured programming languages, one of them being C. Because code becomes difficult to maintain, the use of goto is strongly discouraged in C++ and, hence, will not be discussed at length. In short, the goto permits execution to jump to any section of a program.

Objects and C++

Everything around us is an object. Every object has its own attributes and performs actions in its own particular way. Even though each individual object is an independent entity, a casual observation would indicate that objects share behavioral and structural aspects, some more so than others. Further inspection would reveal that there is a pattern to these observations, leading to the inference that object attributes and functionality can be defined once, with every individual object inheriting these traits. This leads us to classes.

Classes

Objects, as discussed above, can be said to belong to a *class* of objects. The keyword class in C++ permits the definition of a template for an object that has a specific set of attributes and methods. A class example is shown on the next page.

The keyword class in Line 1 begins the definition of a class called counter. The keyword public: in Line 2 is one of three keywords (public, protected, and private) that define the access rights of class elements. These keywords are discussed later in this chapter. Note that the function in Line 3 – counter() has the same name as the class. This function is called the constructor and will be discussed later. Also, all functions defined within a class are commonly referred to as methods.

Line 9 defines the destructor, also discussed later. Lines 4, 5, and 6 define functions to manipulate the counter class. Line 7 sets the access control to private: for the statements in Line 8 and 9. Line 8 defined the integer variable that will hold the value of the counter. The class is now used in the program defined in Lines 12 to 19. Line 13 initializes cntVar1 - an instance of a pointer of the counter class with an initial value of 50. This results in memory being allocated on the heap.

```
1.  class counter {
2.     public:
3.        counter(int val){counterVar = val;}
4.        int getCountValue(){return counterVar;}
5.        void setCountValue(int countVal){counterVar = countVal;}
6.        void incrementCounter(){counterVar++;}
7.     private:
8.        int counterVar;
9.        ~counter(){};
10. };
11.
12. int main() {
13.    counter* cntVar1 = new counter(50);
14.    cntVar->incrementCounter();
15.    cout << "Counter1 val: " << cntVar->getCountValue() << endl;
16.    delete cntVar1;
17.    counter cntVar2(55);
18.    cntVar2.incrementCounter();
19.    cout << "Counter2 val: " << cntVar2.getCountValue() << endl;
20. }
```

Line 14 uses the increment function and Line 15 gets the current value of the counter variable. Note the use of the operator -> to call the incrementCounter function; this is the operator used to access a member of a class through a pointer. Line 16 destroys cntVar1 (see the *delete* section for more information). Lines 17 to 19 define and use another variable, cntVar2, that is used without the new operator. This definition results in memory being allocated memory on the stack. Note the use of the . operator in accessing cntVar2.

Constructor

The constructor is an optional construct of a class that permits the initialization of class variables. In the case when a constructor is not defined for a class, an implicit empty default constructor is provided automatically during compilation. A class may have more than one constructor, as long as the inputs to the constructor vary in type and/or number; this concept is an example of function overloading discussed earlier. The syntax of a constructor is the class name with a set of parentheses enclosing zero or more parameters, as described below:

className(param1, param2,...);

A *copy constructor* is used when a copy of an object is to be made. This occurs when objects are passed by value between functions etc. By default, the compiler generates a copy constructor that performs a bitcopy of the object. This works unless the object contains pointers, etc. The best solution is to define a custom copy constructor. The syntax for this is as follows, where classNameRef is a reference to className:

```
className(const className& classNameRef)
```

Destructor

The destructor is an optional construct of a class. It deals with the cleanup of class variables and is called when the class is destroyed either explicitly through the use of a delete statement or when the object goes out of scope. In the case when a destructor is not defined for a class, an implicit empty default destructor is provided automatically during compilation. A class can have only one destructor. The syntax of a destructor is a ~ followed by the class name with a set of parentheses with no enclosing parameters, as shown below:

```
~className();
```

new

The new statement is one of two methods of instantiating a class. An object created in this way is allocated memory on the heap and a pointer to the variable is returned. Line 13 of the sample program is an example; note the storage of the return value of the new call to the pointer – cntVar1. The syntax of a new statement is the keyword followed by the name of the class to be instantiated with a set of parentheses enclosing zero or more parameters, as described below:

```
className* new className(param1, param2,...);
```

delete

The delete statement is used to destroy an instance of a class created using new. Note that an object created using new has to be specifically deleted. Failure to do so will render the memory allocated for the variable on the heap unusable – this is commonly referred to as a *memory leak*. The syntax of a delete statement is the keyword followed by the name of the class to be instantiated with a set of parentheses enclosing zero or more parameters, as described below:

```
delete pointerToClassObject;
```

Please note that it matters if the pointer being used is instantiated or not. Attempting to delete an unassigned pointer can result in unpredictable behavior, including system crashes. Deleting a pointer assigned to NULL is internally handled by the delete statement and is, therefore, safe.

Access Control

As discussed earlier, C++ facilitates the concept of encapsulation with the use of three access specifiers: public, protected, and private. Encapsulation enables an object to be aware of some of its attributes and methods. This knowledge is made available with the assumption that an object knows how it best handles its internals. The following discussion elaborates on this topic.

Public

Public members, functions, and variables alike are accessible to everyone, all member functions of the class and through objects of the class. For example, Lines 4 to 6 from the example under the *Classes* section define public member functions. These functions can be called using an object of the class as in Line 18 or using a pointer to an object of the class as in Line 14. Please note that if a class does not have any member variables and merely contains functions, the class need not be instantiated. Member functions can be defined as static and accessed as follows:

```
className::func();
```

Protected

Protected members of a class can be accessed only through other member functions of the class and not through objects of the class. In this scenario, if the function in Line 6 of the example were defined with the protected keyword, function calls through the object in Lines 14 and 18 would fail. Member functions of derived classes can also use these protected members; this will become clearer when inheritance is discussed.

Private

Private members, functions and variables alike, are accessible only through other member functions of the class. They cannot be accessed directly through objects of the class. In this scenario, if the function in Line 6 of the example were defined as a private one, function calls through the object in Lines 14 and 18 would fail. Member functions of derived classes cannot use these private members.

Friends

A friend can be a function or class. Just as in the real world, where one has a choice of who is a friend and who is not, C++ syntax allows a class to declare functions or other classes as its friends. Once declared in this way, the rules of encapsulation change. Every friend of a class has access to all members of the class, including private ones. Therefore, it is very important to decide on nominating a friend, just like in the real world.

Here is how classB is declared to be a friend of classA:

```
class classA {
  public:
    friend classB;
...};
```

Friends are used primarily for convenience, especially when relationships between classes are not anticipated at design time and access is required into a class. An important point to remember about friends is that friendship is not inherited, transitive, or reciprocal:

Inherited: Just because a base class has befriended another class, a class derived from it does not inherit this relationship.

Transitive: If classA has befriended classB and classB has befriended classC, it does not mean that classC is a friend of classA.

Reciprocal: If classA is a friend of classB, it does not mean that classB is automatically a friend of classA, unless explicitly declared so by classA.

Inheritance

The ability to *inherit* is one of the most powerful constructs of C++, enabling object-oriented programming. Inheritance is natural. A simple example involves two means of transportation; a car and a motorcycle. Both can be generalized to represent vehicles. Hence, a vehicle class can be defined with a set of common properties and methods as follows:

```
1. class vehicle {
2.   public:
3.     vehicle(){};
4.     void setNumWheels(int wheelCount){numWheels = wheelCount;}
5.     int getNumWheels(){return numWheels;}
6.     virtual void start(){// Basic vehicle stuff};
7.   protected:
8.     int numWheels;
9. };
```

The class above defines a vehicle class that has a certain number of wheels. This number is stored in a protected member variable in Line 7; the reason for using protected will soon become clear. Line 4 defines a simple get method to fetch this value. The virtual function in Line 5 will be discussed later. Let's derive the car class from the base class – vehicle; the motorcycle class definition is similar and, hence, not shown:

```
10. class car : public vehicle {
11.   public:
12.     car(bool AC){airConditioning = AC};
13.     void start(){//Do some car-specific starting work...};
14.   private:
15.     bool airConditioning;
16. };
17. int main() {
18.   car aSedan = new car(true);
19.   aSedan.setNumWheels(4);
20.   aSedan.start();
21. }
```

Lines 10 to 14 implement the inheritance of the car class from the vehicle class. Line 10 declares that class car is being inherited from class vehicle. The keyword public on the same line indicates that public inheritance is occurring, which grants all public and protected members of vehicle access to car. Protected and private inheritance methods also exist, but are not frequently used.

The car class defines an additional Boolean property called airConditioning that is unique to the car class. Lines 18 to 20 create an object of the car class and set its properties. Note that the setNumWheels function that was defined in the vehicle class is now available to the car class due to inheritance. Line 20 will be discussed in the section on virtual functions.

Other considerations when using inheritance concern *constructors* and *destructors*. Constructors are always called in the following order: base class, then derived classes in the order of their derivation. Destructors are called in the reverse order: lowest level of derives class going upwards in the hierarchy, ending with the base class destructor.

Polymorphism and Virtual Functions

Polymorphism is the phenomenon in which an object shows varying behavior depending on circumstances. The implementation of polymorphism in C++ has to do with *upcasting*. Now, let's combine our knowledge of pointers to with what we have learned about inheritance.

Extending our example from the inheritance section, let's examine the following program:

```
int main(){
  vehicle* aHatchback = new car(false);
  aHatchback->setNumWheels(4);
  aHatchback->start();
}
```

In the previous example, we have created a new car object, but assigned the output of the new statement (which is a pointer to a car object) to a pointer to a vehicle object. This is legal since a car is a type of a vehicle. This process is called *upcasting*. Line 3 is a function call to a vehicle member function using the vehicle pointer pointing to a car object.

The start function is called using the vehicle pointer. Although it may seem straightforward, the function that is actually executed is the start function of the car class. The prime reason for this behavior is the use of the virtual keyword while defining the start function in the vehicle class. The use of this keyword results in the delegation of the function call to the object that is pointed to by the vehicle pointer (car) rather than the type of the pointer itself (vehicle).

Other considerations when using polymorphism concerns destructors. Destructors should always be made virtual to ensure that the correct object, pointed to by a base class pointer, is destroyed.

Abstract Base Classes

Abstract base classes (ABCs) are an extension to the use of virtual functions. An ABC permits the definition of an *interface*. ABCs are classes that have at least one pure virtual function. This can be achieved in the previous example by changing Line 6 to:

```
virtual void start() = 0;
```

The presence of the pure virtual function renders the class uninstantiable (an object of this class can never be created). The only way to use this class is to derive from it, define the method in the derived class, and then instantiate the derived class. An attempt to instantiate the ABC would result in a compiler error.

Exceptions and Error Handling

Programs can, and will, generate errors. These may be the result of improper coding or issues in the run-time environment. Occurrences of the former can be significantly reduced by proper testing, but not much can be proactively done about the latter. The best way to handle such exceptions is by the use of the C++ try-catch-throw sequence.

In the following example, myException is a custom class inherited from an Exception class. The vehicle class in the above example is assumed to have been extended from the earlier example to throw exceptions of type myException and myOtherException when exceptions are encountered. This means that member functions of this class have been written to capture exceptions and *rethrow* exceptions of these types. Further, this example catches the exception object, does some processing using the information obtained from the object, and then rethrows another exception object of type, myProcessedException. If the exception is of type myOtherException, it is caught at Line 8.

The syntax of the try-catch-throw sequence is shown in this example:

```
try {
    vehicle* aHatchback = new car(false);
}
catch(myException ex) {
    // Do something with ex
    throw myProcessedException;
}
catch(myOtherException ex) {
    // Do something with ex
}
```

Exceptions propagate outwards; this means that if an exception is thrown from functionC that has been called by functionB which, in turn, has been called by functionA, the exception propagates from functionC if it is not handled there, it moves on to functionB. If it fails to be caught there, it goes on to functionA. If it is not handled there, then it gets thrown to the environment; this usually results in the program coming to an ungraceful end.

Please note that it is always difficult to handle exceptions thrown from constructors or destructors. There are means of doing this, but they are beyond the scope of this book.

Looking Forward

C++ saw great acceptance in the 80s and early 90s when object-oriented programming was the norm. Java technology has since taken over most application programming due to its relative ease of use and platform-independence. This, coupled with the spread of the Internet, has made Java the de-facto standard for Web-enabled applications.

C++ has its niche in areas where throughput is the most important factor. But this percentage is gradually decreasing, primarily due to the great advancements in hardware, which make up for the loss in code performance. Also, Total Cost of Ownership (TCO) has been traditionally higher in C++ based applications.

A good online resource for C++ questions is C++ FAQ by Marshall Cline at http://www.parashift.com/c++-faq-lite/. A good book for detailed coverage of C++ is *Thinking in C++, 2nd edition, Volume 1* by Bruce Eckel (http://www.mindview.net/).

Chapter 3

C#

C# is a new object-oriented, memory-managed programming language developed by Microsoft as a core part of the .NET strategy. Pronounced "C-sharp," this language combines the rapid development and ease of languages like VB and Java without sacrificing the power of C++. Since C# is a memory-managed and garbage-collected language, developers are freed from memory management tasks, such as allocating and deallocating memory, as well as pointer manipulation, allowing them to focus on the bigger picture.

C# is formally defined in ECMA-334, the C# Language Specification, which is available online (http://www.ecma-international.org). Like all .NET languages, C# is compiled into a platform-independent intermediate language (IL). The IL is a bytecode interpreted by the Common Language Runtime and *just-in-time* compiled into machine code for the specific architecture of the machine used at runtime.

Since C# exists as a standard, there are other implementations of the language, including Mono (http://www.mono-project.com) and DotGNU (http://www.dotgnu.org). This chapter will focus on the Microsoft .NET version of C#, though the language concepts should hold true across the various C# implementations.

Fast Facts

- C# is case sensitive. The variable "Hello" is not the same as "hello" in C#.
- Source files end with the .cs extension. Once compiled, the file has an .exe extension for executable programs or a .dll extension for code libraries and ASP.NET pages.
- Code can be compiled in Visual Studio by using the Build menu or csc.exe directly from the command line.
- The syntax for the command line compiler is:

```
csc Filename.cs
```

- The syntax to print a line to the console is:

```
Console.WriteLine("This is my string to print");
```

- Every statement must end with a semicolon (;).
- The plus operator (+) is used to concatenate two strings.
- Garbage collection occurs automatically.
- Block comments are indicated between a slash asterisk (/*) and an asterisk slash (*/). Single-line comments appear to the right of a double slash (//).
- Executable programs written in C# begin in the Main() method, which must have one of the following signatures:

```
static void Main() {...}
static void Main(string[] args) {...}
static int Main() {...}
static int Main(string[] args) {...}
```

- Every method must be defined as a part of a class or a struct.
- Errors are called exceptions, and they either get caught in the method in which they occur by a try/catch block or bubble up to the calling method.
- C# supports single inheritance, but not multiple inheritance.

Sample C# Program

A sample program in C# is shown below. Upon execution, it will print the text "Hello, world!" onto the command line. This text can be put in any file with a .cs extension. Classes do not necessarily have to be in files with corresponding names (unlike other languages, such as Java).

```
//Use classes in the System namespace without the "System." prefix.
using System;

//The namespace that the class below is contained in
namespace BlueLine
{
  /// <summary>
  /// C# and Visual Studio use these XML comments as a
  /// standard method for documentation.
  /// </summary>
  class Hello
  {
    /// <summary>
    /// The main entry point for the application.
    /// </summary>
    static void Main(string[] args)
    {
      //Print the string to the console.
      Console.WriteLine("Hello, world!");
    }
  }
}
```

Main Components of a C# Program

The look of a C# program can vary substantially, but most of the main components included in the example above are consistent from program to program. Some of these basic program components are described briefly here.

Headings

The first things that appear in a C# source file are the namespaces the file will use and the namespace the file itself will belong to. The `using System` clause allows you to use the classes of the `System` namespace without putting `System.` in front of the class name. The `Hello` class is defined in the `BlueLine` namespace, making the fully qualified name of the class BlueLine.Hello. If you wanted to refer to that class as Hello instead of by its fully qualified name, you would put a using BlueLine statement at the beginning of your class file.

Classes

The most common component of the C# language is a class. A class can contain member variables, which can be other class instances or primitive types, such as ints and doubles. Classes may also contain methods, which are constructs that can modify a class's member variables or give information about the current state of the class and the variables contained therein.

Inheritance

In C#, any class can directly inherit from any one class. When a class inherits from another class, it automatically gets the functionality provided by that base class. All classes at the bottom of the inheritance hierarchy extend from the System.Object class. Inheritance is notated with a colon (:). If a base class named BaseClass existed, our Hello class above could inherit from it by changing the class declaration to:

```
class Hello : BaseClass
```

Interfaces

Classes can also implement an arbitrary number of interfaces. An interface provides no implementation details; it is simply a contract spelling out the methods, properties, and events that the class must support. Like inheritance, interface implementation is notated with a colon (:) and appears after the base class (if any). Unlike inheritance, a class can implement multiple interfaces, with each interface separated by a comma. The simple example above could be modified to inherit from BaseClass and implement InterfaceOne, InterfaceTwo:

```
class Hello : BaseClass, InterfaceOne, InterfaceTwo
```

Main() Method

The Main() method is the *entry point* of an executable application—the point in the code where the program starts executing. The program is finished when the Main() method returns or all foreground threads created in the Main() method terminate. Classes can be created and other methods can be called from within Main(). The Main() method must adhere to one of four method signatures, presented in *Fast Facts* earlier in this chapter.

Constructors

A constructor is a method with the same name as the class, but with no return type. When an instance of a class is created with the new keyword, a constructor is called. Constructors are used to initialize a class; initial values should be set in order to get the class ready for use. Constructors can be overloaded, meaning that there can be multiple methods with the same name that accept different parameters. If a constructor is not defined specifically, the compiler implicitly gives the class a default constructor that takes no arguments, which in turn calls the default constructor of the direct base class.

Methods

Methods are the parts of a class that do the work. Methods modify the state of the object by modifying member variables; they can accept input parameters and, optionally, return a value. In the above example, static void Main(string[] args) is a method that takes a string array as an input parameter and returns no value (return type void).

Basics of C#

C# is a core language of Microsoft's new .NET platform. The platform consists of a number of elementary components, one of them being the .NET Framework, which provides a set of common class libraries that can be used in any of the .NET languages. Like any .NET programming language, C# programs can be written in any text editor, but Microsoft Visual Studio is the most commonly used editor. Visual Studio provides a rich set of features that make editing, debugging, building, and deploying easy to do.

If you are not using Visual Studio, you can still write and compile C# programs. The .NET Framework includes a command line compiler, csc.exe, usually found in C:\Windows\Microsoft.NET\Framework\. The basic syntax is:

```
csc filename.cs
```

This will create an executable with the same name as the file, such as *filename*.exe. Additional output targets are supported, including DLLs, Windows (as opposed to command line) executables, and modules. You can compile multiple .cs files into a single executable or DLL file as well. Run 'csc /?' to see all of the compiler options.

To run an executable, simply type the name of the .exe on the command line or double-click it in Explorer. Running the program will start up the .NET runtime, wherein the program actually runs. It is *just-in-time* compiled from the machine-independent IL bytecode produced by the compiler to machine-specific bytecode that is executed on the current machine.

Operators

C# operators allow you to perform logical (Boolean) comparisons, as well as arithmetic operations. Please note that more advanced mathematical functions, including trigonometric and logarithmic functions, may be found in the System.Math class.

Table 3-1. C# Operators

<table>
<tr><th colspan="2">Arithmetic</th><th colspan="2">Relational</th></tr>
<tr><td>+</td><td>addition or concatenation</td><td>==</td><td>equal to</td></tr>
<tr><td>-</td><td>subtraction</td><td>!=</td><td>not equal to</td></tr>
<tr><td>*</td><td>multiplication</td><td><</td><td>less than</td></tr>
<tr><td>/</td><td>division</td><td><=</td><td>less than or equal to</td></tr>
<tr><td>%</td><td>modulus</td><td>></td><td>greater than</td></tr>
<tr><td></td><td></td><td>>=</td><td>greater than or equal to</td></tr>
<tr><td></td><td></td><td>is</td><td>is of type</td></tr>
<tr><th colspan="2">Logical</th><th colspan="2">Unary</th></tr>
<tr><td>&</td><td>bitwise and</td><td>+</td><td>positive</td></tr>
<tr><td>^</td><td>bitwise xor</td><td>-</td><td>negative</td></tr>
<tr><td>|</td><td>bitwise or</td><td>~</td><td>bitwise complement</td></tr>
<tr><td>&&</td><td>logical and</td><td>!</td><td>logical complement</td></tr>
<tr><td>||</td><td>logical or</td><td>++</td><td>increment</td></tr>
<tr><td>? :</td><td>logical ternary, 3 opearands</td><td>--</td><td>decrement</td></tr>
<tr><th colspan="2">Shift</th><th colspan="2">Assignment</th></tr>
<tr><td><<</td><td>left shift)</td><td>=</td><td>assignment</td></tr>
<tr><td>>></td><td>right shift</td><td></td><td></td></tr>
</table>

Conditionals

Conditionals are responsible for the flow control of C# applications and are one of the foundations of any programming language. Depending on the status of variables, certain code will be executed or not executed. If-else and switch-case are the most common forms of flow control used in C#.

if-else

If-else is the primary way to evaluate a condition and, based on that result, evaluate (or not evaluate) certain code. The syntax for if-else is:

```
if (expression)
  statement1
[else
  (statement2)]
```

The *expression* is a Boolean expression. If *expression* evaluates to true, the code in *statement1* is executed. If *expression* evaluates to false, the code in the optional *else* clause is executed:

```
if(val == 0)
{
  Console.WriteLine("val is 0.");
}
else if(val < 0)
{
  Console.WriteLine("val is less than 0.");
}
else
{
  Console.WriteLine("val is greater than 0.");
}
```

switch-case

A switch-case statement allows you to compare the value of a single variable with a set of possible constant values. The syntax is:

```
switch (expression)
{
  case constant-expression:
    statement
    jump-statement
  [default:
    statement
    jump-statement]
}
```

The *expression* is the variable that you wish to evaluate. If *expression* evaluates to being equal to *constant-expression*, the *statement* immediately following that constant expression will be executed.

In C#, the *jump-statement* is usually break. Break indicates that the evaluation is complete, and the switch block may be exited. If you also wish to evaluate the statement in another *constant-expression* block, you may use 'goto *constant-expression*'. Note that in C#, unlike C++, falling through from one case statement to another is not supported. Either break or goto is required at the end of each case statement. Stacking of empty cases, however, is allowed.

The default block will execute if none of the *constant-expressions* match the value of *expression*. The following example illustrates usage of a switch-case expression:

```
switch(val)
{
  case 0:
    Console.WriteLine("val is 0");
    break;
  case 1:
    Console.WriteLine("val is 1. About to evaluate case 0.");
    goto case 0;
  case 2:
  case 3:
  case 4:
    Console.WriteLine("val is 2, 3 or 4.");
    break;
  default:
    Console.WriteLine("val does not match a defined case.");
    break;
}
```

Loops

Loops are used to execute a block of code multiple. In C# there are four main loop constructs: for, do-while, while, and foreach.

for

The for loop executes a block of code repeatedly until a specified Boolean expression evaluates to false. The syntax for a for loop is:

for ([*initializers*]; [*expression*]; [*iterators*]) *statement*

An example follows. When the loop is entered, i is initialized to zero; the loop will keep iterating while i is less than 10; after each iteration, i is incremented:

```
for(int i = 0; i < 10; i++)
{
  Console.WriteLine("val is " + i.ToString());
}
```

do-while and while

The do and do-while loops are similar in their structures. The main difference is that a do-while loop will always execute once, as its continuation expression is evaluated after the block of code executes. A while loop, on the other hand, tests the condition before entering the loop:

```
bool condition = true;
do
{
  //a do-while loop always executes once before testing the condition
  condition = !condition;
}
while(condition);

while(!condition)
{
  //a while loop tests the condition before entering the loop
  condition = !condition;
}
```

foreach

The foreach loop allows you to easily iterate over each and every item in any collection that implements the interface IEnumerable. This includes arrays and all of the classes in the System.Collections namespace. An example follows:

```
foreach (type identifier in expression) statement


int[] ints = new int[] {0,1,1,2,3,5,8};
foreach(int i in ints)
{
  //do something to each integer in the array
  Console.WriteLine("The current value of i is " + i.ToString());
}
```

continue and break

Inside of a loop, you may use continue and break statements to affect the execution of the loop. A break statement exits out of the innermost loop immediately. A continue statement exits the current iteration of the loop and continues on the next iteration if the loop is to continue executing.

```
public void BreakContinue()
{
  int[] ints = new int[] {0,1,2,3,4};
  for(int i = 0; i < ints.Length; i++)
  {
    if(i == 1)
      continue;
    else if(i == 3)
      break;
    else
      ints[i]++;
  }
  //After executing, the contents of the
  //ints array will be:
  //{1,1,3,3,4}
}
```

Arrays

An array is a fixed-size collection of elements of a particular type. Arrays in the .NET Framework are zero-indexed, which means that the first element in the array is indexed with 0 and the last is indexed with the array's length, minus 1. Arrays can be created with the following syntax:

```
//create a new int array of length 5
int[] intArray = new int[5];
//create an int array with rank 1 and length 6, and give it initial values
int[] ia2 = new int[] { 1, 1, 2, 3, 5, 8 };
//create some multidimensional arrays
int[,] ia2d = new int[3,4];
int[,,] ia3d = new int[3,4,5];
```

The .NET Framework also provides some classes that help with the management of data collections. These classes can be found in the System.Collections namespace. Some of the classes provided include ArrayList (a dynamically-resized array), Hashtable, SortedList, Stack, and Queue.

Strings

In .NET, strings are a built-in type representing a sequence of characters. Strings are notated with quotation marks (""). Individual chars are notated with single quotes ('').

Strings are concatenated with the plus (+) operator. If you are building a long string, you may find the System.Text.StringBuilder class to be helpful. The string class has a plethora of helpful methods, such as EndsWith(), SubString(), Split(), Join(), IndexOf(), and many others. Take a look at a small sampling below:

```
string foo = "Hello ";
string bar = "world!";
string foobar = foo + bar;
int x = foobar.IndexOf('!');
string unsure = foobar.Replace("!", "?");
string[] words = foobar.Split(' ');
```

All strings in .NET are immutable; that is, once a particular string exists in memory, that copy cannot be modified. Modifications that you make in your code actually create new copies of strings in memory.

Exceptions

In .NET, exceptions are raised when an error occurs. For example, if you try to divide a number by zero, a DivideByZeroException will be thrown. If you attempt to connect to a Microsoft SQL Server database, but the database is offline, a SqlException will be thrown.

Exceptions indicate that something has gone awry. They should not be used for flow control. Whenever possible, you should test for conditions that could cause an exception (and thus prevent the exception from being thrown). For example, when dividing, you should check to see if the divisor is zero rather than dividing and catching the DivideByZeroException.

The example below illustrates a try-catch-finally block. The code inside of the try block throws an exception. The two catch blocks attempt to handle the exception. The finally block is optional:

```
public void ExceptionExample()
{
  try
  {
    //Code in the try block is executed.
    Console.WriteLine("About to throw an exception!");
    throw new NullReferenceException("Error message");
```

```
    }
    catch(ArgumentException ex)
    {
      //If the exception is or inherits from ArgumentException, it will be caught.
      Console.WriteLine(ex.ToString());
    }
    catch(Exception ex)
    {
      //All Exceptions inherit from the System.Exception class. Thus, this block will
      //catch anything that was not caught by a previous catch block.
      Console.WriteLine(ex.ToString());
    }
    finally
    {
      //code in the finally block is *always* executed, regardless of
      // whether an exception was thrown or not caught or unhandled.
    }
  }
```

Access Modifiers

Access modifiers are used to determine permission levels of classes, variables, and methods. C# offers the following access modifiers:

Table 3-2. C# Access Modifiers

public:	Access is not restricted. Members marked as public can be accessed by other members in the class and by classes in any assembly.
protected:	Access is limited to the containing class or types derived from the containing class.
internal:	Access is limited to other classes that are in the same assembly.
protected internal:	Access is limited to the current assembly or types derived from the containing class.
private:	Access is limited to the containing type.
sealed:	A class that is marked sealed cannot be inherited. Structs are implicitly sealed; therefore, they cannot be inherited. Structs are discussed in the next section.

Classes, Methods and Interfaces

Classes are the building blocks of programs in .NET. They consist of properties, events, and methods. Each can be inherited or extend existing base classes, and are typically used to abstractly represent some logical entity or concept in the system. Classes are reference types, and are allocated in memory on the managed heap.

Value Types and Reference Types

In .NET there are two fundamental classes of data types: value types and reference types. The major difference between value and reference types is how they are allocated and cleaned up in memory. Reference types are allocated in the heap and are garbage-collected when they are no longer being referenced. Value types are allocated on the stack. Memory from variables that are value types is reclaimed when the variable goes out scope.

All types that extend System.ValueType are value types, which include primitive data types like int, double, float, enum etc. To create a value type, use the struct keyword.

Reference types do not derive from System.ValueType. Types created using the class keyword are reference types. Strings are reference types, as are most every class provided in the .NET Framework. The built-in data types are listed in Table 3-3.

Table 3-3. C# Built-In Data Types

Type	Description	Type	Description
object	The base type of all other types.	bool	Boolean type (true or false)
char	Unicode character type	string	A sequence of Unicode characters
byte	8-bit unsigned integral type	sbyte	8-bit signed integral type
short	16-bit signed integral type	ushort	16-bit unsigned integral type
int	32-bit signed integral type	uint	32-bit unsigned integral type
long	64-bit signed integral type	ulong	64-bit unsigned integral type
float	Single-precision floating-point type	double	Double-precision floating-point type
decimal	Precise decimal type, 28 digits		

By default, a variable is passed into a method by value. When a parameter is passed by value, a copy of the data (the value of the object) is passed to the method. This means that when passing a value type, modifications to the variable in the destination method are not reflected in the original calling method.

When a reference type is passed as a parameter, the copy of the data being passed into the method is actually a copy of the reference to that object (a pointer), not a copy of the actual underlying object. This means that modifications to a reference type in the destination method are visible in the original method, since both methods are actually modifying the same object in memory.

This pass-by-value behavior can be modified by using the ref and out keywords, which force value types to be passed by reference. The out keyword, unlike ref, does not require that the variable be initialized before it is passed to the function. The example below illustrates this behavior:

```
public class ValueReference
{
  public ValueReference()
  {
    //int is a value type
    int val = 5;
    //The next line will print "5"
    Console.WriteLine(val.ToString());
    this.PassValue(val);
    //Even though PassValue() modified the parameter, this line will still print "5"
    //since a *copy of the value* was passed into the PassValue()
    Console.WriteLine(val.ToString());

    //Arrays are reference types. It is a pointer to a memory location.
    int[] array = new int[1];

    //Accessing this item in the array will dereference
    //the pointer and modify the value at location [0].
    array[0] = 5;
    //This will print "5"
    Console.WriteLine(array[0].ToString());

    //Passing "array" actually passes a pointer to the
    //array. When PassReference() modifys the passed
    //parameter, it dereferences the pointer to the
```

```
        //array. This means that modifications inside of
        //PassReference() modify the same locations in memory
        //as modifications here.
        this.PassReference(array);
        //This will print "10"
        Console.WriteLine(array[0].ToString());

        //You can use the the "ref" keyword to force a
        //value type to be passed by reference.
        val = 5;
        //The next line will print "5"
        Console.WriteLine(val.ToString());
        //Instruct the compiler to pass a pointer, *not* a copy of the data.
        this.PassValByRef(ref val);
        //This time, the next line will print "10"
        Console.WriteLine(val.ToString());
    }

    public void PassValue(int x)
    {
        //Modify the passed parameter
        x = 10;
    }

    public void PassReference(int[] y)
    {
        if(y.Length > 0)
        {
            //Modify the passed parameter
            y[0] = 10;
        }
    }

    public void PassValByRef(ref int x)
    {
        //Modify the passed parameter
        x = 10;
    }
}
```

While C# frees you from pointer manipulation (such as * and -> that are used in C and C++), it is important to be aware of what is happening behind the scenes. If you are not sure of what is actually being passed and modified, your program could exhibit surprising and unexpected behavior.

Classes

A class is the primary building block in C# (and .NET) and represents some logical entity or concept in the system. A class is a container that holds member variables, provides methods to modify the state of those variables, and may provide events to signal when certain circumstances are met. All objects that are defined with the class keyword are reference types.

Constructors

A constructor is the method that is automatically called when creating a new instance of the class. A constructor follows a new keyword. In the example below, a new instance of System.Uri is created by calling the constructor that takes a single string as an input parameter:

```
System.Uri myUri = new System.Uri("http://www.microsoft.com");
```

Methods

A method is an operation that can be performed on a class instance. Methods can modify the state of the class instance and optionally return some result based on the state. The example below shows the Uri class's ToString() method, which, when called, returns as a string the value of the Uri object (a URI is a location of an Internet resource):

```
myUri.ToString();
```

Methods can be *overloaded*. Overloading is the practice of having multiple methods with the same name and return type that each accepts different input parameters.

Instance Versus Static Methods

When working with classes, typically you'll create an *instance* of the class with the new keyword and then perform some work on that instantiated object. Instance methods are methods in a class that require a class instance in order to be invoked. In addition to instance methods, C# also supports *static* methods. A static method is one that can be invoked without instantiating the class.

The sample below shows a class with both static and instance methods, and illustrates the different syntax used in invoking these two types of methods:

```
public class PublicStaticExample
{
  private int val;
  public PublicStaticExample(int val)
  {
    this.val = val;
  }

  public int AddToVal(int y)
  {
    return this.val + y;
  }
  public static int Sum(int x, int y)
  {
    return x + y;
  }
}
```

Usage:

```
//Use the static method Sum
int nine = PublicStaticExample.Sum(5, 4);
//Create an instance of the class
PublicStaticExample ex = new PublicStaticExample(5);
//and then use the instance method
int ten = ex.AddToVal(5);
```

As you can see, static methods, which are defined with the static keyword, are called by using the class name followed by the method name. Instance methods, on the other hand, require a variable of that class to be created. They are called with the variable name followed by the method name.

The static keyword is not just for methods. Variables and properties can be defined to be static as well. When a member variable is defined as static, it will only exist in memory once. Even if multiple instances of the class have been created, the static member will only point to a single memory location.

Accessors/Properties

An accessor (sometimes referred to as a property) is a way to get and set values inside of a class or struct. It is really just a shortcut for the convenience of the programmer. Before accessors, in order to provide public access to a private member variable, you had to create, get, and/or set methods:

```
private int test;
public int get_Test()
{
  return this.test;
}
public void set_Test(int value)
{
  this.test = value;
}
```

To get and set values, you had to call the methods:

```
TestObject t1 = new TestObject();
t1.set_Test(5);
int x = t1.get_Test();
```

With accessors, you can accomplish this with a more concise syntax. Rather than explicitly creating set and get methods in the class, you instead write a single accessor statement:

```
private int test;
public int Test
{
  get
  {
    return this.test;
  }
  set
  {
    this.test = value;
  }
}
```

Typically, the get will simply return a value from a private member variable, whereas the set can be used to do input validation. (Note that the compiler actually expands the accessors into the get and set methods you see above.)

In the set block, value contains the value the user assigned to the property. The above code would be accessed with:

```
TestObject t2 = new TestObject();
t.Test = 5;
int x = t.Test;
```

You don't have to provide both get and set. You can provide read-only access by providing just a get block, for example.

Structs

A struct is, in many ways, similar to a class in its syntax. However, structs are always value types, whereas classes are always reference types. Structs should be used for lightweight objects that act like primitive types, are immutable, and have a small amount of state.

An example struct is shown here:

```
public struct PhoneEntry
{
  public string Name;
  public string Phone;
  public PhoneEntry(string name, string phone)
  {
    this.Name = name;
    this.Phone = phone;
  }
}
```

Structs are not allowed to have a zero-argument constructor defined by the user. The compiler automatically inserts one that initializes all values to a zero state. Additionally, you cannot inherit from structs.

Enums

An enum allows you to enumerate and name values. Its underlying type can be any integral type, except char. If no base type is specified, a 32-bit integer is used. An enum is a good way to define related constant values.

Following are three valid examples of enums:

```
public enum SimpleEnum
{
   Red,
   Green,
   Blue
}

public enum ByteEnumExample : byte
{
   //Any valid byte value can be used (0-255)
   First = 1,
   Second = 2,
   Third = 3
}

public enum CharEnumExample : int
{
   //It is legal to assign chars as values,
   //since the underlying type is still an int
   //(an implicit cast occurs).
   Alpha = 'A',
   Beta = 'B',
   Gamma = 'G'
}
```

Inheritance and Polymorphism

C# supports single inheritance. Below are examples showing Shape, Polygon, and Triangle classes. A Shape is the most general of the three. A Polygon is more specific than a Shape, and a Triangle is a specific type of Polygon.

```
/// <summary>
/// Shape is the base class that a group of Shape-related classes all inherit from
/// </summary>
public abstract class Shape
{
   /// <summary>
   /// Subclasses must provide an
   /// implementation for Draw
```

```
    /// </summary>
    public abstract void Draw();
}

/// <summary>
/// A polygon is a shape with a certain number of sides that are lines
/// </summary>
public class Polygon : Shape
{
    private int numSides;
    public Polygon(int numSides)
    {
        this.numSides = numSides;
    }

    public override void Draw()
    {
        Console.WriteLine("Polygon with {0} sides", this.numSides);
    }
}

/// <summary>
/// A Triangle is a Polygon with 3 sides
/// </summary>
public class Triangle : Polygon
{
    /// <summary>
    /// Call the base contructor (that of Polygon) with a value of
    /// 3 before processing code in this constructor.
    /// </summary>
    public Triangle() : base(3)
    {
    }

    public override void Draw()
    {
        Console.WriteLine("Triangle");
    }
}
```

If a class is marked with the abstract keyword, it means that the class cannot be instantiated; instead, a class derived from the abstract class must be used. If a method is marked with the abstract keyword, it means that the method does not provide any implementation. It must be provided by the class that directly extends the base class. If a class has any abstract methods, the entire class must be abstract.

The virtual keyword indicates that a method has a default implementation that can, optionally, be overridden. Methods that are not marked virtual cannot be overridden in a derived class. The override keyword denotes that the method overrides an abstract or virtual method that was defined in a subclass.

Interfaces

An interface allows you to define a signature of methods, properties, indexers, or events an implementing class must provide. Interfaces can be used to guarantee a sense of uniformity. Unlike virtual methods with inheritance, an interface cannot provide a default implementation; it is just a contract of a method signature:

```
public interface SampleInterface
{
  //Define a method that implementors of this
  //interface must create
  bool DoWork();
}

public class InterfaceUser : SampleInterface
{
  public InterfaceUser()
  {
  }

  public bool DoWork()
  {
    //Add the implementation for this method
    return false;
  }
}
```

Classes can implement multiple interfaces. Interfaces can also require that the class implement other interfaces (such as ICollection, which requires IEnumerable).

Threading, Events, Delegates

C# and the .NET Framework fully support multithreading. A thread is a unit to which the operating system can allocate CPU time. Working with multiple threads allows an application to perform multiple tasks at once. This is especially important for applications that need to simultaneously present a user interface and perform computations. A Web browser, for example, needs threads to download content, render the pages, and present a responsive UI all at the same time. Without multiple threads, the Web browser would stop responding while it was downloading and rendering, only allowing user interaction once all of the actions were processed in a serial manner.

Events

Classes can publish events that can be consumed by other classes. An *event* is signaled when some condition or action has occurred, such as a button being clicked, a timer ticking, etc. A class that is interested in the notification subscribes to the event. The use of events can be found mostly in applications that involve GUIs, with the events notifying classes of certain user actions. Events are declared with the event keyword.

Delegates

Similar to an interface, a *delegate* represents a contract—a caller agrees to implement a particular method. A delegate declaration actually defines a type in a single statement. Every delegate is declared using the delegate keyword as follows and is a subclass of System.Delegate:

> *attributes modifiers* delegate *resultType delegateName* (*argType argName*);

An instance of a delegate class encapsulates a method. A delegate instance is created using the new keyword:

> new *delegateName* (*expression*)

The *expression* must either be a value of a delegate type or a method group. If the argument is a *delegate type*, it must identify a specific instance in which to create the copy. If the argument is a method group, it must identify the object and method in which to create the delegate. The methods of a class may be overloaded, in which case the signature and return type of the delegate determines which method to implement.

Notice in the following example that the Test.myD field will be initialized with a delegate that refers to the first MyMethod because it matches that signature and return type exactly:

```
delegate int MyDelegate(int x);
class Test {
  MyDelegate myD = new MyDelegate(MyMethod);
  static int MyMethod(int x) {return x * x;}
  static double MyMethod(double x) { return x * x;}
}
```

The following example demonstrates events and delegates working together. It creates a class that performs addition in the background (DelegateSample) and raises an event when that addition has finished. In the real world, a computation that needs to be performed asynchronously such as this would be significantly more complex. To simulate that, a call to Thread.Sleep() is made to wait for five seconds:

```
using System;

namespace BlueLine
{
  /// <summary>
  /// The EventArgs that know about the result of the addition
  /// </summary>
  public class AdditionCompleteEventArgs : System.EventArgs
  {
    public int Result;
    public AdditionCompleteEventArgs(int result)
    {
      this.Result = result;
    }
  }

  /// <summary>
  /// A delegate used for the notification
  /// that the addition has completed.
  /// </summary>
  public delegate void AdditionCompleteEventHandler(object sender,
  AdditionCompleteEventArgs e);

  /// <summary>
```

```
/// A delegate for performing addition.
/// </summary>
public delegate void DoAdditionDelegate(int x, int y);
public class DelegateSample
{
  private int sum;
  public DelegateSample()
  {
  }
  /// <summary>
  /// A method to add two values, sleep 5 seconds,
  /// and signal the AdditionComplete event when finished.
  /// </summary>
  public void Add(int x, int y)
  {
    //Create a delegate that we can
    //BeginInvoke into the background
    DoAdditionDelegate myDel = new DoAdditionDelegate(this.DoAddition);
    myDel.BeginInvoke(x, y, new AsyncCallback(this.AdditionFinished),
    myDel);
  }

  /// <summary>
  /// The internal method used to perform the
  /// addition and sleep.
  /// </summary>
  private void DoAddition(int x, int y)
  {
    this.sum = x + y;
    System.Threading.Thread.Sleep(new TimeSpan(0, 0, 5));
  }

  /// <summary>
  /// A method that is called by Framework internals
  /// when the BeginInvoked method finishes
  /// </summary>
  private void AdditionFinished(IAsyncResult result)
  {
    ((DoAdditionDelegate) result.AsyncState).EndInvoke(result);
```

```
            OnAdditionComplete(this, new AdditionCompleteEventArgs(this.sum));
        }

        /// <summary>
        /// An event that signals that addition has finished.
        /// </summary>
        public event AdditionCompleteEventHandler AdditionComplete = null;

        /// <summary>
        /// Protected virtual method which is used to signal the event.
        /// </summary>
        protected virtual void OnAdditionComplete(object sender,
        AdditionCompleteEventArgs e)
        {
            if(AdditionComplete != null)
                AdditionComplete(sender, e);
        }
    }
}
```

The above example can be used with the following code:

```
class DelegateExecuter
{
    /// <summary>
    /// The main entry point for the application.
    /// </summary>
    static void Main(string[] args)
    {
        DelegateSample sample = new DelegateSample();
        sample.AdditionComplete += new
        AdditionCompleteEventHandler(sample_AdditionComplete);
        Console.WriteLine("About to perform addition in a background thread.");
        sample.Add(2, 3);
        Console.WriteLine("Background invocation complete.");
        System.Threading.Thread.Sleep(new TimeSpan(0,0,10));
        Console.WriteLine("Exiting.");
    }
```

```
        private static void sample_AdditionComplete(object sender,
        AdditionCompleteEventArgs e)
        {
            Console.WriteLine("The result of the addition was {0}.", e.Result);
        }
    }
```

The output will be:

```
About to perform addition in a background thread.
Background invocation complete.
The result of the addition was 5.
Exiting.
```

In the Main() method above, a new DelegateSample class is instantiated. An event handler is *wired up* to respond to the DelegateSample's AdditionComplete event.

When the sample.Add method is called, it creates a delegate and BeginInvokes onto a new thread. On that thread, the addition takes place, followed by it going to sleep for five seconds. Once that sleep expires, the AdditionFinished method is called, raising the AdditionComplete event via the OnAdditionComplete virtual method.

Meanwhile, the thread that is executing the Main() method is sleeping for ten seconds. When the DelegateSample instance finishes its addition, the event that was *wired up* is raised, executing the sample_AdditionComplete method. After a few more seconds of sleeping in the Main() method, the "Exiting" message is written to the console and the program terminates.

Looking Forward

The future of Microsoft programming is the .NET platform. The creation of the C# language is a large part of the .NET initiative; therefore, the popularity and acceptance of C# will be directly tied to the popularity and acceptance of the .NET platform. For more information on the .NET environment, visit the .NET area of the Microsoft Web site (http://www.microsoft.com/net).

At the end of 2001, the ECMA (European Computer Manufacturers Association) standards body ratified the C# and common language infrastructure specifications as international standards. The ECMA consists of representatives of many different companies in the IT industry. This ratification is a significant action, illustrating industry support for C# and .NET technology.

Chapter 4

VB.NET

VB.NET is the object-oriented evolution of Microsoft's proprietary language, Visual Basic. A "first-class citizen" in the world of Microsoft .NET, it is promoted as one of the primary languages directly supported by Microsoft. Because it is based on the .NET Framework, it allows developers who are familiar with Visual Basic to enjoy the power of an object-oriented language while maintaining the rapid development features of Visual Basic. Developers who already know Visual Basic will be familiar with the syntax of VB.NET, enabling them to concentrate on learning the new functionality available to them.

Rather than creating machine code specific to the architecture, the VB.NET compiler translates a program's source files into an executable file (.exe) or DLL library (.dll) that consists of Microsoft's Intermediate Language (IL). When an executable file or DLL library is used, its IL is compiled automatically at runtime by the .NET engine into native machine code. This two step process enables VB.NET programs to move among different platforms that support the .NET Framework, something that wasn't possible before. Platforms that have varying levels of support for .NET assemblies include various Windows versions, Windows Mobile 2002 and 2003, and even Linux. In addition to this portability advantage, the final compilation step during execution allows the VB.NET program to enjoy the speed previously reserved for programs written in C or C++.

VB.NET enables you to quickly create an application with a Graphical User Interface (GUI), as easily as you could a console application, Pocket PC application, or ASP.NET web application. In fact, depending on the design, parts of the same application could be used on all four platforms without modification.

Fast Facts

- VB.NET is case insensitive: public is the same as Public.
- When checking to see if an object has been assigned a value, the object is compared to "Nothing" (as opposed to "null" as with languages like C#). For example:

```
If (MyVariable Is Nothing)
  Console.WriteLine("empty")
```

- VB.NET source files have a .vb file extension.
- To include documentation in VB.NET code, an apostrophe can be used to delineate the start of a comment. For example:

```
' This is a comment
```

- To declare a variable, start a line with Dim.
- To provide immediate visual feedback in a GUI application, use something like MsgBox("You are great").
- Methods that return a value are called Functions. A sample Function is:

```
Public Function AddNums(ByVal Num1 As Integer, ByVal Num2  As Integer)
As Integer
  return Num1 + Num2
End Function
```

- Methods that do not return a value are called Subroutines, or Subs. A sample Subroutine is:

```
Public Sub DisplayMessage(text as String)
  MsgBox(text)
End Sub
```

- VB.NET uses the carriage return as the end of statement character. If you wish to continue a long statement onto a second line, you must use the line continuation character, the underscore '_'.
- All parameters are passed by value unless explicitly passed by reference. This is true for both class instances and primitive types.
- The terse += style operators are valid in VB.NET. This style enables you to condense the statement x = x + 3 to x += 3.
- To exit a looping construct prematurely, use the Exit keyword. This will stop the loop from continuing and will not evaluate the Boolean again. If you do not explicitly name the construct you are exiting, the innermost one will be assumed.

Sample VB.NET Program

The following sample shows a few of the features useful to the VB.NET developer. The Cereal class exposes properties about a cereal type and provides some useful logic. The program asks for information about a type of cereal and then gives back some additional information about the cereal, calculated from the information provided:

```
Imports System

Module SugarServingCalculator

  Sub Main()

    Dim SugarCereal As New Cereal
    Console.Write("How many grams of sugar in the box? ")
    SugarCereal.GramsOfSugar = Convert.ToInt32(Console.ReadLine())

    Console.Write("How many servings are in the box? ")
    SugarCereal.Servings = Convert.ToInt32(Console.ReadLine())

    Console.WriteLine("There are " &
      SugarCereal.SugarGramsPerServing.ToString() &
      " grams of sugar per serving.")

    End Sub
End Module

Public Class Cereal
  Private SizeOfServing As Integer
  Private SugarGrams As Integer
  Private NumServings As Integer

  Public Property Servings() As Integer
    Get
      Return NumServings
    End Get
    Set(ByVal Value As Integer)
      NumServings = Value
```

```
    End Set
  End Property

  Public Property GramsOfSugar() As Integer
    Get
      Return SugarGrams
    End Get
    Set(ByVal Value As Integer)
      SugarGrams = Value
    End Set
  End Property

  Public Property ServingSize() As Integer
    Get
      Return SizeOfServing
    End Get
    Set(ByVal Value As Integer)
      SizeOfServing = Value
    End Set
  End Property

  Public Function SugarGramsPerServing() As Single
    Return SugarGrams / NumServings
  End Function

End Class
```

Main Components

Each VB.NET program is different, but each one uses many of the same basic components. The example above creates a Module (EXE) named SugarServingCalculator. This simple program asks for information about a type of cereal and calculates the number of grams of sugar per serving.

Imports Statements

The very first line of our program is Imports.System. This line was unnecessary, but it enabled us to use the Console.WriteLine and Console.ReadLine statements without having to specify the full namespace every time.

Module Declaration

The declaration of the program follows the Imports statements. This program is a VB.NET Module that is command line executable. Because it is a module, the next line, `Sub Main()`, tells us where the program will start execution from. All of the program's flow is contained within one method, `Main()`. Larger programs should use the `Main()` to begin the execution flow and let other methods and classes do the work.

Classes

Classes are the typical way to represent a non-trivial data type in an object-oriented language such as VB.NET. Classes can encapsulate data, such as variables and constants, as well as behaviors, such as methods and subroutines. Classes allow you to enhance the functionality of an object by allowing inheritance, overloading, and protection. Our `Cereal` class in the above example defines three pieces of data, three property accessors for that data, and a single method for doing calculations.

Basics of a VB.NET Program

To create a VB.NET program, all you need is a text editor, a VB.NET compiler, and the .NET runtime. You can use Notepad in Windows to type in the code from the sample above. From the command line, use the following command to compile the application:

```
vbc.exe /reference:Microsoft.VisualBasic.dll /reference:System.dll MySample.vb
```

Note that your `vbc.exe` may need to be in your path to run it. This will create a file called `MySample.exe` that contains IL, which can then be run on any machine that has the .NET runtime installed. When the program is executed on the target machine, the .NET runtime will convert the necessary IL into machine code for the machine that it is running on and begin executing the program.

This is a very simple command line application; however, VB.NET is often used to create Windows applications. These applications could certainly be written in Notepad, but it would be difficult for any non-trivial application. Microsoft's modern development platform is Visual Studio.NET. VS.NET provides a single development environment for VB.NET, C#, and C++ programs (among others), in order to create Windows applications, command line applications, websites, and even mobile applications. Using VS.NET to write the same sample program is just as simple and also allows you to visually perform tasks such as setting compiler options and drawing forms. In addition, VS.NET integrates the compiler and debugger into a single interface.

Variables

One of the challenges of creating an application that integrates components written in different programming languages is that various programming languages might have different representations of variables. For example, an integer variable in one programming language might be composed of 16 bits, while in another language it is 32 bits. These discrepancies complicate things when components written in one language interact with another. If you have ever created a Visual C++ application that utilized a COM component written in Visual Basic, then you are probably familiar with the nuisances that arise when different programming languages fail to share a common representation of data types.

Fortunately, these problems are a thing of the past. The .NET Framework defines a core set of data types – strings, integers, floating point numbers, date/times, etc. – that *all* .NET programming languages use. That is, an integer in VB.NET is identical in its representation to an integer in C#, J#, or C++.NET. By sharing a common type system, .NET programming languages can seamlessly integrate with one another.

Option Strict

This option, when turned on, requires that the type of every expression be specified. Conversions or casts between variable types must be explicitly declared. That is, if the Option Strict is turned on, you must explicitly specify the resulting type when casting one data type to another. With Option Strict turned off, you can use implicit casting.

Option Explicit

Option Explicit, when turned on, requires that variables be declared prior to their use. Variables are typically declared using the Dim keyword. If you turn Option Explicit off, the compiler will allow a variable to be used without it first being declared. It is highly recommended that Option Explicit be on, since not using Option Explicit can easily lead to bugs due to misspellings. For example, you may create a variable named Age, but might later accidentally mistype the variable name as Aeg. If Option Explicit is not on, the compiler will think that Age and Aeg are two separate variables, when you meant for them to be the same.

In previous versions of Visual Basic, you could use the Variant data type to assign any type of expression to a variable. Because VB.NET is built on top of the .NET Framework, all code must interoperate with code written in other .NET languages. Because of this requirement, the Variant data type has been dropped.

While Visual Basic's particular implementation of Variant has been removed, the concept is still useable in VB.NET through the use of Object.

Every variable and class is a descendent of Object. This means that you could declare a variable of type Object and then assign any type to this variable.

As with methods, variables can have different protection levels such as Private, Protected, Friend, and Public. If a variable is declared Public, it is accessible directly by a caller using the syntax InstanceClass.VariableName. If a variable is declared as Private, it is only accessible to code inside of the class it is defined in. If a variable is declared as Protected, it is only accessible by the code inside of the class and code inside of a class that inherits from the original class. VB.NET also uses the Friend modifier to indicate variables or methods that can be accessed by other classes in the same assembly.

Often, you will need to convert between data types when passing data around. This process is called casting and VB.NET provides many ways to accomplish it. The syntax is similar to casting in Visual Basic. For example, if we had a variable that contained an Integer and we needed to express that variable as a Double, we would use CDbl():

```
Dim MyInt As Integer
Dim MyDouble As Double
MyInt = 4
MyDouble = CDbl(MyInt)
```

There are many built-in ways to convert between data types. They are: CBool(), CByte(), CChar(), CDate(), CDbl(), CDec(), CInt(), CLng(), CObj(), CShort(), CSng(),CString().

These methods are effective for converting between primitive data types. If you want to convert between two of your own data types, use the CType() method. This takes two arguments that are the types you want to convert from and to. This explicit casting will result in faster execution because the runtime does not have to interpret what is implied. For example, to accomplish the example above, you could use the following method:

```
Dim MyInt As Integer
Dim MyDouble As Double
MyInt = 4
MyDouble = CType(MyInt, Double)
```

Properties

Properties are a common way to expose a class variable to a caller. Good design discourages the use of internal variables directly, even if the variable is defined as public. A property lets you specify if the variable should be read-only, write-only, or read-write. It enables you to execute other lines of code when a variable is set or retrieved.

When using a property, a special parameter value is used. However, this parameter will not appear to the caller. If a property is called MyName, a caller might use the line:

```
Class.MyName = "David"
```

In the property definition, a parameter value of the same type as the property is implicitly passed in. The value parameter contains the value assigned to the property, David,in the above example.

```
Private Name As String
Public Property MyName() As String
  Get
    Return Me.Name
  End Get
  Set(ByVal value As String)
    Me.Name = value
  End Set
End Property
```

In this example, the property MyName stores its value using the variable Name, which is declared outside of the property definition. The MyName property has gettors and settors to retrieve and set the value of the variable Name. If we wanted to make the property read-only, we would remove the Set/End Set portion of the property definition. For example:

```
Public Property MyName() As String
  Get
    Return Me.Name
  End Get
End Property
```

Similarly, we could make a property write-only by removing the Get/End Get portion and leaving only Set/End Set.

Strings

In VB.NET, a String is an immutable representation of text or of a collection of characters. We can easily create a string variable and put something in it:

```
Dim MyString As String = "David"
```

Strings can be concatenated using the '&' character:

```
Dim FirstName As String = "David"
Dim LastName As String = "Iffland"
Console.WriteLine(FirstName & " " & LastName)
```

Constants

The keyword Const can be used to declare a primitive variable as a constant. A constant is a variable whose value must be specified at compile time and cannot be changed during runtime. To declare a constant, use the following syntax:

```
Dim Const MyName As String = "David"
```

When a constant is declared, the value must be set at the same time. You cannot declare a constant and then assign a value to it later.

The Const keyword is used when you want a primitive to stay the same. However, it follows the same protection as other member variables. If you want to create a constant that can be used across classes, you might use the Shared keyword. For example, if we want to use the acceleration of gravity as a constant throughout an assembly, we could put the following in our class:

```
Public Class Physics
  Public Shared Const GRAVITY As Single = 9.8
End Class
```

This constant could then be used by other code by using:

```
Dim Height As Single = 10
Dim Velocity As Single
Velocity = Height * Physics.GRAVITY
```

Arrays

An array is a variable that serves as an indexed collection of items of the same data type. The most common way to declare an array in VB.NET is the following:

```
Dim MyArray() As String
```

Notice that it is different from a normal variable definition by the addition of the ' () ' after the variable name. In this case, it will let the compiler know that MyArray is going to be an array of Strings, rather than just a single String. This particular definition does not actually tell us how big the array is going to be. If we wanted MyArray to be a collection of five String objects, we would do the following:

```
Dim MyArray(4) As String
```

This syntax tells the compiler to set aside room in memory for five String objects. But why did we say MyArray(4) instead of MyArray(5)? The number in the parentheses specify the upper bounds of the array, 4, but all .NET programming languages start indexing their array elements at 0, so MyArray(4) has five elements: MyArray(0), MyArray(1), MyArray(2), MyArray(3), and MyArray(4). To assign values to this array, we could then use statements like:

```
MyArray(0) = "Bud"
MyArray(1) = "Tim"
```

You can also pre-fill the array with five names, using the following syntax:

```
Dim MyArray(4) As String = {"Bud", "Tim", "Patrick", "Kent", "Travis"}
```

Modifiers

Modifiers are attributes of a class that change how the class behaves at both design time and runtime. For example, marking a class as NonInheritable tells the compiler that if another class attempts to inherit from this class, an error should be thrown and the build will not succeed. Some examples of modifiers are Public, Private, Protected, Friend, MustInherit, NonInheritable, Inherits, and Implements.

Statements and Expressions

Statements and expressions are the parts of a VB.NET program that perform some action or work. A statement will perform an assignment or define a sequence of events, while an expression will combine operands with operators. Program flow can be altered by statements such as if/then/else and while loops. An example of an expression is x = x + 1.

If/Else

The If/Else is one of the most basic ways to change program flow at runtime. It is called a conditional. It allows the program to do a Boolean comparison and perform one set of instructions if true and another if false. The syntax is:

```
If BooleanCheck Then
  ' do something if true
ElseIf SecondBooleanCheck Then
  ' do something if BooleanCheck is true, but 'SecondBooleanCheck is true
Else
  ' do something if neither check was true
End If
```

There are a couple things to note with the VB.NET syntax. The first is that the Boolean check is not surrounded by parentheses. The second is that instead of brackets as in C# or C++, the clauses are enclosed by Then, Else, and End If. The Then is special and it indicates to the compiler that the conditional check is over and the following code is what should happen if the conditional is True. The Else is optional and can be placed after the code that executes during the True. It provides a branch of code to be executed if the conditional is False. The conditional is completed with End If.

Select Case

Certainly, we could combine many If/Then/Else branches to execute different code branches, but if we are checking a single variable for different values and need to execute a different code path in each case, a better way to do this is to use a Select Case statement. The syntax is:

```
Select Case Variable
  Case option1:
    ' Do something
  Case option2:
    ' Do something
  Case option3:
    ' Do something
  Default:
    ' Do something if none of the other options were true.  This is optional.
End Select
```

While

To execute a sequence of steps repetitively until a given Boolean condition is True, use the While statement. This version of looping will check a condition before the loop is entered. If the expression is False, the steps inside the loop will not be executed. When the series of steps is over, the condition will be checked before executing again. Since the expression is checked before entering the loop, if it isn't True before it enters, the code inside the While .. End While will never be executed:

```
While BooleanExpression
  ' statement1
  ' statement2
End While
```

For/Next

The For/Next control flow style enables you to loop through a block of code a discrete number of times. The syntax is as follows:

```
Dim J as integer
For J = 0 To 10
  ' Do something here.
Next
```

The above block of code will loop through 11 times, each time adding 1 to J. If instead of incrementing by 1 every time, you can increment by an arbitrary amount by specifying the Step clause. If in the previous example, we wanted to increase J by 2 on every iteration, we would write the following:

```
Dim J as Integer
For J = 0 To 10 Step 2
  ' Do something here
Next
```

This block of code will now run six times, rather than 11 – J would start at 0, then go to 2, then 4, then 6, then 8, then 10. After the iteration in which J is 10, the For loop will terminate, as J is incremented to 12, which exceeds the bounds of the loop.

Foreach / Iterators

An iterator is a structure that provides a means to scroll through a collection of objects. While we won't go into how to create iterators, it's important to know how to loop through an existing collection that allows iteration. For this example, we're going to look at the DataTable.Rows collection. There are two primary ways for us to loop through each DataRow in a DataTable. The first is to use a For/Next loop:

```
Dim i As Integer
For i = 0 To MyDataTable.Rows.Length - 1
  ' Do something with each row here – MyDataTable.Rows(i)
Next
```

Please note that the For/Next loop started with zero. This is because the Rows collection – like all collections in the .NET Framework – is indexed starting at zero. While looping through a collection with a For/Next loop is one way to do this, the DataTable.Rows property supports iteration, so we could use the following syntax instead:

```
Foreach r as DataRow In DataTable.Rows
  ' Do something with each row here - r
End Foreach
```

VB.NET Methods

VB.NET classes typically include one or more subroutines or functions; these functions and subs are commonly referred to as methods. Methods are blocks of functionality that you can use to accomplish a task. They break code down into manageable and logical divisions. In the case of a Sub, a method is a block of code that has specific behavior, but does not return anything to the caller. A Function is a method that returns a value to the caller.

Shared vs. Instance

Typically, to invoke a method of a class, an instance of the class must first be created using the New keyword. These types of methods are called Instance methods. There is another class of methods called Shared methods. These methods can be invoked without requiring an instance of the class. Shared methods are denoted by the Shared keyword. Take the following example:

```
Public Class MathHelpers
  Public Shared Function AddNumbers(ByVal Number1 As Integer,
  ByVal  Number2 As Integer) As Integer
    Return Number1 + Number2
  End Function
End Class
```

A method declared in this fashion can be called using the syntax Classname.MethodName. No class instance needs to be created:

```
Dim MyNumber as Integer
MyNumber = MathHelpers.AddNumbers(1, 2)
```

The code in a shared method can only access other shared variables, methods, and events - they cannot access instance variables, methods, and events.

Main()

When a Windows or a command line application starts up, the runtime needs to know where to start execution. The entry point into the application is defined using the Sub Main() declaration. You can tell the compiler which Module to use as the start up module, and that module must contain a Sub Main() definition. This special subroutine can be used for initialization code and other start-up chores. For example:

```
Module MyModule
  Sub Main()
    ' Perform initialization code
  End Sub
End Module
```

Overloading

Overloading a function, subroutine, or constructor means to create multiple versions of the same structure with the same name, but with a different input parameter signature.

Let’s say we have a method that looks like this:

```
Public Function GetDate(ByValue DateString As String) As DateTime
  Return DateTime.Parse(DateString)
End Function
```

This single version of the GetDate method takes in a string representation of the date “3/6/2005” and returns an object of type DateTime that represents the same date. Let’s say we wanted to have a more granular version of this function, but still retain the existing function. In this case, we might also create a version of the method such as:

```
Public Function GetDate(ByValue Month As String, ByValue Day As String,
ByValue Year As String) As String
  Return new DateTime(Year, Month, Day)
End Function
```

This is another version of the same function. In this case, we could call the method in two ways. For example:

```
Dim MyDate As DateTime
Dim YourDate As DateTime
MyDate = GetDate(“3/6/2005”)
YourDate = GetDate(“3”, “6”, “2005”)
```

Overridable/Overrides

A virtual method is one that can be overridden, allowing a descendant class to extend the functionality of that method. For example, we have the following class definition:

```
Public Class Class1
  Public Overridable Function MyFunction() As String
    Return “Class1”
  End Function
End Class
```

In another code block, we have an instance of Class1 and call MyFunction.

```
Dim MyClass As Class1 = New Class1()
Console.WriteLine(MyClass.MyFunction())
```

We expect that “Class1” will be printed to the console.

Let's look at what happens when we inherit from Class1 and override the MyFunction method:

```
Public Class Class2
  Inherits Class1

  Public Overrides Function MyFunction() As String
    Return "Class2"
  End Function
End Class
```

Now, look what happens when MyFunction is called from a Class2 object:

```
Dim MyClass Class2 = New Class2()
Console.WriteLine(MyClass.MyFunction())
```

We expect "Class2" to be written to the console. Together, the combination of these techniques allows for code reuse and programmer flexibility. For example, if an existing class already provides some of the functionality required, you can extend the existing class rather than starting from scratch.

Abstract

An abstract method is one that does not contain any code, but is a simple declaration of what the method signature should look like in a descendent class. The use of abstract methods enables you to declare what behavior a class should expose without having to define what it does, leaving that for a descendent class to define.

Abstract methods in VB.NET need to be marked MustOverride. This syntax creates a very readable note. Abstract methods are defined by a single line in an Abstract class. If a class has an abstract method, it must be marked MustInherit. In fact, if a body is included in the method, an error will occur:

```
Protected MustOverride  Function AddNumbers(ByVal Number1 As Integer, ByVal
Number2 As Integer) As Integer
```

When inheriting from a class that is marked MustInherit, the derived class is required to create a body for every method marked MustOverride in the base class. If an abstract method in the base class is not defined in the descendent class, a compile-time error will be produced, resulting in a failed compilation.

Not Overridable

The opposite of MustOverride is NotOverridable. When required, you can mark a method NotOverridable to keep other developers and classes from creating a descendent that changes the desired behavior.

VB.NET Classes

A class is a basic structure used to define and create an object. An object is a way to hold information and code in an organized manner, typically containing variables, properties, and methods. For example, a store may define a class called "Cereal" for their grocery department and a class called "DVD" for their electronics department. The grocery department may need to know how much sugar is in each type of cereal, while the electronics department may want to know if the DVD is a widescreen version.

While each department needs specific information about the products, the general management may just want to know what the list price is of each product. All of these needs can be accomplished using classes. A base class called Product will store common information about all the store's products, such as price, using properties. The Cereal and DVD classes inherit from the Product class, extending the base functionality by containing information and logic specific to those types.

A class can also contain methods and events. In our store example, there might be an event called PriceChanged that fires whenever the price for a product changes. There might also be a method called ChangeInventory that is common to all product types.

Constructors

A constructor is a block of code that is run when a class is created that typically contains initialization code. A class can have multiple constructors to provide flexibility to users of the class. VB.NET uses the New keyword to create a constructor. A constructor must be a subroutine, since constructors cannot return values. A constructor can be empty, such as:

```
Sub New()
End Sub
```

This constructor would be called by creating an instance of Cereal using the New keyword. For example:

```
Dim BranCereal As Cereal = New Cereal()
Dim CornCereal As New Cereal ()
Dim WheatCereal As Cereal
WheatCereal = New Cereal ()
```

Constructors can be overloaded to provide different behavior when different parameters are available. For example, we could create a class called ZipCode using the default constructor, or one that fills in the class with a 5 digit zip code:

```
Sub New ()
End Sub
```

```
Sub New(ByVal zip As String)
  ' fill in the class
End Sub
```

Abstract

An abstract class is one that defines behavior for other classes and is not intended to be used directly. Abstract classes cannot be instantiated; instead, they must be inherited from. Similar to other inherited classes, they can provide behavior that other classes can use. To mark a class as abstract, use the MustOverride keyword, like:

```
Public MustOverride Class MyClass
  '...
End Class
```

Abstract classes, unlike non-abstract classes, can define abstract methods. Abstract methods are methods that must be defined in a descendant class and are also denoted using the MustOverride keyword at the method level.

Inheritance

To create a class that inherits from another class, the class definition line looks like this:

```
Public Class MySubClass
  Inherits MyBaseClass
End Class
```

This is a very readable way to determine if a particular class may inherit any functionality from another class. The class definition line reads almost like a complete English sentence, minus the punctuation. If you wish to reuse functionality in another class and change only parts of that class, a common solution is to inherit from the base class.

NotInheritable

If a developer creates a class or method and wants to ensure that it cannot be derived from, he or she needs a way to tell the compiler to enforce this rule. For classes, the class modifier NotInheritable is used. When the compiler sees a class that has this modifier set, it will not allow a subclass to extend the base class. An example of this modifier is:

```
Public NotInheritable Class MyClass
  '...
End Class
```

When a class is declared NotInheritable, no method may be marked MustOverride.

Instantiation

VB.NET now uses the New keyword to create an instance of a class:

```
Dim MyClass As Classname = New Classname()
```

Or the class can be declared on one line and instantiated later:

```
Dim MyClass As Classname
  ' other code here
MyClass = New Classname()
```

When you instantiate a class, the class instance is created and put on the heap, with a reference to the class on the stack. As you use the class instance, you are passing around a reference to the class instance. At run time, the CLR converts your reference into an actual memory location for the code to use.

The exact opposite is true if you are using a primitive type. When creating a primitive type – such as Integer, Boolean, Decimal, DateTime, etc. - you are putting the actual variable on the stack. By default, when you pass the variable to functions or subs, you are passing a copy of the variable. If you want to instead pass the reference to the primitive type, use the ByRef keyword. This tells the compiler to pass a reference to the variable, rather than just a copy of the variable.

VB.NET Interfaces

A similar concept to inheritance is the concept of Interfaces. An interface simply spells out what properties, events, and methods a class must contain. It cannot define the behavior. Similar to an abstract class, an interface declaration contains method and property signatures, but no implementation code.

A real world example of an interface is a stereo receiver. All stereo receivers have a volume knob, a power button, and source selection. As consumers, we don't care about the logic behind these controls, just that our stereo has these controls.

An example of where interfaces are used in the .NET Framework is in enumerators that implement the IEnumerable interface. This interface is used by common collections such as Arrays, Hashtables, SortedLists, and Stacks. The IEnumerable interface dictates a single method, GetEnumerator(), which returns an object that provides a means to enumerate through an ordered set of data. Classes that implement IEnumerable are known to be enumerable, and classes that implement this interface can be used in a For Each to loop through the object's items.

Interfaces provide a way to program against a common method signature on classes that are otherwise not related. Take the following example as a sample interface definition:

```
Interface IMyInterface
  Function MyFunction() As String
  Readonly MyProperty() As Boolean
  Sub MySub(MyString As String)
End Interface
```

To declare a class that exposes this predefined behavior, use the Implements keyword in the class definition:

```
Public Class MyClass Implements IMyInterface
  '...
End Class
```

This will tell the compiler to expect that the MyFunction, MyProperty, and MySub methods will be defined in MyClass. You'll need to add the appropriate methods, properties, and events dictated in the implemented interface(s) to create the MyClass class . To utilize the interface, an instance of the class is casted to the interface type. For example:

```
Dim MyInstance As New MyClass()
Dim MyBehavior As IMyInterface = MyInstance
MyBehavior.MySub()
```

You can see that if another class has been defined that implements the same interface, you could assign MyBehavior a different class type and achieve a completely different result, purely based on the class type used.

In this example, our interface was defined using the default access modifier Friend rather than a Public one, so casting our class to the interface type was required. However, if the interface is declared Public, the behavior can be accessed directly from the class instance. The code might instead look like this:

```
Dim MyInstance As New MyClass()
MyInstance.MySub()
```

Exceptions

New to VB is the concept of exceptions. Exceptions are errors that are raised by a method to inform the caller that there is a problem and an instruction cannot be completed. The advantage of exceptions over previous error handling methods in VB - such as On Error Goto statements - is that exceptions are more organized and can be elegantly handled.

Exception Handling

An exception can happen at any time; however, you can plan for an exception by creating an exception handler by enclosing a block of code in a Try/Catch block. An example of this is shown here:

```
Try
   ' do something here
Catch MyException as System.Exception
   ' Handle MyException here
Finally
   ' Code that should execute regardless here
End Try
```

A Try/Catch block includes code that might raise an exception within the Try portion. If the code in this section raises an exception, control flow is diverted to the appropriate Catch portion. Regardless of whether or not an exception is raised and caught, the code in the Finally portion is executed last. In this example, there is only one Catch block; however, there can be multiple Catch blocks, each handling different types of exceptions.

A special section of a Try/Catch is the Finally block. This is a block of code that will execute, regardless if an exception was thrown or not. It will always execute as the last step in any Try/Catch block. This section is helpful for using code that will clean up (close connections, files, etc.), by reducing redundant code blocks.

Throwing

To raise your own exceptions, use the Throw keyword. The Throw syntax allows you to throw exceptions, as well as catch a previously thrown exception, handle it, and *rethrow* it. To raise an exception, you can use the following syntax:

```
Throw New Exception("There was an error")
```

This single line will stop the program execution in its tracks and start bubbling an exception up the call stack. If there is no caller above that has a Try/Catch block enclosing the code where the exception was thrown, the executing program will terminate and display a runtime error.

If you have a Try/Catch block and wish to know about an exception, take some action (perhaps logging the exception information to some data store), but let that exception continue up the call stack and you'll *rethrow* the caught exception. Here's an example:

```
Try
   ' Do something here that causes an exception
```

```
Catch ex As Exception
  ' handle the exception
  Console.WriteLine(e.Message)
  Throw  're-throw the exception
End Try
```

As a general coding practice, you should catch the most specific exception you can. This means that if you know a specific type of exception might occur, you should plan on handling the specific exception rather than allowing a more general Catch block to handle it. Along these same lines, since Catch blocks are evaluated in order, the most general blocks should be after the more specific blocks.

Events

VB.NET continues the event-driven programming model as in earlier versions of Visual Basic. In general, event-driven programming executes code when something happens, an event, rather than in a procedural language where code is executed in order. An example of an event is when the mouse button is pressed. We can write a piece of code that will execute when the mouse button is pressed down. This code will not run until the user pushes one of the mouse buttons.

To respond to an event, use an event handler. An event handler is a subroutine that is executed in response to the firing of an event. We use the Handles keyword to mark an event as the event handler for a specific event. Let's take the mouse button down event as an example. There is no specific mouse click event, but there is a mouse down and a mouse up event. If we have a Windows form application, we can write code to respond to mouse events:

```
Private Sub MyForm_MouseDown(ByVal sender As Object, ByVal e As
MouseEventArgs) Handles MyForm.MouseDown
  ' Do something here.
End Sub
```

Typically, an event will have something like the MouseEventArgs in the above code snippet. Event arguments are passed in by the event raiser and give the handler information about the context of the event. For example, in the MouseEventArgs, we can obtain the following pieces of information:

- Button: Gets which mouse button was pressed.
- Clicks: Gets the number of times the above specified button was clicked.
- X: The x position of the mouse when the event happened.
- Y: The y position of the mouse when the event happened.

Using the event arguments, we can perform different behavior depending on the context of the mouse at the time of the event. The same event, MouseDown, is raised every time any mouse button is pressed, but we are able to change the code behavior based on the context of the event.

We can also create our own events and raise them to allow more sophisticated behavior. To define our own event, we use the following process:

```
Public Delegate Sub MyEvent(ByVal sender As Object, ByVal e As EventArgs)
Public Class MyClass
  Public Event DoSomething As MyEvent
  Protected Sub OnMyEvent(ByVal e As EventArgs)
    RaiseEvent DoSomething(Me, e)
  End Sub
End Class
```

The addition of the OnMyEvent Subroutine is not necessary; we could just as easily use the RaiseEvent operation every time we wanted to raise an event. However, the use of the OnMyEvent lets us perform any addition processing that we might want to do before or even after the event is raised. The RaiseEvent operation will create an instance of our event and any code that is declared as a handler for this event will be executed.

Looking Forward

There are some impressive language enhancements in the upcoming version of Visual Basic, dubbed Visual Basic 2005, to give even more power to Visual Basic users. Two notable enhancements are the addition of partial classes and the Using statement.

Partial classes allow you to put different parts of the same class into different files. This feature is useful for breaking up the same class into different logical divisions. For example, if a team has an automatic code generator, that automatic code can go in one file and code edited by a programmer can go in a different file.

Another useful feature that has previously been available to C# programmers, but not VB.NET users, is the Using statement. The Using statement allows you to create a variable that is only alive for a specific duration during a method and ensures that it is cleaned up when it is done being used. This is especially important when dealing with unmanaged resources such as database connection objects.

Wrapping MyConn in the Using statement ensures that when the End Using statement is reached, MyConn is automatically marked for disposal. Without a Using statement, MyConn would remain in memory until it was explicitly set to Nothing or the variable reference went out of scope.

Chapter 5

PERL

PERL (Practical Extraction and Report Language) is an interpreted scripting language that was written to supplant or compliment UNIX tools and shell scripting languages by combining some of the features of C, sed, awk, and shell. PERL's syntax and function attempt to simplify and add value to the original set of UNIX tools, mostly in the form of reporting, but today's PERL distribution is much more encompassing. PERL's greatest strength is in its text processing capability.

Larry Wall began writing utility code to organize frequently used procedures, eventually forming the initial version of PERL, which was released in October 1987 as version 1.0. Wall's initial intent was to write a language that made 'quick and dirty' small tasks trivial.

At the time, writing code to do some ordinary task would either require relatively arduous coding and debugging in C if it needed to perform quickly or inefficient writing with awk, sed, sh, and other UNIX commands. PERL attempts to satisfy both problems by creating programs to efficiently perform a particular function in regard to development time.

In the almost 20 years PERL has thrived as a well-guided open source (free software) project, it has grown from a small utility and reporting scripting tool to a very efficient language with a huge install base, from academic institutions to large corporations. Currently, PERL has one of the largest and richest APIs containing everything from W3 tools like XML/Schema/XSLT to even Palm Pilot synchronization and database libraries.

It also bears mention that PERL was used as the primary backend Web development with, now obsolete, CGI (Common Gateway Interface) scripting.

Fast Facts

- PERL is an interpreted language and requires the interpreter image (PERL program) to execute programs. PERL programs can be complied as stand alone, but the interpreter is bundled with the binary.
- PERL is a structured language. While it has all the features of the object-oriented paradigm, it is not considered by most to be a truly object-oriented language.
- PERL is not a type casted (statically typed) language; every variable instance is treated either in its context (scalar context) or is dynamically allocated on the heap.
- The primary documentation facility is 'perldoc', which provides documentation for almost every aspect of PERL. Use `perldoc -f open` to view the documentation of the `open` function.
- To execute a PERL program, invoke the command with the PERL interpreter program, such as: `perl <script>` i.e. `perl myscript.pl`.
- PERL has doesn't allow you to de-allocate memory similar to Java or Lisp. However, current implementations of PERL's memory reclamation aren't as mature as Java, so use caution with data allocation.
- Comments are denoted with a pound (#) at the beginning of the line. Comments can appear at the end of any line of PERL code if the pound comes after the end of the valid line of code.
- With some exception, most lines of code in a script end with or are separated by a semi-colon (;).
- The three first class data structures (loosely types) are scalars (i.e. numbers and strings), arrays, and hashes.
- The syntax to indicate a scalar is the dollar sign ($), an array is denoted with the at sign (@), and a hash by a percentage sign (%).
- Variables can, but need not be declared.
- Strings can quote with single quotes ('), double quotes (") or with the `qq` directive (i.e. `qq^string^`).
- PERL has default variables, which many functions act on, either as a default or a modification of a by product of some other action. They include $_ for scalars, @_ for arrays, and %_ for hashes.
- A PERL script should start with `#!<PERL interpreter path>` i.e. `#!/usr/bin/perl` and typically has a '.pl' extension.

Sample Program

This sample program is like the UNIX command wc in the way it reads a text file, counts the number of words and lines, and then prints out the statistics:

```
#!/usr/bin/perl

# put the content in an array and return the array
sub gather {
  my ($filename) = @_;
  my @data;

  open(FILE, $filename)
  or die "$0: can't open file '$filename' for read: $!\n";
  while (<FILE>) {
    chop;
    push @data, $_;
  }

  close FILE;
  return @data;
}

# return the total number of words in all elements of the passed array
sub countWords {
  my @lines = @_;

  for my $i (@lines) {
    my @split_up = split(/\s+/, $i);
    $total += $#split_up + 1;
  }
  return $total;
}

our @lines = gather($ARGV[0]);
our $num_words = countWords(@lines);
print "total number of words: $num_words, lines: ",
  $#lines + 1, " total\n";
```

Main Components of a PERL Program

Like most languages, PERL has syntax that lexically groups statements together. In PERL, this grouping syntax is curly braces ({}). Line 4's curly brace is terminated by line 19's brace.

Line 1 tells the operating system to execute the interpreter /usr/bin/perl to interpret this script. In Microsoft Windows, this might be something like: #!c:\Progra~1\perl\bin\perl.exe. Under UNIX/Linux, the script has to be made executable with chmod a+x <script> and then executed via ./<script>. Note that this isn't needed if you always execute the script with PERL (i.e. '% perl <script>').

Line 3 contains a comment. There can be whitespace before this comment as well.

Line 4 starts a subroutine definition. This isn't technically a PERL function, but for all practical purposes can be thought of as such. Please note that we don't have a prototype for passing arguments. That's because PERL is not a type-casted language.

Line 5 contains a my declaration, indicating that the scalar variable 'filename' is local to this subroutine. This is similar to a local variable in ANSI C. Otherwise, the variable would add to the global name space and be lexically visible to the entire program. The parentheses around the variable mean to allocate the value from the first element of the default array (@_) to the first variable declared in the parentheses, which is 'filename' since there is just one variable mentioned in the parentheses. The default array contains all the parameters passed to the subroutine. We see a call to this subroutine on line 30.

Line 6 contains a declaration of a variable local to the subroutine without initializing it.

Line 8 contains a function call to open, which opens a file for read. Here, FILE is the file handle to the open file. The 'or die' clause says to exit the program with the error message given in the string. In this context, the 'or' is much like '||' or the rest of a Boolean expression that is executed if open returns 0. In PERL, we could rewrite this as:

```
if (open(FILE, $filename) != 0) { die "..."; }
```

However, terse syntax (within reason) is usually the norm in the PERL culture. The $0 variable is the name of this script, which indicates to the user what program failed in the scenario this program was called from or a chain of commands, etc. The $! is a variable that contains the error string of the last error message that occurred in open. If the file that is attempting to be opened doesn't exist, an error message would look something like:

```
sample.pl: can't open file 'dat.txt' for read: No such file or directory
```

Line 10 - 13 is a while loop that reads the input file and terminates when the end of file is reached. The <FILE> statement gets the next line of input from the FILE descriptor and stuffs it in the $_ variable. You can also make an assignment to any variable with the syntax while($myvar = <FILE>). It returns NULL or 0 when there are no more lines to read.

Line 11 calls the chop function to remove the last character of the string passed, or in this case, uses $_ as the string since no string is passed to it. This gets rid of the new line.

Line 12 adds a line of data to the end of the data array variable by calling the push function. Arrays in PERL are not static in length, so this actually increases the size of the array by one for every call to push.

Line 15 closes the file handle and de-allocates the OS side resources, and Line 16 returns the array variable.

Line 21 sets every array element in the variable 'lines' to each parameter passed to the subroutine countWords. This is a slightly different usage of parameter passing we saw earlier, but the semantics are the same. In this case, think of each line as a parameter of a potentially very large list of parameters to pass. This is a very inefficient way to pass data to subroutines because we are passing by value and effectively copying each string, but is provided to contrast with single parameter passing.

Line 23 contains a for loop which sets the scalar variable i to each line as it iterates the entire array variable lines. We could omit the my keyword if we wanted to make the variable global. Because we did include it, the variable is local or private to the for loop.

Line 24 creates a variable that is locally scoped to the for loop with the my keyword. It then uses the split function call to split (tokenize) using whitespace as a delimiter the contents of the i variable, which contain the contents of the line. In this function call, the first parameter (parameters are delimited with a comma) is the regular expression defining the boundaries of each token, or where to split each word in this case. The \s+ means any whitespace.

Line 25 increments the word count to the number of words of the current line. The $#split_up returns the number of elements in array variable split_up minus one. The + 1 makes this the number of words in the array. Notice we don't use the my keyword in front of scalar variable total. By not using the keyword, we create a global variable as soon as the PERL interpreter evaluates this line. This is probably a mistake because if we happen to call another function that uses the same variable name, it will corrupt our value of 'total'. For that reason, it is recommended to declare variables and their scope in each subroutine unless the script will always stay relatively small and limited in scope. However, many times scripts are expanded and going back through the script to add these qualifiers takes time and is problematic.

Line 30 first declares a module level scoped variable with the our keyword, which is like my, but is limited to the lexical scope of this script starting at the point it is declared. This variable is set to the content of the file named by the first parameter, passed to the script, and denoted by $ARGV[0]. The $ARGV is the syntax for an array that addresses a particular element. In this case, the array contains the parameters passed from the command line and [0] is the first element of the array. Gather returns an array by reference and sets copies to the size of the array and all array elements to the lines variable.

Line 31 invokes the countWords subroutine to count the words. The input of the countWords subroutine is the output from the gather subroutine. The number of words in the entire text, which is found in the lines variable array, is returned as a integer scale to the num_words variable.

Lines 32 - 33 print the output with substituted values of the num_words and number of elements in array lines (the number of lines in the file). Any text in the quotes that has variable syntax (i.e. $<variable name>) gets replaced with the value of that variable. The \n symbol means to print a new line at the end of the line.

Basics of PERL

As mentioned, PERL is (primarily) an interpreted language so you only need the PERL interpreter binary instead of a compiler, IDE (per se), or toolkit. You will need a text editor like Emacs, vi, or Windows Notepad.

A popular distribution under Windows is ActivePerl. Another is the ported PERL via GNU tools that come with Cygwin from Cygnus.

Under Linux/UNIX, most distributions have packing systems (i.e. Redhat, Solaris, AIX). Of those systems, most include PERL as optional package. In fact, most include it by default. To find out if you have it under Windows, look for 'perl.exe', under Linux/UNIX, do which perl and whereis perl. This will almost always yield /usr/bin/perl, although /usr/local/bin/perl is another possibility. If you don't have PERL, you can get it from http://www.cpan.org/ports/.

Once you have your PERL interpreter, invoke a script by executing the interpreter with your script as a parameter, then script parameters afterwards. For example:

```
perl <your script> <arg1> <arg2>
```

You'll have to prefix perl with an absolute path if not already in your path.

Namespace

Namespace in PERL is not often used in most PERL programs, but it more prominent in enclosure and lexical scope. While namespace is relevant to the PERL object system, it serves to provide a hierarchy for modules (PERL packages). Namespace is defined by two things only: file system directory structure in relationship to where PERL module files exist (file with the '.pm' extension) and the name of the PERL module file itself.

For example, if you wanted to create your own package Foo and create a module called bar, create a directory Foo and a file called Bar.pm in the Foo directory. Then, include the directory containing Foo in the environment variable PERL5LIB (see the perlrun man page). In the script that uses this module, add use Foo::Bar; to the top of the script, which includes the package into the namespace (like include in C or import in Java).

There are two primary namespaces in PERL. There is the aforementioned module namespace, which is explicitly notated in the code, and another implicit namespace called main, for the script you are running. In our example program mentioned earlier, we forgot to declare the total variable with the my keyword in line 25 to make it scoped only to the subroutine. When you don't qualify the scope of a variable, it is put in the global namespace or more accurately, the main namespace.

Just as the use declarations or any namespace, we refer to the global or main namespace as main::. For instance, our sample program is exactly the same if we use either of the lines below, and both are equivalent to the interpreter:

```
$total += $#split_up + 1;
$main::total += $#split_up + 1;
```

Strict

Many consider global variables undesirable for a variety of reasons. If you want to restrict any script of a PERL module to not 'pollute' the global namespace, you can include use strict vars; at the top of your script to enforce this policy. If a script or module violates the global namespace policy, the interpreter halts the program indicating the line number and infringing variable.

Scope

PERL, like most languages, has lexical scoping of variables, meaning a variable exists or is valid for a literal lexical region of text in the code. Chronologically, the variable is allocated at the beginning of the function. When the function terminates, any variables that were declared for the scope of the function are de-allocated.

There are three main kinds of scope in PERL:

my - this the most restrictive and private and pertains to whatever level of function or control a structure is given. For functions, it is valid for the scope of that function. For a while or for loop, it is valid only in the respective control structure.

local - valid for the function in which it is defined and any functions called from the function in which it is defined.

our - a somewhat recent addition, which enables variables to be valid for the lexical scope of the program file (script or '.pm' module).

Data Structures

The heading for this section would normally be 'Variable Types'. However, PERL is not a type-casted language, so there are no types. This subtle difference between PERL and other dynamically typed languages like Python and Ruby with other statically typed languages like C and Java makes it relative to popular contemporary technology. However, there are three principle first class data structures in PERL that have their own sets of behaviors. They are:

scalars - these are a 'flat' data-like strings and numbers, including floats, digits, etc. These also can be references and any other single element data in PERL.

arrays - these are arrays in the normal definition of the word. Elements of arrays are scalars or references to other first class (primitive) PERL data structures.

hashes - these are hash tables in the normal definition of the word. These are a one to one constant time (time complexity of O(1)) associative data structure of a mapping of key value pairs. Both keys and values are first class PERL data structures.

As implied for each definition, PERL data structures can and often are nested. They can be nested as literal (pass by value) or by reference. The conical ways to initialize literal data structures in PERL follow.

Scalars

Scalar data is included between a quote ('), double quote (") or the qq syntax:

```
qq<delimiter character><scalar data><delimiter character>
```

The qq syntax is nice for literal text you want to include in the PERL script, but don't want interpreted as PERL syntax. To do this, you cannot include the delimiter character in the content itself. For example:

```
$a = "dog";    # a string
$b = 43;       # an integer
$c = 1.23;     # a floating point number
$d = qq^text^; # equivalent to '$d = "text";'
```

Access to scalars is the same as assignment and initialization:

```
print $a;
print "scalar value is $a\n";
```

Arrays

Parentheses are used to create new literal arrays:

```
@a = ('a string', "another string", 234.44);
```

Like scalars, a special syntax qw quotes words. For example:

```
# equivalent to '@a = ("dog", "cat", "fish");
@a = qw(dog cat fish);
```

To access a given element, use the scalar notation since an array element resolves to a scalar when indexed. The index is given in brackets right after the variable name. This is because what we are getting out of the array *is* a scalar. For example:

```
print "element: $a[0]\n";
```

In this example, we use substitution once again. As mentioned, the substitution replaces the PERL variable syntax ($a[0] in this example) with its value at runtime. Since there is a lot more going on here than just a substitution (like syntax pattern matching and evaluation), this has a special name in PERL, which is *interpolation*. The same syntax is used to assign:

```
$a[4] = "fourth";
```

Please note that even if the array has just been created, the above will not cause any errors because of the tolerant and robust approach to PERL. When assigning array elements that don't yet exist like the above, all elements up to the assigned element are not initialized, as shown in this example:

```
for $_ (@a) { print "value: $_\n"; }
```

The line above would yield:

```
value:
value:
value:
value:
value: fourth
```

Hashes

Hashes key and value pairs are given directly in the initialization form:

```
%a = ('animal' => 'dog', food => 'samosa' );
```

In this example, the parentheses group a listing of key/value pairs. Key/value pairs are separated by commas. The => separates the key (on the left) from the value (on the left).

Like arrays, hash values resolve to scalars so scalar notation is used once again:

```
print "animal type: $a{animal}\n";
```

Access is again, the same:

```
# replace the value in the case of already existing entries
$a{animal} = "cat";


# assign what was a
$a{class} = "first";
```

To get the set of keys use the 'keys' function:

```
print "keys: ", join(", ", keys(%a)), "
values: ", join(", ", values(%a)), "\n";
```

Which yields:

```
keys: food, class, animal
values: samosa, first, cat
```

If what you want are the entries, use each:

```
while (($key,$value) = each %a) {
  print "$key -> $value\n";
}
```

In this example, each iteration of each returns a two element array. The first element of the array is the key and the second the value. The parentheses assign these values respectfully to $key and $value. The example yields:

```
food -> samosa
class -> first
animal -> cat
```

References

References in PERL are simply scalar data. They have the same syntax as normal scalars in the context of variable passing. However, the creation of references has a slightly different syntax.

A reference is exactly like a pointer in C or C++, with the exception of direct access or the numerical contents of the variable (think pointer arithmetic), meaning that you can't access reference numbers. In this case, the numbers are memory locations. Instead, you can only assign them and de-reference them. It is the exact same concept of a reference in Java or a variable binding in Lisp.

To create a reference, add a backslash (\) in front of the variable being assigned. To access (dereference) the scalar value, use two dollar signs ($$) instead of one. For example:

```
# create a string scalar
$a = "a string";
# create a reference to the string.
$b = \$a;
```

After the above assignment, $b and $a both refer to the same scalar in memory.

```
# access the scalar data via the reference
print "the contents of the value of the reference is: ", $$b, "\n";
```

Arrays and hashes have a slightly different syntax. Again, like C, they use an arrow to deference data. For example:

```
# create a three element array
@a = qw(cat dog fish);
%y = ( instrument => 'sitar', food => 'samosa' );

# create a reference to the array
$b = \@a;
$z = \%y;

print "$b->[1], $z->{food}\n"; # yields `dog, samosa'
```

Initialization

There is also an initialization form for references as well. Once created, these references are not bound to any variable except that which is assigned to it. Therefore, it is better to not use this form often or in tight loops because of the heap memory allocation and de-allocation. Instead, memory is better handled by creating non-reference data structures and passing them, when necessary, as references.

Non-reference data structures are better because memory reclamation (similar to garbage collection) isn't efficient in current implementations of PERL, and because the interpreter has less control of memory allocation since it is dynamic. When declaring in place variables, the interpreter knows when the memory for those variables are valid and when they go out of scope. To create a new array reference, use brackets instead of parentheses:

```
$a = [ "dog", "samosa" ];
print "tasty: $a->[1]\n"; # yields `tasty: samosa'
$a = []; # creates an empty array
```

To create a new hash reference, use curly braces in place of the parentheses:

```
$a = { animal => "dog", food => "samosa" };
print "man's best friend: $a->{food}\n";
$a = {}; # creates an empty hash
```

Operators

Again, PERL attempts to make both C and UNIX script authors happy. This is manifested in operators. The following table summarizes each operator and its equivalent C/UNIX script form (note that PERL has its own order of operations, so there is a precedence associated with the order in which sub expressions are evaluated). As the table suggests, any conditional syntax is a super set of UNIX 'test' command.

Table 5-1. PERL Operators

UNIX	ANSI C	Description
and	&&	logical and
Or	||	logical or
none	&	bitwise and
none	|	bitwise or
not	!	not
Eq	==	equal
ne	!=	unequal
lt	<	less than
gt	>	greater than
-f	None	true if following string argument is an existing file false otherwise
-d	None	true if following string argument is an existing directory false otherwise

Conditionals and Control Structures

Conditions (i.e. if) and control structures (loops) take two forms, as do many things in PERL. These include a C like syntax and UNIX scripting like syntax. However, much of PERL syntax is truncated or has a syntax that is less verbose or *shortcut*.

if/else

In general, the conditions in PERL have the syntax of both C and traditional UNIX scripting:

```
if (<expression>) {
  ...
} elsif (<expression>) {
  ...
} else {
  ...
}
```

The elsif is an else if and is optional. The end else is also optional. There can be 0 or more elsif blocks but only one if and else block.

Replacing the if keyword with the unless keyword is the equivalent to adding a not (!) or negating the if. For example, these two lines are equivalent:

```
if ( ! $condition_var ) { print; }
unless ( $condition_var ) { print; }
```

Unlike C, in PERL it is illegal to have a one line block when the keyword comes before the block. The above example has a syntax error in the way it is missing the curly braces, whereas the below includes them. The following example is illegal:

```
if ( $condition ) print "yes";
else print "no";
```

However, a slightly more terse syntax exists. In this syntax, put the if or unless after what is to be done. It is helpful if the if or unless block is only one line long. For example:

```
print "yes" if ( $condition );
```

Note that you cannot use if/else with this syntax.

for, while Loops

The while loop has the form:

```
while (expression) {
  ...
}
```

The while loop continues while *expression* evaluates to anything defined but 0. The for loop, on the other hand, can take many forms. A for loop that iterates over a list and assigns a variable to each element of the array follows:

```
for <variable> (<array variable>) {
  ...
}
```

For example:

```
for $i (@array) {
   print $i;
}
```

C programmers might be more comfortable with the form:

```
for(int $i = 0; $i < 10; $i++) {
   ...
}
```

This has the abbreviated form:

```
for $i (1..10) {
   ...
}
```

next, last

The next and last keywords can be used inside either the while or for loop. The keyword next stops execution of the remaining loop and continues at the beginning of the loop. The next keyword is used in the following example:

```
for $i (1..5) {
   next if ($i == 4);
   print "$i\n";
}
```

The lines above would yield:

```
1
2
3
5
```

The last keyword terminates the entire loop prematurely. For example:

```
for $i (1..5) {
   last if ($i == 3);
   print "$i\n";
}
```

The lines above would yield:

```
1
2
```

Labels

Labels aid in jumping to an outer loop level. The syntax is a *termination* keyword and then the label afterward. For example:

```
outer: for $i (1..5) {
  for $j (1..3) {
    last outer if ($i == 2 and $j == 2);
    print "$i, $j\n";
  }
}
```

In this example, when the last outer statement is executed, the interpreter will terminate the for loop with the label outer before it. The output yields:

```
1, 1
1, 2
1, 3
2, 1
```

If the label was omitted, the inner loop is used by default and the outer loop will continue to cycle.

Subroutines and Functions

Subroutines and functions are like methods in Java or functions in C. They break up code not only in easy to understand logical pieces, but also in places where a particular functionality is called more than once and is included to avoid cutting and pasting copies of code.

Calling

Calling subroutines happens much like it does in the C language. List the function name, followed by comma separated parameters in parentheses:

```
function name(parameter1, parameter2, ...);
```

For example, the built-in print function can take as many arguments as we want to give it:

```
print("hello ", "there ", "world");
```

Ampersand Prefix

An ampersand in front of a function is/was used to call a function in PERL 4. Sometimes you see this form as such:

```
&function("hello world\n");
```

As you might have noticed, the parentheses aren't needed, and are usually omitted in PERL. Among other things, PERL allows a more C-like syntax for those who are used to C, or a more shell-like syntax for those who are used to scripting.

The ampersand in front of functions was required in the old PERL 4 version. However, if you see it in newer code, it also has the implication of calling a function defined in the current 'main' namespace.

The my clause isn't needed if you don't need to accept any parameters; however, in general, it is a good idea to use take this form when the subroutine takes parameters.

The my clause illustrates how parameters are passed in the temporary @_ array in PERL. You could pass a large array and only one array, but as mentioned, this is inefficient and doesn't allow for other parameters to be passed in. Instead, it is better to pass large data structures by reference and then let the subroutine operate on the data structure through its reference. For example, consider:

```
sub collect {
  my ($a) = @_;
  for my $i (1..5) { push @$a, $i; };
}
sub printCollection {
  my ($a) = @_;
  for my $i (@$a) { print "collected: $i\n"; }
}
sub main {
  my @array;
  collect(\@array);
  printCollection(\@array);
}
main();
```

In this example, we call the main procedure, which in turn calls collect and printCollection. Instead of letting collect create an array, either by a named variable and passing back by value in a return statement or by creating an array reference on the heap, we create the named variable in the main function where it is created and will be de-allocated quickly in one spot.

The collect function pushes new data into the data structure by de-referencing the array variable. Additionally, we pass by reference and use the data structure to another function, printCollection, where once again, we don't incur pass by value penalties.

CPAN

CPAN is the "Comprehensive PERL Archive Network", which is not only a huge repository (http://www.cpan.org) of all sorts of useful tools and APIs, but it is also a tool for managing the installation of PERL modules and packages.

In fact, CPAN is a very comprehensive, well-organized, and streamlined tool that does everything from dependency generation to querying for packages with PERL regular expressions.

To invoke the CPAN command line interactive tool, simply invoke the "cpan" tool, or invoke the interpreter directly with perl -MCPAN -e shell.

Once in the tool, you will have a cpan> prompt, which has a very good help facility. To install a package, use install <package>. For example, install Package::Foo installs the Package::Foo packages/modules and all of its dependencies directly into the default PERL installation.

Advanced Concepts

This section discusses more advanced concepts in PERL. The power of PERL is demonstrated and becomes evident with more advanced usages like Dynamic Evaluation.

Dynamic Evaluation

Previously, we said subroutines are essentially functions. That is, they are more than just a forward declaration. In other words, a subroutine is something validated at the beginning of running a script, but isn't evaluated until it is called. This is the reason you will often find many compile time errors in other languages at runtime in PERL.

This is another powerful feature of the language that gives it some of the features of a symbolic language like Lisp or Prolog, which allows code to be modified and executed at runtime. An example of this concept is working on an engine while it is running.

One example of anonymous functions where braces are given indirectly as the syntax to a subroutine invocation (i.e. 'grep { ! /^#/, @arr }') would return the contents of @arr but with all lines starting with the hash, like comments. Anonymous functions are like anonymous classes in Java or lambda expressions in Lisp.

To illustrate all of these concepts, consider the code snippet below. This program reads a program from a string, then modifies and executes it:

```
1 @program = split /\n/, qq
2 ^# this is a perl program embedded in another
3 # comment to extract
4 for \$i (1..3) {
5    print "value of \\\$i: \$i\n";
6 }
7 ^;
8
9 $count = 0;
10
11 @nocomment_program = grep {
12    $count++;
13    if ($count == 2) { print "filtering out line: `$_'\n"; undef; }
14    else { $_; }
15 } @program;
16
17 $new_code = join("\n", @nocomment_program);
18 print "executing: \n", $new_code, "\n";
19 eval $new_code;
```

This will yield:

```
filtering out line: `# comment to extract'
executing:
# this is a perl program embedded in another
for $i (1..3) {
  print "value of \$i: $i\n";
}
value of $i: 1
value of $i: 2
value of $i: 3
```

In the above example, we first create an array containing a PERL program, each element is a line of code. We do this by quoting the program (lines 1 - 7) and invoking the split function (functions don't need parentheses around them) to separate into an array using the new line as the delimiter.

Then, we create another version of the program, but strip out the second line of the program, which is a comment in lines 11 - 15. We do this by invoking the grep function with an anonymous function, which is the code content between lines 12 - 14. Line 15 contains the terminating brace and the array to filter, which is our original program. When the grep function runs, it executes our code setting $_ to the current line and returning values we return from our anonymous function as the output as an array, which is the nocomment_program variable.

In line 17, we piece the content of the program back together and print it out in line 18 to see our filtered program line. We then use the eval function in line 19 to invoke the PERL interpreter to run the code as the string we just printed.

Because we can create code in code, this enables more advanced programming like genetic algorithms which are programs that modify themselves with use of a self modifying algorithm, such as a mutation engine.

Scalar Context

Scalar context refers to how data is treated depending on the type of data structure being used. One example is the way an array is used. Consider the following example:

```
1 @list = qw(one two three);
2 @copy = @list;
3 $count = @list;
4 print "$count == ", $#copy + 1, "\n";
```

The lines above yield:

```
3 == 3
```

In this example, line 2 copies the array but in line 3, @list returns a scalar value, which is the number of items in the list. This is because the context is a scalar, since we are setting it to a scalar vs. an array. The determining factor is the data structure we are using for the assignments. In the assignment, we are setting the scalar expression ($count) to @list, which gets evaluated as a scalar resulting in the length of the array. This is just like overloading operators in C++ and operating on two objects (i.e. adding), in turn invoking the overloaded operator function on the object:

```
@arr_output = `ls -l`;
$str_output = `ls -l`;
```

The first line above puts the returned output from the ls command as elements, one element per output line, in @arr_output. The latter line, the entire output, new lines and all, gets set to the scalar.

Regular Expressions

Regular expressions are strings that specify search criteria and what to replace in matched text during searches. Regular expressions are primarily used for three things:

- Match text - determines whether or not text matches a pattern.
- Modify text - replaces some text for other text by pattern matching part of it, either in the regular expression or other matched text.
- Extracting text - matches a pattern and then takes some of the content of the text in or around the pattern.

Regular expressions are very powerful. This is the reason why they are so complicated. However, once you get the hang of it, you'll find you can't do without them.

The PERL regular expression engine (engine for short) takes two things as input: the regular expression pattern (pattern or just `pat' for short) and the text string to match against, replace, or extract from text.

The engine starts reading text from left to right and matches characters one at a time against the pattern given to it. If it matches text, it goes as far as it can with the match and terminates with the results, which is either the extracted text or the replaced text, or simply that it matched something and where. If the engine doesn't find a match for the pattern, it goes to the end of the line and tries to match, reading back from right to left.

The best and perhaps only way to learn and understand regular expressions is with examples. Searching for regular expressions in Emacs real time can be a great learning tool. However, be warned that Emacs regular expressions and PERL regular expressions are slightly different.

Matching

While the scope of this chapter doesn't include an exhaustive coverage of the extremely feature rich set of functionality in PERL regular expressions, it does give the most useful patterns.

In PERL, there are slightly different forms of regular expressions that tell PERL to match, extract, or replace text. However, the syntax is the same across all operations. For the sake of simplicity, we'll start with match patterns.

If you want PERL regular expressions to match on the `$_', the syntax is:

```
/<pattern>/
```

This will return a Boolean indicating whether or not it was found, which is why this form is used with conditionals.

Each of the following is a character or string form used in the regular expression pattern. Any alpha numeric characters that appear in the regular expression pattern indicate to match those characters.

Table 5-2. Characters Used in Regular Expressions

Chars	Description
^	**Match something at the beginning of the line.** This 'anchors' the search by starting at the beginning of the search string and matching only at the beginning. Only after matching the beginning will the engine proceed to match the rest of the search string.
$	**Match something at the end of the line.** This 'anchors' the search at the end, meaning that if the ending text doesn't match what comes directly before the '$', the engine doesn't proceed. For example: $_ = "cat"; if (/cat/) { print "found\n"; } # yields `cat' This prints `cat' and we say that our pattern /cat/ matches. Since `$_' is set to `cat', patterns /^cat/, /cat$/, and /^cat$/ all match, but /^at/ and /^ca$/ don't match. If the pattern doesn't contain either ^ or $, it matches anywhere in the middle as well. For example /c/, /ca/, /cat/, /at/ all match `cat'.
.	**Matches one character of anything.** For example, /^.at$/, /^c.t$/ and /^ca.$/ all match `cat'.
.*	**Matches 0 or more characters.** For example, /^.*t$/ and /^.*cat/ both match `cat'.
.+	**Matches 1 or more characters.** The pattern /^.+at$/ and /^.+t$/ match `cat', but /^.+cat$/ does not.
.?	**Matches 0 or 1 characters.** Both /^c.?t$/ and /^ca.?t$/ match `cat'.

Chars	Description
[]	**Match a character range or set of characters.** This only matches one character instance in the search string and can be qualified with + and *. For example, /^[a-z]at/, which defines the character range from anything from alpha characters from a through z, will match `cat', `pat', `patrick' (note that there is no terminating $ in the pattern which is why 'rick' isn't matched), but would not match `flat', `Cat', or `8at'. Likewise, you include specific characters by simply juxtaposing them: /^[abc]at$/ matchs `cat', `aat', and `bat' only, not `pat'. To qualify character ranges, use the same qualifiers for the dot (.) pattern previously mentioned. For example /^[a-zA-Z]+[0-9]$/ matches `c9', `C9', `Cat9', and `DOG0', but not `9'. In this example, we have two ranges, upper and lowercase alpha characters.
{N,M}	**This is a qualifier that matches a number of occurrences.** It means to match at least N occurrences but no more than M. Ether number can be omitted, meaning that criteria is left out of the picture.
{N}	**Match exactly N occurrences.**
{N,}	**Match at least N occurrences.** For example, /^fo{2,3}$/ matches `foo', and `fooo', but not `fo' or `foooo'. The pattern /^fo{2}$/ matches only `foo', nothing else. The pattern /^fo{2,}/ matches `foo', `fooo', `foooo', etc., but not `fo'.
\s	**Match whitespace.** This includes spaces, tabs, and new line (only used in multi-line `//m' regular expression context). Just like the dot (.) pattern, this can be qualified with `+', `*', `{}', etc.
\w	**Matches words.** This includes all alpha-numeric characters. Just like the dot (.) pattern, this can be qualified with `+', `*', `{}', etc.
\d	**Matches digits (0-9) characters.** Just like the dot (.) pattern, this can be qualified with `+', `*', `{}', etc.

Extraction

Once you get comfortable with matching, extracting text from regular expressions is very straight forward. This concept and regular expression replacements revolve around *grouping*. Groups are recursively marked ranges of text that indicate to the PERL regular expression engine what to *remember* for later retrieval.

As the engine scans (consumes) text, groupings are recorded. This recorded text comes from the instance string being searched. Each grouping is kept in a numbered temporary variable, starting with one. The first recording is placed in $1, the second in $2, etc. Of course, you should record this data directly after the matching and extraction since executing any other code, including other functions or subroutines, might use regular expressions and clobber your results.

In these patterns, groups are used to remember matched text in the parentheses. The first example below matches the first character and remembers it in the first grouping. Any first character in the search string is set to $1:

Pattern: /^(.)[Aa][Tt]$/

Text being matched 'Cat'

Result: $1: 'C'

Text being matched: 'cAT'

Result: $1: 'c'

Text being matched: 'catt'

Result: Doesn't match. When a regular expression doesn't match, it returns 'undef', which evaluates to false if in an 'if' and no numbered temporary variables are set.

This next pattern will match anything after the first 'f' in the search string and then up to 'o'.

Pattern: /^f(.*)o(\w+)/

Text being matched: 'faoz'

Result: $1: 'a', **$2**: 'z'

Text being matched: 'faoz'

Result: $1: 'a', **$2**: 'z'

Text being matched: 'fabcoz more'

Result: $1: 'abcoz m', **$2**: 're'

Greedy

In the last example, first we matched (consume) 'abccoz m' and stopped at the 'o'. This is because, by default, regular expression matching is greedy, meaning it matches as much as it can before quitting. Since our regular expression matches only up to 'o', and we have two o's in our instance string, we matched to the last one. To do this, we must be able to match the second grouping, which is just a word, but 're' is considered a word since a word is alpha-numeric data.

In contrast to greedy, you can specify non-greedy by added a question mark '?' as a qualifier to anything, including groupings. For example, if the last example introduced the non-greedy syntax we would have:

Pattern: /^f(.*?)o(\w+)/

Instance: 'fabcoz more'

Result: $1: 'abc', **$2**: 'z'

Now we only match up to the first 'o'. The 'z' comes from the remainder of the 'fabcoz' word and the rest doesn't match at all since we didn't finish the regular expression with '$'.

Replacement

Regular expression replacement is another natural extension from the match and extraction concepts. It is more a convenient since you can do it with just extraction mechanisms and reformation of the entire instance string. The form adds a little syntax:

s/*search pattern*/*replacement pattern*/

The *search pattern* is no different from what we've seen thus far; however, the *replacement pattern* is new. The replacement pattern is only the interpolation (substitution of text string scalars) of the respective groups. The entire string is replaced, so every part you want to keep has to be grouped.

For example, the pattern 's/^a ([a-z]+) dog$/nice/' with instance string 'a bad dog' yields 'nice' since the entire string of the word is replaced with the replacement pattern. However, if 'a 8 dog' is used instead, the regular expression changes nothing and the original 'a 8 dog' remains because the search pattern did not match. In this example, no interpolation is done. The following examples make use of interpolation in the replacement pattern:

```
s/^a (\w+) dog$/quote $1 unquote/
```

In the above example, $1 gets a value from the search pattern. Since it was able to find a match, the substitution pattern is evaluated and $1 is interpolated. With instance string, 'a quick dog' yields 'quote quick unquote'.

```
s/(\w+)\s+(\w+)/$2 $1/
```

This switches the order of two words. For instance, 'one two' would give 'two one'. Note that we lose the space between the words because we aren't grouping the middle '\s+', so 'one two' still gives 'two one'. If you want to keep the middle space, use:

```
s/(\w+)(\s+)(\w+)/$3$2$1/
```

Escaping

Escaping refers to putting regular expression syntax in the search itself. For example, if you wanted to search for an 'a' followed by an asterisk (*) you can't just use '/a*/' because the engine will interpret it as matching zero to many 'a's in a row.

To avoid this, you must escape the asterisk by putting a backslash (\) in front of it. In our example, we would use '/a*/'.

Bringing it Together

The following example uses many of the techniques we've discussed in this section. Something new we see in this example is the '(?:...)' syntax in the search pattern. This is the exact same thing as using just the parentheses to mark a group. However, it doesn't remember the data and no temporary variables (i.e. $1) are assigned. Instead, that numbered temporary variable is skipped and the next temporary variable is used for the next group, if there are any. In this example, we indicate that the text 'date' is optional because we just want to match the text.

In the example below, we also use the 'or' nomenclature, whose regular expression syntax is a pipe (|). This symbol is used to either match one substring or another. For instance:

```
/^f(ao|u)z$/
```

This pattern matches both 'faoz' and 'fuz':

```
$_ = "the time/date is 11:59pm 3/07/2005";


# strip out English


# below, the (?:...) syntax means don't record the data into
# a numbered temporary variable so we can just use $1
if ( ! s/^the time(?:\/date)? is (.*)$/$1/ ) {
   die "$0: expecting human language at beginning\n";
}
```

```
# if we are here, $_ now has `11:59pm 3/07/2005'
# below, the (?:...) syntax means don't record the data into
# a numbered temporary variable, instead we simply use it to
# utilize the multiple grouping with {}s
if ( /^(\d{2}):(\d{2})(am|pm)\s+(\d{1,2})\/(\d{1,2})\/(\d{4})$/ ) {
   my ($hour, $min, $amOrPm, $day, $month, $year) =
   ($1, $2, $3, $4, $5, $6);
   print "at $hour o'clock at the $min minute ";
   if ("am" eq $amOrPm) { print "before"; }
   else { print "after"; }
   print " a transaction occurred\n";
} else {
   die "$0: invalid format: '$_'\n";
}
```

The example above yields:

```
at 11 o'clock at the 59 minute after a transaction occurred
```

First, we strip the first part of the string 'the time/date is ' by matching up to 'is'. We remember everything from that point to the end and then replace the entire string with the remembered grouping. The $_ string gets the replacement. If the substitution finds do not match, it returns false and the if evaluates to true, killing the interpreter with an error.

However, if it succeeds, meaning we found our expected text, we then match a time/date format. If we match this part, we also grab all of the data from the temporary variables and print what was found, otherwise we will kill the interpreter with an error message.

Looking Forward

As of this writing, the latest stable release is 5.8.6 and PERL 6 is under development. Among various language mechanics like looping mechanisms, the PERL 6 has more efficient compilations.

Another key feature coming out in PERL 6 is UNICODE. Currently, it is difficult to efficiently manage regular expression matching with UNICODE, not to mention the task of making it work.

Chapter 6

COBOL

COBOL (**CO**mmon **B**usiness **O**riented **L**anguage) was designed specifically for commercial applications such as payroll. COBOL is best suited to handle large amounts of data and less suited to handle specific problems where complex calculations are required. COBOL was the first widely used, high-level programming language for business applications. It was originally developed by the CODASYL committee (**C**onference **O**n **DA**ta **SY**stem **L**anguages) in 1959. The Department of Defense united representatives from the business world, computer manufacturers, and academia because they were unhappy with the lack of standards in the computing industry. The first COBOL compilers became available in 1960 as a result of the CODASYL effort. COBOL standards have been further designed by the ANSI (**A**merican **N**ational **S**tandards **I**nstitute).

COBOL is not owned or controlled by any specific vendor and can be formatted to be used in conjunction with any operating systems; i.e. Windows and/or Unix. COBOL is coded using English words instead of complex code and thus is a user-friendly language.

Fast Facts

- COBOL must be compiled. Compiling is the process of converting your source program to machine code.
- The compiler indicates if any of the COBOL language rules have been violated. The source code will not be compiled into machine code until all errors are corrected.
- The result of a compiled program is called the object program. On IBM mainframes, the object program is executed by job control language (JCL).
- A COBOL program is divided into columns. Each set of columns serves a different purpose: Columns 1-6 are used for the sequence number of the program. Column 7 is used for continuation (-) or for a comment (*). Columns 8-11 are known as Area A. Columns 12-72 are known as Area B.
- The following must start in Area A: Division headers, section headers, paragraph headers, and paragraph names.
- All entries in Area A must begin in position 8, 9, 10, or 11 and can extend into area B. All other statements must begin in Area B. All entries in Area B must begin anywhere after position 11.
- Each statement does not need to end with a period. However, each paragraph *does* need to end with a period.
- COBOL is not case sensitive, however, it is standard practice to use all capitals when coding COBOL.
- The word FILLER is used to mark bytes of a record layout that will not be used.
- An 88-level entry gives a name to a specific value for a field.
- Level numbers are the two digits that precede each field item. Any number between 02 and 49 can be used to define the fields within the record you defined at the 01 level.
- A numeric field is indicated with a PIC 9. An alphanumeric field is indicated with a PIC X. The number in parentheses that follows either the X or 9 is the length of the field.
- Defining a field as COMP-3 allows the computer to store two digits in one storage position, except for the rightmost position, which holds a digit and the sign (positive or negative).

Sample COBOL Program

The following example is a simple COBOL program. Its purpose is to demonstrate how the four divisions of a COBOL program are presented chronologically.

```
IDENTIFICATION DIVISION.
PROGRAM-ID.                                   PAYROLL.
AUTHOR.                                       MIKE VANDEWOESTYNE.
INSTALLATION.                                 MY COMPANY.
DATE-WRITTEN.                                 JAN  2005.
DATE-COMPILED.                                JAN 10 2005.
*** HISTORY SECTION:
*** DATE        PROJECT                       PROGRAMMER
*** 01-01-05    PAYROLL PGM                   MIKE VANDEWOESTYNE
***  1) CREATED PROGRAM
***
*** INPUTS:     1. EMPLOYEE DETAIL FILE       EMPLYIN-FILE
*** OUTPUTS:    1. PAYROLL REPORT             PAYROL-FILE
ENVIRONMENT DIVISION.
CONFIGURATION SECTION.
SOURCE-COMPUTER.                              IBM-3033.
OBJECT-COMPUTER.                              IBM-3033.

INPUT-OUTPUT SECTION.
FILE-CONTROL.

SELECT EMPLYIN –FILE
  ASSIGN TO   UT-S-EMPLYIN .
SELECT PAYROL-FILE
  ASSIGN TO   UT-S-PAYROL.
DATA DIVISION.
FILE SECTION.

FD  PAYROL-FILE
BLOCK CONTAINS 0 RECORDS
RECORD CONTAINS 80 CHARACTERS
LABEL RECORDS ARE STANDARD
DATA RECORD IS PAYROL-REC.
```

```
01  PAYROL-REC.
    05  FILLER                      PIC X(80).
FD  EMPLYIN-FILE
BLOCK CONTAINS 0 RECORDS
RECORD CONTAINS 80 CHARACTERS
RECORDING MODE IS F
LABEL RECORDS ARE STANDARD
DATA RECORD IS EMPLYIN-REC.
01  EMPLYIN-REC.
    05  FILLER                      PIC X(80).
WORKING-STORAGE SECTION.
01  WS-EMPLYIN-REC.
    05  EMPLY-DETAIL.
        10  RECORD-TYPE-DETAIL      PIC X(03) VALUE SPACES.
            88   DETAIL-RECORD      VALUE '001'.
        10  NAME-IN.
            15  LAST-NAME-IN        PIC X(15) VALUE SPACES.
            15  FIRST-NAME-IN       PIC X(15) VALUE SPACES.
        10  HRLY-RATE-IN            PIC 999V99 VALUE ZEROES.
        10  HRS-WRK-IN              PIC 9(03) VALUE ZEROS .
        10  FILLER                  PIC X(39) VALUE SPACES.
    05  TRAILER-RECORD REDEFINES
          EMPLY-DETAIL.
        10  RECORD-TYPE-TRAILER     PIC X(03) VALUE SPACES.
            88   TRAILER-RECORD     VALUE '002'.
        10  FILLER                  PIC X(10) VALUE SPACES..
        10  NUM-RECORDS             PIC 9(03) VALUE ZEROS .
        10  FILLER                  PIC X(64) VALUE SPACES.
01  COUNTERS.
    05  TEMP-SALARY                 PIC 9(07) VALUE 0 COMP-3.
    05  TEMP-HOURS                  PIC 9(06) VALUE 0 COMP-3.
    05  TEMP-EMPLOYEES              PIC 9(03) VALUE 0 COMP.
    05  TEMP-NUM-RECORDS            PIC 9(03) VALUE 0 COMP.
01  SWITCHES.
    05  SW-EOF                      PIC X VALUE SPACES.
            88 EOF                  VALUE 'Y'.
01  PROGRAM-LITERALS.
    05  LIT-Y                       PIC X     VALUE 'Y'.
    05  LIT-N                       PIC X     VALUE 'N'.
```

```
01  HEADER-LINES.
    05  RPT-HEADING-1.
        10  FILLER                  PIC X(35) VALUE SPACES.
        10  FILLER                  PIC X(10) VALUE 'MY COMPANY'.
        10  FILLER                  PIC X(35) VALUE SPACES.
    05  RPT-HEADING-2.
        10  FILLER                  PIC X(08) VALUE SPACES.
        10  FILLER                  PIC X(09) VALUE 'LAST NAME'.
        10  FILLER                  PIC X(08)  VALUE SPACES.
        10  FILLER                  PIC X(10) VALUE 'FIRST NAME'.
        10  FILLER                  PIC X(07) VALUE SPACES.
        10  FILLER                  PIC X(12) VALUE 'HOURS WORKED'.
        10  FILLER                  PIC X(09)  VALUE SPACES.
        10  FILLER                  PIC X(03)  VALUE 'PAY'.
        10  FILLER                  PIC X(14)  VALUE SPACES.
01  DETAIL-LINES
    05  RPT-DETAIL.
        10  FILLER                  PIC X(05) VALUE SPACES.
        10  LAST-NAME-OUT           PIC X(15) VALUE SPACES.
        10  FILLER                  PIC X(03)  VALUE SPACES.
        10  FIRST-NAME-OUT          PIC X(15) VALUE SPACES.
        10  FILLER                  PIC X(10) VALUE SPACES.
        10  HRS-WRK-OUT             PIC 9(03) VALUE ZEROES.
        10  FILLER                  PIC X (10) VALUE SPACES.
        10  EMP-PAY-OUT             PIC $999.99 VALUE ZEROES.
        10  FILLER                  PIC X(12) VALUE SPACES.
01  TOTAL-LINES.
    05  RPT-TOTALS.
        10  FILLER                  PIC X(10) VALUE SPACES.
        10  FILLER                  PIC X(17) VALUE 'TOTAL EMPLOYEES: '.
        10  TOT-EMPS-OUT            PIC 9(04)  VALUE ZEROES.
        10  FILLER                  PIC X(13)  VALUE 'TOTAL HOURS: '
        10  TOT-HRS-OUT             PIC 9(05) VALUES ZEROES
        10  FILLER                  PIC X(03) VALUE SPACES.
        10  FILLER                  PIC X(11) VALUE 'TOTAL PAY: '
        10  TOT-PAY-OUT             PIC $$9,999.99 VALUE ZEROES.
        10  FILLER                  PIC X(07) VALUE SPACES.
```

```
PROCEDURE DIVISION.
0000-MAIN-CONTROL.
  PERFORM 1000-INITIALIZATION              THRU 1000-EXIT.
    PERFORM 2000-READ-IINPUT-FILE          THRU 2000-EXIT UNTIL EOF.
      PERFORM 6000-END.
        STOP RUN.
1000-INITIALIZATION.
  OPEN INPUT EMPLYIN-FILE.
  OPEN OUTPUT PAYROL-FILE.
  MOVE SPACES                              TO PAYROL-REC
    DETAIL-LINES
    TOTAL-LINES.
  MOVE LIT-N                               TO SW-EOF.
  MOVE ZEROES                              TO TEMP-SALARY
    TEMP-HOURS
    TEMP-EMPLOYEES
    TEMP-NUM-RECORDS.
  MOVE RPT-HEADING-1                       TO PAYROL-REC
  PERFORM  5000- WRITE-PAYROL              THRU 5000-EXIT
  MOVE SPACES                              TO PAYROL-REC
  MOVE RPT-HEADING-2                       TO PAYROL-REC
  PERFORM  5000- WRITE-PAYROL              THRU 5000-EXIT.
1000-EXIT.
  EXIT.
2000-READ-INPUT-FILE.
  READ EMPLYIN-FILE                        INTO WS-EMPLYIN-REC
    AT END MOVE LIT-Y                      TO SW-EOF
      PERFORM 2000-EXIT
    NOT AT END
      ADD 1 TO TEMP-NUM-RECORDS
      PERFORM 3000-CALCULATE-PAY           THRU 3000-EXIT
      PERFORM 4000-MOVE-TO-OUTPUT          THRU 4000-EXIT
      PERFROM 5000- WRITE-PAYROL           THRU 5000-EXIT.
  END-READ.
2000-EXIT.
  EXIT.
```

```
3000-CALCULATE-PAY.
    MOVE SPACES                                    TO PAYROL-REC
        DETAIL-LINES.
    IF DETAIL-RECORD
        CONTINUE
    ELSE
        PERFORM 3000-EXIT
    END-IF
    MULTIPLY HRLY-RATE-IN TIMES HRS-WRK-IN GIVING  EMP-PAY-OUT
    ADD EMP-PAY-OUT                                TO TEMP-SALARY
    ADD HRS-WRK-IN                                 TO TEMP-HRS
    ADD 1                                          TO TEMP-EMPLOYEES
3000-EXIT.
    EXIT.
4000-MOVE-TO-OUTPUT.
    MOVE LAST-NAME-IN                              TO LAST-NAME-OUT
    MOVE FIRST-NAME-IN                             TO FIRST-NAME-OUT
    MOVE HRS-WRK-IN                                TO HRS-WRK-OUT
    MOVE RPT-DETAIL                                TO PAYROL-REC
4000-EXIT.
    EXIT.
5000-WRITE-PAYROL.
    WRITE PAYROL-REC.
5000-EXIT.
    EXIT.
6000-END.
    MOVE TEMP-EMPLOYEES                            TO TOT-EMPS-OUT
    MOVE TEMP-HOURS                                TO TOT-HRS-OUT
    MOVE TEMP-SALARY                               TO TOT-PAY-OUT
    MOVE RPT-TOTALS                                TO PAYROL-REC
    PERFORM 5000-WRITE-PAYROL                      THRU 5000-EXIT
    CLOSE EMPLYIN-FILE
        PAYROL-FILE.
6000-EXIT.
    EXIT.
```

Main Components of a COBOL Program

The preceding program will serve as a reference as you read about the main components of a COBOL program and various coding rules within these divisions. Every batch COBOL program must contain the four divisions briefly described below. A job that is not run in batch may not have an environment division. A more in-depth look at the four COBOL divisions takes place at the end of this chapter.

IDENTIFICATION DIVISION

The identification division identifies the program to the computer by giving the program a name. The identification division is also commonly used to document a program through the use of comments.

ENVIRONMENT DIVISION

The environment division is the link between the COBOL program, the computer, and the input-output devices the program uses. The coding of the environment division is dependent upon the computer, compiler, and the operating system used.

DATA DIVISION

The data division describes the data that is used in the program. It describes the fields on the input, output, and any additional fields that are used for processing.

PROCEDURE DIVISION

The procedure division contains the logic of the program. It is divided into paragraphs that perform specific functions.

Basics of COBOL

COBOL programs are keyed in a couple of ways. They can be keyed into a PC that has a COBOL compiler, a PC that is linked to a mainframe, or into a terminal that is linked to a mainframe. In most cases, a text editor is used to key a COBOL program. The text editor is similar to a word processing program. The editor allows you to perform common editing functions like inserting, deleting, and moving lines of code.

After the COBOL program has been keyed, it is time to compile it. Compiling is the process of changing the code that has been keyed (source code) into code that the computer can read (machine code). Once a COBOL program compiles successfully, it is ready to be executed.

Programs that are run on a mainframe need JCL to execute them. JCL is not used in a PC environment. JCL is a separate language that is used to execute a COBOL program that has been compiled on an IBM mainframe.

Record Description

The record description gives names to the items that that will be in the record, the order those items will appear in each record, and the relationship each item has to the other. The record description can either follow the file description FD as shown above, or it can go in the working storage section. It is recommended that you use the working storage section for your record description because you are able to assign initial values to your fields in working storage.

The record description is given a name at the 01 Level. In the example program, EMPLYIN-REC is the record name and all the entries below EMPLYIN-REC are a part of that record. Level 01 is always used for the record name and begins in Area A. The name at the 01 Level must match the name you use in the data record clause in order to give them a relationship.

Level Numbers

The elements that make up your record are called fields. A field is a group of consecutive bytes reserved for an item of data with a name assign. Fields are related to each other based upon the level numbers you assign them. Level numbers are the two digits that precede each field item. Any number between 02 and 49 can be used to define the fields within the record you define at the 01 level. Generally, the first field level after the record name is 05 and increases by multiples of 05 thereafter. This is done so that in case you need to break down an item, you will still have the numbers 02, 03, and 04 to do so. All level numbers except for 01 are coded in Area B.

In the example program, 05 defines the first data entry NAME. The NAME field is further broken down into the subordinate fields (LAST-NAME and FIRST-NAME). In order to make these fields subordinate to NAME, they must have a level number that is numerically higher than the field that it is subordinate to and they must be coded directly after the field they are subordinate to. Any reference to the field NAME will now include the fields LAST-NAME and FIRST-NAME because they are subordinate to NAME. The field NAME is known as the group item and it does not contain a picture clause because its length (30 bytes) is the sum of its subordinates. The items that are not broken down further and that do have picture clauses (LAST-NAME and FIRST-NAME) are known as elementary items.

For readability reasons, it is common practice to indent subordinate items. Fields that are not subordinate to each other are coded with the same level numbers. For example, HRLY-RATE is not subordinate to NAME because they have the same level number 05. Any field after NAME cannot have a level number lower than 05.

88-level

An 88-level entry gives a name to a specific value for a field. Consider the following example:

```
05  SW-EOF                    PIC X VALUE SPACES.
    88 EOF                    VALUE 'Y'.
```

The name EOF (end of file) has been given to the value of 'Y' for the end of file switch. The code IF EOF can now be used to check for a value of 'Y' in the switch. Code is easier to read and write when meaningful 88-level entry names are used for conditions that will be checked repeatedly.

Field Names

Each field is assigned a name in the record layout and must be unique. It is good practice to make your field names as meaningful as possible so you will know what the field represents when you see the field name in your code.

Record Layout

A COBOL file is organized according to the record description. Each record is one row. Every time a write statement is executed, one row of data that consists of the fields within the record description is produced. Each byte in the record layout is a column within the record row. COBOL uses the picture clause to define bytes, or columns, of data. The word FILLER is used to mark bytes of a record layout that will not be used. The following is an example of how WS-EMPLYIN-FILE is stored:

Table 6-1. Storage of WS-EMPLYIN-FILE

RECORD-TYPE-DETAIL PIC X(03)	LAST-NAME PIC X(15)	FIRST-NAME PIC X(15)	HRLY-RATE-IN PIC 999V99.	HRS-WRK PIC 9(3)	FILLER PIC X(39)
1-3	4-18	19-33	34-38	39-41	42-80

Picture Clause

The picture clause indicates how many bytes the field contains and if the field is either numeric or alphanumeric. A numeric field is indicated with a PIC 9. An alphanumeric field is indicated with a PIC X. The number in parentheses that follows either the X or 9 is the length of the field. LAST-NAME is an alphanumeric field that is 15 bytes long. You can repeat the X or 9 symbol to represent the length of the field as an alternative to using parentheses. For example, PIC 9999 = PIC 9(4). For longer length fields, it is easier to read the number in parentheses. For fields that are going to be used in any type of calculation, a 9 is used.

Comp

COMP stands for computational. Computational is the form the computer converts numbers to do a computation. Usually this form is binary. Using COMP is advantageous when repetitive math operations are going to be performed on a field. This is often the case with counters that are performed every time a loop is performed. A counter that is defined as COMP will save run time because the computer will not have to convert the counter to computational form every time the counter is performed on. An example COMP definition:

```
05 TEMP-EMPLOYEES                 PIC 9(03) VALUE 0 COMP.
```

Comp-3

COMP-3 is also known as packed decimal. Defining a field as COMP-3 allows the computer to store two digits in one storage position, except for the rightmost position, which holds a digit and the sign (positive or negative). This helps save storage space. Typically, COMP-3 is used on tables and working storage fields. COMP-3 is usually not used on output because packed decimal is not readable. Packed decimal fields become unpacked once they are moved to a field that is not defined as packed decimal. An example COMP-3 definition:

```
05 TEMP-SALARY                    PIC 9(07) VALUE 0 COMP-3.
```

Redefines

The REDEFINES clause allows you to give the same bytes of data numerous definitions. A common use of the REDEFINES clause is to use it to define a field as both numeric and alphanumeric. Consider the following example, which redefines alphanumeric to numeric:

```
05 EMPLOYEE-NUMBER                        PIC 9(5).
05 EMPLOYEE-NUMBER-X
   REDEFINES EMPLOYEE-NUMBER              PIC X(5).
```

EMPLOYEE-NUMBER can now be used as alphanumeric or numeric. Another common use is to allow for two different record layouts within one file.

```
WS-EMPLYIN-REC.
   05 EMPLY-DETAIL.
      10 RECORD-TYPE-DETAIL           PIC X(03) VALUE SPACES.
          88 DETAIL-RECORD            VALUE '001'.
      10 NAME-IN.
         15 LAST-NAME-IN              PIC X(15) VALUE SPACES.
         15 FIRST-NAME-IN             PIC X(15) VALUE SPACES.
      10 HRLY-RATE-IN                 PIC 999V99 VALUE ZEROES.
      10 HRS-WRK-IN                   PIC 9(03) VALUE ZEROS .
      10 FILLER                       PIC X(39) VALUE SPACES.
   05 TRAILER-RECORD REDEFINES
        EMPLY-DETAIL.
      10 RECORD-TYPE-TRAILER          PIC X(03) VALUE SPACES.
          88 TRAILER-RECORD           VALUE '002'.
      10 FILLER                       PIC X(10) VALUE SPACES.
      10 NUM-RECORDS                  PIC 9(03) VALUE ZEROS .
      10 FILLER                       PIC X(64) VALUE SPACES.
```

All of the picture clauses under WS-EMPLYIN-REC add up to 160, however, there are only 80 bytes in this record. There are two types of records that are going to be used in EMPLY-IN-REC; EMPLY-DETAIL and TRAILER-RECORD. In order to reference the fields within both of these types of records, the REDEFINES is used.

Conditional Statements

Conditional operators are used to test a condition before an action is performed. COBOL uses the word IF to test a condition. If the condition following the key word IF is true, then all the statements following the IF will be executed until either an END-IF or a period is encountered. If the condition following the key word IF is false, then the statements following the IF are ignored and the execution continues with the COBOL statements following the next END-IF or period, whichever is used to terminate the IF statement.

An ELSE clause can be added after an IF statement to execute statements when the IF condition is false. The ELSE statement does not need to be coded if no action is necessary when the IF condition is false. Multiple IF statements can be used together to test for multiple conditions.

IF statements can be terminated with a period or an END-IF followed by a period. It is considered good coding to use an END-IF instead of a period. It is also considered good coding to have an END-IF for every IF and to have the two aligned vertically in the code.

In the following example, PERFORM 2500-PROCESS-SMITH is only executed if two conditions are met:

```
IF DETAIL-RECORD
  IF LAST-NAME = 'SMITH        '
    PERFORM 2500-PROCESS-SMITH
  ELSE
    PERFORM 3000-EXIT
  END-IF
END-IF
```

If it is a DETAIL-RECORD and if the LAST-NAME is SMITH. If it is not a DETAIL-RECORD, the condition of LAST-NAME being equal to SMITH is not tested, instead the program goes directly to the last END-IF. If it is a DETAIL-RECORD and the LAST-NAME is not equal to SMITH, the ELSE statement is executed which directs the program to perform 3000-EXIT.

Relational Conditions

Relational conditions are used to test one field compared to another. The three relational tests are EQUAL TO, LESS THAN, and GREATER THAN. The relational conditions are used in IF statements and thus follow the same format of an IF statement. Multiple relational operators can be used together. For example:

```
IF FIELD1 IS GREATER THAN OR EQUAL TO FIELD2
```

The traditional comparison symbols can be used instead of words to compare fields. The equal sign (=) can be used in place of EQUAL TO, less than sign (<) in place of LESS THAN, and greater than sign (>) in place of GREATER THAN. The previous example could be coded with symbols as follows:

```
IF FIELD1 >= TO FIELD2
```

Efficient Programming

Programming efficiency can easily be overlooked to initially save time. However, it is much easier to maintain a program that has been coded efficiently. Once the groundwork for an efficient system has been laid, all subsequent programming takes much less time to code and troubleshoot. Below are some examples of efficient programming.

Copy Statement

The COPY statement is a procedure that brings outside COBOL statements into a program. The statements that are brought into a program are stored in a library and copied into the program. This is an extremely useful tool due to the time saving benefits of not having to reproduce statements that have already been written. ENVIRONMENT, DATA, and PROCEDURE division entries can all be used in a COPY statement.

The most common use of the COPY statement is to copy record layouts that are common to multiple files. For example, if FILE A has the same contents as FILE B, they can share a record layout that is copied into every program that uses either FILE A or FILE B. This process also standardizes field names that are common throughout a company's applications because it forces every program that uses the record layout to use the same field names.

The COBOL statements that are being copied are inserted into the program directly after the COPY statement. The format for a COPY statement varies by installation. Some installations no longer use the word COPY and instead use the word INCLUDE. Check with your installation if you are not sure of the format.

Call Statement

The CALL statement is a procedure that brings entire COBOL programs into another program. The program that is brought into a program is stored in a library and called into the program. To help understand the CALL statement, consider it as a perform statement that executes an entire program. This is an extremely useful tool due to the time saving benefits of not having to reproduce code that has already been written in another module. For example, PROGRAM A converts any given date format into any desired date format. PROGRAM B has a date in MMDDYY format that needs to be converted into Julian format.

There are two options: Write the code to perform this conversion in PROGRAM B or issue a CALL statement to PROGRAM A. The CALL statement improves efficiency by eliminating the duplication of coding efforts. This process also standardizes field names that are common throughout a company's applications because it forces the called and calling program to use the same names for the fields they share. The format for a CALL statement varies by installation. Check with your installation for the standard.

Identification Division, Closer

The only required entry in the identification division is the PROGRAM-ID. The following entries are optional: AUTHOR, INSTALLATION DATE, DATE-WRITTEN, DATE-COMPILED, and SECURITY. Each entry must be followed by a period and at least one space. The entry following the paragraph name must also be followed by a period. The division name (IDENTIFICATION DIVISION) and the entries coded in the identification division are coded in Area A. The identification division is often used to document the program with comments. The comments are important because they provide an overview of the program's purpose and a history of the changes made to the program.

Environment Division, Closer

The environment division is the link between the COBOL program and the computer and input-output devices the program uses. The environment division consists of the CONFIGURATION SECTION and the INPUT-OUTPUT SECTION. The environment that a program runs in varies from company to company and sometimes within divisions of companies. Each environment will have different requirements on how to code the environment division.

Configuration Section

The configuration section identifies the computer that will be used to compile the program (source computer) and the computer that will be used to execute the program (object computer). The best way to determine what the source and object computers in your environment are is to copy the information from a COBOL program that is already running.

Input-output section

The input-output section uses select statements to define a file name and assign that file name to a device name. The device name format is machine dependent. Again, the best way to determine what the device name format is in your environment is to copy the information from a COBOL program that is already running.

Every input and output file that is used in a COBOL program needs to have a select statement. Select statements begin in Area B and are followed by a period. In the example COBOL program, EMPLYIN-FILE is the name assigned to the input file. The UT-S-EMPLYIN name is the machine dependent format that assigns my file to a device. UT-S is used in the IBM Mainframe OS environment. The EMPLYIN portion of the UT-S-EMPLYIN statement comes from job control language statements (JCL) that are independent of the COBOL program.

Data Division, Closer

The data division consists of the FILE SECTION and the WORKING-STORAGE SECTION. All fields that going to be used in the program are found in the data division.

File Section

The file section is used to describe all the inputs and outputs to your program. The file description FD statement is the first entry in the file section. Every file that you have a select statement for must have also have an FD statement. In the sample program, there are select statements for EMPLYIN-FILE and PAYROL-FILE. Each select statement matches an FD statement. The FD statement is coded in Area A and the subsequent file name is coded in Area B. FD clauses follow the FD statement and are used to describe the file. The FD clauses are optional, however, it is important to know what the default values are if you choose not to code them. In older versions of COBOL, these clauses were required and are still used in most corporate environments. If FD clauses are used, the last clause is followed by a period. The FD clauses used in the sample program are:

```
BLOCK CONTAINS 0 RECORDS
RECORD CONTAINS 80 CHARACTERS
LABEL RECORDS ARE STANDARD
DATA RECORD IS PAYROL-REC.
```

Block Contains Clause

The BLOCK CONTAINS clause is optional. The BLOCK CONTAINS clause indicates how many records have been blocked together. Blocking is done for efficiency purposes. It is more efficient to read records together than it is to read one record at a time. The system designer will give you information on how the environment is set up for blocking.

Record Contains Clause

The RECORD CONTAINS clause indicates the total size of each record. In the example program, the EMPLY-IN-FILE has a RECORD CONTAINS clause of 80 bytes, which means the picture clauses that define EMPLY-IN-FILE add up to 80 bytes. The RECORD CONTAINS clause is optional just like the rest of the FD clauses. However, it is highly recommended that you use this clause because the compiler will check your RECORD CONTAINS clause against your picture clauses to see if they match.

For example, the RECORD CONTAINS clause indicates 80 bytes, but the picture clauses only add up to 79 bytes. The compiler will issue a syntax error during compilation. If you did not code the RECORD CONTAINS clause, your file would have 79 bytes when you intended it to have 80 and you would have to debug this at run-time.

Label Records Clause

The LABEL RECORDS clause is optional. If the clause is not coded, the computer uses the standard default value of label records. Standard label records mean that the first record on output files will have an identifier and the last record will have a trailer. These records are used by the system to identify beginning and the end of a file. The other option for this clause is label records are omitted. This would be used for print files that are not being saved to disk and would have no need to mark the beginning and end.

Data Record Clause

The DATA RECORD clause gives your file a record name that you will reference throughout the rest of the program. Like the rest of the FD clauses, it is recommended you use the DATA RECORD clauses for clarity. The name you assign your file in the data records clause must match the name used at the 01 Level in the record description.

If we omitted the FD clauses in the sample program, it would look like this:

```
FD  EMPLYIN-FILE.
01  EMPLYIN-REC.
    05  FILLER                  PIC X(80).
WORKING-STORAGE SECTION.
```

The Working Storage Section

The working storage section stores all the fields that are not stated in the file section. Fields typically used in working storage are for keeping totals and for switches to mark a certain condition. Working storage can also be used to store a version of your record layouts. In the example program, the input and output records are given values of all filler in the FD.

The working storage versions break down the 80 bytes into field names. The advantage to defining the record description in working storage is the ability to assign field values. In the file section, you cannot assign field values. This is an advantage because you can initialize your fields to zero (numeric fields) or spaces (alphanumeric fields). It cannot be assumed that fields begin with an initial value of zero or spaces. Your record area may contain unexpected values and this is one way to make sure you are starting with nothing unexpected in your record.

Working storage can also be used to help make your coding more efficient. In the example program, TEMP-SALARY is stored in working storage. When the program is being coded, you do not have to remember what minimum wage is. You can now use the working storage field TEMP-SALARY whenever you compute an employee's salary that is earning minimum wage. It is more efficient to use working storage for values that are going to be used repeatedly throughout your program because if the value changes you will only have to change the one working storage field instead of every occurrence of that value in your program.

Procedure Division, Closer

The procedure division contains the instructions the computer executes. The instructions are broken up into paragraphs that perform a specific task within the program. Paragraph names should be descriptive of what their purpose is and begin with a numeric prefix.

The numeric prefix determines where within the program each paragraph is placed. Usually paragraphs are coded in the order they are going to be executed. Paragraph names are coded in area A and all statements within each paragraph are coded in area B. The most commonly used instructions and their format are described below. The instructions are described in the order they are normally performed.

Open Statement

Every file must be opened before any statements involving the file can be executed. The verb OPEN is followed by either the word INPUT or OUTPUT, depending on if the file being opened is an input or an output file. The file name comes after the word INPUT or OUTPUT. After the last file name being opened, a period is used. The file name, not the record name, is used in the OPEN statement. If there are multiple input or output files, the OPEN command and the descriptions of INPUT or OUTPUT are only issued once. An example OPEN statement:

```
OPEN INPUT    EMPLYIN-FILE
  EMPVACIN-FILE.
```

Perform / Loop Statement

COBOL statements are executed in the order they are written until a PERFORM statement is encountered. PERFORM statements direct the program to another paragraph and then the program comes back to the statement directly after the PERFORM statement. PERFORM statements can also direct the program to perform a paragraph or a series of paragraphs until a condition is met. This is called a *loop*.

In the example program, the paragraph 2000-READ-INPUT is executed in a loop until the end of the input file is reached. That means that for each record read in EMPLY-IN, 2000-READ-INPUT is executed one time. When there are no more records, the condition of end of file is met and the loop stops executing. Following is an example loop statement:

```
PERFORM 2000-READ-INPUT THRU 2000-EXIT UNTIL EOF.
```

Read Statement

Once a file has been opened, generally a loop is performed that reads each record in a file. The READ statement brings the first record on the input file into the record description area of the file section. The READ statement is performed on a file, not on a record or field. A file can only be read after it has been opened. There can be unexpected characters in the record description area prior to your READ statement. Once the READ is executed, anything that was already in this area will be overlaid with the input record.

When a READ statement is performed in a loop on a sequential file, it brings the records into the record description area one record at a time in sequential order until all the records are read. This allows the program to process the data on every input record. A well written READ statement will state what the program should do if it is at the end of the file and also what to do if there are more records. Each READ statement should be matched with an END-READ statement. The END-READ is called a scope terminator. Following is an example READ statement with NOT AT END and END READ:

```
READ EMPLYIN-FILE
  AT END MOVE LIT-Y TO SW-EOF
    PERFORM 2000-EXIT
  NOT AT END
    PERFORM 3000-CALCULATE-PAY
END-READ.
```

The NOT AT END statement and the END-READ scope terminator are not required, but are considered good coding. The following example is executed the same way even though it omits these statements:

```
READ EMPLYIN-FILE
  AT END MOVE LIT-Y TO SW-EOF
    PERFORM 2000-EXIT.
PERFORM 3000-CALCULATE-PAY.
```

In the example program, a READ INTO statement is used to read each input record directly into the working storage version (WS-EMPLYIN-REC) instead of the FD record description area.

An example READ INTO statement:

```
READ EMPLYIN-FILE INTO WS-EMPLYIN-REC
  AT END MOVE LIT-Y TO SW-EOF
    PERFORM 2000-EXIT
  NOT AT END
    PERFORM 3000-CALCULATE-PAY
END-READ.
```

Move Statement

A simple MOVE statement moves a field or a literal to an output field. A general rule of thumb is to move numeric fields to numeric output fields and alphanumeric fields to alphanumeric output fields. This ensures that you will preserve the data type and not run into any compile errors for an illegal move operation. Some of the more popular uses of the MOVE and some of the issues involving moving data types are listed below:

Initialize a Field

Fields defined in a record description located in the data division often contain unpredictable data that is left in the area from the last time the program was run. Defining fields in working storage where an initial value can be assigned and then moving them to the data division is one way to deal with this issue.

Another way is to move a specific starting value to each field. A group MOVE of spaces to the output record is the best way to deal with this. This will clear out any contents from the last record that was stored in the output record. In addition to output records, switches and other working storage fields may have to be reset at specific times in a program. Consider the EOF-SWITCH in the example program. The initial value assigned to it is 'Y'. If the switch was not initialized to 'N' the NOT AT END portion of the READ statement would never be executed and no processing would take place.

Move an Alphanumeric Literal

To move an alphanumeric literal, you must put the literal in single quotes. Alphanumeric literals can only be moved to alphanumeric fields. This example moves an alphanumeric literal:

```
MOVE 'SANDY' TO FIRST-NAME-OUT.
```

Move a Numeric Literal

The difference between alphanumeric literals and numeric literals is the use of single quotes, not the contents of the literal. '123' is an alphanumeric literal and 123 is a numeric literal. When moving numbers, consult the receiving field to determine if there should be single quotes or not. An example numeric literal move is shown here:

```
MOVE 80 TO TOTAL-HRS-OUT.
```

Numeric move

A numeric field can be moved to other numeric fields and to alphanumeric fields. Once a numeric field is moved to an alphanumeric field, it can no longer be used in any computations because it is considered an alphanumeric field.

Alphanumeric Move

An alphanumeric field can only be moved to other alphanumeric fields. A compile error will be issued when an alphanumeric field is moved to a numeric field.

Group Move

A group move is when a group level item (see level numbers) and all of its subordinates are involved in a move. Consider the following example:

```
05 NAME.
   10 LAST-NAME-OUT          PIC X(15)
   10 FIRST-NAME-OUT         PIC X(15)
```

When a move is performed on NAME, LAST-NAME-OUT and FIRST-NAME-OUT are moved. When spaces are moved to NAME, LAST-NAME-OUT and FIRST-NAME-OUT are filled with spaces. A group move is considered an alphanumeric move. This allows spaces to be moved to any group level item, even if a subordinate item is numeric.

Moving Multiple Fields

Moving one value to multiple fields or multiple fields to one value can be performed with only one move statement. Consider the following example:

```
MOVE SPACES TO              PAYROL-REC
   DETAIL-LINES.
```

PAYROL-REC and DETAIL-LINES will both have SPACES moved to them. There is no limit on the number of receiving fields listed.

Reference modification

Reference modification is a way to access any byte in a field without having to specifically define that byte with a field name. Consider the following example where a field DATE is defined in MMDDYY format:

```
10  DATE                     PIC X(06).
```

In order to use only the MONTH portion of the DATE field, a subordinate field with a picture clause of 2 bytes would have to be created:

```
10  DATE.
   15  MONTH                 PIC X(02).
   15  DAY                   PIC X(02).
   15  YEAR                  PIC X(02).
```

An alternative to creating subordinate fields is to use reference modification. The format for reference modification is:

```
FIELD NAME (STARTING LOCATION:NUMBER OF BYTES)
```

The following example shows how to access only the MONTH portion of the DATE field using reference modification:

```
MOVE DATE (1:2)              TO MONTH-OUT.
```

The number of bytes portion is optional. The entire field is used if it is omitted.

Write Statement

The WRITE statement moves the record that is in the output record area to the output device (report, file, etc). The WRITE statement only writes one record at a time because only one record is stored in the record area at one time. WRITE statements are performed on a record, not a file or field. The record name that is to be used in the WRITE statement is on the 01 Level of the record description. WRITE statements are generally performed in a loop and combined with a read and a move statement. These three statements performed in a loop will sequentially read each record, move each record into the output record area, and then write them to the output device. An example WRITE statement:

```
WRITE PAYROL-REC.
```

Close Statement

All files that are opened must be closed. The verb CLOSE is followed by the file name. The descriptions INPUT and OUTPUT are not used in the close statement. After the last file name being closed, a period is used. The file name, not the record name, is used in the CLOSE statement. If there are multiple files being closed, the close command is only used once. Following is an example CLOSE statement:

```
CLOSE EMPLYIN-FILE
  EMPVACIN-FILE.
```

Stop Run

COBOL programs end with a STOP RUN statement or a variation of the STOP RUN statement. The STOP RUN statement causes the execution of the program to terminate and transfers control to the operating system. Some environments use a GOBACK statement. Both GOBACK and STOP RUN perform the same function. Consult your system to see which statement is standard. It is considered good coding to put the STOP RUN statement in the paragraph that directs the control of your program. Consider an example:

```
0000-MAIN-CONTROL.
  PERFORM 1000-INITIALIZATION THRU 1000-EXIT.
  PERFORM 2000-READ-IINPUT-FILE THRU 2000-EXIT UNTIL EOF.
  PERFORM 6000-END.
  STOP RUN.
```

Looking Forward

Many have predicted the demise of COBOL by C, then by Java, etc. However, COBOL has withstood the test of time and remains the dominant language for business applications. Managers do continue to look to other languages for the future, but they are faced with a number of issues. COBOL is the foundation that almost every major industry was built on. Because COBOL has been in the business world for decades, the investments that have been made in this language are unsurpassed.

There is a lot at risk for a manager who decides to move from an extremely stable COBOL system that has been fine tuned to the needs of the business, to a new and unproven system. COBOL has always played a major role in transactional systems and will continue to do so in the future.

Chapter 7

HTML

HTML stands for *HyperText Markup Language*, a simple markup language used in creating Web pages on the World Wide Web. This language is based on Standard Generalized Markup Language (SGML), and its simplicity is its strength. SGML was recognized by the International Standards Organization in 1986 as a meta language, a language that describes a language. HTML is a less-rigorous, user friendly subset of SGML. Combined with scripting languages and graphics, HTML is behind every website on the Internet.

While an employee of the computing services department of CERN (http://www.cern.ch), Tim Berners-Lee developed several of the components that made the World Wide Web (WWW) feasible, including HTTP, HTML, and the first Web browser. With these tools and an open venue for discussion, the concept of the Web began to gain popularity, and the evolution of Berners-Lee's early ideas were undertaken by groups of enthusiasts around the world.

The HTML 2.0 specification was developed by the HTML Working Group and became the Internet Engineering Task Force (IETF) proposed standard in 1995. The HTML 3.2 specification, which added new features such as tables and applets, became a World Wide Web Consortium (W3C) recommendation in early 1997. HTML 4.0 was recommended by the W3C in late 1997, and a number of bugs were fixed with the December 1999 release of HTML 4.01. In January of 2000, the W3C recommended XHTML (Extensible HyperText Markup Language) 1.0, a reformulation of HTML 4.01 in XML (or Extensible Markup Language, covered in Chapter 8).

The future of the Web is XHTML, but most of the current Web is coded following the HTML specification. Many of the older HTML 4 and earlier Web pages in existence will not be upgraded for a long time, and although browsers will slowly move in the direction of XHTML, HTML will probably always be accepted. HTML is an excellent introduction to the workings of the World Wide Web and the browser's interface to it. This chapter focuses on the HTML 4.01 specification, with an introduction to XTML 1.0.

Fast Facts

- HTML is not case sensitive (though XHTML is).
- Data enclosed in <script> tags or <%...%> tags comes from a scripting language.
- The HTML comment tags (<!--...-->) may be used to hide scripting code from a browser that doesn't support scripting.
- HTML tags can be any case. It is a good idea to use all lowercase letters because they compress better and XHTML requires lowercase tags. However, capitalizing each letter causes the tags to stand out and allows for easier readability.
- Different Web browsers may interpret an HTML document differently. This is due to variances in browser default settings, screen resolution, and extensions to the HTML standard.
- An HTML document file typically ends with .html or .htm.
- Most opening HTML tags should have a matching closing tag, though this is not enforced by Web browsers.
- Whitespace is recognized in HTML data, but the amount of whitespace is irrelevant. These two lines render the same in the browser:

```
<h1>Hello There</h1>
<h1>Hello            There</h1>
```

- To avoid potential errors when using scripting mixed with HTML, always enclose attribute values in quotes (either double or single quotes are okay, but be consistent).
- Although HTML allows some of its rules to be broken, XHTML does not permit this luxury. In January of 2000, XHTML became a W3C recommendation, and more and more browsers now accept XHTML as the default.
- Many Web pages use tables. A simple table is shown here with two cells in one horizontal row:

```
<table>
 <tr>
 <td>cell1</td>
 <td>cell2</td>
 </tr>
</table>
```

Sample HTML Page

The following page demonstrates some of the basics of HTML. It includes the required tags, plus headings, line breaks, a horizontal rule, and an anchor linking to another page. In addition, it contains a rudimentary form which allows a user to enter text and submit it.

Figure 7-1. Type This in Your Editor

```
<!DOCTYPE HTML PUBLIC "-//W3C//DTD HTML 4.01 //EN">

<!-- This is the code for a Web page. These comments will not appear in the
browser, but can be seen using the "view source" function available in most browsers.
This example presents a large heading with one word in red, followed by a horizontal
rule, and a form for the viewer to enter and submit a data field. --><html>

<head>
<title> My PageTitle- this is displayed on the title bar of the browser </title>
</head>
<body>
<h1> This is <font color="red">MY</font> Web Page </h1>
<br><hr><br>
<h2>Click <a href="http://www.myServer.com/sister.htm"> here </a> to see my
sister's page</h2>
<form method="POST" action="http://yourserver.com/scripts/post-query">
  Sign my guestbook. What is your name:
  <input type="text" name="yourName" size="30">
  <input type="submit">
</form>
</body>
</html>
```

Figure 7-2. See This in Your Browser

Main Components of an HTML Page

The look of an HTML page can vary substantially, but most of the main components included above are consistent from page to page. Some of those basic components are described briefly here.

Document Type Definition Tags

The document type definition or <document> tag should be the first line of an HTML document. It indicates what dialect of HTML the document is written in by referring to a Document Type Definition (DTD). The DTD, included as a document attribute, specifies the elements, attributes, and element relationships that are *valid* for the document.

html Tag

The html tag indicates the beginning of the HTML document. It contains only the head, body, and possibly the frameset element.

head Element

The head element often contains meta information, or information about the rest of the document. The head section is used by search engines when organizing Web pages because it contains the title element, among others.

body Element

Most of the elements that appear in an HTML document will be enclosed by body tags. Only one body element may appear per document.

form Element

A form is the most basic means of creating interactive Web pages. The form element and its subelements allow information to be gathered by the Web page and sent back to the Web server, with the content of the subsequent Web page delivered to the user dependent on the information gathered.

Basics of HTML

HTML is a markup language that defines the structure and presentation of content on the Web. The notion today is that HTML should not be used for presentation instructions, but rather for providing document structure. However, current Web sites use HTML for both purposes. Even though it is often difficult to place things in specific positions on a page, sometimes requiring extensive use of tables, it is how most Web pages have been created. The idea behind using HTML as merely a logical language, providing structure instructions only, is that the actual presentation of the information is left to other pieces of the puzzle, such as the browser and Cascading Style Sheets, or CSS (more about the latter in the section *Style Sheets and HTML* later in this chapter).

What is "Markup"?

"Markup" refers to the use of hidden *tags* alongside content to assign various attributes. In other words, you *mark up* your content, and when it is shown in the browser, the content has the attributes you specify. People used to primarily write HTML using Notepad, although now there are a variety of development tools to choose from. All you need are the tags, and the browser will interpret your content with the proper attributes. Through the use of markup tags, HTML describes how the contents of a document are structured and should be presented and formatted on a Web page. For example, one tag may indicate that a particular word should appear red, and another tag may specify that certain data should be displayed in a table. Here's an example:

What You Type	What You See
<b>this is boldface text</b>	**this is boldface text**

Tags consist of up to three parts: tag name, attributes, and attribute settings.

- **Tag Name** (the text after the "<") – there are hundreds of tags, and they all must have the tag name within angle brackets "<>" at a minimum. For example, <DIV> indicates a division of the page.

- **Attributes** – not always required, but if included, it usually has an attribute value setting. For example, you can have a <DIV> tag, but you cannot use <DIV align> without setting the align tag.

- **Attribute Value** – required if you use an attribute within the tag, this text following the attribute and equal sign is usually in quotes (best practice). Extending the previous example, <DIV align="center"> is a valid tag. Multiple attributes can be set within the same tag.

An HTML document is made up of document elements, scripting elements, and content. An opening tag, a closing tag, and the data between them make up an element. Web pages can contain only a finite number of elements, and almost all these elements can include attributes, which encompass details about their respective elements. The basic format for an element with attribute is as follows:

```
<tagname attribute = "value">
```

A typical HTML page follows much of the same format as the sample document shown previously. The document element is the first line, indicating the version of DTD the browser should use to parse the document. An html tag then encloses the rest of the document, with the head being the first child element of the html element. The head element often contains meta data about the rest of the document, and almost always contains the title element—the contents of which will be displayed in the title bar of the browser. The head element is then closed, and unless the frameset element is used, the rest of the document is contained within the body tags (more on framesets in the section *HTML Frames* later in this chapter).

Presentation

Many of the elements defined in HTML are used for presentation instructions. The future of HTML separates presentation and content, and so controlling presentation (such as specifying colors and fonts) using HTML is discouraged by the W3C, and the HTML 4 specification deprecates attributes for which a style sheet alternative exists. However, most of the existing HTML on the Internet today controls presentation. Various HTML elements allow for the control of text placement, color, style, and size. Text can be arranged in paragraphs and lists, with different headings and colors, incorporating links to other Web pages and images throughout.

Cascading Style Sheets (CSS) comprise lists of presentation rules and are the recommended way of conveying presentation instructions in HTML. Cascading Style Sheets can be maintained in a file separate from the HTML file, thus making maintenance easier and keeping HTML file sizes down. In addition, the functionality of CSS is greater than that of HTML.

The use of tables in HTML documents is far more common that you would think. Tables are used, improperly or not, to break up the area of a Web browser screen into smaller areas so that the exact location of text and graphics can be controlled. Tables can also be created inside of other tables (a process called *nesting*), resulting in something of a grid and thereby providing a designer with a great degree of control over the visual outcome of the Web site.

Frames divide one regular-sized Web browser pane into multiple smaller browser panes. Each pane acts individually, loading its own HTML documents. Often, two frames will work together, with one frame being smaller and serving as a table of contents that provides links to other HTML documents. When a link is chosen, the corresponding new document loads in the larger frame, keeping the table of contents as is.

Forms take data in from the user. You can recognize forms by the presence of a text box, list box, or a button on a Web page. Using forms and the associated elements and attributes, interactive Web pages can be created in which the content of a subsequent page is determined by the user's input in the current page.

HTML vs. DHTML

Dynamic HTML, or DHTML, is essentially a way of providing hooks into the elements of an HTML document. Since the generation of 4.x browsers, this technology has allowed scripting code to manipulate individual elements without a page refresh, though the word *technology* in reference to DHTML is somewhat misleading. DHTML is simply a combination of the existing technologies of HTML, style sheets, and client-side scripting that together can create an extremely dynamic Web experience. The details of DHTML are beyond the scope of this chapter.

HTML vs. XML

XML (Extensible Markup Language) is a powerful and flexible subset of SGML that is playing a more and more important role in shaping the increasingly complex evolution of the Web. The newest HTML specification, XHTML, is HTML combined with certain aspects of XML. See the section *XHTML* later in this chapter for more on this latest specification, and refer to Chapter 8 for more about XML.

Text and Layout in HTML

Many HTML tags provide ways to manipulate text and control its appearance in the browser. The font tag has been deprecated in the HTML 4 specification in an effort to separate content from presentation. However, as most of the Internet still includes presentation information in HTML, the presentation tags discussed in the upcoming text are useful to know.

Common Font-Related Tags

Some of the more common tags include <big>, <small>, <i>, <u>, and <b>. Any text included between a <big> and </big> tag will be enlarged relative to the text around it, whereas the <small> tag has the opposite effect. (Note that the <big> and <small> tags, though not deprecated, are strongly discouraged in favor of the <font> tag or use of style sheets.) Text between a <b> and </b> tag becomes boldfaced, while <i> and <u> cause the text to be italicized and underlined. A browser would render the following line with the words "no way" boldfaced and the word "no" in italics:

```
There was <b><i>no </i>way</b> that he would get back on that horse.
```

font and basefont Elements

While the <font> element and its attributes have become deprecated in HTML 4 and XHTML, in order to promote the use of style sheets, it remains a very popular element in existence today. The attributes that may be included in the opening tag of a <font> element include class, dir, id, size, face, color, lang, style, and title.

The size attribute may be set to any number between 1 and 7, with 1 being the smallest. It can also be specified as a relative size with a plus or minus sign, as in the following:

```
<font size="+3">
```

This translates to three sizes larger relative to the basefont.

The face attribute is the name of the font type, such as Arial or Times. If the listed font type does not exist on your system, a default type will be used instead. The color attribute can be specified as a hexadecimal number or a string color name. A style sheet class can be assigned to a group of characters via the class attribute. The id attribute uniquely identifies one use of a tag within a document. When set equal to a two-letter language code, the lang tag identifies the base language used when displaying text (English is indicated by "en").

The basefont element specifies the font qualities for text that has not been enclosed by <font> tags, and it has also been deprecated in HTML 4 and XHTML. Attributes of this element include class, size, face, color, id, and lang. Most of the attributes behave exactly as they do for the font element.

Layout

Beyond the format of the actual text, HTML is most useful in defining the layout of text in the Web page. The following elements are useful in creating a page layout to best display information.

Text enclosed by an <h1></h1> tag set will be rendered as a section heading, which appears larger than the other text on the page. The <h2> tag displays section heading text a bit smaller than the <h1> tag, and this trend continues down to the <h6> tag. In this case, the closing heading tag must be included. The most commonly used heading attribute is align, which can be set to "left", "center", or "right" to align the heading left, center, or right.

The <center> tag, deprecated in HTML 4 in favor of the <DIV> tag with align attribute set to "center", puts the text enclosed in its tags in the horizontal center of the page. Text can be organized into paragraphs using the <p> tag (closing tag is optional). The <br> element inserts a line break into an HTML page. This element does not require a closing tag, so multiple line breaks can be listed in a row, resulting in a larger block of whitespace.

A horizontal rule may be drawn on the Web page by including an <hr> element. Like the <br> element, no closing tag is required or allowed. The attributes allowed include: align, class, color, dir, lang, noshade, size, src, style, title, and width. The size attribute refers to the height of the line in pixels, and the width attribute is the width of the line in pixels. The latter can be specified as a percentage of the window width by adding a percentage sign (%). Both of these attributes have been deprecated in HTML 4.

Lists

A number of elements are available for creating list layouts on a Web page. Possible formats include bulleted (unordered), numbered (ordered), or glossary style (definitions list). To create an ordered list, start with the <ol> element followed by one or more list items, each preceded by an <li> tag.

```
<ol>
  <li> finished ahead of schedule
  <li> finished below budget
</ol>
```

The preceding example creates a list of two statements numbered 1 and 2. Notice that the <li> elements are not required to be closed.

Two attributes of the <ol> element are type and value. The type attribute can be set to one of the following:

1	Arabic numerals (default)
A	Capital letters
a	Small letters
I	Large roman numerals (I, II)
i	Small roman numerals (i, ii)

The value attribute is used to specify the number of the current list item. This attribute, as well as the type attribute, have been deprecated in HTML 4.

When creating an unordered list, you follow the same syntax presented for creating an ordered list, substituting the <ul> element for <ol>. The type attribute for the <ul> element can be set to either "circle", "disc", or "square", thereby specifying the shape of the bullet.

Links

The most common way to link one HTML document to another is by using the anchor element, <a>. The href attribute of the element specifies a target URL. The <a></a> element pair is used to outline the hyperlink *hot spot*. When a user clicks the hot spot, he or she is delivered to the target URL. The following will deliver you to the weather.com page when you click the word "weather":

```
Be sure to check the <a href="http://www.weather.com">weather</a> today!
```

Instead of jumping to another URL, you can jump to a marked section of the same Web page if the link you click is associated with an anchor element that includes the name attribute. Specifically, an <a> element that includes the href attribute and anchor name (indicated with an initial hash mark) specifies the link text, and the section on the page the link jumps to is indicated using an <a> tag that specifies the anchor name via the name attribute. For example, clicking the link created by this line of code:

```
Back to <a href="#paragraph24">Go to paragraph 24</a>
```

This will deliver you to the next line of code, which would be inserted at paragraph 24:

```
<a name="paragraph24">Welcome to Paragraph 24</a>
```

Some other common anchor attributes are:

id	Identifies a target anchor
target	Defines a window or frame destination for the link
title	Sets text to appear when the mouse is held over the hot spot
accesskey	Sets key for keyboard access to link
tabindex	Sets tabbing order for keyboard access to link
rel	Defines relationship of target object
rev	Defines relationship of current object

The *clickable* or hot spot for a hyperlink is not limited to text. You can be delivered to a URL by clicking an image if the <img> tag, used to insert images on a page, is enclosed by the anchor tags. The <link> element provides much of the same function of the anchor element, and additionally provides information about the relationship between the source and target document. It uses the href attribute the same way the anchor element does, as well as the rel attribute to convey the relationship. The rel attribute can be set to a number of values, including 'INDEX', 'HELP', and 'BOOKMARK', used to indicate if the target is an index, a help file, or an arbitrary bookmark.

Style Sheets and HTML

One of the main goals of the W3C when creating HTML 4.0 after HTML 3.2 was to separate the presentation data from the content data. The W3C recommendation is to use HTML to format the page content and Cascading Style Sheets to specify the presentation information.

Separating the structure from the presentation has a number of benefits. One benefit is the degree of control you have when using style sheets, easily creating effects such as shadowing and overlapping text. Keeping the presentation separate allows for one style sheet to be used for multiple HTML pages. This keeps file sizes down because the style code needs to be written only once. It also makes global changes easier, as the style needs to be modified in just one place, the style sheet, and its effect can be instantly applied to every HTML page that uses it.

Basics

A style sheet is basically a list of declarations, or rules. A simple declaration specifies the affected tag, which property of this tag to set, and the value for the property. The basic format for a rule is as follows:

```
tag { property: value }
```

The properties of multiple tags can be set in the same line by separating the tag names with commas. Also, multiple properties can be set for a tag by inserting a semicolon after each property and enclosing them within a set of braces. The following example sets the font color and family for all <h1> and <h2> elements:

```
h1, h2 {
   color: red;
   font-family: sans-serif;
}
```

These tags allow the properties of an outer tag to be carried through to inner tags, a process known as inheritance, which provides an indirect way of setting a default. Setting the font color in the <body> tag to green sets all of the text font within the body to green, unless a particular element overwrites that property. Inheritance can alternatively be used selectively by listing nested tags (without commas) in the rule declaration. The following example would set the font color of any italic heading 2 text to green (other instances of italic text would not be affected):

```
h2 I { color:green }
```

Using Style Sheets

Style sheet declarations can be included within an HTML document, or they can exist in a separate document that the HTML document links to. Including these declarations in the HTML document requires only that they are enclosed in <style></style> tags. The type attribute can be included in the <style> element to indicate the type of style sheet being used (for example, "text/CSS"). This <style> code is often inserted into the <head> of a document so that it loads first.

```
<head>
<style type="text/css">
  h3 {font-family:arial; color: brown}
</style>
</head>
```

To link an external style sheet to an HTML document, use the <link> element as shown in the following line. The href attribute points to the location of the CSS file and the rel attribute indicates the relationship of the link:

```
<link rel="StyleSheet" href="http://myserver.com/stylesheets/MyStyleSheet.css">
```

A style sheet file should contain nothing more than what would be contained within the <style> tags of an embedded style sheet. Style sheet files are typically named with a .css file extension. MyStyleSheet.css could look like this:

```
h1 { color: red }
.myStyle {
  color: blue;
  font-size: 14pt;
}
```

The previous example defines the color for the h1 attribute and also introduces a way to specify a class. MyStyleSheet.css renders any h1 font red, and makes the font blue and 14 point whenever the class is myStyle. While the class attribute is a universal attribute, any tag can be assigned a class, and hence a style. The class is set in a style sheet using the format *element.class*, where the *element* may be omitted (as in the previous example using mystyle). If the element is included, the style is only valid for that particular element.

Assume that the following line was added to MyStyleSheet.css, creating a style class named yourStyle that is valid only when using an <h1> element:

```
h1.yourStyle { color: green }
```

A separate HTML document that linked to the MyStyleSheet.css would render the first line in the following code with green text, the second line in red, and the third line in blue.

Notice how the example shows the span element, which is used simply to apply style to a section of text:

```
<h1 class="yourStyle">Welcome!</h1>
<h1> We are using </h1>
<span class="myStyle"> Style Sheets </span>
```

Using Images in HTML Pages

Anyone who has loaded a Web page over a dial-up modem connection knows that there is more to a Web page than just text—pictures can considerably slow the page speed down. Images come in many flavors, and among those types supported in HTML and rendered in a browser are .gif, .jpg, .jpeg, .xbm, .xpm, and .png.

An image is included in a Web page by using the <img> tag with the source attribute (src) set to the location of the image file. Note that the absolute or relative location of the image file may be specified. Also, it is a good idea to always include the alt attribute, which specifies a string that is displayed to the user if the image fails to show up. The following example loads an image stored in a file named pony.gif, which, because of its location in the same directory as the HTML file, excludes a full path name:

```
<img src="pony.gif" alt="This is my favorite pony.">
```

If the image fails to load, then the alternate text is displayed in its place. The title attribute is used like the title attribute in anchor elements—to specify a small bit of text that gets displayed if the mouse pointer is held over the image.

The exact placement of an image is very important to careful Web designers, and the align, height, and width attributes aid in achieving this. The align attribute is set to either "left", "center", or "right", and indicates the horizontal justification of the image on the screen. The height and width attributes can be set to either a number of pixels or a percentage of the browser window size to specify the height and width of the image.

When an image is placed amongst text, the text flows around the image. The hspace and vspace attributes specify a horizontal and vertical buffer space, respectively, in pixels. Text then flows only up to the edge of the buffer space instead of the image.

An image may also be used as a button or a hyperlink to send you to another URL or another place in the same URL. To achieve this, the anchor tags must surround the <img> element:

```
<a href="http://www.myGrandma.com"><img src="images/gram.gif"
align="left"></a>
```

This would cause a picture of Grandma to be displayed aligned left in the browser, and clicking on the photo would take the user to Grandma's Web site.

HTML Tables

Even though Cascading Style Sheets provide a more precise way of positioning things in a Web page, the <table> element and its associated elements and attributes are more commonly used. With only four main elements, <table>, <tr>, <th>, and <td>, tables can be created and organized to a surprising degree.

The <table> element itself must be the parent element, and the </table> element must close all table instructions or else the table will not render properly. Inside of that tag, a <tr> element specifies the start of a table row. The first row of the table will most likely contain column headings, so a series of <th> elements are used to indicate a table heading. The data inside a heading cell must be closed with a </th> element, and the end of the row must be marked by a </tr> element. Once the heading row ends, the next row begins with a new <tr>, and in place of heading cells, you add table data cells, inserting data between the <td> and </td> elements. A </tr> element specifies the end of that row. Once all of the rows have been created, a </table> element closes the table information. The caption element may enclose text, usually a table title, and that title is usually displayed above the table border.

The following HTML code, if inserted into a properly formatted HTML document, will display a table with four rows and two columns. The table has a title, a header row, a column stating the piece of Tom's clothing, and another column indicating the color of that piece:

```
<table border="1">
  <caption>Tom's Clothing</caption>
  <tr><th>Piece</th><th>Color</th></tr>
  <tr><td>jeans</td><td bgcolor="blue">blue</td></tr>
  <tr><td>shirt</td><td bgcolor="pink">pink</td></tr>
  <tr><td>shoes</td><td bgcolor="gray">gray</td></tr>
</table>
```

The cols attribute specifies the number of columns present. If omitted, the table is created with the number of columns equal to the maximum number of <td></td> pairs in a given row. The rowspan and colspan attributes of <td> and <tr> are used when data needs to be larger or smaller than just one cell, either vertically or horizontally.

The <thead> element is used to group one or more rows into a header group. The <tbody> and <tfoot> elements provide similar organization for a group of body or footer rows. Columns may also be organized using the <colgroup> element, specifying an individual column with the <col> element.

Height and Width

The height and width attributes of the <table> element specify the height and width of the entire table, either in pixels or as a percentage of the window size. The border attribute is used to determine the thickness of the lines drawn between table cells. It is also specified in pixels, and if no border attribute is included, no border gets drawn. The cellpadding attribute indicates the space between the border of one cell and the border of the neighboring one.

The height and width attributes can also be set at the <td> level, specifying the size of a particular table cell. In addition, border colors can be set for the entire table using the bordercolor attribute, and background colors and patterns can be indicated for the whole table or at the cell level using bgcolor:

```
<table border="1" align="right">
  <caption>My Example</caption>
  <tr>
    <td rowspan="2">Element1</td>
    <td bgcolor="red">Element2</td>
  </tr>
  <tr>
    <td>Element3</td>
  </tr>
</table>
```

The preceding code would produce a table titled My Example with two columns and two rows. However, the first cell extends down into the second row due to the rowspan attribute. The cell at the top right is colored red.

A table cell can contain anything—lots of text, an image, nothing, or another table. In fact, this is how page designer programs allow you to place items in exact positions on a Web page, using tables full of smaller tables.

HTML Frames

An HTML document that makes use of multiple frames is divided into multiple panes, each one operating as its own window. Frames are popular for creating a table of contents that remains along the left side of a Web page, and for maintaining a consistent look and feel across multiple pages. Each pane can have its own scroll bars and show its own .htm or .html file.

Although there are benefits to using frames, they are often confusing to use because the true URL is sometimes masked, and refreshing can cause unpredictable results. Note that the body element and frameset element are mutually exclusive; a body tag within a frameset will not render, and a frameset within a body tag will not render.

Three main elements make up a framed Web site: <frameset>, <frame>, and <noframes> (to specify what to display on a browser which does not support frames, a rarity). The <frameset> element must be the first element after the <head> section of a document, and <frameset> elements surround <frame>, <noframes>, and sometimes nested <frameset> elements.

<frameset>

The <frameset> element allows the number of rows and columns of frames to be specified via the rows and cols attributes. These attributes can be set to a list of measurements in pixels, percentages, or ratios. The number of columns or rows is determined by the number of commas, as a comma separates the different column or row size specifications. Pixel amounts are simply specified as numbers, whereas percentages are made up of a number followed by a percent sign. An asterisk can be used in place of a number to act as a placeholder and divide the remaining space up equally. An asterisk can also be included after an integer to signify a ratio is being used. The three rows of the following example have widths that are 30, 20, and 50 percent of the width of the browser from left to right. The second column is larger than the first by a ratio of 3 to 1:

```
<frameset rows="30%, *, 50%" cols="1*, 3*">
  <frame> <frame> <frame>
  <frame> <frame> <frame>
</frameset>
```

<frame>

The <frame> element often has no closing tag, as all of the information that follows it is included as attributes. The attributes include frameborder, marginheight, marginwidth, scrolling, noresize, longdesc, src, and name.

The frameborder attribute indicates whether or not a border is drawn around the frame—a value of "1" or "YES" draws the border (and is the default), "0" or "NO" draws no border. The marginheight and marginwidth attributes specify the number of pixels of space between the edge of the frame and the frames contents. The scrolling attribute determines if a scroll bar will be placed in the frame—possible values being "NO", "YES", or "AUTO", which creates a scroll bar only when necessary. Including the noresize attribute will prevent the frame from being resized in the browser by the user dragging the window boundary. The longdesc attribute specifies a link to a long description of the current frame.

The HTML document that is displayed in a frame is set using the src attribute. The name attribute can be used to name a frame so that it may be targeted by a link in another document. The name attribute of <frame> is used in conjunction with the target attribute of the anchor element.

The following piece of code creates two columns. The smaller column on the left displays a table of contents with links to other documents to be displayed in the main_frame:

```
<frameset cols="20%, *">
  <frame src="contents.html">
  <frame src="welcome.html" name="main_frame">
</frameset>
```

A link placed in the left-hand frame such as the one that follows will cause the specified HTML document to load in the larger main frame:

```
<a href="aboutUs.html" target="main_frame">About Us</a>
```

<noframes>

A <noframes> element may be included within a <frameset> element to provide content to be displayed in browsers that do not support frames. Often included between the opening and closing frameset elements is a link to a no-frames version of the content. Frame-supporting browsers ignore the content between the noframes tags.

<iframe>

HTML 4.0 added the <iframe> element, allowing creation of an inline or *layered* frame. The <iframe> element does not need to be enclosed by the <frameset> container, and it takes attributes similar to those for the <frame> element: align, frameborder, height, marginheight, marginwidth, name, scrolling, src, width, and longdesc. When added to an HTML document, the following lines of code create a large, inlayed frame containing the contents of MyTest.html. Scrollbars are added automatically if they are needed:

```
<iframe src="MyTest.html" width="400" height="500"
  scrolling="auto" frameborder="1">
</iframe>
```

HTML Forms

In addition to presenting information in a browser, many Web sites also offer the option of collecting information from a user. This is done using forms. The data in a form is submitted and then sent to the Web server. A script or service picks up from there, performing any operations called for, and then generates a new document to send back to the user's browser. A form can be recognized in an HTML page any time the following HTML controls are found: free text areas, radio buttons, drop-down list boxes, and click buttons.

The data is sent to the server from the browser in name/value pairs, in the format name="value". The pairs are separated from each other with ampersands (&), and spaces are converted into plus signs (+). Special characters (plus sign, ampersands, and so on) are converted into hexadecimal and preceded by a percent sign (%).

<form>

All forms begin and end with the <form> tag. The <form> tag and its closing tag, </form>, can be placed anywhere within the body of an HTML document, in any multiple, but they cannot nest or overlap. The <form> element encloses HTML control structures, and the following attributes are allowed: action, enctype, method, target, accept-charset, and accept.

The action and method attributes are the most commonly used. The action attribute is set to the URL that will receive the data once the form is submitted. It is the program that will handle the submitted data, and can be an absolute or relative path. The method attribute is set to either POST or GET, thereby indicating the way that the entered data will be sent to the server. The POST method is the newer and preferred method of submission, sending data in a data stream. The GET method is older and limited by the fact that the data sent gets tacked onto the URL with a question mark, and hence is accompanied by a size limitation. Though GET is the default method for some browsers, sending secure data in the URL also poses some security deficiencies, and hence the GET method is deprecated in HTML 4.0. The following line illustrates proper usage of the <form> tag:

```
<form method="POST" action="http://www.myserver.com/cgi/post-
query1"></form>
```

The form element can surround a number of different HTML controls that are used to actually collect the data: <input>, <textarea>, <select>, <optgroup>, <button>, <label>, <fieldset>, and <legend>. These control elements are described in the following sections.

<input>

The <input> element is the simplest of the controls, and it can be modified to do a variety of things. Using this element, a single-line text field is created by setting the type attribute to "text" (a longer text field requires the use of the <textarea> element). If type is set to "checkbox", a check box control is created. Table 7-1 outlines the acceptable values for the type attribute.

The name attribute gives a control a specific name, and the name should be unique to the form. The size attribute can control the size of the text box, whereas the maxlength attribute controls the maximum size of the entered text (when the text size grows larger than the displayed size of the text field, the text scrolls). The align attribute controls the position of the text in relation to the element and can be set to either "top", "middle", or "bottom".

When included, the readonly attribute causes the control to be read-only and the disabled attribute causes the control to be grayed out. The checked attribute sets a default radio button, while text or numeric controls provide the value attribute to be set as the default.

Table 7-1. Type Attribute Values

Value	Description
text	Creates a single-line text field.
password	Specifies that letters typed in the text field will appear as asterisks, keeping input hidden.
hidden	Hides entire field.
checkbox	Creates a check box control.
radio	Creates a radio button control in which only one option may be chosen.
reset	Creates a button that resets all fields to initial values when clicked.
submit	Creates a button that submits entered data to server.
image	Creates an image map that when clicked submits entered data to server.
button	Creates a button with no default action, used to initiate scripts.
file	Creates a text box that is used to enter name of file to send to server.

The button element can be used in place of an input of type button. The tag <button> is equivalent to saying <input type="button">.

<textarea>

The <textarea> element is used to generate an area larger than one line for entering text into a Web page. Each line of text entered into a text area is submitted to the server separated by a carriage return and line feed. The cols and rows attributes set the width and height of the area in number of characters. The name attribute should specify a unique name for the control. When included, the disabled attribute causes the control to appear grayed out, and the readonly attribute keeps the appearance normal, but forces the control to remain read-only. The closing </textarea> tag is required.

<select>

List boxes and drop-down combination boxes are created through the <select> element. The <option> tag specifies the different value options that appear in the list, as described in the next section. The most significant attribute of this element is the size attribute, which dictates the number of options shown at one time on the screen. When set to "1", the control appears as a drop-down list box.

Setting the size to more than "1" makes the control a list box and determines the number of options displayed in the box at one time. The inclusion of the multiple attribute allows the user to make more than one selection at a time by holding down the Ctrl button and clicking. Inclusion of the disabled attribute causes the control to appear grayed out. The closing </select> tag is required.

<option>

Items entered between the opening and closing <option> tags appear as the choices in the list boxes and drop-down combination boxes created using the <select> elements. The default choice for a list box or drop-down box can be specified by including the selected attribute in the <option> tag. Including the disabled attribute will cause the option to appear grayed out. The value attribute is set to the value that is sent to the server if that option is chosen and submitted.

Form Example

The following example demonstrates the use of some common form elements. A text box is created to enter a string value license plate number. A drop-down list box displaying a few car makes is then created. A group of radio buttons specify the color of the car, and a Submit button at the bottom submits the form via an HTTP POST:

```
<form method="POST" action="http://yourserver.com/scripts/post-query">
License Plate Number:
  <input type="text" name="plateNum" size="10">
  <p>Car make:
  <select name="makeName" size="1">
  <option selected>Honda
  <option>Ford
  <option>GM
  </select>
  <p>Car Color:</p>
  <input type="radio" name="color" value="BL">Blue
  <input type="radio" name="color" value="RD">Red
  <input type="radio" name="color" value="BK">Black
  </p>
  <input type="submit" value="Submit">
</form>
```

XHTML

In January 2000, XHTML 1.0, a reformulation of HTML 4 in XML, became a W3C recommendation. This was followed in May 2001 with XHTML 1.1, which is the current specification as of this writing (though an XHTML 2.0 specification is in its sixth working draft). Although Web browsers are not going to immediately change to accept XHTML as the standard for Internet Web pages, XHTML is going to be the way of the future. Therefore, the W3C recommends transitioning to XHTML when possible, but also remaining backward compatible with existing HTML 4 design.

A valid XHTML 1.0 document conforms to one of three defined Document Type Definitions (DTD). A DTD is a list of legal elements that defines a document structure. The DTD provides the framework for the elements, attributes, and entities contained within the document they restrict. A DTD may be included in an XML file, or it may exist as a separate document to which the original document links.

XHTML 1.0 is different from HTML in the following ways:

- Documents must be well-formed. This means that each opening tag must have a closing tag, nested elements must close in order, and the syntax rules of the XML 1.0 specification must be followed.
- Element and attribute names must be lowercase, as XML is case sensitive.
- End tags are required for nonempty elements. The <p> tag must have a matching </p> tag.
- Attribute values must be quoted, even numeric values.
- Attribute-value pairs are required to be written in full. Although it is acceptable in HTML to write certain attributes as <input readonly> and <frame noresize>, in XHTML they must be <input readonly="readonly"> and <frame noresize="noresize">
- Empty elements must have end tags or else opening tags must include closing slash: <hr></hr> or <hr/>
- Leading and trailing white space in attribute values are stripped and mapped to a single space character (for Western scripts).
- The script and style elements are declared as having #PCDATA (parsed character data) content, which means that characters such as "<" or "&" will be interpreted by the browser as markup and may not render properly.
- DTDs cannot *exclude* elements from being contained within an element.
- The id attribute must be used as an element identifier wherever the name attribute was formerly used, because this attribute has been formally deprecated in XHTML 1.0.

XHTML Variants

XHTML 1.0 has three variations, each indicated by a corresponding DTD included at the beginning of an XHTML document. The DTD tells the tool that to what degree the document should be validated. There are also three DTDs for the validation levels of HTML 4.01, though these are slightly different.

The XHTML 1.0 *Strict* DTD should be used when creating a clear division between the structure of XHTML and the style of Cascading Style Sheets. This DTD does not contain any of the deprecated elements or attributes, and therefore demands that everything be up to the current specification. The following lines should be included at the top of a document when using the Strict DTD, immediately following the line <?xml version="1.0" ?>:

```
<!DOCTYPE html PUBLIC "-//W3C//DTD XHTML 1.0 Strict//EN"
  "http://www.w3.org/TR/xhtml1/DTD/xhtml1-strict.dtd">
```

The XHTML 1.0 *Transitional* DTD should be used when trying to remain compatible with older browsers that cannot handle style sheets. The Transitional DTD includes deprecated attributes and elements. The following line should be included when the Transitional variant is desired:

```
<!DOCTYPE html PUBLIC "-//W3C//DTD XHTML 1.0 Transitional//EN"
  "http://www.w3.org/TR/xhtml1/DTD/xhtml1-transitional.dtd">
```

The XHTML 1.0 *Frameset* DTD should be used when a Web page is divided into frames. This DTD includes the deprecated elements of the Transitional DTD, in addition to the <frame> tags. To use the Frameset DTD, include this:

```
<!DOCTYPE html PUBLIC "-//W3C//DTD XHTML 1.0 Frameset//EN"
  "http://www.w3.org/TR/xhtml1/DTD/xhtml1-frameset.dtd">
```

Strictly Conforming

The following items outline the qualifications that a document must meet to become a strictly conforming XHTML document.

- The document must validate against one of the three DTDs described earlier.
- The root element of the document must be <html>.
- The root element, <html>, must use the xmlns attribute to designate the XHTML namespace (see http://www.w3.org/1999/xhtml for more).
- The DOCTYPE declaration must come before the root element and must reference one of the three DTDs described previously.
- No parameter entity of the referenced DTD can be overridden by a DTD subset.

HTML 4.01 Element Tags

These deprecated tags are not listed: <u>, <plaintext>, <listing>, <xmp>, <strike>, <s>, <isindex>, <dir>, <menu>, <font>, <basefont>, <center>, and <applet>.

Element	**Description**
<!DOCTYPE>	Defines the doc type
<html>	Defines HTML doc
<body>	Defines the body
<h1>..<h6>	Defines header 1 to header 6
<p>	Defines a paragraph
 	Inserts a line break
<hr>	Defines a horizontal. rule
<!-->	Defines a comment

Character Format

<b>	Defines bold text
<strong>	Defines strong text
<i>	Defines italic text
<em>	Defines emphasized text
<big>	Defines big text
<small>	Defines small text
<sup>	Defines superscripted text
<sub>	Defines subscripted text
<bdo>	Defines of text direction

Output

<pre>	Defines preformatted text
<code>	Defines computer code text
<tt>	Defines teletype text
<kbd>	Defines keyboard text
<var>	Defines a variable
<samp>	Defines sample computer code

Blocks

<acronym>	Defines an acronym
<abbr>	Defines an abbreviation
<address>	Defines an address element
<blockquote>	Defines an long quotation
<q>	Defines a short quotation
<cite>	Defines a citation
<ins>	Defines inserted text
<del>	Defines deleted text

Input

<form>	Defines a form
<input>	Defines an input field
<textarea>	Defines a text area
<button>	Defines a push button
<select>	Defines a selectable list
<optgroup>	Defines an option group
<option>	Defines an item in a list box
<label>	Defines a label
<fieldset>	Defines a fieldset
<legend>	Defines a title in a fieldset

Links

<a>	Defines an anchor
<link>	Defines a resource ref

Frames

<frame>	Defines a sub window
<frameset>	Defines a set of frames
<noframes>	Defines a noframe section
<iframe>	Defines an inline frame

Lists

<ul>	Defines an unordered list
<ol>	Defines an ordered list
<li>	Defines a list item
<dl>	Defines a definition list
<dt>	Defines a definition term
<dfn>	Defines a definition term
<dd>	Defines a definition descrip.

Images

<img>	Defines an image
<map>	Defines an image map
<area>	Defines area in image map

Tables

<table>	Defines a table
<caption>	Defines a table caption
<th>	Defines a table header
<tr>	Defines a table row
<td>	Defines a table cell
<thead>	Defines a table header
<tbody>	Defines a table body
<tfoot>	Defines a table footer
<col>	Defines column attributes
<colgroup>	Defines groups of columns

Styles

<style>	Defines a style definition
<div>	Defines document segment
<span>	Defines document segment

Meta Info

<head>	Defines document info
<title>	Defines the document title
<meta>	Defines meta information
<base>	Defines default reference

Programming

<script>	Defines a script
<noscript>	Defines a noscript section
<object>	Defines an embedded object
<param>	Defines a object parameter

Looking Forward

The future of Web development does indeed lie with XHTML. However, XHTML will not cause immediate changes across the Web. If XHTML suddenly became the default language used by Internet browsers, every existing page would fail to display. Web browsers will be configured to accept both HTML and XHTML. Existing Web pages will remain as they are and will continue to work, and new documents should probably be written using XHTML. In time, browsers will begin looking for XHTML first, but will probably always accept HTML. The initiative to separate the format markup from the presentation information is well underway. The use of style sheets will continue to grow, as they provide expanded functionality and are easier to maintain.

If migrating existing Web page HTML to the newer standards is in the plan for you, consider using HTML Tidy. HTML Tidy is a free utility that can be used to clean up sloppy HTML code that was (and still is) accepted as proper HTML by today's Web browsers. Things like missing end tags are added by the utility, while questionable situations are marked for you to attend to. A link to the HTML Tidy utility can be found on the W3C homepage (http://www.w3c.org).

The W3C site is a good source for many things relating to HTML (including the latest and past HTML specifications as well as specs for XML and CSS), and it also contains a list of guidelines that should be followed in order for XHTML documents to render on HTML browsers (http://www.w3.org/TR/xhtml1/#guidelines). In addition, you can view the recent actions of the standards group to prepare for changes to come.

If you are writing Web pages using HTML, remember to adhere to the standards as closely as possible. Not all browsers "forgive" HTML syntax errors. Download a variety of browsers, and view your pages in each of them, so you will have a good idea of the quirks each has when rendering your HTML.

Another important piece of advice is to find a good HTML editor. Different companies have different standards for which editors they allow, but *Notepad* just won't cut it for writing good HTML anymore. There are numerous inexpensive products out there to help you write consistent HTML.

Finally, one *big* secret: if you see a Web page that you particularly like, or one which has formatting features you'd like to incorporate into your Web page, most browsers offer a *view source* function, which will show you the page including all the tags. Use the source to advance your learning of HTML.

Chapter 8

XML

XML, extensible markup language, is a standard format for storing structured data. This standard format enables the development of tools and utilities. More precisely, XML is a meta-language, meaning it is used to define other languages. For example, if you use XML to output expense reports, you can create a special purpose "expense report" language.

XML is the base technology for the other tools and standards described in this chapter, and it has many different applications. It is not tied to a specific industry or type of data and can easily represent hierarchical or tree-structured data. XML is the most important data format for new development in the enterprise.

Initial development on the World Wide Web used HTML displayed in a browser. HTML is a data format with a fixed set of tags designed to define document layout. With widespread availability, the Web began to be used for machine to machine communication, and HTML is not suited for this task. The main data standard for communication between systems prior to XML was a difficult to use binary format called EDI (Electronic Data Interchange). The ubiquity and simplicity of HTTP/HTML led to the development of something new.

XML was created under the sponsorship of the W3C in 1996, and that organization maintains the current standard. Like HTML, it is based on SGML (Standard Generalized Markup Language). XML defines a basic syntax, but allows you to create tags. It can be used as a part of a large scale system where the specific XML format is defined by an international standards body, or it can be used on an ad hoc basis to create a data format for a single program. HTML defines layout, XML defines content.

Fast Facts

- There are many related standards. XML, XSL, XPath, and XML-Schema will be covered here. See http://www.w3.org for more details.
- XML is composed of elements and attributes.
- Every XML document should start with an xml declaration.
- There must be a single top level tag.
- Every element must have a begin and an end tag (which can be combined <tag/>).
- Tags cannot overlap, <a><b></a></b> is not allowed.
- Attributes must always be enclosed in quotes.
- Whitespace between elements is not significant (this means it does not matter if a document is all on one line or formatted with indentations). Whitespace inside element content is preserved.
- XML schemas and DTDs are used to define the structure of an XML document.
- XML is read by programs using XML parsers. The availability of standard parsers makes this task much easier.
- SAX and DOM are types of XML parsers.
- XML text is Unicode, a standard that can represent any language.
- A DTD can define elements (tags), attributes, and entities.
- An entity is a keyword or abbreviation that is replaced by its value when parsed.
- XML-Schema can fully define the structure of an XML document.

Sample XML

This small example shows the basic structure of an XML document:

```
<?xml version="1.0" encoding="UTF-8"?>
<parent>
  <child firstname="fred"> child text... </child>
</parent>
```

Main Components of an XML Document

Every XML document can be broken down to the basic building blocks explained here.

XML Declaration

The first line in this example is the XML declaration. The current XML version is 1.0, so this is always the same. The encoding defines the Unicode code page (character mapping) that is used.

<parent>

The second and last lines contain the <parent> start element and </parent> end element. These form the topmost (root) element that contains the rest of the document. The parent start and end elements contain the parent data, in this case, a nested child sub-element.

<child>

The third line contains a <child> element, a sub-element of parent that has a firstname attribute. The value of the firstname attribute is "fred", that is, the child's first name is fred. The <child> element also contains some text content "child text...". Elements, attributes, and text content are the basic building blocks of XML.

Basics of XML

XML is a document format. Some other formats are easier to read and write, such as attribute-value files (like the ini file format in Windows):

```
firstname=fred
```

The problem with simple formats is they cannot easily represent complex data. Even our simple XML example, where a *parent* contains a *child*, is hard to represent in an ini file format. XML strikes a good balance between simplicity and expressiveness.

You can create an XML document with any text editor. There are many free and commercial tools available to parse, analyze, and work with XML documents. The technologies outlined in this chapter are free (see the *Looking Forward* section at the end of the chapter for URLs).

The most basic concept in XML is *well-formedness*, that is, the definitions that specify the syntax of the language. Several of the *Fast Facts* define aspects of well-formedness: attributes are quoted, elements are nested, and there is a single top level element. Well-formedness is the minimum requirement for an XML document.

The XML Declaration

An XML document should start with an XML declaration. In practice, many parsers will accept a document that does not have one:

```
<?xml version="1.0" encoding="UTF-8"?>
```

The version is always "1.0" as of this writing. The encoding defines the Unicode character representation; UTF-8 matches the European languages.

Elements

Elements are the foundation of XML. Each element (or *tag* in HTML) consists of a name surrounded by angle brackets <child>. Element tags must be used in pairs, each start element is followed by a corresponding end element: <child></child>. The end element has a slash in front of the name. Element content, consisting of text or other elements, is contained between the start and end tags. There is a shorthand notation for use when there is no content, <simpleElement/>, which is the same as <simpleElement></simpleElement>.

This is an example containing text content:

```
<child>child text..</child>
```

This is an example containing element content:

```
<child><pet></pet></child>
```

Tags cannot overlap. This is not allowed:

```
<child></pet></child></pet>
```

XML is extensible because the element names can be whatever you want - whatever makes sense for your application. Element names are case sensitive and can contain dashes and underscores, but not spaces. It is generally considered good style to capitalize adjacent words, like <grandChild>, for better readability.

Attributes

Attributes add some data to an element. Attributes consist of name="value" pairs, where the value part must be in quotes:

```
<child name="fred">
```

In this example, the element child has an attribute name with a value fred.

Character Entities

XML syntax is very flexible, but that creates a problem. Consider the following content:

```
<expression>x < y > z</expression>
```

This is supposed to be an arithmetic expression, "x < y > z". However, it looks like the expression has a child element with the name, "y".

To avoid this confusion, use the following character entities in the place of the characters they stand for. Character entities start with an ampersand and end with a semicolon.

Table 8-1. Character Encoding

Character	Entity
<	<
>	>
"	"
&	&

The ampersand and angle brackets are special characters in XML, they are not allowed inside element content or attribute text. To get around this restriction, you should use the character entities for these special characters. The correct way to write the example above is:

```
<expression>x &lt; y &gt; z</expression>
```

CDATA

Element content can be simple text, as in the examples we have shown, or it can be arbitrary data. The CDATA element is used to define a blob of data that will be treated as a unit and will not be parsed. Angle brackets and ampersands are allowed:

```
<content><![CDATA[this can be anything...]]></content>
```

Grammar == Structure

The XML standard defines the syntax of the language, but as soon as one program needs to communicate with another, you need a way to specify how the message will be structured. This is a *grammar*. The XML specification defines well-formed documents. A grammar allows you to determine if a document is *valid* for that application.

How would you describe and define the structure of this sample XML document?

```
<?xml version="1.0" encoding="UTF-8"?>
<contacts>
  <contact name="greg">
    <email>gmunger@isp.com</email>
    <phone type="cell">219-222-3456</phone>
    <phone type="home">219-945-1234</phone>
  </contact>
</contacts>
```

DTD

XML is derived from SGML, and the mechanism used to define a grammar in SGML is a document type definition (DTD). The XML standard described above can be defined by a DTD. However, a DTD is not a valid XML document, it is a separate document format (so it cannot be parsed by an XML parser). This is more important than you might think. Most new development uses the XML-Schema specification (described in the following section) to define XML structure.

Element

A DTD consists of grammar rules. The ELEMENT rules consist of a tag name followed by a specification of the allowed contents. The allowed contents (right hand side of the rule) can be a parenthesized list of child element names: PCDATA, for text content; EMPTY when no content is allowed; and ANY, meaning any element or text is allowed.

Each child element name can be followed by a *, ?, or + symbol, indicating the number of times it can repeat.

? - child is optional (zero or one time)

+ - child appears one or more times

* - child appears zero or more times

Each child element in the list is separated by a comma or bar. The comma defines a sequence. Here, the one or more addr elements are followed by a city element, followed by an optional state element:

```
<!ELEMENT address ( addr+, city, state?) >
```

The vertical bar defines a choice. Here, the preferredContact element contains either a cellPhone or a homePhone child element:

```
<!ELEMENT preferredContact (cellPhone|homePhone) >
```

Attribute

The ATTLIST rules define what attributes are allowed in the elements. In this example, the contact element is defined to have a name attribute. The type of the attribute follows its name. In this case, CDATA allows any character string:

```
<!ATTLIST contact name CDATA #REQUIRED >
```

It is also possible to define a parenthesized list of enumerated values for the type. In this example, the phone element contains a phonetype attribute that can be either "cell" or "home":

```
<!ATTLIST phone phonetype (cell|home) >
```

Entities

ENTITY rules are currently the most important use for DTDs. Entities define constant placeholders with replacement values. In the XML document, they are referenced by preceding with an ampersand and following with a semicolon. We have already seen the standard entities in the previous section, for example:

```
&lt;
```

The line above is defined by the declaration:

```
<!ENTITY lt "<">
```

A possible DTD for the XML example is the following:

```
<?xml version="1.0"?>
<!ELEMENT contacts (contact+)>
<!ELEMENT contact (email?, phone+)>
<!ATTLIST contact name CDATA #REQUIRED >
<!ELEMENT email (#PCDATA) >
<!ELEMENT phone (#PCDATA) >
<!ATTLIST phone type (cell|home)  #REQUIRED >
```

The above defines that there are zero or more contacts in a contactList. The contact name attribute is required, the phone element must be present one or more times, and the email element is optional.

Applying a DTD to an XML document

A DTD is applied to an XML document by the DOCTYPE declaration. The DTD can be referenced as either PUBLIC or SYSTEM:

```
<!DOCTYPE dtdName PUBLIC "public_identifier" "url_of_dtd">
<!DOCTYPE dtdName SYSTEM "url_of_dtd">
```

SYSTEM indicates that the DTD is private and is intended only for local use. PUBLIC indicates that the DTD is intended for general use. In our original example, assuming the DTD is saved in a file named contacts.dtd, the XML file would contain the following change:

```
<?xml version="1.0" encoding="UTF-8"?>
<!DOCTYPE contacts SYSTEM "contacts.dtd">
<contacts>
```

XML-Schema

Like a DTD, an XML-Schema is used to define the grammar or structure of an XML document. The XML-Schema standard was published by the W3C in 2001. It is more powerful, more verbose, and more complex than DTD. The lengthy (and highly recommended) primer on the W3C site contains more detail than we can cover on these few pages. See the *Looking Forward* section for the URL. The following is a fragment of a schema:

```
<?xml version="1.0" encoding="ISO-8859-1"?>
<xsd:schema xmlns:xsd="http://www.w3.org/2001/XMLSchema">
<xsd:element name="contacts">
  <xsd:complexType>
    <xsd:sequence>
      <xsd:element name="contact" type="contactType"/>
    </xsd:sequence>
  </xsd:complexType>
</xsd:element>
```

Namespaces

An XML document can and often will be defined by more than one schema. Namespace declarations are used to keep track of which schema applies to each part of the document. Any element in a document can have a namespace associated with it (the namespace will apply to the sub-tree of elements), but usually all namespace declarations are applied to the top element.

A namespace can be defined with a prefix, and each use of an element from the schema is prepended with the prefix. One schema can be declared to be the default namespace. Any element or type without a prefix is assumed to belong to the default namespace. A namespace declaration consists of:

```
<elementName xmlns:prefix="URI">
```

elementName is the tag the namespace is applied to.

xmlns is the keyword that specifies a namespace declaration.

prefix is the optional prefix used to identify usage of the namespace.

URI is a unique identifier, generally the URI (URL) of the schema.

Schema documents must start with a schema namespace declaration:

```
<?xml version="1.0" encoding="ISO-8859-1"?>
<xsd:schema xmlns:xsd="http://www.w3.org/2001/XMLSchema">
<xsd:element name="contacts">
```

By convention, xsd is the prefix used for the schema namespace:

```
<xsd:complexType>
```

In use, the prefix (xsd:) shows that this element is associated with the XML-Schema namespace (the schema that defines XML-Schema documents). The fundamental building blocks of a schema declaration are xsd:complexType, xsd:element, and the grouping elements like xsd:sequence or xsd:choice. Together they form the definition of a tag.

Complex Type

A complex type at the top level of the schema document defines a tag *type* that can be used elsewhere in the document. These top level types must have a name element that is used to make this connection. This works very much like a type definition in a programming language, as shown in the *Parsing* section.

In this example, the contact top level complex type is defined to contain a series of sub-elements. Without further constraints, each sub-element in a sequence must appear once, in order. The types of the sub-elements are specified by the type attributes. In this case, they are string and integer. There will be more information about this in the section on built in types:

```
<xsd:complexType name="Contact">
  <xsd:sequence>
    <xsd:element name="id"  type="xsd:int"/>
    <xsd:element name="name" type="xsd:string"/>
  </xsd:sequence>
</xsd:complexType>
```

The xsd:element statements act like variable declarations. In Java this would be something like:

```
class Contact {
  int   id;
  String name;
}
```

Though the schema is not complete, sample valid XML could look like this:

```
<contact>
  <id>12321</id>
  <name>fred</name>
</contact>
```

Occurrence Constraints

The example above is not precise. We also need to define the number of sub-elements allowed. In XML-Schema, this is done with min-occurs and max-occurs constraints. The default minOccurs and maxOccurs for xsd:sequence is one and one. It is only necessary to specify values that are different than the default. The values used for the constraints can be any positive integer, or the keyword unbounded:

```
<xsd:complexType name="contact">
  <xsd:sequence>
    <xsd:element name="name"  type="Name"/>
    <xsd:element name="phone" type="Phone" maxOccurs="unbounded"/>
    <xsd:element name="email" type="Email" minOccurs="0"/>
  </xsd:sequence>
</xsd:complexType>
```

Here, name has no constraints, so it must occur exactly once in the contact element. This is followed by one or more phone elements. Finally, there is an optional email element.

Top Level Element

An XML document can have only one top level element, but a schema can be defined to specify documents with different top level elements. For example, a schema defining a B2B message might allow either a request or a response top level element. Each top level tag (element) of an XML document must be defined using a schema element declaration. An element will either contain a complex type or reference one by name:

```
<xsd:element name="contacts" type="Contacts"/>
```

Here, the top level element contacts references the type Contacts by name.

Grouping

Besides the xsd:sequence grouping element, the most commonly used is xsd:choice. A choice element only allows one of its children to be present in the document. If we wanted to allow either a cell phone or a home phone number, we could use this schema:

```
<xsd:complexType name="phone">
  <xsd:choice>
    <xsd:element name="cellPhone" type="phoneNumber"/>
    <xsd:element name="homePhone" type="phoneNumber"/>
  </xsd:choice>
</xsd:complexType>
```

We haven't defined how the phoneNumber will be represented, but this example shows how XML that matches this could look:

```
<phone><cellPhone>219-999-1213</cellPhone></phone>
```

When designing a schema for a new specification, it makes sense to use the simple building blocks we have described here. However, if you are writing a schema to define an existing format, it may be necessary to carefully nest the grouping elements to match what is needed.

Built-in Types

The types and elements in XML-Schema are analogous to types and variables in a programming language. Also, like programming languages, there are a number of built-in types that are fundamental to defining what content is allowed in an element or attribute.

There are about 50 built-in types defined in the standard. All of the Java types have direct analogs. The most commonly used are shown in Table 8-2.

Table 8-2. XML Built-In Types

Type	**Definition**
string	Any text string
token	A string with no spaces in it
Int	Positive integer
integer/long	A signed 32/64 bit integer
float/double	A floating point 32/64 bit number
date/time	A specially formatted string representing a date or time value

Simple Types - Extension

It is also possible to create a user-defined type based on a built-in type. A simple type is an element that does not contain child elements. An xsd:simpleType is commonly used to create enumerations - in this example, restricting a string to a set of values. Here, we wish to define phoneType to be the string "cell" or "home". A restriction base of xsd:integer could be used to define a set of numeric values:

```
<xsd:simpleType name="phoneType">
  <xsd:restriction  base="xsd:string">
    <xsd:enumeration value="phone"/>
    <xsd:enumeration value="home"/>
  </xsd:restriction>
</xsd:simpleType>
```

Another common approach is to define a simple type with attributes:

```
<xsd:complexType name="Phone">
  <xsd:simpleContent>
    <xsd:extension base="xsd:string">
      <xsd:attribute name="type" type="phoneType"/>
    </xsd:extension>
  </xsd:simpleContent>
</xsd:complexType>
```

Types and Anonymous Types

As we have mentioned, XML-Schema elements correspond to *variables*, and complexTypes and simpleTypes correspond to types in a programming language. However, if there are many elements in the schema, this can result in numerous types that really only exist for a single use. To avoid this, an element can contain its type rather than refer to one. This makes the type anonymous:

```
<xsd:element name="contacts">
  <xsd:complexType>
  <xsd:sequence>
   <xsd:element name="contact" type="ContactType" maxOccurs="unbounded"/>
  </xsd:sequence>
  </xsd:complexType>
</xsd:element>
```

In this example, the contacts element consists of a sequence of contact elements, but the definition of this structure is anonymous - used only for this element.

Putting It All Together

The following schema defines the Contact xml file. It can be used to validate the XML example at the start of this section:

```
<?xml version="1.0" encoding="ISO-8859-1"?>
<xsd:schema xmlns:xsd="http://www.w3.org/2001/XMLSchema">
  <xsd:element name="contacts" type="ContactList"/>
  <xsd:complexType name="ContactList">
    <xsd:sequence>
      <xsd:element name="contact" type="ContactType" minOccurs="0"
      maxOccurs="unbounded"/>
    </xsd:sequence>
  </xsd:complexType>

  <xsd:complexType name="ContactType">
    <xsd:sequence>
      <xsd:element name="phone" type="Phone" minOccurs="1"
      maxOccurs="2"/>
      <xsd:element name="email" type="xsd:string" minOccurs="0"/>
    </xsd:sequence>
    <xsd:attribute name="name" type="xsd:string"/>
  </xsd:complexType>

  <xsd:complexType name="Phone">
    <xsd:simpleContent>
      <xsd:extension base="xsd:string">
      <xsd:attribute name="type" type="phoneType"/>
      </xsd:extension>
    </xsd:simpleContent>
  </xsd:complexType>

  <xsd:simpleType name="phoneType">
    <xsd:restriction base="xsd:string">
      <xsd:enumeration value="cell"/>
      <xsd:enumeration value="home"/>
    </xsd:restriction>
  </xsd:simpleType>
</xsd:schema>
```

The top level element is contactList that contains 0 or more contact elements. Each contact element contains one or two phone elements followed by an optional email element that has a name attribute. The phone element contains string content (the phone number) and a type attribute that is either "cell" or "home".

Complex Schemas

XML-Schema provides a number of ways to specify the type of content allowed in an element or attribute. This example defines an email type that is based on string, but is restricted to match a regular expression pattern:

```
<xsd:simpleType name="email">
  <xsd:restriction base="xsd:string">
    <xsd:pattern value="[\w_]+@[\w_.]+"/>
  </xsd:restriction>
</xsd:simpleType>
```

This pattern, [\w_]+@[\w_.]+, matches strings like my_name@aol.com. For details on regular expressions, refer to *Chapter 5* which covers the PERL language.

XML-Schema also provides an inheritance facility for complex types. This is especially useful to document relationships between elements (a cat is-a mammal). It also provides a way to share common structures between elements.

In this example, the Person type contains a name sub-element. The Employee type extends Person (so that it has a name sub-element) and it adds an employeeid:

```
<xsd:complexType name="Person">
  <xsd:sequence>
    <xsd:element name="name" type="xsd:string" />
  </xsd:sequence>
</xsd:complexType>
<xsd:complexType name="Employee">
  <xsd:complexContent>
    <xsd:extension base="Person">
      <xsd:sequence>
        <xsd:element name="employeeid" type="xsd:string" />
      </xsd:sequence>
    </xsd:extension>
  </xsd:complexContent>
</xsd:complexType>
```

The two definitions are merged, so this is the same as the following:

```
<xsd:complexType name="Employee">
  <xsd:complexContent>
    <xsd:sequence>
      <xsd:element name="name" type="xsd:string" />
      <xsd:element name="employeeid" type="xsd:string" />
    </xsd:sequence>
  </xsd:complexContent>
</xsd:complexType>
```

An XML fragment that matches this schema is:

```
<employee><name>greg</name><employeeid>100</employeeid></employee>
```

The extension relationship exists only at the modeling level. It does not show up in the XML documents. However, it does have important ramifications for schema-based parsing, which is covered later.

Wrapup

XML-Schema provides for a fine-grained specification of what is allowed in a document. When the designer is in the position of creating a new schema, this power must be balanced with practical concerns. The most important issue is that input not matching the schema will be rejected by a parser as invalid - it will be unreadable. This could make error handling difficult. On the other hand, a strict schema may provide a valuable contract between producer and consumer, protecting the receiving system from erroneous data.

Parsing

Parsing XML is difficult. Fortunately, all modern programming languages provide libraries that handle most of the complexity. The first two of these approaches, SAX and DOM, are language independent. They have largely been supplanted by toolkits that generate parse trees of schema-specific objects (or XSLT, covered in the next section).

SAX

SAX (Simple API for XML parsing) was developed by David Megginson as a standard interface between the various XML parsers and the programs that use them. It is available in Java, Perl, C++, and most other languages. SAX is an event-driven approach, each entry and exit of an element generates a callback. It is the program's responsibility to maintain state between these calls. Because there is no extra state maintained, SAX has the fastest performance and is often used in the implementation of the other higher level parser interfaces.

SAX provides a one time pass through the source file. There is no way to look ahead or correlate the content except through state maintained by the caller. For that reason, it is seldom used except where the source file is too large to read in at once or only a small subset of the data is of interest. Today, most performance-critical applications use schema-generated objects:

```
import java.io.*;
import org.xml.sax.*;
import org.xml.sax.helpers.*;
import org.apache.xerces.parsers.SAXParser;

public class SaxTest extends DefaultHandler {
  int count = 0;
  public void startElement(String namespaceURI, String
  localName, String qName, Attributes atts) {
    count++;
  }

  public static void main(String[] args) {
    Saxtest saxer = new SaxTest();
    SAXParser p = new SAXParser();
    p.setContentHandler(saxer);
    try { p.parse("contacts.xml"); }
    catch (Exception e) {e.printStackTrace();}
    System.out.println(saxer.count);
  }
}
```

In this example, the saxer object is registered as the content handler with the parser. In this case, it only implements the method that is called when an event is entered. For this example, SAX is a good choice.

DOM

The document object model (DOM) is another W3C standard (see the references section for links). Like SAX, it is a language neutral interface for parsing XML. A DOM parser creates a generic object model that reflects the content of the XML file. The objects created mirror the base components of XML: element, attribute, text node, etc. Also, because the DOM standard is targeted at languages with limited OO support, the DOM object model is very flat. Type information is conveyed through attribute values instead of subclasses. This results in a model that is clumsy and tedious to use.

The base class/interface for most DOM objects is Node. Traversal of the document tree takes place at the node level. Occasionally, it is necessary to downcast to obtain data.

Schema Generated Parsing Objects

The most promising contemporary technique for parsing XML is schema generated objects. Using this approach, the XML elements and types are mapped to pre-generated domain specific classes. The parser creates an object hierarchy using these objects as the model. This allows the programmer to work with objects that correspond to the structure of the document being parsed. In our example, parsing would result in a Contacts object that contains a collection of Contact objects.

There are several tools that use this approach: JAXB, Çastor, and XMLBeans (all for the Java language). Other technologies are available for languages such as C# and Python. These examples generate the domain objects using a compile time tool. The resulting objects are very close to what one would write if doing this task by hand, except that it is not easy to extend them. It is the equivalent of using a SAX parser and building a custom representation in the program of all of the data read. These tools avoid the significant development time that would entail.

Transformation

XML is a data format. XML-Schema and DTD define its structure. The parsing approaches in the last section take advantage of the regularity of the data format and the structure information in the schema. This section shows another advantage of working with a standard data format like XML. XPath and XSLT are special purpose languages that manipulate XML. They are higher level constructs than what we have seen so far in that each provides an abstract view of XML data.

XPath

XPath is a foundation technology for manipulating XML data. The purpose of XPath is to specify or select part of a document. XPath models an XML document as a tree of nodes, somewhat like the DOM. The nodes correspond to elements and attributes, as well as text and other aspects of the XML data.

The notation we will describe here is the abbreviated form. It is concise, but cannot express the esoteric features of the standard. There is also a long form that will not be covered here.

The selection of elements in XPath looks like a Unix file path. The top level element is matched with a slash ("/") character. Each child in the tree is separated by a slash. There is a current context, a current point in the tree that is used as a basis for relative selections. The results of an XPath expression are either a (possibly empty) set of nodes or a value, such as an integer or string.

Location Paths

The expression /contacts/contact/email will start at the root and find the contacts element, then the child contact elements, then the email elements that are their children. For example:

<contacts><contact>**<email></email>**</contact></contacts> will match.

<contacts><info><email></email></info></contacts> will not match.

The // delimiter matches a child or descendent of the current node. So the expression /contacts//email will match any email node that is a child or descendent of a child of contacts. Given the previous example, this expression will match both email elements. An expression that does not start with a slash is a relative path. The expression contact/email will match the email children of contact relative to the current position. If the current position is the contacts element, the result is the same as the first example.

The concept of current node is a part of the XPath standard, but it is determined by the technologies such as XSLT that are based on XPath. For now, assume the current position is set somehow; we will cover this further in the next section. As with the file system, "." is the current node and ".." is the parent node (relative to the current node). Also, "*" is a wild card:

- ./contact is the same as contact
- ../contact selects the contact children of the parent of the current node.
- */email selects the email children of any child node of the current node.

In the XPath specification, the concepts child, parent, and descendent are referred to as axis.

Node Tests

The location paths reference the tree structure of the XML document. It is also possible to add constraints on the nodes selected using Node Tests. In the examples above, the named nodes in the XPath (/contacts/contact/email) are simple tests against the node names in the XML document.

As with regular expressions, the vertical bar is the OR symbol: contact/email|phone and selects the email and phone children of the contact nodes that are children of the current node. Node tests other than these simple ones are enclosed in brackets. Attributes are selected with an ampersand, node[@attribute]:

- @attr checks for the existence of an attribute attr.
- @attr="true" checks for an attribute named attr with the value true.

Nodes returned by the XPath expression are numbered based on the document order in the original document. They can be selected by a one-based index in brackets:

- elmt[2] selects the second elmt child of the current node.

Assume the current node is at contact in the following example:

```
<contact name="greg">
  <email>gmunger@isp.com</email>
  <phone type="cell">219-222-3456</phone>
  <phone type="home">219-945-1234</phone>
</contact>
```

In the example above, phone[@type="cell"] selects the first phone element, while phone[2] selects the second phone element. These tests can be combined using phone[@type][1] to select the first phone from the list of phones that has a type attribute (i.e. the first phone is selected).

Functions

XPath comes with a set of logical, numeric, and string functions that can be applied to the current context. This is a part of the XPath standard, but it cannot really be used without one of the frameworks based on XPath such as XSLT.

XSLT

The XSL (EXtensible Stylesheet Language) specification associates a style sheet with an XML document, specifying the appearance separately from the content. XSLT, which stands for XSL Transformations, generalizes this approach. Usually the output of the XSLT transform is another XML document, often from one schema to another. However, it can also be used to transform an XML document to plain text, HTML, and other formats.

The model for XSLT is quite different from most programming languages. It is declarative rather than imperative. Meaning, you specify what you want as a result rather than how you want it done. The control-flow is largely implicit. This makes some tasks easy that would be tedious with a parser based approach, and visa versa.

An XSLT document is an XML document and must satisfy proper nesting and quoting. Maintaining this structure can be inconvenient, especially if the target of the transform is not XML. XSLT selects data from the input XML file and merges it with the XSLT templates. This is much easier if the data used is localized. If data from distant parts of the input are needed together in the output, a DOM or object-based parser may be better. On the other hand, when the path through the source document is straightforward and the output can be expressed as a template with substitution, XSLT may be the best choice. Please note that evaluating XSLT expressions is a complex task. Employing this technology at runtime is likely to be less efficient than the alternatives.

Top Level Elements and Default Actions

The following example shows the required scaffolding for a stylesheet:

```
<?xml version="1.0"?>
<xsl:stylesheet xmlns:xsl="http://www.w3.org/1999/XSL/Transform"
version="1.0">
<xsl:output method="xml"/>
</xsl:stylesheet>
```

All XSLT documents have an xsl:stylesheet element at the top level. The first element is the xsl:output element that specifies the output format. The output method attribute could be "text", "html", or "xml". This example does not specify any actions, so the default actions will be called. The default action for an element node is to traverse the child nodes. The default action for a text node is to print the contents. Running this stylesheet outputs the text content of the source document. Applying this stylesheet to the following XML:

```
<?xml version="1.0" encoding="UTF-8"?>
<contacts>
  <contact name="greg">
    <email>gmunger@isp.com</email>
    <phone type="cell">219-222-3456</phone>
    <phone type="home">219-945-1234</phone>
  </contact>
  <contact name="fred">
    <email>flo@isp.com</email>
    <phone type="cell">219-242-1234</phone>
  </contact>
</contacts>
```

Which yields the following output:

```
<?xml version="1.0" encoding="UTF-8"?>gmunger@isp.com219-222-3456219-
945-1234flo@isp.com219-242-1234
```

Select - Tree Traversal

The basic unit of work in XSL is the template. A template has a match attribute that specifies the element it applies to. Or, as we will see later, templates can also be called by name. This transform renames the top level element from contacts to contactList, and it merges the text content of the contact elements into an element called contactNew:

```
<?xml version="1.0"?>
<xsl:stylesheet xmlns:xsl="http://www.w3.org/1999/XSL/Transform"
version="1.0">
<xsl:output method="xml" omit-xml-declaration="no" indent="yes"/>
  <xsl:template match="contacts">
    <contactList>
      <xsl:apply-templates select="*"/>
    </contactList>
  </xsl:template>

  <xsl:template match="contact">
    <contactNew>
      <xsl:apply-templates select="email|phone"/>
    </contactNew>
  </xsl:template>
</xsl:stylesheet>
```

The result of running this is:

```
<?xml version="1.0" encoding="UTF-8"?>
<contactList>
  <contactNew>gmunger@isp.com219-222-3456219-945-1234</contactNew>
  <contactNew>flo@isp.com219-242-1234</contactNew>
</contactList>
```

The output of a template is the content inside the template tag. Processing will stop at this point unless another template is called. The apply-templates element will select some or all of the children of the current node for processing.

The first xsl:template that matches "contacts" contains contactList start and end elements. These are just hard-coded text - they could be anything (as long as the stylesheet is well-formed XML). The first xsl:template also contains an xsl:apply-templates element that has a select="*" attribute. The apply-templates element will continue processing with the node that matches the select attribute as a child of the current node. The * pattern matches any child of the current node. Since the template matches the top level contacts element, the apply-templates will match each child of this node, that is, each contact child.

The second xsl:template element in the stylesheet matches the contact element. It contains hard-coded contactNew start and end elements. Inside these is another call to apply-templates, this time selecting the email and phone child elements (using the vertical bar as the OR symbol). Because these are the only possible children of the contact node, this is functionally the same as select="*", but specifying the expected elements is a better use of style.

There is no template defined for the phone or email children of contact, so the default actions are called. This causes the text content of these elements to be concatenated. This is for illustration only. In practice, matched element types generally have a template defined for them.

Value-of

The contents of an xsl:template element are assumed to be hard-coded: XML, HTML, or plain text. To access dynamic data from the document being processed, the value-of element grabs data from the context of the current node. The select attribute is an XPath expression. The following line selects the text content of the phone element that is a child of the current node:

```
<xsl:value-of select="phone"/>
```

This next line selects the name attribute of the current node:

```
<xsl:value-of select="@name"/>
```

Creating Attributes

Because the content of apply-templates elements is hard-coded, it is easy to add hard-coded attributes, as well as elements:

```
<xsl:template match="contact">
  <contactNew name="example1"></contactNew>
</xsl:template>
```

This example matches a contact element and outputs a contactNew element:

```
<contactNew name="example1"></contactNew>
```

It is possible to use this approach for dynamic content, but quoting can get complicated and the result can be hard to read. The xsl:attribute element creates an attribute in the current element. The following example creates a name attribute in the contactNew element and populates it with the id attribute of the current node in the input document. If the id attribute of the current contact was "example1", the result would be the same as the previous example:

```
<xsl:template match="contact">
  <contactNew>
    <xsl:attribute name="name"><xsl:value-of select="@id"/></xsl:attribute>
  </contactNew>
</xsl:template>
```

Variables

XSLT is based on a declarative model, but it does have features of a (normal) imperative language. Variables are used to store the result of a computation, or to make the style sheet easier to read. Variables are created with the xsl:variable element. The name attribute defines the name of the variable. The select attribute assigns it a value:

```
<xsl:variable name="num" select="125"/>
```

This example creates a variable named num with the value of 125. Variables are accessed by name prefixed by the dollar sign. This example returns "125":

```
<xsl:value-of select="$num"/>
```

Functions

Most of the functions used in XSLT come from the XPath standard. Because these expressions are often verbose, variables are often used to make the results more legible. The translate function modifies the first argument and replaces each character in the second argument with the corresponding char in the third argument:

```
<xsl:variable name="num" select="translate(.,'-','+')"/>
```

In this example, each "-" in the value of the current node "." is replaced by a "+". So the value "1-2-3" would result in "1+2+3", assigned to the variable num. There are a number of other functions, but compared with a standard programming language, they are incomplete and hard to use.

The following example uses this function to change the hyphen in the phone number to a period:

```
<xsl:template match="contact">
  <contactNew>
    <xsl:variable name="num" select="translate(phone,'-','.')"/>
    <xsl:attribute name="phone"><xsl:value-of select="$num"/></xsl:attribute>
  </contactNew>
</xsl:template>
```

Partial output from running against our standard test case follows:

```
<contactNew phone="219.222.3456"/>
```

Conditionals

Another feature of most programming languages that is available in XSLT is conditional expressions. In the following example, an if test is used to avoid creating empty attributes. If the email sub-element is non-empty (the test evaluates to true), then an email attribute is created in the current output element:

```
<xsl:if test="email">
  <xsl:attribute name="email"><xsl:value-of select="email"/></xsl:attribute>
</xsl:if>
```

There is another conditional statement, xsl:choose, that is like a select in C or Java. Unfortunately, there is no else statement, though either choose or successive if statements can be used to achieve the same result.

Call-Template Actions

XLST provides the xsl:call-template element that acts like a function call. This is used to share common code and make the stylesheet more readable. In the body of the xsl:call-template, there can be xsl:with-param elements that pass data to the called template. The called template operates from the current context of the caller.

The called template is an xsl:template with a name attribute instead of a match attribute. The name matches the name in the call element. The values that were passed with xsl:with-param, are retrieved by xsl:param elements. The name in the caller is used to match the name in the called.

The following stylesheet displays several of the techniques discussed:

```
<?xml version="1.0"?>
<xsl:stylesheet xmlns:xsl="http://www.w3.org/1999/XSL/Transform"
version="1.0">
  <xsl:output method="xml" omit-xml-declaration="no" indent="yes"/>
  <xsl:template match="contacts">
    <contactList>
      <xsl:apply-templates select="*"/>
    </contactList>
  </xsl:template>

  <xsl:template match="contact">
    <xsl:variable name="name" select="concat( 'mr. ', @name)"/>
    <xsl:if test="email">
      <xsl:call-template name="contact-email">
        <xsl:with-param name="name" select="$name"/>
        <xsl:with-param name="email" select="email"/>
      </xsl:call-template>
    </xsl:if>
 </xsl:template>
```

```
<xsl:template name="contact-email">
  <xsl:param name="name"/>
  <xsl:param name="email"/>
  <xsl:variable name="isp" select="substring-after($email,'@')"/>
  <contactEmail>
    <xsl:attribute name="name"><xsl:value-of select="$name"/></xsl:attribute>
    <xsl:attribute name="isp"><xsl:value-of select="$isp"/></xsl:attribute>
  </contactEmail>
</xsl:template>
</xsl:stylesheet>
```

The resulting output is as follows:

```
<?xml version="1.0" encoding="UTF-8"?>
<contactList>
  <contactEmail name="mr. greg" isp="isp.com"/>
  <contactEmail name="mr. fred" isp="isp.com"/>
</contactList>
```

Handling Content

XSLT is well-suited to transformations that examine all of the XML input. If the source XML elements contain XML or HTML data, by default this data will be quoted on output. This can be a problem if you want to merge this content (as XML) with the other XML output. For example, this template matches the description element and outputs its content inside a descript element:

```
<xsl:template match="description">
  <descript><xsl:value-of select="."/></descript>
</xsl:template>
```

If the content of the original description element contained HTML, it would be quoted on output. For example:

```
<description>a very <b>nice</b> person</description>
```

The above line would result in:

```
<descript>a very &lt;b&gt;nice&lt;/b&gt; person</descript>
```

Adding the disable-output-escaping attribute turns off this quoting:

```
<xsl:value-of disable-output-escaping="yes" select="."/>
```

This results in output like this:

```
<descript>a very <b>nice</b> person</descript>
```

XSLT is a large topic and is the subject of a number of books. The most important concept to grasp is how templates are applied because they match the nodes of the input data.

Looking Forward

The major focus of activity in the near future is the proliferation of industry standard schemas. Examples include OASIS, BCPEL, and OFX. The goal is to create a common grammar to describe data in a problem domain. The scope of these projects is large, and the political and financial implications often outweigh the technical issues.

Longer term development must address the more fundamental problem of semantics. A standard schema can specify how a document is structured, but schema does not specify semantics - it doesn't define meaning. Even a simple concept like employee may be subtly different in a census domain versus a corporate information system. Progress here requires a framework for knowledge representation and this will not be solved soon. But, without standard semantics, schemas will only be able to tell us what was said - not what was meant.

- http://www.w3.org/schema primer - an excellent introduction to schema.
- http://www.w3.org/TR/xslt - the XSLT standard specification
- http://www.w3.org/DOM/ - the document object model specification
- http://java.sun.com/xml/jaxb/ - JAXB, the schema object compiler from Sun.
- http://sax.sourceforge.net/ - SAX, the event driven parser.
- http://xml.apache.org/ - XML parsers (both DOM and SAX) from the Apache foundation.

Chapter 9

ASP.NET

ASP.NET is Microsoft's server-side Web programming technology, developed as part of the .NET initiative. ASP.NET integrates the user markup of a Web page and server-side logic, allowing you to easily work with elements of an HTML Web form via source code. This integration is possible thanks to a large number of HTML element-like objects, called server controls, that render W3C-compliant HTML markup. These server controls, which map to built-in classes in the .NET Framework's System.Web.UI.WebControls namespace, can be programmatically accessed through the ASP.NET page's source code.

ASP.NET is radically different from its predecessor, ASP (also called "classic ASP"). ASP version 3 was the last "classic" ASP version, and still ships with Microsoft's Web server software. While some similarities exist, ASP.NET is an entirely new implementation of server-side Web programming.

In order to use ASP.NET, you need to have the .NET Framework installed on a computer that has the IIS Web server version 5 or later. While other implementations of ASP.NET do exist (such as mod_mono for Mono and Apache), for our purposes, Microsoft's implementation will be used.

ASP.NET pages are composed of two portions: a markup portion (which contains a mix of standard HTML syntax along with ASP.NET server controls) and a source code portion. The source code portion consists of a class that can be written in any .NET-compatible language, such as C#, VB.NET, or J#. For this chapter, it is assumed that you are already familiar with HTML and at least one .NET language. While examples in this chapter will be done in VB.NET, realize that any .NET language may be used when creating an ASP.NET application.

Fast Facts

- ASP.NET pages usually end with .aspx.
- ASP.NET mixes standard HTML markup with special HTML-like server controls.
- Server controls in an ASP.NET page are denoted in a familiar HTML-like syntax, such as <asp:ControlType id="ControlName" runat="server" otherAttributes="otherValues" />.
- ASP.NET server controls map to classes in the .NET Framework namespace System.Web.UI.WebControls.
- ASP.NET pages use an event-driven model: code is run in response to events such as the page being requested, a button being clicked, etc.
- When the page is sent to the client, the server controls render to various standard HTML form inputs, such as <input type="text">.
- ASP.NET pages emit standards-compliant HTML and therefore can be viewed with any browser on any platform.
- ASP.NET pages usually contain a Web Form. A Web Form is a server control that renders as a standard <form> element.
- A *postback* occurs when the form is submitted, which commonly happens by clicking a button or changing the status of an auto-postback control.
- A postback is a submittal of the HTML form back to the page via HTTP-POST.
- Controls that participate in the postback - such as Buttons, TextBoxes, DropDownLists, and so on - must exist inside of the Web Form.
- ASP.NET is language agnostic. Any .NET language can be used on the server side.
- The server-side code is compiled and deployed as a DLL, thereby improving performance over script-based Web technologies.

Sample ASP.NET Page

An ASP.NET page has three main parts: the HTML markup, the ASP.NET server controls, and the code to respond to control events. The following example has three server controls: a Label (labelName), a TextBox (textBoxName), and a Button (buttonSubmit). When you visit this page through a browser, you will see a textbox along with a button. When something is typed into the textbox and the button is clicked, the Web Form will postback and the code in the <script> block will execute, setting the value of the TextBox in the label:

```
<!DOCTYPE HTML PUBLIC "-//W3C//DTD HTML 4.0 Transitional//EN" >
<HTML>
  <head>
    <title>Employee List</title>
    <script language="visualbasic" runat="server">
      Sub SubmitClick (Sender as Object, e as EventArgs)
        Me.labelName.Text = Me.textBoxName.Text
      End Sub
    </script>
  </head>
  <body>
  <form id="Form1" method="post" runat="server">
    Name: <asp:Label id="labelName" Runat="server"></asp:label><br />
    New Name: <asp:TextBox ID="textBoxName"
    Runat="server"></asp:TextBox>
    <asp:Button ID="buttonSubmit" Runat="server"
    Text="Change" OnClick="SubmitClick"></asp:Button>
  </form>
  </body>
</HTML>
```

When you request this ASP.NET page through your browser, the ASP.NET page's source code is executed on the Web server and its server controls are converted into standards-compliant HTML markup. The resulting HTML markup is sent back to the requesting client and displayed on their browser's screen.

The following markup shows the HTML the browser receives when requesting the ASP.NET page we just examined. Note that the server-side <script> block is not sent down to the client, and that the server control syntax has been replaced with corresponding HTML elements:

```
<!DOCTYPE HTML PUBLIC "-//W3C//DTD HTML 4.0 Transitional//EN" >
<HTML>
  <head>
    <title>Employee List</title>
  </head>
  <body>
  <form name="Form1" method="post" action="TbLblBtn.aspx" id="Form1">
    <input type="hidden" name="__VIEWSTATE"
    value="dDwtMTc1MjgxMTQ0Mjs7PnpZUu3aMcYiVzRJTaslc70dkn9K" />
    Name: <span id="labelName"></span><br />
    New Name: <input name="textBoxName" type="text" id="textBoxName" />
    <input type="submit" name="buttonSubmit" value="Change"
    id="buttonSubmit" />
  </form>
  </body>
</HTML>
```

In addition to the expected HTML markup, there is also a hidden form field element named __VIEWSTATE. This hidden input field is used internally by ASP.NET to keep track of the state of controls in the page across postbacks. It can also be used by ASP.NET page developers; see the *State Management* section later in this chapter for more details.

This received HTML markup will be rendered in a Web browser as:

Figure 9-1.

Main Components of ASP.NET

Each ASP.NET page is different from the next, but they all use the same basic components. The example above has three main parts, which are described here.

HTML Markup

An ASP.NET page starts out as a standard HTML page. As you can see, most of the example above is HTML markup.

Server Controls

Server controls are notated with HTML-like tags that have the form <asp:ControlType>. Server controls are items on the page that the user and/or the server can interact with: buttons, textboxes, images, etc.

Server-side Code

Server controls can raise events to which the server-side source code may respond. For example, if you click a button it raises that Button server control's Click event. The Click causes the <form> to submit the current page back to itself via an HTTP-POST operation. During this *postback*, changes in the state of the page are evaluated by the ASP.NET engine on the server. Changes cause events to be raised. If code is in place to respond to the event, that code will be evaluated. Please note that the event handling code resides on the server. In order for a server control to raise an event it must cause a postback, as the Button control does when clicked.

Basics of ASP.NET

Pages written in ASP.NET are just plain text and can be created with any text editor. Microsoft Visual Studio provides a rich interface to aid in editing, but the markup and code that is created is no different than what could be created with something as simple as Notepad.

In order for a machine to serve an ASP.NET page, you must be running Windows Server 2000 or later or Windows XP. The .NET Framework must be installed, as well as Microsoft's IIS Web server. When pages are served to the client, the ASP.NET server controls are converted into standards-compliant HTML that can be viewed by any modern Web browser. You can then interact with the page as you would any other Web form.

You can cause a postback by clicking a button or modifying the state of an AutoPostBack control. A checkbox, drop-down list, and other controls can be set to be AutoPostBack="True". When such controls are marked as AutoPostBack, changing the state of the control - selecting a different item from the drop-down list or changing the checked state of a checkbox, for example - automatically causes a postback.

The postback is how work is accomplished in ASP.NET. The <form> in the page submits a POST back to the page itself, making a round-trip from the client to the server. The ASP.NET engine evaluates the state of the page and determines what has happened. Events are raised for changes in the page, and code that responds to those events is executed on the server. Once the code finishes running, the page is sent back to the user, and the cycle repeats.

ASP.NET Server Controls

Server controls are the building blocks for ASP.NET pages. They all have a similar syntax:

```
<asp:ControlType ID="ControlName" runat="server" xxAttributes="xxValues" />
```

Every ASP.NET server control maps to a class in the System.Web.UI.WebControls namespace. These classes have various properties that affect how the server controls are rendered. The attributes in the tag's syntax specify the default values for the properties of the control. Every control must have runat="server", otherwise the control will not be recognized by the ASP.NET engine as a server control; instead, it will interpret it as HTML markup that will be sent to the browser. All of the controls have the following attributes in common:

- **Runat**: Required. Must be set to "server".
- **ID**: Required. A name for the control that is unique on the page. Can be any alpha-numeric string, plus underscore (_).
- **Visible**: Determines whether or not the control will be included in the rendered page. Can be either "True" or "False".
- **CssClass**: If using CSS, the name of the class to be applied to this control. Along with specifying a CSS class, you may also use properties like Font, ForeColor, BackColor, etc, to specify the style.

A number of controls that accept user input have the following property:

- **AutoPostBack**: Determines if a change to the control will cause the form to postback. Can be "True" or "False". Defaults to "False" if omitted.

Events

Server controls can have events associated with them. When you perform an action, it can cause a postback during which a particular server control's event may fire. For example, when a button is clicked, the Web Form is posted back and the button's Click event fires; if a Checkbox is checked or unchecked, the CheckBox's CheckChanged event will fire when the Web Form posts back; when the selected value of a DropDownList changes and the Web Form is posted back, the DropDownList's SelectedIndexChanged event fires. On the server during a postback, ASP.NET compares the previous state of the page to the current state of the page. This comparison allows the server to determine what has changed and which events need to be fired.

ASP.NET makes it easy to have server-side code executed in response to these events, thereby allowing you to build functionality into your Web application. To respond to an event, you must create an *event handler*. An event handler is a method that is executed when its associated event fires.

The event handler method must match the expected signature of that event. Typically, this is:

```
Sub MethodName (sender as Object, e as EventArgs)
  ...
End Sub
```

The parameter sender is the object that raised the event, e.g., the Button or the CheckBox. The parameter e can contain additional information about the event.

Every time a page is visited—be it the initial visit to the page or a visit due to a postback—the Page_Load event fires. You can create an event handler for this event to initialize data in the page or perform other tasks before the control-specific events fire.

Label, TextBox, and Button

In our earlier example, we examined an ASP.NET Web page that consisted of three server controls: a Label, a TextBox, and a Button. Let's examine each of these common server controls in more detail.

A Label control is a container that simply holds text. It has a Text property that indicates the text to display in the Label. When the Label is rendered, it is converted into a <span> tag with the Text property as the inner content of the <span>.

A TextBox control allows you to input an arbitrary text value. The TextMode attribute determines which type of textbox to use. If not set, the default is "SingleLine" which renders as <input type="text">, displaying a single-line Textbox in the user's browser. TextMode can alternately be set to "Password". This renders as <input type="password">, enabling you to enter sensitive data without it being visible on screen. The third and final option for TextMode is "Multiline". Multiline renders as a <textarea>, which displays a multi-line TextBox in your browser. Use the Rows and Columns properties of the TextBox Web control to specify its dimensions.

When a Button control is clicked, the Web Form that contains the Button is posted back and the Button's Click event is raised. Often, ASP.NET pages will be designed such that the logic for processing a user's input occurs in the Click event handler of a particular Button on the page. For example, an ASP.NET page might have a series of TextBox controls and a Save Button control. Upon entering data into the TextBoxes, you would click the Save Button, causing a postback and execution of the Button's Click event handler. This event handler would then process the data entered into the TextBox controls, perhaps saving the information to a database.

In addition to the Click event, the Button control contains a Text attribute that determines the text displayed on the button. The Button control renders as <input type="submit" value="Text">.

Let's take another look at our earlier example. In addition to the HTML markup and server control syntax, there is also a server-side script block that contains the SubmitClick event handler. This event handler is executed when the Button's Click event is fired. Notice that the Button's Click event is wired to the SubmitClick event handler in the Button control's syntax (OnClick="SubmitClick"). Due to this association, the SubmitClick event handler will be run when a postback occurs after clicking the button. Our code in SubmitClick then reads the value of the TextBox (the Text property) and assigns it to the Label's Text property:

```
<!DOCTYPE HTML PUBLIC "-//W3C//DTD HTML 4.0 Transitional//EN" >
<HTML>
  <head>
    <title>Employee List</title>
    <script language="visualbasic" runat="server">
      Sub SubmitClick (Sender as Object, e as EventArgs)
        Me.labelName.Text = Me.textBoxName.Text
      End Sub
    </script>
  </head>
  <body>
    <form id="Form1" method="post" runat="server">
    Name: <asp:Label id="labelName" Runat="server"></asp:label><br />
    New Name: <asp:TextBox ID="textBoxName"
    Runat="server"></asp:TextBox>
    <asp:Button ID="buttonSubmit" Runat="server"
        Text="Change" OnClick="SubmitClick"></asp:Button>
    </form>
  </body>
</HTML>
```

As previously discussed, when this page is requested, the server-side code and server controls will be processed and simple HTML will be returned to the client's browser. The image below shows what this page will look like when rendered in a Web browser. Clicking the Change button initiates a postback cycle.

Figure 9-2.

DropDownList and ListBox

A DropDownList allows you to present the user with a pre-defined set of values, from which exactly one must be chosen. You can specify the items within a DropDownList in one of two ways: statically, by nesting ListItems inside of a DropDownList; or dynamically, such as from a database. A DropDownList requires that the user pick precisely one item from the list of items.

A ListBox provides more functionality than the simpler DropDownList. If the ListBox's SelectionMode="Multiple" is specified, the user is allowed to select more than one element from the list. Additionally, with a ListBox, the user is not required to pick an item; they may opt to not choose any items from the list.

Both the DropDownList and ListBox render as <select> with their selectable values as <option> elements. The following builds on the previous example:

```
<!DOCTYPE HTML PUBLIC "-//W3C//DTD HTML 4.0 Transitional//EN" >
<HTML>
  <head>
    <title>Employee List</title>
    <script language="visualbasic" runat="server">
      Sub SubmitClick (Sender as Object, e as EventArgs)
      Me.labelName.Text = Me.textBoxName.Text & " (" & _
      Me.ddlRole.SelectedItem.Text & ")"
      End Sub
    </script>
  </head>
  <body>
    <form id="Form1" method="post" runat="server">
      Name:
      <asp:Label id="labelName" Runat="server"></asp:Label><br>
      New Name:
      <asp:TextBox ID="textBoxName" Runat="server"></asp:TextBox>
      <asp:DropDownList ID="ddlRole" Runat="server">
      <asp:ListItem Value="Manager">Manager</asp:ListItem>
      <asp:ListItem Value="Employee">Employee</asp:ListItem>
      </asp:DropDownList>
      <asp:Button ID="buttonSubmit" Runat="server" Text="Change"
      OnClick="SubmitClick"></asp:Button>
    </form>
  </body>
</HTML>
```

The preceding code adds a DropDownList with ID="ddlRole", which allows the user to specify whether the person is a manager or an employee. The label's text will be assigned Name (Role) when the button is clicked.

Validators

Validator server controls greatly simplify the process of validating user input. ASP.NET includes multiple validator controls: the CompareValidator, RangeValidator, RequiredFieldValidator, RegularExpressionValidator, and CustomValidator. These controls share a number of common properties. For example, the ControlToValidate property, which all validators have, is used to specify the ID of the control on the page whose data is being validated. In the example below, a TextBox is added, textBoxHireDate. A CompareValidator with Operator="DataTypeCheck" and Type="Date" performs validation on the textBoxHireDate, ensuring that the user enters a valid date.

Validation is an important part of any program that accepts user input. When you take a value from a TextBox (or other control that accepts free input), it is text; a string. When it becomes necessary to use or convert the user-supplied string into another data type - a DateTime in the following example - input validation is critical. Not only does it prevent the user from accidentally making a mistake (such as accidentally typing the employee's name in the hire date field), but it helps prevent visitors with malicious intent from succeeding:

```
<!DOCTYPE HTML PUBLIC "-//W3C//DTD HTML 4.0 Transitional//EN" >
<HTML>
  <head>
    <title>Employee List</title>
    <script language="visualbasic" runat="server">
      Sub SubmitClick (sender as Object, e as EventArgs)
      If Page.IsValid Then
        Me.labelName.Text = Me.textBoxName.Text & " (" & _
        Me.ddlRole.SelectedItem.Text & ")"
      End If
      End Sub
    </script>
  </head>
  <body>
    <form id="Form1" method="post" runat="server">
      Name:
      <asp:Label id="labelName" Runat="server"></asp:Label><br>
      New Name:
      <asp:TextBox ID="textBoxName" Runat="server"></asp:TextBox><br>
      Hire Date:
```

```
        <asp:TextBox ID="textBoxHireDate" Runat="server"></asp:TextBox>
        <asp:CompareValidator ID="validatorDate" Runat="server"
        ControlToValidate="textBoxHireDate" Type="Date"
        ErrorMessage="Please enter a valid date."
        Operator="DataTypeCheck"
        /><br>
         Role:
        <asp:DropDownList ID="ddlRole" Runat="server">
        <asp:ListItem Value="Manager">Manager</asp:ListItem>
        <asp:ListItem Value="Employee">Employee</asp:ListItem>
        </asp:DropDownList>
        <asp:Button ID="buttonSubmit" Runat="server" Text="Change"
        OnClick="SubmitClick"></asp:Button>
      </form>
    </body>
  </HTML>
```

If the value of the Text property of textBoxHireDate cannot be recognized by the validator as a valid Date, a red error message is displayed asking the user to correct their mistake. The form will not submit (a postback will not occur) until validation succeeds.

Validation occurs in two stages: ASP.NET attempts to use JavaScript to validate the value client-side. To ensure validity (in case the client has disabled JavaScript in their browser), validation is always performed server-side upon postback, after the Page_Load event, but before the individual controls' events fire. You may force page validation with the Page.Validate method, or test for validity with Page.IsValid.

DataGrid

The DataGrid is one of the most powerful server controls that ASP.NET has to offer. It allows you to easily display a table of information from an arbitrary data source, such as a database, an XML file, etc. The DataGrid supports in-grid editing, pagination, headers and footers, sorting by columns, and a whole host of other useful features, all of which can be accomplished with just a few lines of code.

In the example below, clicking the button will add a new employee to the DataGrid, building a three column table. As one employee is added after the other, a table is built listing all employees and their information:

```
<!DOCTYPE HTML PUBLIC "-//W3C//DTD HTML 4.0 Transitional//EN" >
<HTML>
  <head>
    <title>Employee List</title>
    <script language="visualbasic" runat="server">
      Protected Property Table as System.Data.DataTable
        Get
          If ViewState("table") Is Nothing Then
            Dim dt as System.Data.DataTable = New System.Data.DataTable
            dt.Columns.Add("Name")
            dt.Columns.Add("Role")
            dt.Columns.Add("Hire date")
            ViewState("table") = dt
          End If
          Return CType(ViewState("table"), System.Data.DataTable)
        End Get
        Set
          ViewState("table") = Value
        End Set
      End Property

      Sub SubmitClick (sender as Object, e as EventArgs)
        Dim dr as System.Data.DataRow = Me.Table.NewRow()
        dr("Name") = Me.textBoxName.Text
        dr("Role") = Me.ddlRole.SelectedValue
        dr("Hire date") = Me.textBoxHireDate.Text
        Me.Table.Rows.Add(dr)
        Me.dgEmployees.DataSource = Me.Table
        Me.dgEmployees.DataBind()
        Me.textBoxName.Text = ""
        Me.textBoxHireDate.Text = ""
      End Sub
    </script>
  </head>
```

```
<body>
  <form id="Form1" method="post" runat="server">
    New Name:
    <asp:TextBox ID="textBoxName" Runat="server"></asp:TextBox><br>
    Hire Date:
    <asp:TextBox ID="textBoxHireDate" Runat="server"></asp:TextBox>
    <asp:CompareValidator ID="validatorDate" Runat="server"
    ControlToValidate="textBoxHireDate"
    Type="Date" ErrorMessage="Please enter a valid date."
    Operator="DataTypeCheck" /><br>
    Role:
    <asp:DropDownList ID="ddlRole" Runat="server">
    <asp:ListItem Value="Manager">Manager</asp:ListItem>
    <asp:ListItem Value="Employee">Employee</asp:ListItem>
    </asp:DropDownList>
    <asp:Button ID="buttonSubmit" Runat="server" Text="Add"
    OnClick="SubmitClick"></asp:Button>
     <asp:DataGrid ID="dgEmployees" Runat="server">
    </asp:DataGrid>
  </form>
</body>
</HTML>
```

When viewed in a Web browser, the above code (after a few people have been added) will look like the following:

Figure 9-3.

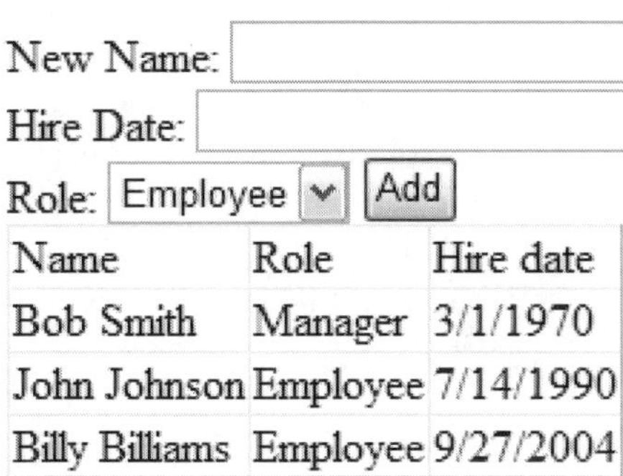

In this example, the code is very important. A DataTable is constructed in the Table property and stored in the ViewState (see the *State Management* section). It has three columns, corresponding to the inputs on the page. When the button is clicked, the SubmitClick event handler reads the values in the page and adds them as a row to the DataTable. The DataTable is then bound to the DataGrid. Finally, the values of the TextBoxes are cleared. The end result is a <table> that the client sees.

In the above example, the table that is built is not stored anywhere other than on the current page that the current user sees. With the addition of more code, it would be possible to save the table to a database, XML file, or some other method of storage.

For more advanced DataGrid features, please see the documentation on http://msdn.microsoft.com, or check out Scott Mitchell's excellent book, *ASP.NET Data Web Controls Kick Start.*

Other Server Controls

ASP.NET includes over 40 built-in server controls. A few of the most common ones have been highlighted above, but there are others worth noting.

- **CheckBox**: Renders a single checkbox using <input type="checkbox">. By setting its AutoPostBack property to true, changing the checked state of a checkbox will cause a postback. You can respond to a change in the checkbox's checked state via the OnCheckedChanged event. The Checked property returns True if the checkbox is checked, False otherwise.

- **RadioButton**: A radio button is another way to present multiple options from which one may be chosen. Multiple RadioButtons with the same GroupName attribute are logically grouped, allowing only one radio button in the group to be selected. Renders as <input type="radio">. Like the CheckBox server control, the RadioButton server control has an OnCheckedChanged event and AutoPostBack and Checked properties.

- **Panel**: A panel is a container that holds other controls and is often used to logically group related controls. You can turn off the visibility of a panel to hide its entire contents. Panels are rendered as a <div> or a <table>, depending on the Web browser used to view the page.

- **LinkButton**: A link button allows you to present a standard link, <a href="">, that invokes a postback when clicked. Therefore, you can respond to the link being clicked with server-side logic in the control's OnClick event.

- **Image**: A placeholder for an image. Renders to an <img src=""> tag. Set the ImageUrl property to specify the URL of the image to display. If you need a clickable image, use either an ImageButton (to respond to the OnClick event in code) or a HyperLink (to navigate to another URL when the image is clicked).

- **ImageButton**: Renders an image that, when clicked, causes a postback and raises its OnClick event.
- **HyperLink**: Renders to an <a href=""> tag. Set the NavigateUrl property to determine the destination. You may also set ImageUrl to have the link be an image instead of text.
- **Calendar**: Renders a one-month calendar with clickable days and navigation to change the visible month. Handle the OnSelectionChanged event to react to a specific date being clicked. The SelectedDate property contains the date that was selected.

State Management

A variable created in an ASP.NET page's source code doesn't exist across postbacks; it only exists for the time that the server is processing a particular request. If you need to remember the value of a page's variable across postbacks, you must use some sort of state management.

ASP.NET provides a number of mechanisms for state management, all of which are relatively similar in their syntax. Essentially, these state management techniques work using name/value pairs: you provide a string that is a key to an object. If the key has no object associated with it, the resulting object will be Nothing (null in C# or J#).

Client Side

Client side state management means that the data is stored on the client's machine. With every page request, the data must be transferred to and from the server. Keep this in mind when using client side state management, as large amounts of data will negatively impact the speed and performance of your application, especially for clients on lower-bandwidth connections.

ViewState

The view state exists only on the current page from postback to postback for a specific user. It is stored as the hidden input <input type="hidden" name="__VIEWSTATE"> in the form. The view state implements security features to help prevent client tampering of the data. To access data in the view state, use ViewState("keyname").

Hidden Form Inputs

A hidden form input is slightly lower-level than the view state. It only holds a single value. To use a hidden input, use a System.Web.UI.HtmlInputHidden variable in your code with the same ID as that of the hidden field.

Cookies

A cookie is a small file kept on the remote user's machine that stores some data related to the Web site from which that cookie originated. Cookies are accessible to the entire Web application. Care must be taken with what data is placed in cookies since they offer no implicit security. Avoid storing sensitive information, such as usernames or passwords, in the cookie. Instead, store a token that can be used to look up the sensitive information.

Cookies also have size limitations. Typically, the limit is 4096 or 8192 bytes, depending on the Web browser being used. To set a value for a cookie, use Response.Cookies("*keyname*").Value. To get the value from a cookie, use Request.Cookies("*keyname*").Value. To destroy a cookie, use Response.Cookies.Remove("*keyname*"). The Response.Cookies object also controls other functionality related to the cookie, such as the expiration of the cookie, the domain on which the cookies are valid, and whether or not the cookies must be transferred over an HTTPS connection.

Query String

A query string is additional information added to the URL of the Web page, following a question mark (?). Additional values are separated with an ampersand (&). A query string may look like this:

http://www.domain.com/cart.aspx**?item=num422&quantity=1**

The value of item is accessed with Request.QueryString("item"); the value of quantity is similarly retrieved.

Be wary of data in the query string! Not only is it plainly visible, but it is also easily manipulated. Additionally, it is possible for the user to input invalid HTML or even <script> blocks that could break the rendering of your page.

Server Side

Server side state management uses memory resources on the server. This means the data does not have to make a round-trip to the client's machine.

Session

Session state contains values that are available to a user's current browser, available across all pages in the site. If the user closes their browser, the information will be lost. Session state has a timeout associated with it, meaning that if a user does not visit a page on the site within the timeout period, ASP.NET abandons the user's session. The default timeout is 20 minutes, but this can be lowered or raised if needed. Session variables are available using Session("*keyname*").

Application

The application state is available to all pages across all users of the application. The data remains valid as long as the Web server is not restarted. Access values with Application("*keyname*").

User Controls

There are times when, for reasons of reusability or simply encapsulation, you may wish to create a composite user control. A user control is very similar to a regular ASP.NET page, containing a mix of HTML markup, server controls, and server-side code. However, a user control is meant to encapsulate common user-interface functionality. A visitor to your site won't browse directly to a user control; rather, an existing ASP.NET page can include one or more user controls. The file extension of a user control must be .ascx.

If you have a Web site that allows a user to log in, you might want a login control on many pages in the site. Rather than repeating this markup and programmatic logic on each page that requires it, you can encapsulate the logic within a user control and then add the user control as needed. Instead of adding the required functionality again and again to each and every page, you simply add the logic to this user control, which can be repeated with ease on any number of pages:

```
<%@ Control Language="vb" AutoEventWireup="false"
Codebehind="Login.ascx.vb" Inherits="AspNetVb.Login"
TargetSchema="http://schemas.microsoft.com/intellisense/ie5" %>
<script language="visualbasic" runat="server">

Public Property LoggedInUser As String
  Get
    Return ViewState("LoggedInUser")
  End Get
  Set
    ViewState("LoggedInUser") = Value
  End Set
End Property

Public Sub LoginClick (sender as Object, e as EventArgs)
   'Add code to verify login credentials
  Me.LoggedInUser = Me.TextBoxUsername.Text
  Me.TogglePanels(False)
End Sub
```

```
Public Sub LogoutClick (sender as Object, e as EventArgs)
  'Add code to log out the current user
  Me.LoggedInUser = Nothing
  Me.TogglePanels(True)
End Sub

Public Sub TogglePanels (showLogin as Boolean)
  Me.PanelLogin.Visible = showLogin
  Me.PanelLogout.Visible = Not showLogin
End Sub
</script>

<asp:Panel ID="PanelLogin" Runat="server" Visible="True">
  Username:
  <asp:TextBox id="TextBoxUsername"  runat="server"></asp:TextBox> <BR>
  Password:
  <asp:TextBox id="TextBoxPassword" runat="server"
  TextMode="Password"></asp:TextBox><BR>
  <asp:Button id="ButtonLogin" onclick="LoginClick" runat="server"
  Text="Login"></asp:Button>
</asp:Panel>
<asp:Panel ID="PanelLogout" Runat="server" Visible="False">
  <asp:LinkButton id="LinkButtonLogout" onclick="LogoutClick"
  Runat="server">Logout</asp:LinkButton>
</asp:Panel>
```

In the markup above, there are two panels: PanelLogin contains the username and password TextBoxes, as well as a Button. When the Button is clicked, it causes a postback and the sub LoginClick to be executed. At that point, the username of this user is cached in the ViewState via the property LoggedInUser. Code to actually verify the credentials—against a database or other means—has not been included, as it is site-specific. Additionally, the visibility of the two panels is toggled, making the PanelLogin invisible and PanelLogout visible.

Figure 9-4.

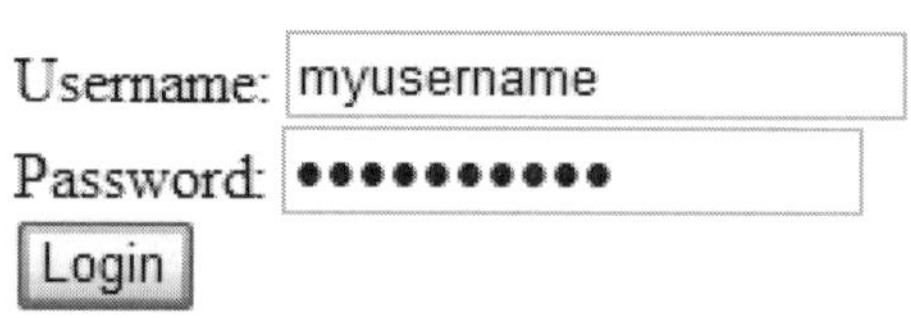

Now that the user is logged in, they see a LinkButton that will allow them to log out. The sub LogoutClick will handle that and toggle the visibility of the panels back to the previous state.

Figure 9-5.

Logout

It is simple to use this control from an ASP.NET page. If you are using the visual designer in Visual Studio, you may simply drag-and-drop the user control from the Solution Explorer onto the page to which you wish to add this control.

If you are writing the code by hand, you must add a page directive at the very top of the markup:

```
<%@ Register TagPrefix="uc1" TagName="Login" Src="Login.ascx" %>
```

Inside of your <form runat="server"> tag, you can then add the control where desired:

```
<uc1:Login id="Login1" runat="server"></uc1:Login>
```

After those two lines have been added to your ASP.NET page, you get all of the functionality—markup, controls, and code—that the user control provides. Code reuse like this offers a great advantage: if the login routine for your site changes, you simply make the change once in the .ascx. Every page that consumes the control will reflect the change automatically.

Code-behind vs. inline

There are two ways to write your server-side code in ASP.NET. Throughout this chapter, the *inline* code model has been used. That is, we've used <script runat="server"> blocks to contain the code.

The second method, which is used by Visual Studio .NET 2003, is the *code-behind* model. The code-behind model separates the markup (HTML and server controls) and the server-side code into two separate files. To use this model, the very first line of your page that contains the markup must look like the following:

```
<%@ Page Language="vb" AutoEventWireup="false"
Codebehind="CodeBehind.aspx.vb"
Inherits="MyNamespace.MyCodeBehindClass"%>
```

The Language="" attribute must match the language of your code (Visual Basic .NET, in this case). The Codebehind="" attribute must be the file that contains the code. The Inherits="" attribute is the fully qualified name of the class that contains the code for the page.

The source-code portion in the code-behind model must be created as a class. This class's name is what is specified in the markup page's Inherits attribute. The code-behind class must inherit from System.Web.UI.Page class in the .NET Framework. In Visual Basic, an empty class would look something like this:

```
Public Class MyCodeBehindClass
  Inherits System.Web.UI.Page
  Private Sub Page_Load(ByVal sender As System.Object, ByVal e As
    System.EventArgs) Handles MyBase.Load
    'Put user code to initialize the page here
  End Sub
End Class
```

When you add a server control to the markup, you must define the corresponding class as a member variable in your class. For example, if your markup defines a button such as:

```
<asp:Button id="MyButton" runat="server" Text="I am a button"></asp:Button>
```

Your class must add a member variable of the same name as the ID and add code to handle that button's events, such as its click event:

```
Protected WithEvents MyButton As System.Web.UI.WebControls.Button
Private Sub MyButton_Click(ByVal sender As System.Object, ByVal e As
  System.EventArgs) Handles MyButton.Click
  'Add code to handle the buttons click event
End Sub
```

Another important difference with code-behind is that the code must be compiled before visiting the ASP.NET page. The code for the site's pages' code-behind classes are compiled as a DLL that needs to be placed in the bin subfolder of the Web application root.

Typically, the code-behind model is only used when creating ASP.NET pages with Visual Studio .NET, as Visual Studio .NET will automate many of the tedious tasks required to use the code-behind model. For example, when you create a new ASP.NET page in Visual Studio .NET, it automatically creates a bare-bones code-behind class along with an appropriate @Page directive in the markup page. Furthermore, when new server controls are added through the Visual Studio .NET designer, a class reference to the control is automatically inserted into the page's corresponding code-behind class. Also, compiling the code-behind classes into a DLL with Visual Studio .NET is as simple as going to the Build menu and choosing the Build Solution menu option.

Looking Forward

At the time of this writing, ASP.NET 2.0 is in beta and is slated for release in late 2005. ASP.NET 2.0 will be built around the .NET Framework 2.0. ASP.NET 2.0 offers many exciting improvements and enhancements over ASP.NET 1.0. For example, whereas ASP.NET 1.0 contains 40 or so built-in server controls, ASP.NET 2.0 has over 100. Furthermore, the 2.0 server controls will have the option to render XHTML-compliant markup.

ASP.NET 2.0 includes a number of data source controls, which are Web controls that are used for accessing database data. These controls have properties that you can set to specify how to connect to the database, and what data to retrieve. This allows for these data source controls to be able to access database data without having to write a single line of code - you simply set the control's properties and the data is automatically retrieved.

New controls like the GridView are designed to work seamlessly with the data source controls. The GridView control in 2.0 takes the place of ASP.NET 1.0's DataGrid control and is designed to display database data on an ASP.NET page. Once you have added a data source control to a Web page and specified its data-specific properties, you can then add a GridView to the same page and set its DataSourceID to the ID of the data source control. This will display the data returned from the data source control in an HTML <table>.

Additionally, you can configure the GridView to page through the data a certain number of records at a time; you can add sorting capabilities to the GridView so that the end user can sort the data in either ascending or descending order; and you can allow users to insert, update, and delete existing data through the GridView control. Best of all, this entire workflow can be accomplished without writing a single line of code! All logic can be handled internally by the GridView and data source control - you just need to set the control's properties to provide the proper information for retrieving, inserting, updating, and deleting the data.

Microsoft's code editor, Visual Studio .NET, has been greatly improved for version 2.0, and will be named Visual Studio 2005. Visual Studio 2005 offers a number of tools that are missing in Visual Studio .NET. For example, Visual Studio 2005 allows project files to be transferred from the local machine to a remote Web site using FTP, a feature missing from the current version of Visual Studio .NET. Additionally, whereas Visual Studio .NET essentially forces the code-behind model, Visual Studio 2005 allows you to employ either the inline script-block or code-behind model.

Chapter 10

JavaServer Pages

JavaServer Pages (JSP) technology is an integral part of the Java 2 Platform, Enterprise Edition (J2EE) suite of enterprise-class client-server technologies. Intimately tied to markup languages such as HyperText Markup Language (HTML) and Extensible Markup Language (XML), scripting languages (most often the Java programming language), and the Java Servlets API, JSP is a technology that was created to simplify the generation of dynamic Web content.

Sun Microsystems released version 1.0 of the JavaServer Pages specification in September 1999, followed by version 1.1 only two months later. However, the two versions that are most popular at the time of this writing are version 1.2, released in August 2001 as part of J2EE version 1.3, and the recently implemented version 2.0, released in November 2003 as part of J2EE version 1.4. The latter release officially moved the Expression Language (EL) from the JavaServer Pages Standard Tag Library (JSTL) specification into the JSP specification.

Fast Facts

- A JSP page is a text file with a .jsp extension that, once requested by a client (most often a Web browser), is compiled by the Web application server into a servlet, processes the client's request, and returns a response back to the client.
- JSP pages are entirely case sensitive, with the possible exception of the markup, depending on the client's requirements. For example, an HTML client (Web browser) may process tags case-insensitively, whereas an XML client may not.
- Although the JSP specification allows for scripting languages other than Java, this is the only language that is currently supported by all application servers for this purpose (although a few application servers are beginning to support other languages, such as JavaScript).
- Directives (<%@ ... %>) give the JSP container instructions about how to compile and execute a JSP page.
- The scripting code that makes a JSP page dynamic may be placed within declarations (<%! ... %>), scriptlets (<% ... %>), and scriptlet expressions (<%= ... %>), or within the corresponding XML-compliant <jsp:declaration>, <jsp:scriptlet>, and <jsp:expression> tags. There is no limit to how many of these elements may be present in a single JSP page, although they may not be nested within one another.
- Scripting code in scriptlets and scriptlet expressions automatically has access to a number of *built-in* objects that provide access to various components of the JSP container. These objects are known as *implicit scripting variables* and include page, pageContext, request, response, session, application, config, out, and exception.
- The pageContext, request, session, and application implicit scripting variables each has a Map in which a JSP page can store *scoped attributes*, which are the mechanism by which the scripting code can pass data to other components and JSP pages.
- In a JSP page, an *action* is any tag that is processed by the JSP engine, rather than merely written verbatim to the output stream. This term should not be confused with the term "action" as it applies to Model-View-Controller frameworks, such as Jakarta Struts.
- JSP technology provides a set of standard actions, as well as a mechanism to extend the technology's functionality by providing implementations for custom actions.
- A JSP page essentially becomes a servlet, so it must follow standard servlet conventions (e.g., instance variables are not thread-safe by default).

Sample JSP Page

The following code listing shows a fairly complex sample JSP page, mainly for the purpose of serving as a reference to those already familiar with JSP technology. If you are fairly new to JSP technology, it is recommended that you move on to the *Basics of a JSP Page* section, which explains in more detail all of the code elements shown here:

```
<%@ page language="java" contentType="text/html; charset=ISO-8859-1"
pageEncoding="ISO-8859-1" %>
<%@ page import="" %>
<%@ taglib uri="/jstl-c" prefix="c" %>
<%@ taglib uri="/xavtech" prefix="xavtech" %>
<%! // Declarations
  public static Integer myInteger = new Integer(27);
  private String myString = "Hello, world!";
  public String getMyString() {
    return myString;
  }
%>

<!DOCTYPE HTML PUBLIC "-//W3C//DTD HTML 4.01 Transitional//EN">
<HTML>
<HEAD>
<META http-equiv="Content-Type" content="text/html; charset=ISO-8859-1">
<TITLE>index.jsp</TITLE>
</HEAD>
<BODY>

<P>Welcome to my <B>JSP</B> page!</P>
<P>
Let's first get the formalities out of the way:
<%
  // Here we use the implicit scripting variable "out" to write to the
  // JSP's output stream from inside a scriptlet; notice that, because
  // this JSP compiles to a Servlet class, we can access its member
  // variables and methods as we would those of any other Java class
  out.print(this.getMyString());
%>
</P>
```

```
<P>
Now let's output a weather report:
<%
  String weather = null;
  if (Math.random() < 0.5) {
    weather = "sunny";
  }
  else {
    weather = "cloudy";
  }

  // Use the implicit scripting variable "request" to set an attribute on the request
  request.setAttribute("temperature", new Integer((int)(Math.random() * 100)));
%>
Tomorrow it will be <%= weather %> and <%= request.getAttribute("temperature")
%> degrees.
</P>
<P>
<jsp:useBean id="temperature" scope="request" class="Integer" />
<% if (temperature.intValue() < 20 || temperature.intValue() > 80) { %>
That's right, I said <%= temperature %> degrees, so dress appropriately!
<% } %>
</P>

<c:if test="${temperature < 20 || temperature > 80}">
You heard me, buddy, ${temperature} degrees!
</c:if>

<%-- This is a JSP comment.  It will not be included in the generated servlet,
  so it will not get back to the client. --%>
<!-- This is an HTML comment, which does get included in the generated servlet,
  and is sent back to the client.  It will not show up in the client's
  browser, but if they "View Source", they will be able to see it. -->

<P>Have a <xavtech:adjective index="<%= (int)(Math.random() * 5) %>" />
day!</P>
<%@ include file="/common/copyright.html" %>
</BODY>
</HTML>
```

Main Components of a JSP Page

The sample JSP page above outputs a "Hello, world!" message followed by a randomized weather report to the client, which exhibits the principal elements of a JSP page:

Directive Elements <%@ ... %>

Directives are messages to the JSP engine about how to compile and execute the JSP page.

Scripting Elements

Scripting elements enclose the scripting code that generates and arranges the JSP page's dynamic content. Scripting elements include declarations <%! ... %>, scriptlets <% ... %>, scriptlet expressions <%= ... %>, and comments <%-- ... --%>. Scripting elements also provide access to several *implicit scripting variables* (pageContext, page, request, response, session, application, config, out, exception) that provide access to various components of the JSP container.

Action Elements

Actions are tags belonging to *tag libraries* that are declared in the JSP page via a taglib directive and processed by the JSP engine, rather than being output verbatim in the response back to the client. Action elements include standard actions <jsp:tag ...>, JSTL actions <c:tag ...> <fmt:tag ...> <sql:tag ...> <x:tag ...>, and custom actions <xyz:tag ...>.

EL Expressions ${expr}

Expression Language (EL) expressions are special elements that allow page authors who aren't familiar with the scripting language to more easily generate and arrange a JSP page's dynamic content.

Basics of a JSP Page

A JSP page is a text document containing both static and dynamic content. The static content (usually in a markup language such as HTML or XML) makes up most of the document, with several dynamic elements (some of which may contain scripting code) interspersed to generate and arrange the dynamic content.

A JSP page is compiled into a Java servlet by a JSP engine running within a Web server. A Java servlet is a pure Java class that extends the functionality of the Web server by providing custom behavior to generate a response to a client's request. Such a servlet provides an implementation of the javax.servlet.Servlet interface, often accomplished by extending either the javax.servlet.GenericServlet or javax.servlet.http.HttpServlet abstract classes.

JSP technology follows the typical client-server computing model, whereby a client sends a request to the server, the server processes the request, and then sends a response back to the client. In a typical Web application, not every page must be a JSP page. Pages which contain only static content may be HTML pages. However, at some point, a client will send a request and the server will realize that it must return a response with dynamic content. In this case, the server will try to find the generated servlet for the JSP page that would provide that dynamic content. If the servlet has not been generated or has a timestamp older than that of the JSP page, the server will recompile the JSP page. Once the servlet has been generated, it will execute, with the client's request object being passed in as a parameter. The servlet will then generate a response object typically containing HTML, XML, or some other markup language, and this response will then be returned to the client.

Since JSP pages may contain Java code, a JSP page may directly perform any operation made available by the Java Virtual Machine (JVM). This includes connecting to databases via Java Database Connectivity (JDBC) technology, invoking remote objects via Remote Method Invocation (RMI) or Common Object Request Broker Architecture (CORBA), and interacting with Enterprise JavaBeans (EJBs). However, you are encouraged to use the Model-View-Controller (MVC) pattern of Web application development, which promotes JSP pages as *view* components, and thus limits the logic that they should contain to presentation logic. Conversely, most business logic should live within separate Java *controller* components, such as Action classes in the Jakarta Struts framework, which interact with the back-end *model* components, all of which is beyond the scope of this chapter.

Benefits of JSP Technology

JSP technology promotes separation of roles and division of labor: developers can write components that interact with the back-end, while authors can use those components to concentrate on presentation instead of business logic. JSP technology also provides for the separation of static and dynamic content by allowing for the insertion of dynamic content into static templates.

Although structurally similar to Microsoft's Active Server Pages (ASP) technology, JSP provides several benefits that ASP does not. First, it provides "Write Once, Run Anywhere" characteristics common to the rest of the Java platform. This means that users are not limited to a certain implementation, tool set, server, or platform, but rather are free to choose the best-of-breed of each.

Second, it follows an open development process (meaning anyone is free to contribute) and is open-source (meaning source code may be freely downloaded, facilitating reuse and debugging). As a consequence, there are enterprise-class implementations, tool sets, and application servers that support

JSP technology and may be used free of charge, even in commercial production environments. Third, JSP technology promotes reusability by allowing developers to define custom tags and tag libraries to be reused by authors to abstract them from the complexities of the Java programming language.

Finally, JSP technology uses Java as its scripting language, which, unlike ASP's VBScript and JScript, is a mature and powerful object-oriented programming language that allows full access to the enterprise.

JSP Technology Motivation

Before JSP technology was born, Java developers would create Web applications by extending the functionality of a web server via *servlets*, which were Java classes that would respond to requests by generating dynamic content in a markup language and sending it via an output stream back to the client. Unfortunately, markup languages are often more difficult to debug than programming languages, and they benefit greatly from proper indentation and organization. The appearance of markup language fragments as Strings littered throughout Java code made readability difficult and maintenance a nightmare. It soon became clear that the coupling of a markup language with a programming language needed to be rethought, and JSP technology was born.

JSP revolutionized this coupling by turning it inside out. Instead of the markup language inside the programming language, the programming language was placed inside the markup language. Recognizing the fact that the markup language was more significant with respect to the output to the client than the Java code, JSPs looked very much like markup language files, with a sprinkling of Java code here and there to say which portions of markup should be repeated iteratively, which portions should be output conditionally, etc. Furthermore, JSP gave developers the ability to define their own behavioral tags. These tags would be implemented in separate Java classes, but their markup language interface would theoretically be simple enough for non-programmers to use.

This promoted the idea that a company could hire one set of developers to develop the front-end of a Web application, and another set of developers to develop the back-end. The front-end developers would have to be well-versed in markup languages and UI design, with only minimal programming experience, whereas the back-end developers would have to be well-versed in programming languages, with only minimal experience with markup languages and the complexities of developing front-ends supporting all the various clients.

JSP Translation and Execution

The prerequisite to understanding how JSP pages work and how to best utilize them is an understanding of what they get translated into.

Essentially, a JSP page gets translated and compiled into a class implementing either javax.servlet.jsp.JspPage or javax.servlet.jsp.HttpJspPage (depending on the request protocol), both of which extend javax.servlet.Servlet. One of the most important things to realize is that everything you see in a JSP page, with the exception of directives, declarations, and JSP comments, ends up living inside a method named _jspService, which has the following signature:

```
public void _jspService(ServletRequestSubtype request, ServletResponseSubtype
response) throws ServletException, IOException
```

This _jspService method will live inside the servlet class into which the JSP page gets translated. Consider the following simple JSP page named helloWorld.jsp:

```
<%! private String[] greetings = { "Hello", "Hi", "Greetings" }; %>
<HTML>
<HEAD><TITLE>helloWorld.jsp</TITLE></HEAD>
<BODY>
<% for (int i = 0; i < 3; i++) { %>
<P><%= this.greetings[i] %> world!</P>
<% } %>
</BODY>
</HTML>
```

This gets translated into the following servlet class (when compiled under the IBM WebSphere Application Server; each brand of server will compile a given JSP page slightly differently, to conform to their J2EE implementation):

```
public class helloWorld_jsp_0 extends
com.ibm.ws.webcontainer.jsp.runtime.HttpJspBase {
  ...
  private String[] greetings = { "Hello", "Hi", "Greetings" };
  ...
  public void _jspService(HttpServletRequest request, HttpServletResponse
    response)
    throws java.io.IOException, ServletException {
```

```
    JspFactory _jspxFactory = null;
    PageContext pageContext = null;
    HttpSession session = null;
    ServletContext application = null;
    ServletConfig config = null;
    JspWriter out = null;
    Object page = this;
    String  _value = null;
    java.util.Stack _jspxTagObjects = new java.util.Stack();

    …

    _jspxFactory = JspFactory.getDefaultFactory();
    response.setContentType("text/html;charset=ISO-8859-1");
    pageContext = _jspxFactory.getPageContext(this, request, response, "", true,
    8192, true);
    application = pageContext.getServletContext();
    config = pageContext.getServletConfig();
    session = pageContext.getSession();
    out = pageContext.getOut();

    …

    out.write(
    "\r\n<HTML>\r\n<HEAD><TITLE>helloWorld.jsp</TITLE></HEAD>\r\n
    <BODY>\  r\n" );

    for (int i = 0; i < 3; i++) {
      out.write( "\r\n<P>" );
      out.print( this.greetings[i] );
      out.write( " world!</P>\r\n" );
    }
    out.write( "\r\n</BODY>\r\n</HTML>\r\n" );
    …
  }

}
```

This generates the following output when executed via an HTTP request:

```
<HTML>
<HEAD><TITLE>helloWorld.jsp</TITLE></HEAD>
<BODY>
<P>Hello world!</P>
<P>Hi world!</P>
<P>Greetings world!</P>
</BODY>
</HTML>
```

Thus, each type of element of a JSP page is translated into a corresponding type of element in the generated servlet Java class. Static content is translated into out.write() calls with the static content as the String parameter. A scriptlet expression that occurs in static content is translated into an out.print() call, with the Object resulting from the scriptlet expression as the parameter. A scriptlet expression that occurs as the value of an action attribute gets translated into a setter call on the property of the action's corresponding tag handler, with the Object resulting from the scriptlet expression as the parameter.

A scriptlet gets translated into actual Java code inside the _jspService method, and this code manipulates the aforementioned out.write() and out.print() calls. Although not present in the above example, an action would get translated into Java code that instantiates the supporting tag handler object, performs initial setup, and invokes the tag handler's various template methods at the appropriate times.

Directive Elements <%@ ... %>

Directives are messages to the JSP container about how to compile and execute a JSP page. Directives have the form:

```
<%@ directive { attr="value" }* %>
```

page

The page directive lets you define several page-level attributes. An example of a page directive would be:

```
<%@ page language="java" import="java.math.*" buffer="16kb" %>
```

Attributes of the page directive are described in Table 10-1.

Table 10-1. Attributes of the page Directive

Attribute	Description [default values in brackets]
autoFlush	A value of "true" means that the output buffer should be automatically flushed when it reaches full capacity; a value of "false" means that an exception should be raised instead. [true]
Buffer	A value of "none" means the output should not be buffered; otherwise, the output will use a buffer of the specified size in kilobytes (a number plus the suffix "kb"). [8kb]
contentType	The MIME type of the response. [text/html]
errorPage	The URL of the page to forward to if an error occurs.
Extends	An alternate superclass for the generated servlet. Use of this attribute is discouraged, as it may limit the ability of the JSP container to use service-enhancing superclasses.
Import	The fully-qualified names of Java classes and packages to be imported by the generated servlet.
Info	A comment about the page that can be obtained via the getServletInfo method of the generated servlet.
isELIgnored	A value of "true" means EL evaluation is deactivated. [*dependent on web.xml version*]
isErrorPage	A value of "true" means current page can be used as the target errorPage of another JSP page, and that the implicit scripting variable exception will be made available. [false]
isThreadSafe	A value of "true" means page can be concurrently executed by multiple threads. As of the Servlet 2.4 specification, authors are discouraged from setting this attribute to "false", since SingleThreadModel has been deprecated. [true]
Language	The name of the scripting language used in the page; as of JSP 2.0, the only defined and required value is "java". [java]
pageEncoding	The IANA name of the character encoding that this page was written in. [for standard JSP pages: ISO-8859-1; for XML JSP pages: *same as XML prolog*]
Session	A value of "true" means the page participates in a session, and thus may use the implicit session scripting variable. [true]

taglib

The taglib directive lets you define which tab libraries are used in the JSP page. Either the uri or tagdir attribute should be used, but not both. If specifying the uri attribute in this directive, a tag library must be accompanied by an explicit tag library descriptor file, which is an XML document with a .tld extension that should reside in the /WEB-INF directory or a subdirectory thereof (except /WEB-INF/classes or /WEB-INF/lib). An example of a taglib directive would be:

```
<%@ taglib uri="myURI" prefix="myPrefix" %>
```

Table 10-2. Attributes of the taglib Directive

Attribute	Description
prefix	The prefix string that tags in this tag library will use in this JSP page.
tagdir	The path (must begin with "/WEB-INF/tags/") where these tag extensions are installed. Using this attribute means that no explicit tag library descriptor must be provided, since in this case the JSP container is required to create an implicit descriptor for all tags installed in /WEB-INF/tags/ or its subdirectories.
uri	An absolute or relative URI that serves to uniquely identify and locate this tag library's descriptor via the Web application deployment descriptor.

include

The include directive allows another page (HTML, JSP, etc.) to have its content inserted into this page before it is translated into a servlet. The only attribute is file, which specifies the relative URL of the page to be included. See the <jsp:include> standard action in the *Action Elements* section for an alternate but semantically different way to include content dynamically. An example of an include directive would be:

```
<%@ include file="/common/copyright.html" %>
```

Tech Tip: Since the include directive (unlike the include standard action) actually inserts the contents of another page into the current JSP page, the including JSP page *must be* recompiled in order to pick up changes made to the included page.

Scripting Elements

Scripting elements are the mechanism by which the scripting language (Java) may be used to generate and organize the dynamic content. The code within a scripting element must conform completely to the syntax rules of the scripting language. You may use any elements of the scripting language, including comments:

Declarations <%! ... %>

A declaration element is an actual declaration of member variables and methods to be included in the generated servlet class. These members may then be accessed by the various other JSP page elements via the implicit this reference. Some examples of declarations would be:

```
<%! private int i = 0; %>

<%! public String foo(Double d) { return d.toString(); } %>
```

Scriptlets <% ... %>

A scriptlet is a section of Java code that will be included verbatim in the _jspService method amidst the translated versions of other JSP elements. For example, you may place an if statement around static content in order to have the generated servlet conditionally execute the out.write() call that the static content gets translated to. Some examples of scriptlets would be:

```
<% if (request.getParameter("showCopyright") != null) { %>
<A HREF="/common/copyright.html">Copyright 2005, XavTech Solutions</A>
<% } %>
```

Scriptlet Expressions <%= ... %>

A *scriptlet expression* is similar to a scriptlet, in that it's a single Java statement (although it may be as complex as necessary) whose result is used in a manner dependent on where the scriptlet expression appears. If the scriptlet expression appears where static content is expected, the result of the expression is passed to an out.print() call, which then prints the parameter to the implicit out JspWriter. Some examples of scriptlet expressions would be:

```
<A HREF="/common/copyright.html">Copyright <%= currentYear %>, XavTech
Solutions</A>

<xyz:tag attribute1="<%= pageContext.getAttribute(key) %>" />
```

Tech Tip: The JSP specification says that when a scriptlet expression appears as the value of an action's attribute, it should be the entire value. The use of static strings in conjunction with a scriptlet expression is not supported, and any strings should be moved inside the scriptlet expression as String literals. Furthermore, the use of more than one scriptlet expression as an action attribute's value is also not supported.

Comments <%-- ... --%>

A JSP comment is not included in the generated servlet. It is important to understand the distinction between this and an HTML or XML comment (denoted by <!-- … -->), which is included in the generated servlet as HTML or XML that is output to the client via a call to out.write(). Thus, clients will be able to see an HTML or XML comment in the output that they receive from the server (albeit their browser may choose not to show it to them), whereas they will not be able to see a JSP comment at all, since it won't even make it back to them. An example of a JSP comment would be:

```
<%-- This comment will never be seen by the client, even if they use their
browser's "View Source" command. --%>
```

Implicit Scripting Variables

The _jspService method of the generated servlet will have certain parameters passed into it by the servlet container, and will also declare several local variables. These parameters and variables are collectively known as *implicit scripting variables*, since they are available for use in scriptlets and scriptlet expressions. However, implicit scripting variables are *not* available for use in declarations, since declarations are used to declare member variables and methods that would live outside the _jspService method.

We will now go over the various implicit scripting variables. Although a complete discussion of their types and all of their member variables and methods would be too lengthy for this chapter, we will cover the most important ones. The actual type of each variable is given in parentheses.

pageContext (javax.servlet.jsp.PageContext)

This implicit scripting variable represents the context that this JSP page is executed in, and provides access to the various attribute scopes, as well as to other page properties. See Table 10-3 for the methods of the pageContext variable.

page (javax.servlet.jsp.HttpJspPage or javax.servlet.jsp.JspPage)

This implicit scripting variable represents the *generated servlet* that the JSP page was translated and compiled to. It has several template methods that are called by the container. See Table 10-4 for the methods of the page variable.

Table 10-3. Methods of the pageContext Variable

Method	Description
ErrorData getErrorData()	Provides access to error information that is meaningful if the isErrorPage attribute of the page directive is "true".
Object findAttribute(String *name*)	Searches for the named attribute in the four attribute scopes in order of increasing persistence (page, request, session, application), and returns the first attribute found, or null if not found in any scope.
Object getAttribute(String *name*)	Returns the named attribute from the page scope, or null if not found.
Object getAttribute(String *name*, int *scope*)	Returns the named attribute from the specified *scope*, or null if not found.
JspWriter popBody()	Returns the "out" JspWriter that was pushed via the last pushBody() call, and sets it as the "out" page scope attribute.
BodyContent pushBody()	Saves the current "out" JspWriter to the stack, instantiates a new BodyContent object, sets it as the "out" page scope attribute, and returns it.
void removeAttribute(String *name*)	Removes the named attribute from all scopes.
void removeAttribute(String *name*, int *scope*)	Removes the named attribute from the specified scope.
void setAttribute(String *name*, Object *value*)	Sets the named attribute in page scope.
void setAttribute(String *name*, Object *value*, int *scope*)	Sets the named attribute in the specified scope.

Table 10-4. Methods of the page Variable

Method	Description
void _jspService(HttpServletRequest *request*, HttpServletResponse *response*)	The method that is executed by the container when a request for the JSP page is received; this method contains the main body of the *generated servlet*.
void jspDestroy()	This method is invoked by the container when the JSP page is about to be destroyed.
void jspInit()	This method is invoked by the container when the JSP page is about to be initialized.

request (javax.servlet.http.HttpServletRequest or javax.servlet.ServletRequest)

This implicit scripting variable represents the client's request to the server for this JSP page. It provides an attribute map, as well as information about the various components of the client's request.

10-5. Methods of the request Variable

Method	Description
Object getAttribute(java.lang.String name)	Returns the named attribute from this request's attribute map, or null if it doesn't exist.
Cookie[] getCookies()	Returns all cookies sent by the client with this request.
String getHeader(String name)	Returns the specified request header.
String getMethod()	Returns the name of the HTTP request method (GET, POST, PUT, etc.).
String getParameter(String name)	Returns the named parameter from this request's parameter map, or null if it doesn't exist.
String getQueryString()	Returns the query part of the requested URL (the part after the question mark).
String getRequestedSessionId()	Returns the session ID that the client sent along with this request.
String getRequestURI()	Returns the part of the requested URL from the protocol up to the query string.
String getServletPath()	Returns the part of the requested URL that specifies the servlet.
HttpSession getSession(boolean *create*)	Returns the session associated with this request's session ID, optionally creating it if such a session doesn't exist.
boolean isRequestedSessionIdFromCookie()	Returns true only if the requested session ID came in as a cookie.
boolean isRequestedSessionIdFromURL()	Returns true only if the requested session ID came in via the requested URL.
boolean isRequestedSessionIdValid()	Returns true only if there is still a session corresponding to the requested session ID.
void removeAttribute(String *name*)	Removes the named attribute from this request's attribute map.
void setAttribute(String *name*, Object *value*)	Sets the named attribute in this request's attribute map.

response (javax.servlet.http.HttpServletResponse or javax.servlet.ServletResponse)

This implicit scripting variable represents the response that will be sent back to the client. It provides facilities for adding cookies and headers to the response, as well as for redirecting the client to another URL.

10-6. Methods of the response Variable

Method	Description
void addCookie(Cookie *cookie*)	Adds a *cookie* to this response.
void addHeader(String *name*, String *value*)	Adds a header to this response.
boolean containsHeader(String *name*)	Returns true only if the specified header has already been added to this response.
boolean isCommitted()	Returns true only if this response has been committed to the client.
void reset()	Clears any data from the response buffer, and also clears the status code and headers.
void resetBuffer()	Clears any data from the response buffer, without clearing the status code or headers.
void sendError(int *sc*, String *msg*)	Sends an error response to the client with the specified status code and message.
void sendRedirect(String *location*)	Sends a response to the client to redirect to the specified URL.
void setHeader(String *name*, String *value*)	Sets the specified header on this response, or adds it if it hasn't been added yet.

session (javax.servlet.http.HttpSession)

This implicit scripting variable represents the client's current session in the server. A session is represented by a server-generated ID that is passed back to the client, and which the client then includes with every subsequent request. This ID ties every subsequent request to the same conceptual session, and allows the server to access the data that it has stored under that session on behalf of the client. The session variable provides an attribute map, as well as facilities to access information about the client's current session. The methods of the session variable are described in Table 10-7.

Table 10-7. Methods of the session Variable

Method	Description
Object getAttribute(String *name*)	Returns the named attribute from this session's attribute map, or null if it doesn't exist.
String getId()	Returns the unique session id.
long getLastAccessedTime()	Returns the last time a request was received with this session's id.
void invalidate()	Invalidates this session and unbounds its attributes.
boolean isNew()	Returns true if the client doesn't yet know this session's id or if it chose not to join this session.
void removeAttribute(String *name*)	Removes the named attribute from this session's attribute map.
void setAttribute(String *name*, Object *value*)	Sets the named attribute in this session's attribute map.

application (javax.servlet.ServletContext)

This implicit scripting variable represents the Web application, and thus exists at an even higher level than sessions, since all sessions in a given Web application will have the same ServletContext reference. This variable provides an application-level attribute map and several methods for getting at application-level information.

Table 10-8. Methods of the application Variable

Method	Description
Object getAttribute(String *name*)	Returns the named attribute from this application's attribute map, or null if it doesn't exist.
String getInitParameter(String *name*)	Returns the named initialization parameter, or null if it doesn't exist.
URL getResource(String *path*)	Returns a URL to the resource given by the specified path relative to the current context root, or null if no such resource exists.
String getServletContextName()	Returns the context root of this Web application.
void removeAttribute(String *name*)	Removes the named attribute from this application's attribute map.
void setAttribute(String *name*, Object *value*)	Sets the named attribute in this application's attribute map.

config (javax.servlet.ServletConfig)

This implicit scripting variable contains configuration information passed to the generated servlet by its container. It has a few methods for obtaining configuration information about the servlet.

Table 10-9. Methods of the config Variable

Method	Description
String getInitParameter(String *name*)	Returns the named initialization parameter, or null if it doesn't exist.
String getServletName()	Returns the name of this servlet.

out (javax.servlet.jsp.JspWriter)

This implicit scripting variable represents the output stream going to the client. It has various methods for interacting with the underlying buffer.

Table 10-10. Methods of the out Variable

Method	Description
void clear()	Clears the buffer.
void close()	Flushes and closes the stream.
void flush()	Flushes the stream.
int getBufferSize()	Returns the size of the buffer.
void newLine()	Writes a newline separator.
void print(Object *o*)	Prints the specified object's toString() value.
void println(Object *o*)	Prints the specified object's toString() value, followed by a newline separator.

exception (java.lang.Throwable)

This implicit scripting variable is only made available to JSP pages that have the isErrorPage page directive attribute set to "true". The scripting variable would be set to the Throwable that caused the navigation to the error page. We will not cover its methods, as it is an instance of Throwable, and should be well-known to any Java developer.

Scoped Attributes vs. Scripting Variables

By now this may be a well-understood point, but its significance justifies its repetition. A JSP page operates on variables defined in several ways.

Scoped attributes are Objects that were set in at least one of the four available attribute scopes: page, request, session, and application. That order also happens to be the order in which scoped attributes are sought, because it is an order of increasing persistence. A page-scoped attribute will only exist as long as the JSP page in which it was defined is still being evaluated. A request-scoped attribute may exist across several JSP page evaluations, as long as the client request in which it was defined is still being processed. A session-scoped attribute may exist across several requests, as long as the session in which it was defined has not expired. Each client request contains a "requested session ID", and as long as the session corresponding to that ID has not yet expired, the session's expiration time is reset and it continues to be valid until no request with its ID is received for an entire timeout interval.

Finally, an application-scoped attribute may exist across several client sessions (even of differing clients), as long as the Web application keeps running. Scoped attributes may be accessed via scriptlets or scriptlet expressions, as follows:

```
<%= session.getAttribute("myScopedAttribute") %>
```

However, they are more often accessed via actions, as such:

```
<bean:write name="myScopedAttribute" scope="session" />
```

Scripting variables are Objects or primitives that were defined as parameters or locals in the _jspService method of the generated servlet. Thus, they implicitly only live as long as the JSP page they were defined in is still being evaluated, and may not be accessed from declarations (since declarations are outside the _jspService method). Furthermore, they may be accessed in scriptlets or scriptlet expressions simply by their names:

```
<%= myScriptingVariable %>
```

Action Elements

Actions look like other markup language tags, with the exception that they have a prefix and a colon before the tag name. This difference lets the JSP container know that they are not static content and, as long as corresponding tag handler classes can be found, that they should be processed rather than output verbatim to the client.

With the exception of standard actions (which the JSP container is automatically aware of), groups of action tags (known as *tag libraries*) are declared at the beginning of a JSP page via the use of a taglib directive. Actions whose tag libraries are not declared via a taglib directive are treated as static content and are output verbatim to the client.

The value of an action's attribute may be specified as a static value or as a *request-time attribute value*, which may be either a scriptlet expression or an EL expression.

If a request-time attribute value contains a String literal then, in order to avoid compilation conflicts, the request-time attribute value should be enclosed by single-quotes instead of double-quotes (which should be used for the String literal):

```
<jsp:include page='<%= MyConstants.COMMON_DIR_NAME + "/copyright.html"
%>' />
<c:out value='${user.preferences["notify"]}' />
```

If a scriptlet expression is used as a request-time attribute value, the JSP specification says it should be the entire value of the attribute; no static strings outside the scriptlet expression and no other scriptlet expressions should be used. The following examples of request-time attribute values are both *illegal*:

```
<jsp:include page="<%= MyConstants.COMMON_DIR_NAME %>/copyright.html"
/>
<jsp:include page='<%= MyConstants.COMMON_DIR_NAME %><%=
"/copyright.html" %>' />
```

If an EL expression is used as a request-time attribute value, the JSP specification allows multiple EL expressions mixed with static strings to be used in a single attribute's value:

```
<jsp:include page="${commonDirName}/${copyrightPage}" />
```

Standard Actions <jsp:tag ...>

Standard actions are action elements whose prefix is jsp. They are called *standard* because they are part of the JSP specifications, rather than tags created by third parties. The jsp prefix is reserved for standard actions, and should not be used by third-party tags.

Although a detailed description of each standard action and all attributes would be too lengthy for this chapter, we will briefly mention the most commonly-used standard actions and their intended purpose.

Table 10-11. Standard Actions

Action	Description
<jsp:useBean>	Creates either a scripting variable or EL variable and sets it to a specified scoped attribute.
<jsp:setProperty>	Sets a property on a scripting variable using a value obtained from either request parameters or a request-time attribute expression.
<jsp:getProperty>	Gets a property from a scripting variable and writes it to the out implicit scripting variable.
<jsp:include>	Invokes a resource (such as a JSP page, HTML page, etc.) using the current request, and writes its response to the out implicit scripting variable; evaluation of the current page is then resumed.
<jsp:forward>	Forwards the current request to a resource (such as a JSP page, HTML page, etc.), thereby ending the evaluation of the current page.
<jsp:param>	Used in <jsp:include>, <jsp:forward>, and <jsp:params> standard actions to provide key/value pairs.
<jsp:attribute>	Used to provide an action attribute value in the body of an XML element rather than in the value of an XML attribute (thereby allowing the further use of other actions to generate the value, for example).
<jsp:body>	Used to specify the body of an action if a <jsp:attribute> action is used.
<jsp:element>	Used to dynamically invoke an action by specifying its name, attributes, and body at runtime.

Tech Tip: Since the include standard action (unlike the include directive) actually forwards the request to another page and includes its output in the current JSP page, the including JSP page *does not have to be* recompiled in order to pick up changes made to the included page.

JSTL Actions <c:tag ...>, <fmt:tag ...>, <sql:tag ...>, <x:tag ...>

The JavaServer Pages Standard Tag Library (JSTL) is a collection of actions developed under the Java Community Process (JCP). These actions are organized into four groups of tags, or "tag libraries": core actions (prefix "c"), formatting and internationalization actions (prefix fmt), relational database actions (prefix sql), and XML processing actions (prefix x). The most current JSTL specification at the time of this writing is version 1.1, developed in November 2003.

The group of core actions consists of general-purpose actions (<c:out>, <c:set>, <c:remove>, <c:catch>), conditional actions (<c:if>, <c:choose>, <c:when>, <c:otherwise>), iteration actions (<c:forEach>, <c:forTokens>), and URL-related actions (<c:import>, <c:url>, <c:redirect>, <c:param>).

The group of internationalization actions (<fmt:setLocale>, <fmt:bundle>, <fmt:setBundle>, <fmt:message>, <fmt:param>, <fmt:requestEncoding>) consists of actions that facilitate formatting for the specific purpose of internationalizing JSP page output.

The group of formatting actions (<fmt:timeZone>, <fmt:setTimeZone>, <fmt:formatNumber>, <fmt:parseNumber>, <fmt:formatDate>, <fmt:parseDate>) consist of actions that facilitate more general-purpose formatting of JSP page output.

The group of SQL actions (<sql:query>, <sql:update>, <sql:transaction>, <sql:setDataSource>, <sql:param>, <sql:dateParam>) consists of actions that facilitate relational database access.

The group of XML actions consists of core actions (<x:parse>, <x:out>, <x:set>), flow control actions (<x:if>, <x:choose>, <x:when>, <x:otherwise>, <x:forEach>), and transformation actions (<x:transform>, <x:param>).

Custom Actions <xyz:tag ...>

The JSTL actions discussed above are examples of custom actions, which is one of JSP technology's most important characteristics: a built-in mechanism that allows page authors and developers to extend the capabilities of existing actions and to define new custom actions.

A custom action is implemented by defining a *tag handler* class. This class must either implement one of several interfaces or extend one of several support classes. The interface option exists especially so that existing Java classes may be converted into tag handlers simply by implementing the additional interface.

The tag extension mechanism is fairly large and highly configurable. As such, we will not cover all of its aspects in full detail, but will rather highlight the most significant ones.

Classic Tag Handlers

A *classic* tag handler is one that implements one of the three principal interfaces of the tag extension mechanism: javax.servlet.jsp.tagext.Tag, javax.servlet.jsp.tagext.IterationTag, or javax.servlet.jsp.tagext.BodyTag. There are also two support classes that may be extended instead, javax.servlet.jsp.tagext.TagSupport and javax.servlet.jsp.tagext.BodyTagSupport, since they provide default implementations for all of the interface methods.

Table 10-12. Methods of the javax.servlet.jsp.tagext.Tag Class

Method	Description
int doEndTag()	Called when the container encounters an end tag for this action; should return EVAL_PAGE to continue evaluating the page, or SKIP_PAGE to stop evaluating the page.
int doStartTag()	Called by the container when it encounters a start tag for this action; should return EVAL_BODY_INCLUDE to evaluate the body of the tag into the existing output stream, or SKIP_BODY to skip the evaluation of the body.
Tag getParent()	Returns a reference to the tag enclosing this one; the parent tag's state may be consulted by a child tag in order for the child tag to determine how to proceed.
void release()	Called by the container to signal the tag handler to release its state.
void setPageContext (PageContext pc)	Sets the current page context.
void setParent(Tag t)	Sets the tag that is enclosing this one.

Table 10-13. Methods of the javax.servlet.jsp.tagext.IterationTag Class

Method	Description
int doAfterBody()	Called by the container after it finishes evaluating this action's body; should return EVAL_BODY_AGAIN to re-evaluate the body of the tag, or SKIP_BODY to skip the evaluation of the body.

Table 10-14. Methods of the javax.servlet.jsp.tagext.BodyTag Class

Method	Description
void doInitBody()	Called by the container before the first time this action's body is evaluated.
void setBodyContent(BodyContent *bc*)	Called by the container before doInitBody() to set the BodyContent.

Support Classes

javax.servlet.jsp.tagext.TagSupport and javax.servlet.jsp.tagext.BodyTagSupport are the two support classes that classic tag handlers may extend. These two classes provide implementations of all of the interface methods, as well as a few additional helper methods that may come in handy.

Most tag handlers simply override the doXXX() methods that they are interested in and perform some logic or manipulation inside them in order to write to the output stream and to determine which constant to return.

Simple Tag Handlers

With the arrival of the JSTL and the EL, it became apparent that many JSP pages would no longer need to evaluate many scriptlets and scriptlet expressions. This led to the notion of being able to define *simple* tag handlers, as opposed to *classic* ones.

To this end, javax.servlet.jsp.tagext.SimpleTag and javax.servlet.jsp.tagext.SimpleTagSupport were created for JSP version 2.0. These simple tag handlers have only one method called by the container: doTag(). Instead of doStartTag() and doEndTag() and their return values, simple tag handlers rely on the much simpler interface of having doTag() called once and only once by the container, performing all necessary body manipulation and iteration within that one method, and not having to return any value.

Tag Files

As we alluded to at the beginning of this chapter, JSP technology was created because developers wanted to turn servlets inside out, and write Java code inside markup language rather than the other way around. JSP technology was well received, but the advent of tag libraries caused some developers to scratch their heads in unison and wonder, "Isn't this just moving back towards the *markup-language-within-Java* philosophy?"

Fortunately, as of JSP version 2.0, another option to the tag extension mechanism was introduced: tag files. With tag files, you can once more return to the *Java-within-markup-language* ideal, since a tag file is little more than a section of a JSP page used as the implementation of a tag handler. This allows page authors to implement tag extensions without requiring the help of a Java developer, and it also gives Java developers an easier time when defining tag handlers that contain a lot of static content (which would otherwise be unruly to output from within Java code).

EL Expressions ${expr}

Although scriptlet expressions allowed developers to supply action attribute values dynamically and relatively succinctly, they still required proficiency in Java and seemed somewhat unnatural. So, along with the JSTL, a parallel effort was born to define an Expression Language (EL).

The EL is simple enough for non-developers to use, yet powerful enough to give access to all attribute scopes and contexts. It is also usable practically anywhere in a JSP page, even several times within one action attribute value (whereas a scriptlet expression was only usable as the entire attribute value, no more and no less).

The EL can appear both as an action attribute's value, as well as within static content. The construct used to invoke the EL is ${expr}, where "expr" is an expression. The expression can start with a scoped attribute name (which will be sought in the usual attribute scope order: page, request, session application), followed by property and subproperty accesses via periods. Lists may be indexed via [i] notation, and maps may be keyed via ["key"] notation. Furthermore, the indexes and keys may be expressions that must be evaluated in order to determine their values. This makes EL very expressive and powerful.

There are several implicit objects available in EL expressions: pageContext, pageScope, requestScope, sessionScope, applicationScope, param, paramValues, header, headerValues, cookie, and initParam. Most, if not all, of these implicit objects should be self-explanatory given the previous discussions in this chapter.

Finally, the EL also allows many operators to be used in order to compute a result that is then substituted in the expression's place. The almost full complement of Java operators is available. Some examples of EL expressions would be:

```
<c:if test="${account.balance < account.minBalance}">
You are below your minimum balance of ${account.minBalance}!
</c:if>
<c:out value="${products[5].name}" />
<c:out value="${products[paging.currentIndex]}" />
<c:out value='${user.preferences["notify"]}' />
```

Functions

Functions are a feature provided to extend the capabilities of the EL, just like custom actions extend the capabilities of JSP tags. Just as JSTL provides a standard set of custom actions that is widely needed by most page authors, it also provides a standard set of EL functions:

> fn:contains, fn:containsIgnoreCase, fn:endsWith, fn:escapeXml, fn:indexOf, fn:join, fn:length, fn:replace, fn:split, fn:startsWith, fn:substring, fn:substringAfter, fn:substringBefore, fn:toLowerCase, fn:toUpperCase, fn:trim

As you might guess from their names, most of these functions work on Strings. The one exception is fn:length, which returns either the length of a String or the size of a Collection. Some example usages of functions would be:

```
<P>There are ${fn:length(counties)} counties in ${fn:toUpperCase(state)}.</P>
```

Cookies

A Cookie is a small piece of data (name/value pair) that a server can send to a client's browser in order to tell the browser how to identify itself to the server on subsequent requests. Cookies are typically used to store session management data. The Web application automatically sends the browser a cookie containing its session ID. A browser submits all cookies that it has received from a Web server with each subsequent request.

Many Web applications have used (and abused) cookies to store more data on the client side than cookies were designed for. Data concerning user browsing patterns is typically the goal of this kind of abuse. For this reason, many users turn off their browser's cookie-handling capabilities (although the storing of a session ID is still permitted, since sessions are an essential part of any serious Web application).

The Cookie class is a Java bean with getters and setters for several properties, including one for the maximum age that the cookie should live on the client side and another for the URL domain name that the cookie should be associated with.

A JSP page can set a Cookie on the response object using its addCookie method. If the Web application must interact with clients who may have cookies turned off, the Web application may store client-side data in HTML input elements of type hidden. The values of these elements will be submitted along with all other form data, but will not show up in the form in the browser. However, use of this technique is discouraged due to security issues (especially when the request method is GET, which means that even the hidden field values will be visible in the URL line after the request is made). In fact, most Web applications do not rely on storing any client-side data other than the session ID.

Error Handling

Exceptions may be raised during the processing of a request by a JSP page. If an exception is caught within the _jspService method by the JSP page's scriptlets, the exception will be handled as the page developer's code specifies. Otherwise, if the exception is caught outside the scope of the developer's custom code, the JSP container will attempt to forward both the request and the exception objects to a separate error-handling JSP page specified by the errorPage attribute of the page directive.

The error-handling JSP page should declare the isErrorPage attribute of its own page directive as "true" in order to gain access to a special implicit scripting variable named exception. This variable will be a reference to the javax.servlet.jsp.JspException object that contains the exception data, which may then be printed to the output stream or logged for analysis.

An error page also has access to a javax.servlet.jsp.ErrorData object via the pageContext implicit scripting variable, under the errorData attribute. This object should be initialized with the appropriate exception information, and is provided especially for access from the EL.

Looking Forward

As of July 2005, the JSP version 2.1 specification (JSR 245) has just recently completed its public review draft stage. The principal goals of this next release will be to improve alignment with the next release of JavaServer Faces (JSF) technology and to further improve ease of development. Namely, JSP version 2.1 will seek to enhance the EL so that it meets the minimum requirements of the JSF technology's own "EL" (which had to be developed in parallel, prior to JSP version 2.0), so that the JSF EL may be phased out in the next JSF release in favor of the JSP EL.

With no end in sight for the further integration and enhancement of JSP technology, its future seems fairly bright as the J2EE platform seeks to further improve ease of development for its users, while at the same time maintaining the openness and other benefits of the Java Community Process that have made it a technology of choice in large, demanding, enterprise-class applications.

Chapter 11

PHP

PHP is a cross-platform scripting language that is mostly used for server-side Web applications. PHP supports many Web-specific language features and can be easily embedded into HTML. PHP is also an object-oriented language, supporting features such as inheritance and interfaces.

PHP is a recursive acronym, standing for "PHP: Hypertext Processor." An open source language with a large community following, PHP originated in 1995 as the successor to a language called "PHP/FI," which means "Personal Home Page / Forms Interpreter." PHP has evolved significantly since then. Currently at version 5, PHP has grown from a simple scripting language into a full-featured Web application platform.

Since PHP is regarded as a Web platform, it includes many useful features for manipulating and working with HTML forms. Values that have been submitted to the Web form by various methods - including POST, GET, cookies, and server variables - can be easily accessed with built-in arrays. There are a whole host of Web-related helper functions, such as `htmlspecialchars()`, which convert characters that have special meaning into their proper HTML equivalents.

In an effort make it a rapid development platform, PHP is a dynamically typed language. Variable types are not declared in advance, rather, their type is determined at runtime depending on how you use the variables. PHP also supports a powerful built-in array data type that can be used to quickly store and access various types of data with minimal effort.

Fast Facts

- PHP syntax is a mixture of Perl and C.
- All variables in PHP start with $. Their types are determined by their usage.
- Variable names in PHP are case sensitive.
- Function and class names in PHP are case insensitive.
- A PHP block begins with <?php and ends with ?>.
- Text can be printed to standard output with echo or printf.
- When printing text, use double quotes ("") to evaluate variables. Use single quotes ('') to treat $ as a character, not a prefix to a variable.
- Strings are concatenated with a period (.) in PHP.
- The filename of a PHP script usually ends in .php, though Web servers can be configured to handle other extensions.
- Single-line comments are noted with a double slash (//). Block comments start with /* and end with */.
- Statements in PHP end with a semicolon (;).
- Functions, methods, and classes are enclosed in curly braces ({ }).
- Code that exists outside of functions and classes is executed immediately.
- In PHP, function arguments are passed by value unless explicitly specified to be passed by reference, while objects are passed by reference (see the *Values and References* section).
- HTML form values can be accessed by using the special array that is appropriate for the method: $_GET['*name*'], $_POST['*name*'], $_COOKIE['*name*'], or $_REQUEST['*name*'], which contains the contents of all of the previous three.
- Documentation for built-in functions can be found at http://php.net/function_name.

Sample PHP Script

PHP is usually found inside of HTML pages. The following example presents a textbox wherein a user may enter their name. When the user clicks the button, that name is displayed inside of an <h1> tag:

```
<html>
  <head>
    <title>Student info</title>
  </head>
  <body>
    <h1><?php echo htmlspecialchars($_GET['name']); ?></h1>
    <form action="<?php echo $_SERVER['PHP_SELF']; ?>" method="get">
      Name: <input name="name" type="text" value="<?php echo
      htmlspecialchars($_GET['name']); ?>" />
      <input name="button1" type="submit" value="Add Student" />
    </form>
  </body>
</html>
```

The output and a screenshot of the output rendered in a Web browser follow:

```
<html>
  <head>
    <title>Student info</title>
  </head>
  <body>
    <h1></h1>
    <form action="/student.php" method="get">
      Name: <input name="name" type="text" value="" />
      <input name="button1" type="submit" value="Add Student" />
    </form>
  </body>
</html>
<html>
```

Figure 11-1.

After typing a name into the box and clicking the “Add Student” button, the rendered page will look similar to the screenshot below:

Figure 11-2.

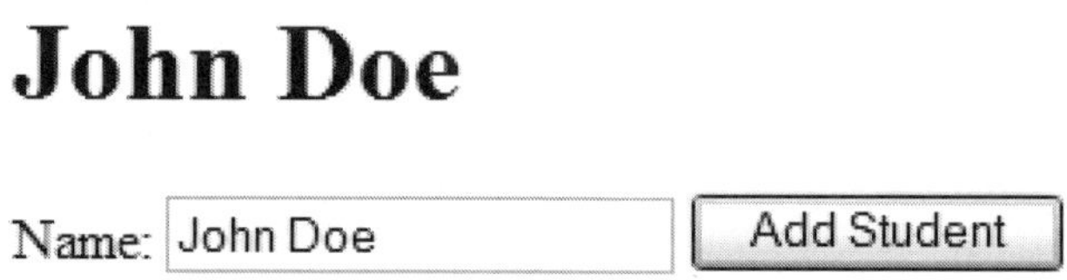

Main Components of PHP Script

To run the above script, you should place it on a Web server that is configured for use with PHP and navigate to the page (PHP also supports a command line mode in the form of `php filename.php`). Some of the components above are basic parts of any PHP script, and are defined here.

<?php...?>

The most important part of a PHP script is the code block delimiter. Everything found in between `<?php` and `?>` is interpreted as code. Anything found outside of those blocks is just printed as is. There can be multiple `<?php ?>` blocks in a script, and logic can even be interspersed between various blocks. In the example below, a form is shown if the user is not logged in, otherwise it shows a logout link. Notice how the `if{ }` blocks start and end in different `<?php ?>` blocks:

```
<?php
  $showLogin = !($_COOKIE['loggedin']);
  if($showLogin) {
?>
  <form action="/login.php" method="post">
    Username: <input type="text" name="username" /><br />
    Password: <input type="password" name="password" />
    <input type="submit" name="doLogin" value="Log in" />
  </form>
```

```
<?php
  }
  else
  {
?>
  <a href="logout.php">Logout</a>
<?php
  }
?>
```

include, require

To promote code reuse, you may wish to include other PHP files that you have already written. If you had another file that defined some helper functions or other classes that you needed to use, you could load it with an include_once('helpers.php') statement, where helpers.php is the name of the file. This will attempt to load the file, issuing a warning if there is an error. The _once directive makes sure that the file is only loaded once, preventing certain issues - such as a class being redefined - should the same file be loaded more than once. In addition to the include() and include_once() directives, there are also require() and require_once() statements which load code from another file. The difference between include and require is that require fails with a fatal error if there is a problem, whereas include simply issues a warning and attempts to continue.

Basics of PHP

PHP files are text files that can be created with any text editor, such as Vim, Emacs, or even Notepad. You may also use PHP-specific editors, like NuSphere PHPEd, or Dev-PHP.

PHP is an interpreted language. You do not compile your code in advance; you just execute your script with the PHP runtime engine.

There are two ways to execute your PHP scripts. Most likely, you'll want to place your pages on a Web server (usually Apache) that is configured for use with PHP. When you navigate your Web browser to your page written in PHP, the code will be executed on the server and the resulting output will be sent to the client's Web browser. The extension of your file when executed on a Web server is typically .php, but different servers may have different configurations.

The second way to run a PHP script is to use the command line. All of your output will be displayed in your terminal window, instead of in a Web browser. Use the following syntax:

```
php filename.php
```

On Unix or Linux systems, there is a third way that you can execute scripts. By making the first line of the script #! followed by the path of the PHP executable, you may then simply execute the script on the command line as you would any other executable. The shell will then execute the script against the command referenced in the first line. The first line of your script might look similar to the following:

```
#!/usr/local/bin/php -q
```

Variables

When working with a variable in PHP, one does not define the type of the variable, nor does one have to declare the variable before using it; the type of the variable is determined at runtime by its usage. Variables in PHP always start with $. Consider the example below, which demonstrates how strings and integers can be effortlessly converted between one another:

```
<?php
  $one = 1;
  $two = $one * 2;
  $twelve = $one . $two;
  echo $twelve;
  $thirteen = $twelve + 1;
  echo $thirteen;
?>
```

The variable $one starts out as an integer. When $one is used to create $two, it remains an integer because it is used in a multiplication operation. In the next line, where $twelve is initialzed, $one and $two are converted to strings because they are accessed with the string concatenation operator, period (.). When echo $twelve is evaluated, it prints the string "12" to the output. The next line uses a plus operator to create $thirteen, so the string "12" is converted back to an integer 12, and then one is added to it to result in 13. The last line converts it back to a string and prints "13" to the output.

Types

PHP has eight built-in types. There are four scalar types: boolean, integer, float (sometimes called double), and string. PHP supports two compound types: array and object. There are also two "special" types: resource and NULL.

Booleans

Booleans are either true or false. In PHP, the keywords true and false are case insensitive. When converting to Boolean from other types, all of the following values evaluate to false:

- The integer 0
- The float 0.0
- The empty string ""
- The string "0"
- A zero-element array
- An unset or NULL value
- An object with no member variables (PHP 4 only)

All other values will convert to true. Explicit casts may be done with $boolval = (bool) $otherval;

Integers

Integers are all natural numbers (1, 2, 3…), the negatives of all of those numbers (-1, -2, -3…), and zero (0). Integers can be specified in decimal (base-10), octal (base-8), or hexadecimal (base-16). Numbers preceded with a zero (0) are treated as octal; numbers preceded with 0x (zero-x) are treated as hexadecimal.

To explicitly convert a scalar type (string, float, or Boolean) to an integer, use the intval() function. Numbers converted in this manner will *always be rounded toward zero*. You can also use the cast syntax:

```
$intval = (int) $scalarval;
```

Floats

Floats are decimal numbers. The range of valid numbers is platform-dependent. The most common maximum value is the 64-bit IEEE standard, 1.8e308 with 14 decimal digits.

It is important to note that there is no integer division in PHP. In some languages (such as C), the integer division of 1/2 == 1. In PHP, the division operator treats all of the values involved as floats. As such, in PHP 1/2 == 0.5.

To explicitly convert a scalar to a float, use floatval(). You may also cast using $floatval = (float) $scalarval;

Strings

A string is a sequence of characters. As of version 5, PHP does not yet have native Unicode support. As such, a character is a single byte. The two most common ways to express a string are to wrap it in either single quotes ('') or double quotes (""). It is important to understand the difference between the two: text inside of double quotes will be evaluated for variable expressions; text inside of single quotes is treated literally.

```
<?php
  $name = "Bob";
  echo "Hi, my name is $name.\n";
  echo 'Hi, my name is $name.\n';
?>
```

The above snippet will output:

```
Hi, my name is Bob.
Hi, my name is $name.\n
```

Notice how, inside of double quotes (the first echo statement), the variable and the escaped character are evaluated. Inside of single quotes, they are all taken literally. In fact, inside of single quotes, the only escapable character is '; all others are treated literally (including the backslash character (\)).

The third way to express strings is to use the *heredoc* syntax (<<<). You provide an identifier after <<< and the string terminates when that identifier, followed by a semicolon, is seen again. Like double quotes, variables will be evaluated inside of a heredoc block:

```
<?php
  $var = <<<EOF
  This string spans
  multiple lines using
  the heredoc syntax.
  EOF;

  echo $var;
?>
```

The above snippet outputs:

```
This string spans
multiple lines using
the heredoc syntax.
```

Take care to not include any extraneous whitespace with your terminating identifier. The final line *must* be just the identifier and a semicolon. Anything extra makes the identifier invalid, and thus your string continues:

```
<?php
  $var = <<<EOF
  Heredoc ends with the identifier
  and a semicolon on its own line
  and nothing more.
    EOF;
  EOF;

  echo $var;
?>
```

The output of the script above is:

```
Heredoc ends with the identifier
and a semicolon on its own line
and nothing more.
  EOF;
```

Arrays

Arrays in PHP are really more than just arrays: they are actually *ordered maps*. They can be used as hashtables, dictionaries, lists, stacks, queues, or simply arrays. An array can be used in any situation that has a need to map a key to a value or to store a collection of values. The easiest way to create an array is to just use it with the square bracket syntax:

```
<?php
  $toolBox[0] = 'hammer';
  $toolBox['one'] = 'drill';
  print_r($toolBox);
?>
```

The function print_r() will print out the entire contents of an array. The above snippet yields the following output:

```
Array
(
  [0] => hammer
  [one] => drill
)
```

The more formal method of creating an array is to use the array() language construct. You can either pass a comma separated list of values into array() or you can pass a comma separated list of key => value pairs into array(). The example below initializes the same array as above:

```
<?php
  $toolBox = array(0 => 'hammer', 'one' => 'drill');
  print_r($toolBox);
?>
```

By nesting array() constructs, you can create multi-dimensional arrays:

```
<?php
  $toolBox = array('topdrawer' => array('screwdriver', 'tape measure'),
  'bottomdrawer' => array('hammer', 'drill'));
  print_r($toolBox);
?>
```

The output of the snippet above will be:

```
Array
(
  [topdrawer] => Array
  (
    [0] => screwdriver
    [1] => tape measure
  )

  [bottomdrawer] => Array
  (
    [0] => hammer
    [1] => drill
  )
)
```

The same array can be constructed using square brackets:

```
<?php
  $toolBox['topdrawer'][0] = 'screwdriver';
  $toolBox['topdrawer'][1] = 'tape measure';
  $toolBox['bottomdrawer'][0] = 'hammer';
  $toolBox['bottomdrawer'][1] = 'drill';
?>
```

Another important distinction when working with arrays is how they are evaluated inside of double-quoted strings. You need to use the complex syntax (called "complex" because it allows complex expression evaluation). All you have to do is wrap your variable expression in curly braces ({}) and the expression inside of it will be evaluated. The complex syntax will only be recognized if the first character following the opening curly brace is a dollar sign ({$):

```
<?php
  $favTool = "My favorite tool is a {$toolBox['topdrawer'][0]}!\n";
?>
```

Without the curly braces, PHP doesn't know what to do, so it will either raise an error or result in unexpected output.

When you convert a Boolean, integer, float, string, or resource to an array, the result is a one-dimensional array of length 1 with the value at index [0]. Converting an object to an array yields an array whose keys are member variable names and whose values are member variable values.

Resources

A resource is a special type of variable. It holds a reference to some external (non-PHP) resource. A resource is typically returned by a function that accesses a database, a function that opens a file, or any other function that accesses an external library. Each type of resource is different; see the specific documentation for detailed information.

NULL

A variable that is null is one that has been set to the constant NULL, unset with the unset() function, or one that has been created but has not yet been assigned a value. The NULL keyword is case insensitive.

To see if a variable has a null value, use the function is_null().

```
<?php
  $myVar = NULL;
  if(is_null($myVar))
    echo "myVar is null";
?>
```

In Boolean logic, NULL evaluates to false. Thus, if you compare null to another variable that also evaluates to false (such as zero or an empty string) with the == (equal to) operator, you may get unexpected results (because the expression "false == false" evaluates to true). If you intend to determine if the value of the variable is NULL, you must use the === (identical to) operator.

The identical to operator returns true if and only if the two variables being compared have the same value and are of the same type. Thus "12" == 12 is true, while "12" === 12 is false. In the following example, the output will be "The value of var evaluates to false."

```
<?php
  $var = "";
  if($var == NULL)
  {
    echo "The value of var evaluates to false.\n";
  }
  if($var === NULL)
  {
    echo "var is explicitly NULL.\n";
  }
?>
```

Classes and Objects

PHP supports object-oriented language features, allowing developers to create classes and objects. A class is usually created by a developer to model some logical concept in the application. This section will focus on PHP 5 syntax.

A class definition always starts with the class keyword. The content of the class is delimited with curly braces ({}).

Methods are notated with the function keyword. Similar to the behavior of variables, return types of methods are not specified; they are determined at runtime. A value can be returned from a method with the return keyword.

Member variables and functions may be prefixed with a visibility keyword. The valid visibility keywords are public, protected, and private. Public means that the item may be accessed anywhere, by any class. Protected items are only visible to inheriting classes and the defining class. Private items are visible only in the defining class. Member variables must have their visibility declared, while the visibility keywords are optional for functions. Functions default to public if the visibility keyword is omitted.

Access to variables and functions is made available through the -> (arrow) operator. Inside of a class definition, the special variable $this means the current instance of the class. Thus, to access member variables and methods from inside of the class, you use the $this->varname or $this->methodname($args) syntax.

Classes can have constructors. A constructor is what is called when you create a new instance of the class with the new keyword. A constructor is a method with the name __construct(). If you wish to call the constructor of the class from which the current class inherits, call parent::__construct() from within the child class.

In order to use inheritance in PHP, use the extends keyword. The following example demonstrates a simple object-oriented example. Note that as each class extends and builds upon a base class, the definition becomes more specific. Starting with the general notion of a "Shape," a "Polygon" is then built on top of it. Finally, a special 3-sided "Polygon" (a "Triangle") is created. Near the end of this example, an instance of the Triangle class is created using the new keyword. The Draw function of that object is then called:

```
<?php
  class Shape {
    function __construct() {
      //this is the constructor
    }
    public abstract function Draw();
  }

  class Polygon extends Shape {
    private $NumSides;
    function __construct($sides) {
      $this->NumSides = $sides;
    }
    function Draw() {
      echo "Polygon with $this->NumSides sides.\n";
    }
  }

  class Triangle extends Polygon {
    function __construct() {
      $this->NumSides = 3;
    }
    function Draw() {
      echo "Triangle\n";
    }
  }

  $tri = new Triangle();
  $tri->Draw();
?>
```

Methods and member variables of classes can also be defined as static. Static methods and members are able to be called without first creating an instance of the class. Notice how in the following example, no instance of the SiteValues class is created; the method is called just by referencing the class name followed by the name of the method:

```
<?php
  class SiteValues {
    private static $domain = 'www.blpress.com';
    public static function getDomain() {
      return self::$domain;
    }
  }
  echo SiteValues::getDomain();
?>
```

Interfaces

PHP also supports interface-based polymorphism. An interface is simply a set of method definitions that an implementing class agrees to create. Unlike base classes used with inheritance, interfaces that do not specify implementation details—they just define method signatures. Classes which implement interfaces do so with the implements keyword.

Consider the following example, which defines an iSitePage as interface for a page template. Homepage is a concrete class that implements the interface and provides details for the methods defined in the interface. Finally, a RenderPage function expects an object that implements iSitePage and creates an entire HTML page from it:

```
<?php
  interface iSitePage {
    public function getTitle();
    public function getBody();
  }
  class Homepage implements iSitePage {
    public function getTitle() {
      return 'Welcome to the home page.';
    }
    public function getBody() {
      return '<p>This is the body of my homepage.</p>';
    }
  }
```

```
    function RenderPage($sitepage) {
        $s = "<html><head>";
        $s .= "<title>{$sitepage->getTitle()}</title></head>";
        $s .= "<body>{$sitepage->getBody()}</body></html>";
        return $s;
    }

    echo RenderPage(new Homepage());
?>
```

Conditionals and Flow Control

Conditionals are used in code to control the flow of the application. By evaluating the values of variables at runtime, conditionals allow you to optionally execute one block of code or another. Conditionals are the foundation on which you may build functionality into your applications.

If, elseif, else

In PHP, there are a few ways to do conditionals. The most commonly seen syntax follows that of C:

```
<?php
    function getRole($username) {
        if($username == 'root') {
            return 'root';
        }
        elseif(($username == 'bob')
            || ($username == 'john')) {
            return 'owner';
        }
        else {
            return 'user';
        }
    }
?>
```

An alternate (and less common) if/else syntax also exists. The code below is functionally equivalent to the code above:

```
<?php
  function getRole($username) {
    if($username == 'root'):
      return 'root';
    elseif(($username == 'bob')
      || ($username == 'john')):
      return 'owner';
    else:
      return 'user';
    endif;
  }
?>
```

Finally, there is a concise if/else syntax—referred to as the ternary operator—which is especially useful during variable assignment. The syntax is:

```
condition ? code_to_evaluate_if_true : code_to_evaluate_if_false;.
```

The snippet below will return "Billing" if the argument to the function is 1, otherwise it will return "Shipping."

```
<?php
  function addressType($i) {
    return $i == 1 ? 'Billing' : 'Shipping';
  }
?>
```

Switch

The switch statement can be used to compare the value of a variable against a set of specific values. It is similar to a series of if/elseif/else statements. The example below shows how the value of $cond is compared to different values. The break statement inside of a switch means to stop comparing and exit out of the switch statement. The following example has a function that evaluates a username parameter and determines the appropriate role group for the specified user.

Notice how there is no break statement after the bob case. It will cascade down to the john case and they will both return the same role type of owner:

```
<?php
  function getRole($username) {
    $role = 'user';
    switch($username) {
      case 'root':
        $role = 'root';
        break;
      case 'bob':
      case 'john':
        $role = 'owner';
        break;
      default:
        $role = 'user';
    }
    return $role;
  }
?>
```

Loops

Loops are used to execute a block of code multiple times. A condition is evaluated after each iteration of the loop; if that condition is true, the loop continues executing. If it is false, the loop breaks and the code following the loop executes. Loops are often used to perform work on every item in an array.

For loop

The syntax of a for loop is shown here:

```
for(initializations; continue condition; evaluate every iteration)
 { statement }
```

The following example creates an array containing three elements. It uses a for loop to iterate over each of the elements printing the value to the console.

```
<?php
  $a = array('alpha', 'beta', 'omega');
  for($i = 0; $i < count($a); $i++) {
    echo "$a[$i]\n";
  }
?>
```

Foreach loop

A foreach loop is similar to a for loop. If you need to do something to each element in an array, a foreach loop is a good choice. The syntax is:

```
foreach(array as $value)
  { statement }
```

If the array is keyed and you need to know the key name:

```
foreach(array as $key => $value)
  { statement }
```

The following example again creates an array containing three elements:

```
<?php
  $a = array('alpha', 'beta', 'omega');
  foreach($a as $value) {
    echo "$value\n";
  }
?>
```

The previous example loops over each value of the array and prints the value to the console. The output from the above code is:

```
alpha
beta
omega
```

The following example demonstrates the key/value syntax:

```
<?php
  //create an array with a few elements
  $a = array('one' => 'alpha', 'two' => 'beta', 'three' => 'omega');
  //loop over each element in the array
  foreach($a as $key => $value) {
    //print the value at index $i
    echo "$key holds $value\n";
  }
?>
```

The preceding snippet outputs:

```
one holds alpha
two holds beta
three holds omega
```

The loop variables used in a foreach (the key and/or value) are copies, not references. Thus, changes made inside of the loop using those variables will not be visible outside of the loop. Following the preceding example, a change such as $value = 'newvalue' won't be visible outside of the loop. To modify the actual array, use $a[$key] = 'newvalue' instead.

Do-while loop

A do-while loop will always execute at least once before evaluating the continue condition. If the condition evaluates to true, the loop will continue executing:

```
<?php
  //return an array of the first 3 or $num
  //Fibonacci numbers (whichever is greater)
  function fib($num) {
    $fib[0] = 0;
    $fib[1] = 1;
    $i = 2;
    do {
      $fib[$i] = $fib[$i-1] + $fib[$i-2];
    } while (++$i < $num);

    return $fib;
  }
?>
```

While loop

A while loop is very similar to a do-while loop except that the condition is evaluated *before* entering the loop:

```
<?php
  //build an HTML drop down list of all values between 1 and 100
  function getAgeDdl() {
    $s = "<select name=\"age\">\n";
    $i = 0;
    while ($i++ < 100) {
      $s .= "<option value=\"$i\">$i</value>\n";
    }
    $s .= "</select>\n";
    return $s;
  }
?>
```

Break and Continue

Break and continue can be used inside of loops. A break statement will exit out of the loop and immediately continue executing whatever comes after the loop. A continue statement will end the current iteration of the loop. The loop will evaluate its condition and continue looping if the condition dictates that it do so.

Continue and break both take an optional numeric argument that tells it how many levels of nested loops to continue or break out of. Specifying no argument is the same as specifying 1.

Exceptions

PHP 5 introduced a try/catch style of exception handling, similar to that of other languages such as Java and C#:

```
<?php
  try {
    $error = 'An error has occured';
    throw new Exception($error);
    echo 'Code in the try block that follows a thrown exception won\'t execute.';
  } catch (Exception $e) {
    echo 'Exception message: ' . $e->getMessage() . "\n";
  }
  echo 'No errors here!';
?>
```

A try block must be followed by at least one catch block. Developers may extend the base Exception class to create more specific and detailed exception handling. The catch block would catch a specific type of Exception, rather than the base class Exception.

Values, References, and Scope

PHP 5, by default, passes objects by reference and everything else by value. You may tell PHP explicitly to pass by reference with the & operator. References are *symbol table aliases*, not pointers. By using a reference, two differently named variables can point to the same variable contents.

The example below illustrates this point. The two functions, Value and Reference, do nearly the same thing but have very different consequences:

```
<?php
  function Value($temp) {
    for($i = 0; $i < count($temp); $i++) {
      $temp[$i] = "changed";
    }
  }

  function Reference(&$temp) {
    for($i = 0; $i < count($temp); $i++) {
      $temp[$i] = "changed";
    }
  }

  $var = array(0, 1, 2, 3, 4);
  Value($var);
  print_r($var);
  Reference($var);
  print_r($var);
?>
```

The previous code snippet will output:

```
Array
(
  [0] => 0
  [1] => 1
  [2] => 2
  [3] => 3
  [4] => 4
)
Array
(
  [0] => changed
  [1] => changed
  [2] => changed
  [3] => changed
  [4] => changed
)
```

Notice the ampersand (&) before the parameter of the Reference function. The ampersand means that a reference to the array will be passed into the function instead of a copy of the array. Since the reference actually points to the same variable contents, the modifications remain visible outside of the scope of the function. Since a copy of the array is passed to Value(), the modifications don't "stick" outside of the scope of the function.

Variables defined in the global scope are not visible inside of functions. To put it another way, functions introduce their own local scope, inside of which globals are not available. Consider the following code snippet:

```
<?php
  //defined globally
  $username = 'bob';
  function Scope() {
    //a locally scoped (and undefined) variable
    echo $username;
  }
  //Execute the Scope function.
  Scope();
?>
```

The code will produce no output, since $username is defined in the global scope. Inside of the function, $username takes on an entirely new meaning; its value is undefined at the time it is echoed.

Web Forms & PHP

As mentioned earlier in this chapter, PHP is primarily used as a Web scripting language. The following example illustrates a basic Web form using PHP:

```
<html>
  <head>
    <title>Student info</title>
  </head>
  <body>
    <h1><?php echo htmlspecialchars($_GET['name']); ?></h1>
    <form action="<?php echo $_SERVER['PHP_SELF']; ?>" method="get">
      Name: <input name="name" type="text" value="<?php echo
      htmlspecialchars($_GET['name']); ?>" />
      <input name="button1" type="submit" value="Add Student" />
    </form>
  </body>
</html>
```

In this example, any text that is put into the text box will show up inside of the <h1> tag and stay in the text box when the submit value is clicked. First, notice that the form uses method="get". Inside of the form, there are two inputs: a "text" (name) and a "submit" (button1). When the form is submitted, PHP provides an easy way to get the values of those form inputs by using the special $_GET array. If this form was submitted with a POST action, the special array would be $_POST. There is also a built-in array called $_REQUEST that includes all of the get, post, and cookie variables in one.

Since the text input is named student, we can get the value of (the text contained inside of) that text box with $_GET['student'].

Notice that—before outputting the value with echo—the input is passed through the htmlspecialchars() function. This ensures that characters that have special meaning in HTML get converted to their HTML-safe representations (< becomes <, > becomes >, & becomes &, double-quotes become "). This ensures that not only will the page render properly, but also that malicious users trying to input script blocks will not be able to succeed.

The form action is set to $_SERVER['PHP_SELF']. $_SERVER is a special variable array that holds lots of useful information about the currently executing script. The PHP_SELF value is the name of the currently executing script from the remote Web user's perspective. This provides a nice way to create a form whose action is itself without having to worry about the name of the file. Table 11-1 shows some of the more commonly used items in the array.

Table 11-1. Useful Values of $_SERVER Array

Value	Description
PHP_SELF	The name of the currently executing script from the remote Web user's point of view.
Argv	An array of command line arguments passed to the script.
Argc	Number of command line arguments passed to the script.
HTTP_HOST	The host name part of the script's URL.
HTTP_USER_AGENT	The client's user agent (Web browser).
REMOTE_ADDR	The IP address of the client.
PHP_AUTH_USER	The username if using PHP and basic auth.

Cookies

Cookies are a simple way to store persistent data on a remote user's computer. They are typically used to store login information or machine-specific preferences. To set a cookie, use the setcookie() function. The setcookie function requires at least a name and a value:

```
<?php
  setcookie('mycookie', 'mycookievalue');
?>
```

Setcookie() returns a Boolean indicating whether or not the cookie was set successfully. Setcookie has some optional parameters that control the cookie's lifespan and accessibility:

```
setcookie( string name [, string value [, int expire [, string path [, string domain
  [, bool secure]]]]] )
```

Name and value are straightforward. The expire parameter is a Unix timestamp (epoch time), usually created from time() or mktime(). To set a cookie that expires in seven days, set the expire parameter to "time()+60*60*24*7".

Path is the location on the server for which the cookie is valid. Set it to '/' to make it valid for the entire site; set it to '/path/' to restrict it to /path/ and all subdirectories.

Domain is the domain on which the cookie is valid. Set it to '.mydomain.com' to make it valid on all subdomains of mydomain.com. Set it to 'www.mydomain.com' to make it valid only on that specific domain.

Secure is a Boolean that when set to true ensures that the cookie will only be transmitted over encrypted (HTTPS) channels. If this parameter is omitted, it defaults to false. To unset or delete a cookie, set the expiration to a value in the past.

Note that cookies do not become visible until the next loading of the page. Thus, if you try to set a cookie and, in the same request, get the value of that cookie from the $_COOKIE array, it will be an old value (or NULL if you are setting the cookie for the first time).

File Uploads

Sometimes it is necessary to have the remote user upload a file. Continuing the earlier example, a user will be able to add a picture of themselves in addition to supplying their name.

```
<?php
  if(count($_FILES) > 0) {
    move_uploaded_file($_FILES['picture']['tmp_name'],
    'images/uploaded.jpg');
  }
?>

<html>
  <head>
    <title>Student info</title>
  </head>
  <body>
    <h1><?php echo htmlspecialchars($_REQUEST['name']); ?></h1>

<?php
    if(count($_FILES) > 0) {
      echo "<img src=\"images/uploaded.jpg\" alt=\"uploaded pic\" />";
    }
?>
    <form enctype="multipart/form-data" action="<?php echo
    $_SERVER['PHP_SELF']; ?>" method="post">
    <input name="MAX_FILE_SIZE" type="hidden" value="10000000" />
    Name: <input name="name" type="text" value="<?php echo
    htmlspecialchars($_REQUEST['text1']); ?>" /><br />
    Picture: <input name="picture" type="file" />
    <input name="button1" type="submit" value="Add Student" />
    </form>
  </body>
</html>
```

There are a few requirements for this to work:

- The enctype attribute of the form tag is required with the value "multipart/form-data" as shown.
- The form method must be post (get will not work).
- The hidden input named MAX_FILE_SIZE (specified in bytes) must come before the file type input.

Once the file has been uploaded, it may be accessed in the $_FILES array. The $_FILES array is keyed by the name of the file input. In the example above, it would be $_FILES['picture']. That item contains another array with the following keys:

- ['name'] is the original name of the file from the client's machine.
- ['type'] is the MIME content-type of the uploaded file.
- ['tmp_name'] is the full path to the location on the Web server where the file is temporarily being stored. The file will be deleted when the script finishes executing.
- ['error'] is an error code. 0 indicates success.
- ['size'] is the size of the posted file in bytes.

In the above example, notice that the form now uses action="post" instead of get. Additionally, the MAX_FILE_SIZE hidden field, as well as the input type="file", have been added. Some important code has been added to handle the file upload: the move_uploaded_file() function is called to the move the file from the temp location to a location that is visible on the Web. As a security measure, this PHP function verifies that the file is actually a file that was uploaded during this request. You may also use is_uploaded_file() if you don't need to move it, or realpath() to see if the path specified by the user is in fact a valid path.

You should also be wary of invalid client-supplied filenames (that include invalid characters, for example) that could cause problems on your server. Remember, you must plan for the fact that malicious users *will* attempt to attack your Web site.

Finally, if a file has been uploaded, an <img> tag is inserted into the HTML to display the uploaded image.

Session Handling

Sessions provide a means of creating persistent storage across subsequent page requests for a given user. This allows you to create a more dynamic and custom Web site to attract visitors.

Amending an earlier example, instead of simply printing out the visitor's name in an <h1> tag, we'll also store it in the session. That way, as the visitor navigates around the multiple pages of our site, we'll always have their name, ready to display:

```
<?php
  //required call to enable the session
  session_start();
  if(isset($_GET['name'])) {
    //copy the name into the session for later use
    $_SESSION['name'] = $_GET['name'];
  }
?>

<html>
  <head>
    <title>Student info</title>
  </head>
  <body>
    <h1><?php echo htmlspecialchars($_SESSION['name']); ?></h1>
    <form action="<?php echo $_SERVER['PHP_SELF']; ?>" method="get">
    Name: <input name="name" type="text" value="<?php echo
    htmlspecialchars($_SESSION['name']); ?>" />
    <input name="button1" type="submit" value="Add Student" />
    </form>
  </body>
</html>
```

The session is very simple to use. Simply enable session tracking with a call to session_start(). After that, you may use the $_SESSION array to store and retrieve persistent values. If this user, after setting his name, navigates to another page that also uses the $_SESSION['name'] variable, the value will “stick.”

Sessions store a unique session identifier in a cookie. That identifier is used to find files stored on the server (usually in /tmp on UNIX variants), which stores the data. Data in the session is only valid for the duration of the session.cache_expire configuration option.

For a complete description of session features in PHP, see the official documentation at http://www.php.net/session.

Looking Forward

PHP is an open source language that is being actively developed. Community feedback drives the effort, so your feedback can be incorporated into the next PHP release. If you think you have found a bug, check the bug database at http://bugs.php.net to see if it has already been reported. If not, report it and contribute to the generation of a stronger code base.

At the time of this writing, the most recent version is PHP 5.0.4, and there are typically minor bug fix releases every couple of months, so it may be outdated by the time you read this.

The PHP community has been growing steadily since its inception in 1995, and continues to grow today. According to statistics at http://www.php.net/usage.php, the number of Web domains using PHP has grown from 2 million to around 20 million between 2000 and 2005. See http://www.php.net to get involved and answer any additional questions you have.

Chapter 12

JavaScript

JavaScript is a user-friendly object scripting language designed for creating live online applications that link together objects and resources on both clients and servers. JavaScript is designed for use by enterprise application developers to dynamically script the behavior of objects running on either the client or the server and HTML page authors to reach a very high level of interaction between the user and the document.

JavaScript can be run on the client-side that processes data like validations without further communication with the server. In addition, the language can be run on the server-side, allowing things like database access. A page might contain scripts that run on both the client and the server. JavaScript is related to Java in its C++ object flavor. JavaScript is object-based language and is platform independent like Java, but unlike Java, JavaScript is loosely typed.

Client-side JavaScript exposes objects and properties related to the browser's window, forms, links, etc. Most Web servers provide support for JavaScript (or JScript), allowing server-side scripting such as Netscape Web servers and Microsoft Internet Information Server (IIS).

There have been several formal versions of JavaScript including 1.0, 1.5, and 2.0. Version 1.3 is supported by versions 4, 5, and 6 browsers. Version 1.4 is not supported by browsers. It is used only on Netscape servers. Version 1.5 is the same as the latest ECMAScript.

Fast Facts

- JavaScript is case sensitive (unlike VBScript).
- JavaScript can be embedded in HTML as statements and functions using the <script> tag:

```
<script language="JavaScript"> [Statements, Functions] </script>
<script language="JavaScript" src="file1.js"> [Additional] </script>
```

- The extension of a JavaScript source file is ". js" and it resides on the Web Server. It contains the common functions and statements. A referenced external script is interpreted as if it precedes the local script.
- JavaScript can also be embedded as event handlers using HTML tag attributes:

```
<a href="www.sun.com" onMouseOver="javascript:thankyou();">Thanks</a>.
```

- JavaScript can also be embedded as short statements resembling URLs. Below, thankyou() is a JavaScript function:

```
<a href="javascript:thankyou();">Thanks</a>.
```

- There are two types of comments in JavaScript, // to begin a short comment, and /* ... */ to enclose a comment in multiple lines. In addition, the HTML comment tags may be used to shield a browser that does not interpret JavaScript.
- JavaScript programs may be run on the client or the server. JavaScript is interpreted on the client, but needs to be compiled when run on the server. Not all servers support server-side JavaScript.
- JavaScript is loosely typed. The type of a variable is not specified in the variable declaration. All variables are declared using the keyword var.
- Each statement in JavaScript should end with a semicolon (;). While the JavaScript interpreter will assume one even if it is left out, it is good practice to include them.
- You can use single quotes and double quotes to delimit strings. Two strings can be concatenated together using the plus sign (+).
- The equals sign operator is written as '==' when comparing values, and as '=' when assigning values.
- Server-side JavaScript is an extended version of JavaScript that enables back-end access to databases, file systems, and servers. This includes the Netscape Enterprise Server. This is embedded between <SERVER> ...</SERVER>. This is compiled into byte code (.web) unlike client-side JavaScript.

Sample JavaScript

JavaScript can be executed either on the client (Web browser) or on the server (Web server). The JavaScript code, when run on the client, is embedded within the HTML code of a Web page, and is used to create dynamic page content. The following code is an example of Web page that uses client-side JavaScript:

```
<html>
  <head>
    <script language="JavaScript">
    <!--
    // Declare global variables
    var globalVar1;
    // Define functions
    function checkNum(num) {
      if(num > 10){
        alert ("Sorry. Number must be less than 10");
      }else{
        confirm("You have entered " + num);
      }
    }
    //-->
    </script>
  </head>
  <body>
    <h1>Welcome to this Web Site! </h1><br>
    <form>Enter Your Number: <input type = "Text" Name = "txtNum">
    <input type="button" Name="chkNbr" value="Check Number" onClick =
    "checkNum(this.form.txtNum.value)"> </form>
  </body>
</html>
```

Main Components of a JavaScript Page

While every JavaScript application is different, a few consistencies are described here.

Variables

These are defined with the var keyword, and JavaScript variables are loosely typed. No type is specified when creating the variable, and the language handles all type conversions automatically.

<script>

All the client-side JavaScript code must be enclosed in the HTML <script> tags.

Functions

JavaScript functions can take in arguments and return a value as well, although they need not return a value. In addition, more arguments may be passed to the function than are defined, as JavaScript stores all arguments in a special array.

Objects

There are a number of built-in objects with useful functions that may be used in JavaScript programming. The objects supplied for server-side scripts are different from the objects supplied for client-side scripts.

Events

There are a number of events that are triggered by the actions of a user with a Web browser. These events can in turn be used by a JavaScript program to execute certain pieces of code when a certain event occurs.

Basics of JavaScript

JavaScript uses built-in objects with no inheritance, while JavaScript is platform independent, similar to Java. A JavaScript application can run on a client, like a Web browser, or it can run on a server.

When run on a Web server, the JavaScript code must be compiled with the executable file stored on the server. The file is compiled into another file with a .web extension that contains the HTML and the executable script code. Netscape provides a command line compiler, JavaScript Application Compiler, which can be used to compile files. When a client browser makes a request to the server, the script executes and helps form the reply HTML to be sent back to the browser. Server-side scripts are commonly used to access data from a database or to maintain state information during a particular client's visit to a Web site.

When run on a Web client, the JavaScript is often embedded in the HTML code of a Web page. When the client Web browser receives a Web page to display, it parses out the JavaScript by looking for the <script> tag and executing the code. Client-side scripts are often used to validate input to a Web page, because it is able to immediately notify the user of errors without generating a round trip to the Web server.

Figure 12-1. Client-side and Server-side JavaScript

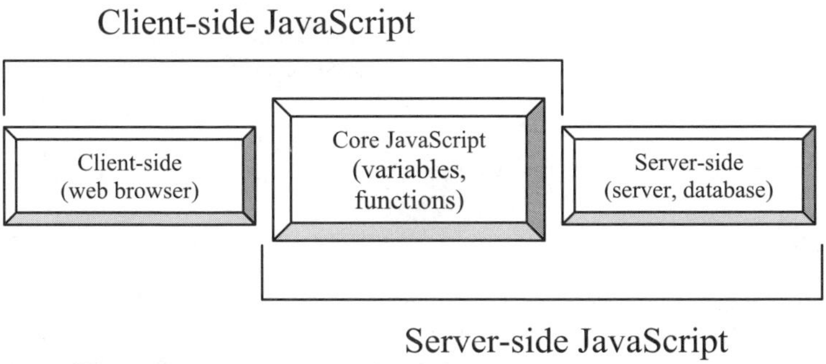

Data Types

JavaScript supports a relatively small number of data types, but its methods and objects compensate for that. As opposed to other languages, a variable data type is not declared explicitly, but rather implicitly according to its initial value assignment. The four different data types in JavaScript are described next.

Number

JavaScript supports most numeric data types, including integers and floating point values. Any numeric value without quotes is a number. However, at the lowest level, the language actually stores all numeric types as floating point values, but converts them to the chosen type at a higher level. Integers, decimal, octal, and hexadecimal values are all stored as floating point values. An octal literal always begins with a leading zero, while a hexadecimal literal always begins with a leading zero x (0X or 0x). Floating point values can include decimals, exponents (e or E), and a positive or negative sign (+ or -) in front of the exponent. For example, *232*, *2.323*, and *2.3e-8* are all valid numbers. The initial value is 0.

String

Enclosing characters between quotation marks, either single or double quotes, makes a string. If the string contains single quotes, the string should be enclosed in double quotes, and vice versa. Alternatively, the escape sequence for a single or double quote (\' or \") can be used within a quoted string to represent the quotation characters. The initial value is "".

Boolean

A Boolean data type holds the value of either True or False. The numeric translation of '1' for True and '0' for False is also acceptable. The initial value is False.

Null

The null value is often used to initialize variables that do not have any meaning. The null value is automatically converted to initial value of other data types. JavaScript interpreter uses the null value on two occasions:

- Built-in functions return null under certain circumstances.
- Non-existent properties evaluate to null.

Variables

All variables must be declared using the var keyword. You can omit the var keyword, but scope confusion often arises (see the *Scope* section), so it is best to always use var. No matter what data type is to be stored in the variable, they are all declared simply by using the var keyword. Once declared, data types can be changed freely, and JavaScript handles the conversion internally. A variable may be declared, assigned a numeric value first, and then immediately assigned a string value and JavaScript handles it all:

```
var myVar;
myVar = 'Hello Reader';
document.write(myVar);
myVar = 2.09;
document.write(myVar);
```

In JavaScript, there are strict rules for naming variables. The first character of an identifier must be either a letter or an underscore (_). All other characters can be letters, underscores, or digits (0-9). An identifier cannot be one of the reserved words. The $ character is not legal in some of the Netscape versions and it is recommended to avoid using it.

Scope

A variable that is created within a function is a local variable, with a scope that stops at that function. If a variable is declared outside a function, it is a global variable and can be accessed from anywhere within the JavaScript application. When a local variable is declared omitting the var keyword, the variable is actually a global variable, and has a scope outside that function. This is why var should always be used when declaring variables.

If a global and local variable exist with the same name, the local variable is accessed while within the local function, and the global variable is accessed when outside the function.

Arrays

An array is a collection of values that are referenced through an index of the same variable name. An array is an object of the Array type, which is a JavaScript built-in object. There are a number of ways to create a new array. Since JavaScript supports dynamic arrays, the number of elements in the array need not be stated at the time of creation. A new array is created like any object is created, by using the new keyword:

```
var myArray = new Array();
```

The number of elements in the array may be passed as a parameter to the Array constructor, but it is not necessary. Actually, JavaScript 1.2 does not accept a size upon creation, and passing a value into the constructor causes that value to be stored as the first element of the array. All elements of an array are initially null. The values of the array can be specified at creation time, as shown here:

```
var myArray = new Array('Hello', 1, 99, 'Books');
```

Even more direct than this method is the use of array brackets, foregoing the new keyword, and entering the elements into the array:

```
var myArray = ['Hello', 1, 99, 'Books'];
```

Notice that the first element of an array is numbered 0.The individual elements of an array may be accessed using the traditional numeric index and square brackets, but also in a way similar to a hash table using key/value pairs. To set the value of the third element equal to 5, the following method could be used:

```
myArray[2] = 5;
```

JavaScript also supports a hash-table (associative arrays) quality in that a value can be stored with a key string, and the value of the element is then accessed by specifying the key string, as shown here:

```
myArray['myKeyValue'] = 5;
```

JavaScript arrays may contain more than one dimension. The elements of these multidimensional arrays are accessed using multiple array brackets. JavaScript does not support true multidimensional arrays, but it does allow you to approximate them with arrays of arrays. To access a data element in an array of arrays, simply use the [] operator twice:

```
var multiArray = new Array([0,1,2], [3,4,5,6], [7,8,9]);
var myValue = multiArray[2][1];
```

You can build a multi-dimensional array as deep as you want, but they can be as unreadable and confusing as they are useful.

Control Structures

This section describes code flow control constructs, including loops and conditional statements. An integral part of a code flow in JavaScript applications is the use of dialog boxes. The alert (*message*) provides the capability to display a short *message* in a separate dialog box with an 'OK' button. The confirm(*message*) similarly displays a brief *message*, and a 'Cancel' button, in addition to the 'OK' button. This dialog returns a value of true if the user chooses 'OK'. The prompt (*message*[,*inputDefault*]) dialog displays the *message* in the dialog box and provides an input field with an optional default value to display. This dialog also returns true if the user chooses 'OK'.

if...else

The if...else structure is used to test a condition and react accordingly. If the Boolean condition tested is True, block1 will execute. Else, block2 will execute:

```
if (condition) {
  // block1
} else {
  //block2
}
```

An else if statement may be used in place of nested if...else statements:

```
if (condition1) {
  // block1
} else if (condition2) {
  // block2
} else {
  // block1
}
```

switch

The switch statement can be used in place of multiple if...else statements. The value of expression is compared against each of the labels of the statement. When a match is found, the following statements are executed. A break statement should be included after each case, otherwise, execution will continue with the following case statements.

A default case can be included to execute in the event that the expression does not match any of the cases. Note that the *expression* and the test values may be string values that get compared, character by character:

```
switch (expression) {
   case label1:
      statement1;
      break;
   default:
      statement3;
}
```

In C and C++, all of the case values must be the same type as the switch value. You cannot switch on the contents of a string. All case values must be unique. In JavaScript, there is no such restriction. The first matching case value is recognized, regardless of duplicates.

for Loop

The for loop is used to execute a statement or group of statements for a known number of repetitions:

```
for (initialization; condition; operation) {
   // block1
}
```

while Loop

The while loop is used to execute a statement or group of statements for an unknown number of repetitions. In order to avoid an infinite loop, a variable in the *expression* should be modified in the loop:

```
while (expression) {
   // block1
}
```

do... while Loop

This loop is a variation of the while loop in which the statements are executed first and then the expression is evaluated, thereby guaranteeing the statements will get executed at least once.

```
do {
   counterVal++;
   // block1
} while (counterVal < 10);
```

for...in Loop

This is a special loop construct in JavaScript that allows each of the enumerated properties of an object to be accessed. The for...in loop uses a variable, an object, and the keyword in. The property name of the *object* specified that is being accessed is temporarily assigned to the *variable* on the left of the in keyword. The loop continues until each property has been accessed:

```
for (variable in object){
  // block1
}
```

break, continue

In each loop, the break statement will cause execution to jump out of the current loop or structure and continue execution immediately following the statement. The continue statement, if called during a looping construct, will cause execution to jump to the next loop iteration. Usually, that means that a Boolean condition will have to be tested again before the next iteration begins.

with

The with command is provided to make coding a little easier. When assigning properties to an object, the long full path name of a particular object can be omitted when the with keyword is used, and instead included only one time in parenthesis:

```
with (document.form) {
  theColor.value="BLUE";
  theSize.value="23";
}
```

Functions

A function groups a sequence of statements to perform a specific task. A function can be passed in values to be operated upon, and it can also return values to the caller of the function. A function is defined using the keyword function followed by the name of the function:

```
function myAddition(arg1, arg2) {
  return arg1 + arg2;
}
```

In order to call that function, or execute the code of a function, the function name is written followed by the arguments to the function in parentheses. Some functions can return a value out of the function back to the caller. Since

JavaScript is loosely typed, it is not necessary to specify the variable type in the function definition, just the name.

Additionally, JavaScript doesn't require that the number of arguments in the function definition match the number passed in when calling a function. This is because all arguments can be accessed through a default array. The array is always called *function_name.arguments[]*, where the actual function name is substituted for *function_name*. A recursive function is usually one that calls itself. It is similar to a loop with or without a terminating condition. The factorial is a classic recursive algorithm.

Objects

An object type is a group of related procedures and properties. An object type in JavaScript consists of a constructor function, object properties, and object methods. JavaScript provides a number of built-in object types, including Array, Date, Math, and many others (see *Built-In Object* section). In addition, JavaScript provides a way to create new object types. A basic object type in JavaScript is much like a constructor in other object-oriented languages. It includes a function definition, any arguments that are passed in, and properties and methods defined using the this keyword:

```
function House (color, length, width) {
  this.color = color;
  this.length = length;
  this.width = width;
  this.getArea = getArea; // method
}
```

The this keyword always refers to the current object. The above function actually creates an object type called House with three properties – color, length, and width. To create a House object, specify the object name, use the new keyword, and pass the arguments to the object type function:

```
myHouse = new House ('red', 20, 40);
```

This is consistent with the method used to create any object using the new keyword, like an Array object. The properties of an object are then accessed using the dot modifier (.):

```
document.write(myHouse.color);
```

Methods

Object types can contain properties and methods. A method is a function that is attached to an object. First, the method is defined like any other function using the function keyword and then it is assigned to the object type using the this keyword.

Suppose, for example, we create the following method:

```
function getArea() {
  return this.length * this.width;
}
```

The this reference refers to the object to which the method belongs. The getArea function then belongs to the House object type, and that function, or method as it can now be called, can be invoked using the format *object.method_name (params)*. The method must be called on an actual object, not just the object type, using the dot modifier (.):

```
myHouse = new House('red', 20, 20);
var houseSize = myHouse.getArea();
```

Adding Properties

A prototype is a property of any object created with the keyword new. Properties can always be added to an object once it is created, simply by moving the property to the other side of the equals sign:

```
myHouse.age = 14;
```

The above line will add the property age to the myHouse object. However, this line affects only the myHouse object. Future objects created will not have an age property, because the change was made to the object, not the object type. In order to add the property to the object *type*, the prototype property of the object type is used:

```
House.prototype.age = 0;
```

Now, each House object that is created using the new keyword will have the property 'age' with an initial value of '0'. Note that while JavaScript allows you to *prototype* prebuilt objects, this only applies to those that are created with the new keyword. Prototypes refer not only to properties, but also to an object's methods. The object prototypes refer to instances of the object created before the definition of the prototype, as well as the instances that are created later.

Events

Events are generated in a Web page when the user does something, usually like clicking a button or moving the mouse over a *hotspot*. The power of these events can be harnessed in JavaScript, coding the actions to occur as a result of particular events. This occurs by using an *event handler*, which is code to execute on occurrence of an event. Event handlers have the same name as the event they handled, preceded by the word 'on'. For instance, the event handler for a click event is called onClick.

Event handlers are defined in HTML tags by including the event handler as an attribute to an HTML tag and specifying the JavaScript code to execute in quotation marks. The following code will cause a JavaScript function, verifyFunct, to be executed when the user clicks the button:

```
<input type="button" value="check Values" onClick="verifyFunct()">
```

Built-In Objects

While the list of built-in objects differs for client-side and server-side scripts, there are a few useful objects that are consistent across JavaScript, and they are described in this section.

Date

The Date object type takes a variety of different parameters in its constructor, creating a date object with the new keyword. JavaScript handles dates similarly to Java. An empty constructor creates today's date. Due to a bug in Netscape Navigator 2.0x on Mac, the Date object represents current date one day into the future:

```
var today = new Date();
var bday = new Date(72, 03, 02);
```

Following is a list of useful methods on the Date object. In addition to these, there are methods used to manipulate Universal Time:

getDate()	Returns the date of a Date object (from 1-31).
getDay()	Returns the day of a Date object (from 0-6. 0=Sunday, 1=Monday, etc.).
getMonth()	Returns the month of a Date object (from 0-11. 0=January, 1=February, etc.).
getFullYear()	Returns the year of a Date object (four digits).
getYear()	Returns the year of a Date object (from 0-99).
getHours()	Returns the hour of a Date object (from 0-23).
getMinutes()	Returns the minute of a Date object (from 0-59).
getSeconds()	Returns the second of a Date object (from 0-59).
getMilliseconds()	Returns the millisecond of a Date object (from 0-999).
getTime()	Returns the number of milliseconds since midnight 1/1-1970.
leapYear()	Returns true if year of the date Object is leap year.
parse()	Returns a string that holds the number of milliseconds since January (01 1970 00:00:00).
setDate()	Sets the date of the month in the Date object (from 1-31).
setFullYear()	Sets the year in the Date object (four digits).
setHours()	Sets the hour in the Date object (from 0-23).
setMilliseconds()	Sets the millisecond in the Date object (from 0-999).

setMinutes()	Sets the minute in the Date object (from 0-59).
setMonth()	Sets the month in the Date object (from 0-11. 0=January, 1=February).
setSeconds()	Sets the second in the Date object (from 0-59).
setTime()	Sets the milliseconds after 1/1-1970.
setYear()	Sets the year in the Date object (00-99).
toGMTString()	Converts the Date object to a string, set to GMT time zone.
toLocaleString()	Converts the Date object to a string, set to the current time zone.
toString()	Converts the Date object to a string.

Math

The Math object in JavaScript is based on two general elements of the language: Mathematical operators and the built-in Math object. A few of the useful properties and methods on the Math object are listed here:

LN10	Returns the natural logarithm of 10.
PI	Returns PI.
SQRT2	Returns the square root of 2.
abs(x)	Returns the absolute value of x.
ceil(x)	Returns the nearest integer greater than or equal to x.
floor(x)	Returns the nearest integer less than or equal to x.
random()	Returns a random number between 0 and 1.
round(x)	Rounds x to the nearest integer.

Number

The Number object is a built-in JavaScript object very similar to the Math object. It is different from the Math object in that Number object is dynamic one requiring a creation step, while Math object is static. Some of the useful properties on the Number object include MAX VALUE (returns the maximum numeric value represented in JavaScript), MIN_VALUE (returns the number closest to 0, approximately 2.22E -308), and Nan (returns a special value representing "Not-A-Number").

The Number object has no specific methods. You can still use the generic methods eval(), toString(), and valueOf(), which are applicable to every object. You can also use the following math-related functions:

parseInt()	Accepts a numeric string of an integer and returns its corresponding numeric value.
parseFloat()	Accepts a string and returns a numeric value without rounding off.
eval()	Accepts a numeric value or mathematical expression and returns the value it evaluates to.

String

A String object may be created using the new keyword, passing to it any string value. The length property returns the number of characters in a string. Following are some of the useful methods on the String object:

toLowerCase()	Converts a string to lower case.
toUpperCase()	Converts a string to upper case.
charAt()	Returns the character at a specified position.
concat()	Returns two concatenated strings.
indexOf()	Returns the first occurrence of a specified string inside another string. -1 if it never occurs.
replace()	Replaces some specified characters with some new specified characters.
substring()	Returns the specified characters. 4,10 returns all characters from the 4th up to, but not including, the 10th (starts at 0).
isNaN()	Evaluates an argument to determine if it is not a number or "NaN".

Array-Related Functions

Because JavaScript arrays are dynamic, there are a number of useful qualities that can be taken advantage of in JavaScript that are not provided in other languages. The length attribute of the Array object is one of these advantages. It can be modified at any time, controlling the number of elements that the array contains. Following are some of the functions useful when working with arrays:

join()	Returns all elements in the array as a string, separated by specified delimiter.
sort()	Sorts the array elements in dictionary order or using a compare function passed in.
split()	Splits a string using the delimiter and returns an array (called on a String object).

Browser Objects (Client-Side)

The default objects stem from the root objects window and navigator (for Netscape Navigator), including commonly used object types such as the document and form object. Browser objects are special objects that correspond to elements of a page. The object hierarchy is illustrated here, and the objects are described in this section:

Figure 12-2. JavaScript Object Hierarchy

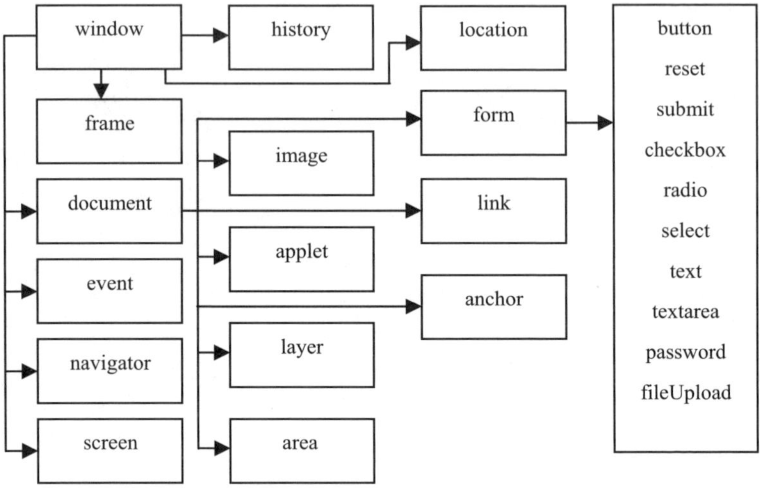

window

The window object is the top-level object of the hierarchy. It contains properties that apply to the whole window. With frames, you can display more than one HTML document in the same browser window. Each HTML document is called a frame, and each frame is independent of the others. Following are some of the useful properties and methods of the window object:

frames[]	Returns all named frames in the window.
closed	Returns true if the referenced window has been closed.
opener	Sets or returns a reference to the window that created the window.
parent	Returns the parent window.
self	Returns a reference to the current window.
top	Returns the topmost window.
alert(), confirm(), prompt	Each of these three display dialog boxes.
blur()	Removes focus from the current window.
close()	Closes the current window.
focus()	Sets focus on the current window.
open()	Opens a new browser window with the specified URL.

document

The most useful property of the window object is the document object. The document object is used to write text to the HTML page. A page has only one document object. Some of the useful collections are anchors[], applets[], forms[], and plugins[]. Following are some of the useful properties and methods of the document object:

cookie	Sets or returns all cookies associated with the document.
domain	Returns the document server's domain name.
referrer	Returns URL of the document that loaded the current document.
URL	Returns the URL of the current document.
clear()	Clears all elements in the document.
getElementById()	Returns a reference to the first object with the specified ID.
getElementsByName()	Returns a collection of objects with the specified NAME.
write()	Writes a text string to a document opened by open().
writeln()	Writes a text string followed by a new line character to a document opened by open().

history

The history object is also a property of the window object. It contains properties of the URLs the user has previously visited. The actual URLs maintained in the list cannot be extracted or modified by a script. Its useful methods are back(), forward(), and go(). It has only one property, length, which returns the number of elements in the list.

location

The location object contains properties of the current URL. If you use this location object to specify an event handler script, you must specify the full window location. Following are some of the properties and methods of the location object:

hostname	Sets or returns the hostname of the location or URL.
href	Sets or returns the entire URL.
search	Sets or returns the part of the href property that follows the question mark (?).
assign("URL")	Loads a new document.
replace("URL")	Replaces the current document with the one specified.

event

This object represents the state of an event, such as the element in which the event occurred, the state of the keyboard keys, the location of the mouse, and the state of the mouse buttons. The event object is available only during an event. You can use it only in event handlers. Following are some of the properties and methods of the event object:

clientX	Sets or returns the x-coordinate of the mouse pointer - relative to the screen.
keyCode	Sets or returns the UNICODE of the key pressed.
offsetX	Sets or returns the x-coordinate of the mouse pointer relative to object firing the event.
screenX	Sets or returns the x-coordinate of the mouse pointer - relative to the screen.
shiftKey	Returns a Boolean value that indicates the state of the SHIFT key.
x, y	Sets or returns the coordinate (in pixels) of the mouse pointer - relative to parent element.

navigator

This object contains information about the client browser plugins[]. It returns a reference to all embedded objects in the document. Following are some of the useful properties and methods of the navigator object:

appName	Returns the name of the browser.
appVersion	Returns the platform and version of the browser.
browserLanguage	Returns the current browser language.
cookieEnabled	Returns a Boolean value that specifies if cookies are enabled.
userAgent	Returns value of the user-agent header sent by the client to server.
javaEnabled()	Returns Boolean value that specifies whether the browser has Java enabled.

screen

The JavaScript runtime engine automatically creates the screen object and it contains information about the client's display screen. Following are some of the useful properties of the screen object:

availHeight	Returns the height of the display screen - excluding the Windows Taskbar.
availWidth	Returns the width of the display screen - excluding the Windows Taskbar.
colorDepth	Returns the bit depth of the color palette on the destination device or buffer.
height	Returns height of the display screen.
width	Returns width of the display screen.

form

The form object(s) of a Web page are used to submit values to the server. The form[] array allows each form to be accessed in numeric order, with the first form called form[0], the second form[1], etc. Following are some of the useful properties and methods of the form object:

elements[]	Returns an array containing each element in the form.
action	Sets or returns the URL of where the input data will be submitted.
encoding	Sets or returns the MIME encoding for the form.
length	Returns the number of elements in a form.
method	Sets or returns how form data is submitted to the server ("get" or "post").
reset()	Resets the default values of all elements in the form (same as clicking the Reset button).
submit()	Submits the form (same as clicking the Submit button).

image

This object represents an HTML img element. Some of the methods are blur(), click(), and focus(). Following are some of the useful properties of the image object:

isMap	Sets or returns a Boolean value that specifies if the image is a server-side image map.
src	Sets or returns the URL of the image.

applet

This object represents an HTML applet element. The applet element is used to place executable content on a page. Following are some of the useful properties of the applet object:

code	Sets or returns the URL of the file containing a compiled Java class.
codeBase	Sets or returns the URL of the component.
form	Returns a reference to the applet object's parent form.

area

This object represents an area of an image-map. An image-map is an image with clickable regions. Following are some of the useful properties of the area object:

coords	Sets or returns a comma-separated list of lengths that defines the clickable area.
href	Sets or returns the entire URL.
noHref	Sets or returns if the area should be inactive.

anchor

The anchor object represents an HTML anchor element. Following are some of the useful properties and methods of the anchor object:

href	Sets or returns the URL of the linked resource.
target	Sets or returns the window/frame where to open the target URL.
blur()	Removes focus from the link.
focus()	Gives focus to the link.

layer

JavaScript allows you to define precisely positioned, overlapping layers of transparent or opaque content. We can use JavaScript to move layers, hide them, and change the order in which they overlap. Some of the useful properties of a layer object are name, width, height, left, top, zIndex, and visibility. Some of the useful methods are offset(), moveTo(), resize(), moveAbove(), moveBelow().

frame

This object represents an HTML frame. Following are some of the useful properties and methods of the frame object. Similar objects exist for frameset and Iframe.

marginHeight	Sets or returns the top and bottom margins of the frame.
marginWidth	Sets or returns the left and right margins of the frame.
noResize	Sets or returns whether the frame can be resized.
scrolling	Sets or returns whether the frame can be scrolled.
src	Sets or returns the URL to be loaded by the frame.
blur()	Removes focus from the frame.
focus()	Gives focus to the frame.

FileUpload

For each instance of an HTML <input type="file"> tag on a form, a FileUpload object is created. All FileUpload objects are stored in the elements array of the corresponding form. The useful methods include blur(), click(), and select().

button, reset, submit

These represent corresponding buttons on an HTML form. Some of the useful methods include blur(), click(), and focus(). Following are some of the useful properties of these objects:

disabled	Sets or returns whether or not the reset button should be disabled.
tabIndex	Sets or returns the tab order for the reset button.
type	Returns the type of the form element. For a reset object it will always be "reset".
value	Sets or returns the value of the value attribute of the reset button.

text, textarea, password

These represent a text field on an HTML form. Some of the useful methods include blur(), click(), focus(), and select(). Following are some of the useful properties of these objects:

defaultValue	Sets or returns the initial value of the text field.
disabled	Sets or returns whether or not the text field should be disabled.
type	Returns the type of the form element, "text" for a text object.
value	Sets or returns the value of the value attribute of the text field.

radio

This represents radio buttons on an HTML form. Some of the useful methods include blur(), click(), focus(), and select(). Following are some of the useful properties of the radio object:

checked	Sets or returns the current state of the radio button as Boolean.
disabled	Sets or returns whether or not the radio button should be disabled.
size	Sets or returns the size of the radio button.
value	Sets or returns the value of the value attribute of the radio button.

checkbox

This represents a checkbox on an HTML form. Some of the useful methods include blur(), click(), and focus(). Following are some of the useful properties of the checkbox object:

checked	Sets or returns the current state of the checkbox (true if checked and false if not).
defaultChecked	Sets or returns the default value of the checked attribute.
disabled	Sets or returns whether or not the checkbox should be disabled.
value	Sets or returns the value of the value attribute of the checkbox.

select

This represents a selection list on an HTML form. Some of the useful methods include blur(), click(), and focus(), remove(). Following are some of the useful properties of the select object:

options	Returns an array of all the options in a dropdown list.
multiple	Sets or returns the Boolean value indicating whether multiple items can be selected.
selectedIndex	Sets or returns the index of the selected option in dropdown list.
size	Sets or returns the number of rows in the dropdown list.
value	Sets or returns the value to be returned to the server when the form is submitted.

option

This represents an option in a selection list on an HTML form. Following are some of the useful properties and methods of the option object:

defaultSelected	Sets or returns the value of the selected attribute of the option.
index	Sets or returns the position of the option in the select box.
selected	Sets or returns the current state of the option.
value	Sets or returns the value to be returned to the server when an option is selected.
click()	Simulates a mouse-click on the option.

Client Side Events

The table below lists the events that can occur on client-side objects.

Table 12-1. Client Side Event Description

Event	**Event Handler**	**Applies To**	**Occurs When**
Abort	onAbort	images	image loading is aborted
Blur	onBlur	button, anchor, checkbox, images fileupload, frames frameset, iframe, reset, password, radio , select, submit, text, window	user removes focus from object
Click	onClick	area, button, text, checkbox, select, document, fileupload images, password, radio, reset, submit	user clicks links, radio buttons

Event	Event Handler	Applies To	Occurs When
Change	onChange	select, text	user changes element
Error	onError	images, window	loading element causes error
Focus	onFocus	anchor, button, select checkbox, submit, images, fileupload, frameset, document, frames, iframe, radio, reset, password, text, window	user gives focus to object
Load	onLoad	images, links, window	user loads page
Mouseout	onMouseOut	area, document	user moves mouse out of area
Mouseover	onMouseOver	area, document	user moves mouse over link
Reset	onReset	forms	user clicks reset button
Select	onSelect	text	user selects input field
Submit	onSubmit	forms	user clicks submit button
Unload	onUnload	window	user exits page
Keypress	onKeyPress	password, text, document	an alphanumeric key is pressed in the password field
Keyup	onKeyUp	password, text, document	a key is released in the password field
Keydown	onKeyDown	password, text, document	a key is pressed down in the password field
selectStart	onSelectStart	fileupload, text, password, radio, reset submit	some text in the password field is selected
doubleClick	onDblClick	area, document	user double clicks
mouseDown	onMouseDown	button, checkbox, document	mouse down occurs
mouseUp	onMouseUp	button, checkbox, document	mouse up occurs
mouseMove	onMouseMove	document	the mouse moves
Resize	onResize	document, window	the window resizes

RegExp

A regular expression object contains the pattern of a regular expression. It has properties and methods for using that regular expression to find and replace matches in strings.

In addition to the properties of an individual regular expression object created using the RegExp constructor function, the predefined RegExp object has static properties that are set whenever any regular expression is used. The constructor function is used as follows:

```
new RegExp("pattern"[, "flags"])
```

Where pattern is the text of the regular expression, and flags, if specified, can have one of the following values: g (global match), i (ignore case), or gi (global match and ignore case). The following is an example that uses RegExp:

```
var regExp = /^[0-9]*$/;
regExp.test("98982"); // returns true.
regExp.test("abvdd"); // returns false.
```

Following are some of the important methods of the RegExp object:

exec()	Returns the match information.
test()	Returns true if matching, false if not.
match()	Returns just the first match or if no match is found returns null.
search()	Returns the index of the beginning of the match if found, -1 if not.
replace()	Returns the edited string.
split()	Returns an array splitting at the match in the string.

Implementing Cookies

An HTTP cookie is introduced to the client in an HTTP request, usually by a CGI script. There are two types of cookies - persistent cookies and session cookies. The format used when setting a cookie is:

```
Set-Cookie: name=name_val; expires=date; path=path_name;
domain=dom_name; secure.
```

Where name is the name of the cookie, expires is an optional expiration date, domain is the domain name, path is a subset of URLs in the domain for which the cookie is valid and secure specifies if the cookie is transmitted over a secure communication.

We can get the HTTP cookie back in the following format using document.cookie method. This can be parsed to get the cookie values (*value1*, *value2*..).

```
Cookie: name1=value1; name2=value2; ....
```

Debugging

Navigator and Internet Explorer indicate an error by producing an alert box with the line number and description of the problem. Common errors include:

"string is not defined" usually uninitialized variable problem.

"string is not a function" usually there is a mismatch in function name.

"unterminated string literal" usually mismatch in the quotes open and close.

"missing } after function body" usually curly braces missing.

"string is not a number" usually problem with an operator that requires a number.

"string has no property named property" did not find the property.

The JavaScript typeof function can be used to determine the data type of a variable or an object. It returns one of the following strings("number", "string", "boolean", "object", "function", "undefined").

Server-Side Objects

JavaScript that is to be run on the server is enclosed by <server> tags as opposed to <script> tags. Server-side scripts have a set of default objects to use that are provided by the Web server. The root objects are DBPool and database, and other objects are derived from these.

On the server-side, the connect() method of the database object is very useful. This method is called from a server-side script before a database can be queried. Once the database connection is no longer needed in a script, it should be disconnected using the disconnect() method. The database execute() method is used to execute the SQL string that is passed to it.

Netscape began to refer to the database access engine as *Livewire* to distinguish it from the language that the database applications are written. Livewire, the access engine, has the following characteristics:

- Provides state management capabilities.
- Is based on a standardized language (ECMA Script/JavaScript).
- Provides built-in database access via the Livewire Database Service.
- Includes the Visual Development Tool (VJS).
- Means that client and server programs can be written in JavaScript.
- Allows code reuse between client and server applications.
- Extends functionality using Java (via LiveConnect).
- Caches database connections for faster performance.
- Runs three times faster and scales better than CGI.

The following objects are available for server-side JavaScript only.

Table 12-2. Server-side JavaScript Objects

Object	Description
DbPool	To connect to a database, you should first create a pool of database connections and then access individual connections as needed. DbPool creates a pool of database Connection objects and optionally connects the objects to a particular configuration of database and user. Following are some of the useful methods: connect, connected, connection, disconnect, majorErrorCode, and storedProcArgs.
Connection	The DbPool.connection method creates a Connection object. You do not call a Connection constructor directly. Once you have a Connection object, you use it for your interactions with the database. Following are some of the useful methods: beginTransaction, commitTransaction, connected, cursor, execute, release, and rollbackTransaction.
database	The database object is used when accessing a database. Following are some of the useful methods: beginTransaction, commitTransaction, connect, connected, cursor, disconnect, execute, majorErrorCode, rollbackTransaction, storedProc, and storedProcArgs.
cursor	The cursor method of a Connection object or of the database object is used to get the cursor. You do not call a Cursor constructor. Following are some of the methods: close, columnName, columns, deleteRow, insertRow, next, and updateRow.
resultSet	The resultSet represents a virtual table created by executing a stored procedure. This is created by the resultSet method of a Stproc object. The resultSet object does not have a constructor. Following are some of the useful methods: close, columnName, columns, and next.
blob	This provides functionality for displaying and linking to BLOB data. blobImage and blobLink are some of the useful methods.
File	The file object is used to read and write to a file on disk. A new file object may have to be created using the new keyword. The following methods are often useful: close, eof, exists, flush, getLength, open, read, and write. To create a new file object, use. 'file = new File();'.
SendMail	This sends an email message. The To and From attributes are required. All other properties are optional. This can be created by the SendMail constructor:
Client	This contains data specific to an individual client. The runtime engine constructs and destroys the client object for each client request. The destroy and expiration methods are often useful.
Server	This contains global data for the entire server. The JavaScript runtime engine on the server automatically creates a single server object to store information common to all JavaScript applications on the Web server.
request	This contains data specific to the current client request. The JavaScript runtime engine on the server automatically creates a request object for each client request.

Object	Description
Java	This is a top-level object used to access any Java class in the package java.*. The Java object is a top-level, predefined JavaScript object. You can automatically access it without a constructor or calling a method.
JSObject	The public final class netscape.javascript.JSObject extends Object. JavaScript objects are wrapped in an instance of the class netscape.javascript.JSObject and passed to Java. JSObject allows Java to manipulate JavaScript objects. When a JavaScript object is sent to Java, the runtime engine creates a Java wrapper of type JSObject. When a JSObject is sent from Java to JavaScript, the runtime engine unwraps it to its original JavaScript object type. The JSObject class provides a way to invoke JavaScript methods and examine properties.
JSException	This object constructs a JSException. You specify whether the JSException has a detail message and other information. Other Predefined functions on the server-side JavaScript include addClient, addResponseHeader, callC, debug, deleteResponseHeader, flush, getOptionValue, getOptionValueCount, redirect, registerCFunction,and write.

Looking Forward

JavaScript is Netscape's implementation of the ECMAScript standard. The original ECMA Script became standard in June 1997. The ECMA edition 3, corresponding to JavaScript 1.5, was standardized in 1999. The proposal for ECMAScript edition 4, or JavaScript 2.0, is being reviewed at the time of this writing.

The objectives for the new JavaScript 2.0 are to improve on its strength as a dynamic language that executes quickly from source (not compiled), allowing the source to be distributed in Web pages. While its intent is not to compete with powerful languages like C++ and Java, the new version will be able to interface with other languages better than it currently does. It is proposed that JavaScript 2.0 introduce optional data types and type-checking. A package mechanism should be introduced for easy reuse of existing code. JavaScript 2.0 should introduce proper classes like those used in other programming languages, using the class keyword, allowing subclasses to be defined much easier than in the current version. Getters and setters should also be introduced, which are functions used to retrieve or set object properties or variables. The details of the proposed specification can be found at http://www.mozilla.org/js/language/js20/index.html.

Language news and version standards can be found at http://www.mozilla.org/js/language/. A useful JavaScript guide is available at http://developer.netscape.com/docs/manuals/js/core/jsguide15/contents.html. In addition, http://www.javascript.com contains much information, including links to reusable JavaScript source. More about ECMA can be found at http://www.ECMA.ch.

Chapter 13

VBScript

VBScript is short for Microsoft's Visual Basic Scripting Edition. It is most commonly used in Microsoft's 'classic' Active Server Pages (ASP) and for client-side scripting in Microsoft's Internet Explorer. VBScript is a subset of Visual Basic for Applications (VBA), and its similarities to VB and VBA allow developers who are familiar with these languages to quickly learn and use VBScript. Unlike compiled Visual Basic code, VBScript is interpreted at runtime. This slows down performance, but offers great flexibility because VBScript can be deployed quickly and easily as plain text. The current version of VBScript is 5.0, which has been stable for quite some time.

Microsoft has implemented the VBScript language in a variety of hosts, the most common being Internet Explorer (browser scripting), Internet Information Server (Active Server Pages), Outlook (email automation), and the Windows Script Host (scripting within Windows). Active Server Pages is by far the most frequently used VBScript host. The Windows Script Host object model provides a logical, systematic way to perform many administrative tasks such as network administration, application development and deployment, and automation of personal tasks. You may encounter VBScript in a variety of other hosts from Microsoft and other companies.

Besides its portability, VBScript is also powerful because most hosts enable the usage of any of the thousands of ActiveX/COM components that can be purchased commercially or custom built. Using VBScript and external components like ADO, the Scripting Runtime, or components you build yourself, you can do just about anything that can be done with Microsoft Windows.

Fast Facts

- VBScript is used in 'classic' ASP pages (ASP v3 and before). ASP.NET pages must use one of the .NET languages.
- VBScript is not case sensitive.
- Unlike VB or VBA, there is no integrated development environment (IDE) for VBScript.
- VBScript files typically have the following file extensions .vbs (VBScript file), .vbe (VBScript Encoded script file), .asp (Active Server Page), .inc (Include file), or .wsc (Windows Script Component).
- Anything to the right of a single quote (') on a line of VBScript is a comment, unless the single quote character appears within double quotes (" ").
- A long statement may be broken into multiple lines by placing the line-continuation character, a space, and an underscore (_) at the end of each line.
- Multiple statements can be combined into a single line by separating each statement with a colon (:). VBScript treats them as individual statements.
- Strings can be concatenated using an ampersand (&).
- VBScript is untyped - that is, all variables are of the same type, Variant. However, data is physically stored as one of the few dozen subtypes.
- A variable does not have to be declared before it is used. However, it is common practice, in order to eliminate the possibility of spelling errors and hard-to-find bugs, to make declarations required by placing the Option Explicit statement at the top of any VBScript modules.
- In an HTML page, VBScript code must be surrounded by <script> and </script> tags. In an ASP page, VBScript code may also be surrounded by <% and %> tags.

VBScript Examples

The following Web page displays a text box in which to enter a text string. When the Submit button is clicked, a message box pops up. If the string entered is longer than eight characters, the message says so:

```
<html><head><script language="VBScript" runat="client">
<!-- Option Explicit
'declare sub procedure
Sub submitButton_OnClick
  Dim name
  name = hello.txtName.value
  If Len(name) > 8 Then
    MsgBox "The name is too long"
  Else
    MsgBox "Hello, " & hello.txtName.value
  End If
End Sub  //-->
</script></head><body>
<h1>Welcome to this Web Site!</h1><br>
<form name="hello">Enter your Name: <input type = "text" name = "txtName">
<br><input type="button" name="submitButton" value = "Submit">
</form></body></html>
```

Although the above approach is probably the most common, you can attach VBScript code to events in two other ways. Internet Explorer allows you to add short sections of inline code in the tag defining the control. For example:

```
<input name="submitButton" type="button" value="Submit" OnClick='MsgBox
"Welcome Message."'>
```

Notice that the function call is enclosed in single quotation marks, and the string for the MsgBox function is enclosed in double quotation marks. You can use multiple statements, as long as you separate the statements with colons (:). You can also use a <script> tag so that it applies to an event for a specific control:

```
<script language="VBScript" event="OnClick" for="submitButton">
<!--  MsgBox " Welcome Message."  -->
</script>
```

The following example uses VBScript to create a 'classic' ASP page. It displays a dropdown box, which has a range of years to select starting with current year:

```
<% Option Explicit %>
<html><body><h1>Welcome to this Web Site!</h1><br><form>
<select size="10" name="year"><option>Please select a year</option>
<% Dim intYearCounter, intCurrentYear
  intCurrentYear = Year(Date)
  for intYearCounter = intCurrentYear to (intCurrentYear + 7)
    Response.Write "<option>" & CStr(intYearCounter) & "</option>"
  next
%> </select></form></body></html>
```

Main Components of VBScript

Although every VBScript application is a bit different from the next, a few consistencies are described here.

<script>

The script tags demarcate the VBScript from the surrounding HTML. Unless it is part of an ASP page, the VBScript must be enclosed in these tags. An ASP page may use either the script tags or <% . . . %> around the script code. There can be multiple script sections in a given page, and the script blocks may be of any scripting language.

Dim

Variables are defined with the Dim keyword. A variable temporarily holds data that is often manipulated and reassigned to another variable.

Procedures

Procedures are blocks of code that perform various operations, and they fall under either one of two categories: Sub or Function. A Sub does not return a value and a Function can return a value (though the compiler does not force you to). In client-side browser usage, the Sub keyword can also be used between <script> tags to define an event procedure.

Basics of VBScript

VBScript is a subset of Visual Basic for Applications, so many of the same rules for VB apply to VBScript, including the structure of variables and procedures. Although VBScript has only one data type (the Variant), each of the VB data types is represented as a *subtype* of the Variant type. With a few exceptions (like ASP include files), the code of a VBScript program is usually contained in a single file. In some hosts (like client-side browser scripting), VBScript also supports VBA's event-driven model, with automatic event handler procedures created by combining the control name and the event name, with an underscore between the two.

Although VBScript is used in coding Outlook forms, etc., this chapter focuses on the three main uses of VBScript: ASP programming, client-side scripting in Internet Explorer, and general Windows scripting and automation.

- ASP employs server-side scripting to create dynamic Web content on the server, allowing for maximum functionality on a Web page.
- Client-side scripting is most often used for validation checks when a user inputs data, thus avoiding a round trip to the server. However, only Microsoft's Internet Explorer supports VBScript, which has decreased the usage of VBScript for client-side scripting in the browser.
- Windows scripting is used to develop and run scripts from both the Windows desktop and the command prompt. Please refer to the *Windows Script Host* section later in the chapter for more information on the use of VBScript for general Windows scripting and automation.

Web Scripting Syntax

VBScript for client-side or server-side should be enclosed in the <script> tags. The <script> tag may include any of these four attributes: runat, src, language, and for. The <script> tag causes the script to be run on the client by default (as opposed to the server).

The runat attribute may be set to "client" or "server". ASP must be run on the server, so if the <script> tag is used to mark ASP code (as opposed to <% . . . %>), the runat attribute must be included and set to "server". When the <% . . . %> tags are used in an ASP file, the code is run on the server by default.

The language attribute is used to specify which scripting language engine the browser will use to execute the scripted code. If the language attribute is not specified, most browsers will default to using the JavaScript engine (Microsoft Internet Explorer included). When specifying VBScript as the language, either "VBS" or "VBScript" is acceptable (case insensitive).

Inclusion of the src attribute indicates that the actual scripted code is contained in another file. The URL of the file must be specified, and that file must contain only scripting code of the selected language. Any HTML tags in that file will result in an error. The src file is then read in by the browser as if that script were included in the actual page itself, allowing for easy maintenance.

The for attribute allows an event handler to be defined for a specified event by attaching the enclosed code to a specific event of a specific control in Internet Explorer.

The HTML comment tags <!-- and --> should be used to enclose any script code in client-side scripting. This way, if a particular browser is not able to interpret the code, that code will not be displayed on the screen, but will remain hidden from the viewer.

Data Types

Unlike Visual Basic and VBA, VBScript is an untyped language. There is only one main data type, called Variant. A Variant is a special kind of data type that can contain different kinds of information, depending on how it is used. Because Variant is the only data type in VBScript, it is also the data type returned by all functions in VBScript.

However, VBScript does incorporate a number of *subtypes* within the Variant type that correspond to data types of Visual Basic and VBA. Unless you use an explicit conversion function (see below), the VBScript runtime automatically selects what it thinks is the best Variant subtype in which to store a piece of data. For example, a Variant behaves as a number when you use it in a numeric context, and as a string when you use it in a string context.

Because strange bugs can arise from automatic changes to the subtype that you might not expect, it is a good idea to be as explicit as you can about your intent for one subtype or another. To do this, you can use the conversion functions and be explicit about any constants in your code: for example, put quotation marks (" ") around data you want treated as a string, pound signs (# #) around dates, and nothing around numbers. The description of the different subtypes used in VBScript is explained in table 13-1.

Note that VBScript does not support Visual Basic's Type.. End Type for user-defined types. However, VBScript does support classes.

Because all variables are of the same type, the situation in which you need to know the subtype of the variable will inevitably arise. VBScript includes two functions that can test for the subtype of any Variant variable. The VarType function returns an integer, each with a corresponding intrinsic constant, indicating the subtype. The TypeName function returns a string value that describes the subtype of the variable. The return values for these functions appear in the *VBScript Miscellany* section.

Table 13-1. VBScript Subtypes

Subtype	Description
Empty	Every variable has the subtype Empty when it is first declared. The value is 0 for numeric variables or a zero-length string ("") for string variables.
Null	The Null subtype indicates that the variable does not contain valid data. A variable is Null when it is specifically assigned Null, or often when an error occurs.
Boolean	A variable of the Boolean subtype that contains the constant values True or False.
Byte	This is the smallest subtype, with one byte of storage space. It can hold values between 0 and 255.
Integer	A variable of the Integer subtype uses two bytes of memory. It can hold values between -32,768 and 32,767.
Long	A Long variable uses four bytes of memory. It can hold values between -2,147,483,648 and 2,147,483,647.
Single	A Single variable stores a floating-point number using single precision. It can hold values between -3.402823E38 and -1.401298E-45 for negative values; 1.401298E-45 and 3.402823E38 for positive values.
Double	A Double variable stores values much more precisely than a Single subtype can. It can hold values between -1.79769313486232E308 and -4.94065645841247E-324 for negative values; 4.94065645841247E-324 and 1.79769313486232E308 for positive values.
Date/Time	A variable of the Date/Time subtype can hold a specially formatted number of date or time.
Currency	The Currency subtype stores monetary values. It can hold values between -922,337,203,685,477.5808 and 922,337,203,685,477.5807.
String	A String variable automatically allocates just enough memory for a string.
Object	The Object variable contains a reference to an object that was created somewhere in script.
Error	A variable of the Error subtype will hold a number corresponding to an error.

VBScript also provides various functions for converting data from one type to another. All of these functions take only one argument, as follows:

```
function_name(expression)
```

The expression represents the value to convert, and the function called returns the value converted to a different subtype. The functions are explained in Table 13-2.

Table 13-2. Converting Functions in VBScript

Function	Description
Asc	Returns the decimal ASCII character code corresponding to the first letter in a string. If the argument contains no characters, a run-time error occurs.
CBool	Returns an expression that has been converted to a Variant of subtype Boolean. If the expression evaluates to a nonzero value, it returns True. Otherwise, it returns False. If the expression can't be interpreted as a numeric value, a run-time error occurs.
CByte	Returns an expression that has been converted to a Variant of subtype Byte. If expression lies outside the acceptable range for the Byte subtype, an error occurs.
Ccur	Returns an expression that has been converted to a Variant of subtype Currency. The format is recognized depending on the locale setting of your system.
CDate	Returns an expression that has been converted to a Variant of subtype Date. It recognizes date literals and time literals, as well as some numbers that fall within the range of acceptable dates. When converting a number to a date, the whole number portion is converted to a date. Any fractional part of the number is converted to a time of day, starting at midnight. It recognizes date format according to the locale of the system.
CDbl	Returns an expression that has been converted to a Variant of subtype Double.
Cint	Returns an expression that has been converted to a Variant of subtype Integer.
CLng	Returns an expression that has been converted to a Variant of subtype Long. If expression lies outside the acceptable range for the Long subtype, an error occurs.
CSng	Returns an expression converted to a Variant of subtype Single.
CStr	Returns an expression that has been converted to a Variant of subtype String.
CVErr	Returns the subtype Error. It takes any valid error number as an argument. Using Err.Raise is recommended instead of CVErr.

Variables

Variables function as placeholders in memory for unknown values of named types. VB programmers should notice there is no "As type" in the declaration, because all variables are of the same type, Variant. Variable declaration is optional in VBScript. This can lead to strange bugs if you ever misspell a variable since VBScript will treat the two spelling variations as two unique variables.

To prevent accidental implicit variables, it is highly recommended that you use the Option Explicit statement, which indicates that within the scope of the script all variables must be explicitly declared. Typically, this statement is placed at top of the script file, module, or ASP page.

There are a few restrictions in choosing a variable name:

- It must begin with a letter.
- It cannot be more than 255 characters long.
- It cannot contain an embedded period.
- It must be unique to its scope.

Scope

A variable's scope refers to the areas of code in which that variable functions. Variables in VBScript may have script-level, class-level, or procedure-level scope. Variables can be declared using the Dim, Public, and Private keywords (depending on scope) as below:

```
Dim|Public|Private varname[([subscripts])][, varname[([subscripts])]] . . .
```

Script-level scope is equivalent to a global variable in other languages. Script-level variables must be created outside of procedures and classes, and they remain in memory for the life of the script. At the script level, many programmers use the Dim keyword for variable declarations because the Public and Private keywords are not very meaningful at the script level since script-level scope is by definition top-level scope.

The boundary that defines script-level scope can be different depending on the host. For example, in an HTML file hosted in IE, it can be either the whole page or only between the <script> and </script> tags. In ASP it would be the file itself, plus any other files that are brought together using the include directive. With the Windows Script host, the boundary is defined by the physical boundaries of the script file.

Class-level scope is within Class and End Class statements within a script file (which may contain multiple classes). When declaring variables at the class level, it is a good idea to use the Private and Public keywords to differentiate between variables that should be part of the class's public interface and variables that should remain private to code within the class. The lifetime of a class-level variable is the same as the lifetime of an object instantiated from the class.

Procedure-level scope is within Sub or Function procedures, including event handlers, class methods, and properties. Lifetime is limited to the length of the call to the procedure.

Constants

A variable that holds the same, unchangeable value throughout a program is known as a constant. Although VBScript provides a number of predefined constants, user-defined constants can be created with the following declaration:

```
Const CONSTANT_NAME = literalvalue
[Public | Private] Const CONSTANT_NAME = literalvalue
```

The *CONSTANT_NAME* must follow the syntax rules of a variable as defined earlier. In addition, most VBScript programmers follow the convention of capitalizing all of the letters in the constant name and separating words with an underscore (_) character; however, this is not required. The value assigned to the constant must be a literal value, not a function call or variable. A constant declared within a procedure is known only to that procedure, because constants have scope just like normal variables. VBScript will raise a runtime error if your code attempts to change the value of a constant.

Operators

When expressions contain operators from more than one category, arithmetic operators are evaluated first, comparison operators are evaluated next, and logical operators are evaluated last.

Arithmetic: Exponentiation (^), Unary negation (-), Multiplication (*), Division (/), Modulus arithmetic (Mod), Addition (+), Subtraction (-), String Concatenation (&).

Comparison: Equality (=), Inequality (<>), Less than (<), Greater than (>), Less than or equal to (<=), Greater than or equal to (>=), Object equivalence (Is).

Logical: Logical negation (Not), Logical conjunction (And), Logical disjunction (Or), Logical exclusion (Xor), Logical equivalence (Eqv), Logical implication (Imp).

The string concatenation (&) operator is not an arithmetic operator, but in precedence it falls after all arithmetic operators and before all comparison operators. The Is operator is an object reference comparison operator. It does not compare objects or their values; it checks only to determine if two object references refer to the same object.

VBScript Arrays

An array represents a set of values referenced through an index of the same variable. Arrays are declared similarly to variables, by including the Dim keyword followed by the array name and the upper bound in parentheses:

```
Dim myArray(30)
```

The upper bound of an array cannot exceed the range of a Long data variable, and a lower bound can only be 0 in VBScript. So myArray(30) creates an array of 31 Variants that can be accessed using index values 0 through 30.

Note that since all variables have the malleable Variant data type, you do not have to declare a variable as an array in order to later change it into an array. For example, you can use the Array function to transform a comma-delimited list into an array:

```
anyVariable = Array(1,2,3,4,5)
```

You can use the IsArray function to see whether a variable is an array or not.

As with VB, multidimensional arrays are allowed in VBScript. In the array declaration, a comma separates the extra dimensions. The following declaration creates a 10-by-10 array of Variants:

```
Dim multiArray(9, 9)
```

An array can also be declared without an upper bound, in which case it is known as a dynamic array. Such an array is useful when the number of elements is not known. A dynamic array is declared as shown in the following example, with empty parentheses and the number of elements stated with ReDim:

```
Dim theArray()
Dim x
'Calculate x in a loop perhaps
ReDim theArray(x)
```

This example dynamically creates an array the size of *x*. The next time ReDim is called on theArray, the elements return to their default values, which means the old elements will be lost. The new elements of a dynamic array can be preserved through the Preserve keyword. Preserve is often used to keep the current data, but increase the upper bound:

```
ReDim Preserve theArray(x +1)
```

Only the upper bound of the last dimension of a multidimensional array may be altered with the Preserve keyword. Also, a dynamic array only allows the size of an array to be altered; the number of dimensions must stay the same.

The UBound intrinsic function is also useful when working with dynamic arrays. This function returns the upper bound value of the last dimension. (In VBScript, the LBound intrinsic function, which returns the lower bound value, is not useful at all, since all lower bounds must be 0.) Substituting the UBound function in the last example results in the following:

```
ReDim Preserve theArray(UBound(theArray) + 1)
```

Also note that VBScript does not support Visual Basic's Option Base statement since the lower bound must always be equal to 0.

VBScript Control Statements

VBScript, like all procedural programming languages, provides a number of statements to create program branches and loops. VBScript requires an End statement for each of these constructs; a runtime error is generated if this statement is missing.

If . . . Then

This structure tests for and reacts to a condition. If the *condition* is True the statements, which need to be closed by End If, are executed. The *condition* may be a comparison that results in a Boolean True or False, or an expression that evaluates to a numeric value. A zero is equivalent to False, and any nonzero number is True:

```
If <condition> Then
  'statements
End If
```

If . . . Then . . . Else

The statement can be expanded to test multiple conditions using the ElseIf and Else statement:

```
If <condition1> Then
  'statements1
ElseIf <condition2> Then
  'statements2
Else
  'statements3
End If
```

Select Case

This statement represents an alternative to using If . . . Then . . . Else structures in situations with many conditions to test. The *testExpression* is first compared against *expressionList1*, and if it matches, the statements between it and *expressionList2* are executed. If this expression does not match *expressionList1*, the next one is compared, and so on. If two expression lists match *testExpression*, only the statements of the first one are executed. If there are no matching expression lists, and if a Case Else section is present, the code in that section will execute (the Case Else is optional).

The Select Case structure is shown here:

```
Select Case <testExpression>
Case <expressionList1>
  'statements1
Case <expressionList2>
  'statements2
Case Else
  'statementsN
End Select
```

Do . . . Loop

This loop repeatedly executes a statement or block of statements, testing a *condition* between each iteration. Once the statement evaluates to False, the loop exits and execution proceeds with the statement following the closing of the loop. The *condition* must be an expression that evaluates to True or False. There are variations of the loop that allow the *condition* to be tested either before or after the first iteration. The difference is that when tested after the first iteration, the statements are guaranteed to execute at least once, but when testing the *condition* first the *statements* may never be executed.

This code tests the *condition* first:

```
Do While <condition>
  'statements
Loop
```

This code executes the statements once before testing the *condition*:

```
Do
  'statements
Loop While <condition>
```

In addition, the *statements* can be made to execute while the condition is False and stop once the condition becomes True. This is done by replacing the While keyword with Until. This code tests the *condition* first:

```
Do Until <condition>
  'statements
Loop
```

This format executes the statements at least once:

```
Do
  'statements
Loop Until <condition>
```

While...Wend

This executes a series of statements as long as a given *condition* is True:

```
While <condition>
  'statements
Wend
```

For . . . Next

The For loops are used when the number of loop iterations is known. The construct uses four numeric arguments: *counter*, *start*, *end*, and *increment*. The *counter* is a variable, set equal to the *start* value initially, that keeps track of the number of iterations. The *counter* value is compared to the *end* value, and if the *counter* value is less, the statements of the loop execute. Immediately following the execution of the last statement, the value of the *counter* is incremented by the number specified as the *increment* argument, and the *counter* is again compared to the *end* value.

In the following example, when *counter* has become greater than *end*, the loop exits. Note that restating the *counter* variable after the keyword *Next* is not required. If no step value is defined, the *increment* defaults to 1. Also note that *increment* is allowed to be a negative number, in which case the loop exits when the *counter* becomes less than the *end* value:

```
For counter=start To end [Step increment]
  'statements
Next [counter]
```

For Each . . . Next

When it is necessary to operate on each of the elements of a collection or each object of an array, a For Each . . . Next loop should be implemented. The statements are repeated for each element in the group. It should be noted that an array used as a group may not contain user-defined types and the element may be only a Variant variable. When specifying a collection as the element, the element may be a Variant variable, a generic Object variable, or an object listed in the object browser:

```
For Each element In group
  'statements
Next element
```

Exit . . .

To immediately exit a loop, the Exit keyword can be implemented, followed by either Do or For. Exit Do exits any variation of a Do loop, and the Exit Do statement may appear more than once in a Do loop. Execution jumps out of the loop and continues with the first statement following the loop. Similarly, multiple Exit For statements may appear in one For loop. Note that the Exit keyword is also used to exit procedures, and is discussed in *VBScript Procedures*.

VBScript Procedures

A procedure performs one or more operations on variable data. Procedures can enclose a repeated task, receive values to perform their operations on, and/or return values to the caller of the procedure. A Function procedure is used to return a value, and a Sub procedure is used when no value needs to be returned to the caller.

Sub Procedures

A Sub procedure has no return value. The declaration for a Sub is as follows:

```
Sub procedurename (arguments)
  'statements
End Sub
```

When called, the statements between the Sub and End Sub lines are executed. The subroutine name cannot begin with a number and cannot contain spaces. To cause execution to jump to the end of a particular procedure, the Exit Sub statement can be inserted anywhere within a Sub. A Sub can further be divided into two categories: general and event procedures.

Event procedures within a Web page in Internet Explorer are considered attached to a form or a control because they are called automatically whenever their associated events occur. An event procedure name is created by joining the control and the event name with an underscore (_). For instance, the code that executes when a button called myButton is clicked would go in an event procedure named myButton_click.

General procedures applicable to all the hosts must be specifically called from somewhere else in the code. General procedures are mainly to promote code reuse and keep code easier to read and maintain.

Invoking a Sub procedure can be done in two ways. The first includes the word Call followed by the procedure name and the arguments to pass into the function enclosed in parentheses and separated by commas. This is in contrast to the second way of calling a Sub procedure, in which the function is called by listing the function name, followed by the arguments. Including parentheses here results in error. Both calling procedure syntaxes are shown here:

```
Call MyProc(ArgOne, ArgTwo)
MyProc ArgOne, ArgTwo
```

Function Procedures

A Function procedure is very much like a Sub procedure, except for the capability to return a value to the caller of the procedure. When a Function is called, the statements between the Function and End Function, shown in the syntax example, are executed, and the procedure then returns a value of the type specified in the declaration to the caller:

```
Function procedurename (arguments, arguments)
  'statements here
  procedurename = value
End Function
```

The same naming requirements exist for a Function as for a subroutine: the name must not begin with a number, and must not contain spaces. Unlike in VB, the As keyword is not supported, and all functions return a type Variant value. The return value is determined by setting a variable with the same name as the function (automatically initialized through the use of the Function statement) equal to the value to be returned in the code. This return variable should not be explicitly initialized using the Dim keyword.

A function can be invoked using both methods described in the section *Sub Procedures*. The first involves the Call keyword followed by the function name, parentheses, and the arguments within the parentheses. A function can also be called with the function name followed directly by arguments. Using these two methods, the return values are simply disregarded. In order to use the return value, the function name is inserted in an expression that includes an equal sign, which assigns the return value to a variable. Two examples of invoking function are shown here:

```
Dim x, y, z
z = myFunctionOne(x, y)
myFunction x, y
```

Note that when capturing the return value of a function with at least one argument, parentheses must be used. This is shown in the preceding example, which sets the return value equal to z.

Procedure Arguments

Arguments may be passed to procedures either by reference or by value in VBScript (the option to pass by reference was not available in VBScript version 1 or 2). To pass by reference means that the function is passed a pointer to the actual address in memory. This is the default manner of passing variables in VBScript, so if nothing is specified, a variable is passed by reference:

```
Sub MySub (ByRef var1)
Sub MySub (var1)
```

These two subroutine declarations are equivalent. Any changes made to *var1* within *MySub* will persist once *MySub* returns.

When passing a variable by value, only a copy of the variable is passed into the procedure so that when the procedure returns, the original value of the argument variable will still exist:

```
Sub MySub2 (ByVal var2)
```

Any changes made to *var2* in *MySub2* will be ignored once *MySub2* returns. The value of *var2* will be the same as it was before *MySub2* was called. Using ByVal is safer in most cases because it encourages encapsulation and prevents hard to find bugs caused by unexpected changes to argument variables.

VBScript Classes

A class is a template for an object. Classes contain variables, methods, and properties; when instantiated, the public methods and properties can be accessed via the interface of the class. Classes have only been supported in VBScript since version 5.0. Unlike many object-oriented languages, in VBScript the class must be defined in the same script where it is used. It cannot be imported or included.

A class is defined between the Class and End Class statements, as shown in the following syntax. Included may be procedures, variables, events, and properties. Code within a class may exist within the Class and End Class statements and within public and private procedures and functions defined within the Class and End Class statements:

```
Class classname
  'methods and variables here
End Class
```

Variables A class may have class variables defined outside of an included function, and therefore constitute a type of global variable, accessible by any of the functions included in the class. These variables are declared using the Dim, Public, or Private modifier.

Methods A class may have methods, subroutines, or functions, and they may be declared either Public or Private. A Private method is visible to only the class in which it is defined, whereas a Public method can be called outside of the class. Unlike VB, VBScript does not support the Friend modifier. A class method is simply a method that is enclosed within a class and typically operates on the class itself.

Properties A class has a way of wrapping its private variables in an accessor method, which are called properties. Properties are most often used to allow outside access to a private class variable, while at the same time doing some sort of data validation. Property methods come in three varieties: Property Let, Property Get, *and* Property Set. The Property Let method assigns a value to a variable. If that variable is an object, then the Property Set method assigns the value. In order to retrieve the value of a variable, the Property Get method is called. Similar to the other members of a class, properties may be either Public or Private. See below in the *Events* section for an example.

Events There are two private events fired automatically during the lifecycle of a class object, Class_Initialize and Class_Terminate. Therefore, the code in a procedure that has the same name is executed automatically when the event fires. The Class_Initialize event is fired when a class is instantiated using the New keyword. Code can be put into this method to handle variable initializations that only need to be done once for the life of the object. The Class_Terminate event is fired when an instance of a class is destroyed. This occurs when an object goes out of scope or is set to Nothing. This procedure can be used to do any class clean up, such as ending database connections or closing files. The following example describes a class and its variables, properties, and, event procedures:

```
Class MyClass
  'declare variables
  Private myCount
  Private myTypeVar

  'property methods
  Public Property Let MyType (strType)
    myTypeVar = strType
  End Property
  Public Property Get MyType()
    MyType = MyTypeVar
  End Property

  'event procedures
  Private Sub Class_Initialize()
    myCount = 0
  End Sub
  Private Sub Class_Terminate()
    'housekeeping code here
  End Sub
End Class
```

The class defined above contains two class variables declared at the top. The property Get and Let methods handle variable values. The event procedures contain code that is executed when a MyClass object is created or destroyed. In order to execute the code contained within a class, an instance of the class must be created.

Objects A VBScript class is instantiated with the New keyword and assigned with the Set keyword. (The New keyword can only be used to instantiate VBScript classes. Externally defined classes must be instantiated using a variation of the CreateObject() function.) This process creates an object of the class, and the object has its own copy of all of the class variables, methods, properties, and events that the class has defined. The following line creates an instance of the class *MyClass*, and assigns a reference to that object to the variable *myObject*:

```
Set myObject = New MyClass
```

Once this is done, *myObject* contains its own copy of all of the members of *MyClass*. The members are accessed by concatenating the object name, a period (.), and the member name.

Regular Expressions

A regular expression is a pattern of text that consists of ordinary characters (for example, letters a through z) and special characters, known as metacharacters. The pattern describes one or more strings to match when searching a body of text. The regular expression serves as a template for matching a character pattern to the string being searched. With VBScript 5.0 engine, VBScript supports the pattern-matching capabilities of regular expressions:

```
Dim RegEx, myStr, myMatches
Set RegEx = New RegExp
RegEx.Pattern = "th"
RegEx.Global = True
RegEx.IgnoreCase = True
myStr = "The fourth time that this happens will be the last."
Set myMatches = RegEx.Execute(myStr)
```

The preceding example creates a RegExp object and sets its properties to search for any occurrence of the string "th". The code also searches for both upper- and lowercase values, and returns every match that is found. Notice the Execute method of the object, which is used to do an expression search and returns a Matches collection as its result.

The Matches collection is a group of Match objects that can only be created as a result of RegExp.Execute. Matches have two properties: the Count property returns the number of items in the collection, and the Item property returns a specific item based on the key. The individual Match objects have a number of properties that can be used to retrieve information about the pattern matches. The FirstIndex property returns the position in the search string where the match occurred. The Length property returns the length of the match, and the Value property returns the text of the match found.

A SubMatches collection contains individual submatch strings, and can only be created using the Execute method of the RegExp object. The SubMatches collection's properties are read-only. When a regular expression is executed, zero or more submatches can result when subexpressions are enclosed in capturing parentheses. Each item in the SubMatches collection is the string found and captured by the regular expression.

The complete list of metacharacters and their behavior in the context of regular expressions can be found at http://msdn.microsoft.com.

VBScript Error Handling

When an error occurs in a VBScript program, the system-defined error object, Err, is automatically set with various properties relating to the error, including an error number and a description of the error. This information can be used within a procedure to handle the error without interrupting the application, with the proper error handling techniques. Although not as extensive as VB or VBA, VBScript provides useful error handling techniques so that errors can be handled within the code instead of allowing the error to halt the program in an inconvenient place.

On Error

It is important to understand that VBScript does not offer the structured or block-based exception handling found in some other languages. There are only two error handling modes which are *toggled* by the On Error statement. When On Error GoTo 0 (the default mode) is in effect, any runtime error will cause the VBScript engine to immediately stop the execution of the script at the place of the error. On the other hand, when On Error Resume Next is in effect, all errors are completely ignored by the VBScript runtime (though you can check for them yourself using the Err object).

The error handling mode is limited to the current scope of the script code. You can think of each procedure or function as having its own scope and any script-level code as having its own scope. Within any given scope, if no On Error statement has yet been executed or if On Error GoTo 0 has been executed, the "immediate stop" mode is in effect; if the last On Error statement was On Error Resume Next, then the "ignore all" mode is in effect, meaning that if an error occurs, execution will resume with the line immediately following the line that caused the error. This requires the anticipation of potential errors, and any error handling code must be placed in the line immediately following the questionable line. An On Error statement follows one of these formats:

```
On Error Resume Next
On Error GoTo 0
```

Be careful leaving On Error Resume Next in effect because you can suppress errors without knowing, which can lead to hard-to-find bugs. Different error handling strategies apply depending on the host in which the VBScript code is running. For example, IIS and ASP provide the ability to customize a default runtime error handling page, which allows you to centralize error handling. However, in a command line Windows Script Host script that runs on a schedule in the middle of the night, you would not have the luxury of a central handler, so you would want to adjust your error handling strategy accordingly.

Err Object

The Err object is automatically set with the properties of a VBScript runtime error. These properties can be retrieved to get some insight into the type of error that has just occurred. Anticipated runtime errors can be handled without halting a VBScript program if used in combination with an If . . . Then statement. The Number property of this object is populated with the error number of the most recent error that has occurred. You can also check the specific error number to decide on an error-handling path. This example puts an explicit error trap around the opening of a database connection:

```
On Error Resume Next
'error prone operation
dataConnection.Open()
If Err.Number <> 0 Then
  MsgBox "An error occurred trying to open the database connection: " &
  Err.Description Err.Clear
End If
```

The Description property describes the error that has occurred. The Clear method clears all of the current properties of the object. The Source property holds the object or application that has caused the error. The HelpContext property returns the context ID of the topic in the help file, and the HelpFile property returns the path to the help file.

Err.Raise

The Raise method of Err provides a way to intentionally generate an error from within the program. When calling the Raise, the properties of this error can be set as below:

```
Err.Raise number, [source], [description], [[helpfile], helpcontext]
```

The *number* can correspond to a VBScript-defined or a user-defined error between 0 and 65535. The *description* is a string that describes the error, and if one is not provided, the *number* value is examined. If a VBScript run-time error code matches, a descriptive message is provided. Otherwise, a default error message is used. The *source* refers to the application that generated the error, and if not specified, the program ID of the current VBScript project is used.

The *helpfile* is a fully qualified path to the help file for the error. The *helpcontext* is a context ID pointing out the useful topic within the *helpfile*.

Windows Script Host (WSH)

Windows scripting brings simple, powerful, and flexible scripting to the Windows platform. It provides objects for manipulation of script execution, as well as functions for other actions. Using these, we can print messages, map drives, connect to printers, modify registry keys, etc. WSH is built into Microsoft Windows 98, 2000, XP and Millennium Editions. Several areas of functionality have been addressed in the latest version, 5.6.

When running scripts from Windows, WScript.exe provides a Windows-based dialog box for setting script properties. Whether you use WScript.exe (Windows) or CScript.exe (Command Prompt), you still run the scripts in the same manner. The difference is only in the output — WScript generates windowed output, while CScript sends its output to the command window. Windows Script Host offers several objects and constants for interacting with the Windows environment and shell. For information on object model, visit http://msdn.microsoft.com/scripting and click on Windows Script Technologies. The following basic Windows script verifies whether a file has required permissions:

```
Dim Signer, File, ShowUI, FileOK
Set Signer = CreateObject("Scripting.Signer")
File = "c:\newfile.wsf"
ShowUI = True
FileOK = Signer.VerifyFile(File, ShowUI)
If FileOK Then
  WScript.Echo File & " is trusted."
Else
  WScript.Echo File & " is NOT trusted."
End If
```

VBScript Included Objects

VBScript has two types of special objects available to it: built-in and runtime objects. Although both types of objects are provided to a VBScript script by Microsoft products, there is a difference between the two (minor though it is). The VBScript interpreter provides the built-in objects, whereas an external DLL file provides the runtime objects.

Built-In Objects

The VBScript engine is contained in a file named vbscript.dll. This file features support for the base VBScript language, and provides a number of built-in objects.

Err The Err object is automatically set with information relating to the most recent error that occurred in the script execution. More can be found about Err in the *VBScript Error Handling* section of this chapter.

RegExp With VBScript 5.0 engine, VBScript supports the pattern-matching capabilities of regular expressions using the RegExp object. More can be found about RegExp in the *Regular Expressions* section in this chapter.

Class Object A class is the template for an object. Classes have variables, methods, and properties. When instantiated, these elements are used. Classes have been supported in VBScript only since version 5.0. More can be found about Class in the *VBScript Classes* section of this chapter.

Debug Object The Debug object cannot be created directly, but it is always available for use. The Write and WriteLine methods of the Debug object display strings in the immediate window of the Microsoft Script Debugger at run time. If the script is not being debugged, the methods have no affect:

```
Debug.Write "The value of counter is " & counter
```

Match Object More can be found about Match Object in the *Regular Expression* section of this chapter.

Matches Collection More can be found about Match Collection and SubMatches Collection in the *Regular Expression* section of this chapter.

Runtime Objects

The Scripting Runtime Object Library is a DLL file (scrrun.dll) that is included in Microsoft products by default and provides additional objects that can come in handy in VBScript. There are two main runtime objects that can be used, Dictionary and FileSystemObject. These objects are created using the CreateObject method. The FileSystemObject provides access to other objects, including Drive, File, Files, Folder, Folders, and TextStream.

Dictionary Object The Dictionary object provides a way to store key/value pairs, and has the following methods:

Add	Adds a key/value pair.
Remove	Removes a key/value pair.
Exists	Tests for the existence of a key.
Items	Returns an array of all of the items.
Keys	Returns an array of all of the keys.
RemoveAll	Removes all elements from the dictionary.

The following shows how some of these Dictionary object methods can be used:

```
Dim myDictionary
Set myDictionary = CreateObject("Scripting.Dictionary")
myDictionary.Add "myKey1","myVal1"
If (myDictionary.Exists("myKey1")) Then
  MsgBox "The value for myKey1 is " & myDictionary.Item("myKey1")
End If
```

The Scripting in the CreateObject method of the previous example indicates that the Scripting library is to be used, and the Dictionary is the object type that is created. The Item property accesses the value stored when the key is passed. The Count property returns the total number of elements. The Key property writes the key value, and the CompareMode property decides between binary and text comparisons.

FileSystemObject The FileSystemObject object allows access to the file system where the code is running. Because accessing the local file system is often a security breach, Internet browsers do not allow client-side use of FileSystemObject by default. The FileSystemObject Object Model (FSO) is comprised of FileSystemObject and the other objects that can be accessed through FileSystemObject.

The first step in using the FSO is to create a FileSystemObject object through the CreateObject method (using the Scripting library). The methods of this object are then used to create other objects, such as Drives, Folders, and Files. The following example accesses an existing File object and pulls the DateLastModified property from that object:

```
Dim myFso, myFile1, myFile2
Set myFso = CreateObject("Scripting.FileSystemObject")
Set myFile1 = myFso.GetFile("C:\temp\hello.txt")
Set myFile2 = myFso.CreateTextFile("C:\temp\goodbye.txt")
MsgBox "This file has last been modified " & myFile1.DateLastModified
```

A new file is also created through the CreateTextFile method. Similarly, Folders, TextFiles, and Drives can be accessed and created using similar Get and Create methods of the FileSystemObject. Each object has its methods that can be used and its properties that can be retrieved. However, the FSO is too vast to cover in detail in this chapter. For more on the FSO, refer to the Microsoft Developer Network Web site: http://msdn.microsoft.com.

VBScript Miscellany

Coding conventions are suggestions designed to help you write code using Microsoft Visual Basic Scripting Edition. Constants were implemented as variables and distinguished from other variables using all uppercase characters.

Variables should always be defined with the smallest scope possible – procedure level or script level. Script level scope is prefixed with (s). Similarly, we can use prefixes for objects you may encounter. To enhance readability and consistency, most VBScript developers use descriptive variable names with the following prefixes: Boolean(bln), Byte(byt), Date(dtm), Double(dbl), Error(err), Integer(int), Long(lng), Object(obj), Single(sng), String(str).

Table 13-3. VBScript Keywords

Keyword	**Description**
Empty	Indicates an uninitialized variable. A variable is uninitialized when it is first created and no value is assigned to it, or when a variable value is explicitly set to empty. This is not the same as Null.
False	Has a value equal to 0.
Nothing	Disassociates an object variable from an object to free resources.
Null	Indicate that a variable contains no valid data. Not the same as Empty.
True	Has a value equal to –1.

Table 13-4. Values Returned by VarType and TypeName Functions

Subtype	**VarType**	**TypeName (name of the subtype)**
Empty	0 (vbEmpty)	Empty
Null	1 (vbNull)	Null
Integer	2 (vbInteger)	Integer
Long integer	3 (vbLong)	Long
Single	4 (vbSingle)	Single
Double	5 (vbDouble)	Double
Currency	6 (vbCurrency)	Currency
Date	7 (vbDate)	Date
String	8 (vbString)	String
Error	10 (vbError)	Error
Boolean	11 (vbBoolean)	Boolean
Byte	17 (vbByte)	Byte
OLE automation	9 (vbObject)	<classname of the object>
Decimal	14 (vbDecimal)	Decimal
Nothing	9 (vbObject)	Nothing

Table 13-5. Useful VBScript Functions

Date/Time functions

Date	Returns the current system date.
DateValue	Returns a date.
Day	Returns a number that represents the day of the month (1 - 31, inclusive).
FormatDateTime	Returns an expression formatted as a date or time.
Hour	Returns a number that represents the hour of the day (0 - 23, inclusive).
IsDate	Returns a Boolean if the evaluated expression can be converted to a date.
Minute	Returns a number that represents the minute of the hour (0 - 59, inclusive).
Month	Returns a number that represents the month of the year (1 -12, inclusive).
Now	Returns the current system date and time.
Second	Returns a number that represents the second of the minute.
Time	Returns the current system time.
Weekday	Returns a number that represents the day of the week (1-7, inclusive).
Year	Returns a number that represents the year.

Format functions

FormatCurrency	Returns an expression formatted as a currency value.
FormatDateTime	Returns an expression formatted as a date or time.
FormatNumber	Returns an expression formatted as a number.
FormatPercent	Returns an expression formatted as a percentage.

Array functions

Array	Returns a variant containing an array.
IsArray	Returns a Boolean value that indicates whether a specified variable is an array.
Join	Returns a string that consists of a number of substrings in an array.
Split	Returns a zero-based, 1-D array that contains a specified number of substrings.

Table 13-6. Additional Functions

String functions

InStr	Returns the position of the first occurrence of one string within another.
Lcase	Converts a specified string to lowercase.
Len	Returns the number of characters in a string.
Ltrim	Removes spaces on the left side of a string.
Rtrim	Removes spaces on the right side of a string.
Trim	Removes spaces on both the left and the right side of a string.
Replace	Replaces a part of a string with another string a specified number of times.
StrReverse	Reverses a string.
Ucase	Converts a specified string to uppercase.

Other functions

Eval	Evaluates an expression and returns the result.
GetObject	Returns a reference to an automation object from a file.
InputBox	Displays a dialog box, where the user can write some input and/or click on a button, and returns the contents.
IsEmpty	Returns a Boolean that indicates whether a specified variable has been initialized or not.
IsNull	Returns a Boolean that indicates whether a specified expression contains no valid data.
IsNumeric	Returns a Boolean that indicates whether a specified expression can be evaluated as number.
IsObject	Returns a Boolean that indicates whether the specified expression is an automation object.
ScriptEngine	Returns the scripting language in use.
ScriptEngineBuildVersion	Returns the build version number of the scripting engine in use.
MsgBox	Displays a message box, waits for the user to click a button, and returns a value that indicates which button the user clicked. MsgBox(prompt[, buttons] [, title] [, helpfile, context]).
CreateObject	Creates and returns a reference to an ActiveX object. (In VBScript, the *New* statement can only be used to instantiate classes defined within the script itself. CreateObject is used to create objects from externally defined types.) CreateObject(*class*,[*servername*]).

Looking Forward

The latest version of VBScript is 5.0. Although VBScript Microsoft's new directions favor the new .NET framework, VBScript remains a powerful, compact, and portable scripting language that will continue to play an important part of client-side scripting, general Windows scripting, and Active Server Pages (ASP). The new ASP.NET is evolving and gaining popularity, but the number of current traditional ASP applications is great, and these applications will continue to require traditional maintenance.

The Microsoft Web site is an excellent source for VBScript information. Visit http://msdn.microsoft.com/scripting, click the VBScript Documentation link, and select either the VBScript User's Guide or the VBScript Language Reference to view the information. Another useful, quick online reference for VBScript functions and syntax can be found at the DevGuru VBScript Quick Reference Web page: http://www.devguru.com/Technologies/vbscript/quickref/vbscript_intro.html.

Chapter 14

Microsoft Windows

Microsoft Windows is the most popular operating system in the world, and no matter your opinion of Microsoft, you cannot work in the computer world without knowing the fundamentals of Windows.

The good news is that Windows is very intuitive and should not take long for you to understand. This chapter is designed to provide some background about Windows, cover the basics of Windows along with some tips to make you more productive, and delve into some more technical tips to get you started writing some of your own command scripts in Windows.

This chapter is written based on Windows XP Professional, though most of its content is applicable to all Windows versions, beginning with Windows 95. Windows XP is the latest Operating System (OS) release at time of press, but Microsoft is constantly enhancing it in preparation for the next release. Most of the commands and instructions in Windows are *backward-compatible*, meaning that they will run on the earlier versions. Microsoft is pretty reliable about maintaining these commands, so this chapter should support your needs for years to come.

Fast Facts

- The Windows OS is an entirely GUI-based application, but there is a command shell for command line utilities and many OS operations.
- Windows is not case sensitive.
- Any number of windows may be open at one time.
- The taskbar along the bottom of the desktop displays all open programs. You can switch from one to the next by clicking on the mini-title bar in the taskbar, or by using the Alt-Tab shortcut.
- Start Menu can be used to invoke almost every program by choosing Start > (All) Programs and navigating to the file that is to be executed.
- Windows Explorer is used to do most folder navigation and file/folder modifications. Explorer can be started by right-clicking on the Start menu and choosing 'Explore'.
- Pressing Ctrl-Alt-Del at any time summons a useful pop-up window that includes the following options: Shut Down, Log Off, Lock Computer, Task Manager, and Change Password.
- All Windows applications share a clipboard. Pressing Ctrl-C copies highlighted text or data to the clipboard. Ctrl-V pastes the contents of the clipboard to any window. Ctrl-X cuts highlighted portions and places them on the clipboard for use by any other window.
- In Windows Explorer, drag a file to another location to move it. However, if the destination is on a separate logical drive, the file is copied rather than moved.
- To select multiple files or folders using Windows Explorer, hold down the Ctrl key while clicking each file or folder.
- A shell window can be invoked by choosing Start > Run and then entering 'cmd'. It can also be invoked by choosing Start > (All) Programs > Accessories > Command Prompt.
- In a shell script, anything to the right of rem is a comment and not executed.
- A shell substitutes the value of an environment variable for the variable name when the name is surrounded by percent signs (e.g., %PATH%).
- Usage rules and hints for commands can be found by typing help followed by the command name from the command prompt.

Windows Basics

The popularity of the Windows OS is based on the fact that the software is represented entirely by a graphical user interface. Almost everything can be done using the mouse and the point-and-click, drag-and-drop, or double-click techniques. Programs are listed in menus and stored in files, so the only thing you need to know to find and execute a file is how to click a mouse button. Of course, even in its most recent releases, Windows still provides command line access to most of the basic OS operations.

The name "Windows" comes from the fact that each program runs in its own distinct window which can be resized and moved, and each window has its own set of controls.

The first thing you must do in order to use the Windows OS is log on. Windows machines are often networked together, and groups of resources are organized into domains. A user can connect to different domains, or sub-networks, simply by logging into that domain from the logon screen. Logging on to systems on corporate networks can be subject to administrative policies; if so, consult your system administrator.

Once logged in, you will notice the Windows Desktop that is loaded and displayed. The Desktop consists of the Start menu in the bottom left corner, the task bar along the bottom of the screen, and the workspace containing some default shortcuts along the left side. Most operations are preformed by pointing to an icon or file name on the desktop or in Windows Explorer and clicking or double-clicking.

The task bar along the bottom can hold shortcuts to applications and will display a small title bar for each window that is running. Clicking on a small title bar here will bring that window in front of all other windows. Any window that is opened can be minimized (click the box in the top right of a window with an underscore '_'), at which time the window will disappear from the workspace and shrink down to a small title bar in the task bar. Clicking on this title bar will restore the window to its maximum size. While the task bar is important, the path to almost everything in Windows begins with the Start Menu, which is covered in the next section.

Vocabulary

The popularity of Windows is not necessarily based on its high resolution graphics, nor its ease of use. The Windows advantage comes from *standardization*: a predictable, consistent model for the way things work on a PC running Windows.

The following list is not in alphabetical order, but rather from the most fundamental components to the more incidental, with virtually every term related in some way to the term before it. These vocabulary words are the building blocks of the Windows OS.

Many of these terms you have already seen, and some of them ("mouse") are downright obvious. Read through these anyway, you might find them interesting.

Figure 14-1. Screen Capture

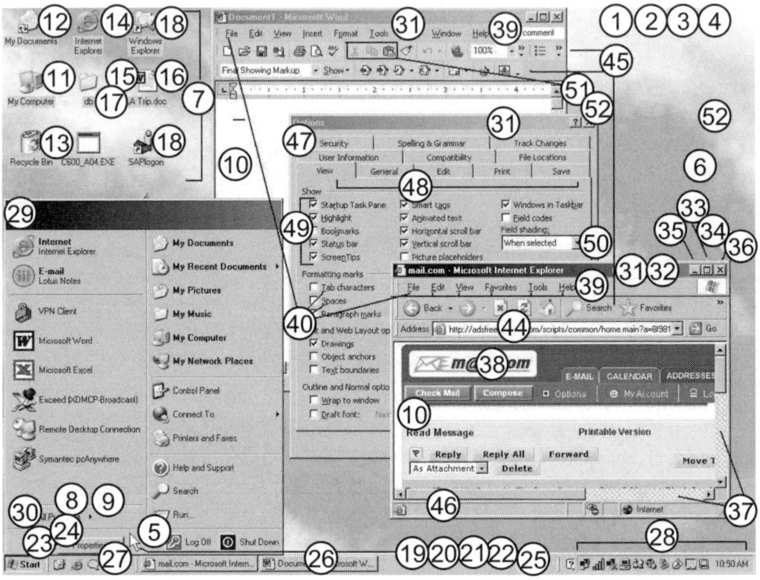

1. **Operating System** – "Operating" means "functioning" or simply, "working." "System" means a methodology based on a set of organized procedures. So, an operating system is a set of procedures that defines how things work. Windows defines how things work on your PC and provides the standard for how applications in Windows should work. If you ever write an application for the Windows OS, pay attention to how Windows does things, and try to make your application conform to those features. The term "Operating System" should convey *predictability*. As boring as that may sound, predictability is one big reason for the success of Windows.

2. **Graphical User Interface (GUI)** – pronounced "gooey", it is a means to interact with the computer using a mouse to manipulate bitmapped graphics instead of typing commands in a text-based interface. In fact, often the text in a window is not actual text, but a graphic of that text.

3. **Microsoft Windows** – the brand name of the Operating System in this chapter. Other operating systems employ "windows", but the functionality discussed in this chapter is specific to Microsoft Windows.

4. **Mouse** – the pointing device used to navigate and manipulate objects in the GUI. Although mice are now built into laptops (often as glidepads, joysticks, or other pointing devices) and many have multiple buttons, wheels, etc., for the purposes of this chapter, the mouse is defined as the two-button, right-handed kind.

5. **Mouse Pointer** – movement of the mouse on the table or mouse pad causes a graphic pointer to move around the screen, usually appearing in the shape of a white arrow, but it can also be shaped as cross-hairs, an I-beam, or a hand, depending on the application.

6. **Desktop** – The desktop is the background screen with the icons on top of it. It is always in the background, no matter what applications are running or how many windows are open. The latest versions of Windows include "show the desktop" as a shortcut menu item and often as a "quick launch" button on the taskbar.

7. **Icon** – in religion, an *icon* is a picture with special meaning and power. In Microsoft Windows, that definition also applies. The icon is a picture that represents the application that will be run if the picture is clicked.

8. **Program** – synonymous with *Application*, a program is code that is executed when you click its icon. Programs are organized in Microsoft Windows through the Start > All Programs buttons on the task bar, but can also be accessed through icons on the desktop.

9. **Application** – synonymous with *Program*, an application is code that is executed when you click its icon. Applications generally refer to programs that you run to achieve an objective (such as word processing, creating spreadsheets, etc.). Programs also include built-in functions with Windows that are designed to make the operating system run, but not necessarily achieve objectives.

10. **Window** – the window is a box that appears on the screen as it runs a program. In the diagram, the windows are running Microsoft Word and Internet Explorer.

11. **My Computer** – a built-in icon that allows you to navigate or view information about the computer.

12. **My Documents** – a built-in icon linked to the default location of your documents.

13. **Recycle Bin** – a built-in icon which holds "deleted" items so that they can be recovered before final deletion (called *emptying the recycle bin*).

14. **Internet Explorer** – a built-in icon which connects your system to the Internet.

15. **File** – a file is a collection of data which can contain information, graphics, or executable programs. On the desktop, a file is an icon that varies in appearance based on the application that uses the file. In the diagram, "LA Trip.doc" is a file that is a Word document, while "C600_A04.exe" is a file that is an executable program.

16. **File Association** – based on the file extension (the three to four characters appended to the file name after the last period in the name, for example "exe", "doc", or "html"), file association determines which program will run when an icon is clicked, also the appearance of the icon (which is why the "LA Trip.doc" icon resembles a document with the large "W" for Word in the top left corner).

17. **Folder** – folder icons look like manila folders, and represent collections of files together in a single area. Folder is synonymous with "directory" and the terms "subfolder" and "subdirectory" are also synonymous, referring to a folder within another folder. It is recommended that you use the term "folder", which is the term used in most documentation of Windows.

18. **Shortcut** – a shortcut is a special icon with an arrow in the lower left corner, as shown: . In the diagram, "SAPlogon" is not a program on the desktop, but rather a shortcut which links to a program in an entirely different location.

19. **Click** – sometimes called *single-click*, clicking is *navigational* by default. In other words, you click an icon to "go to" it, but you *double*-click to actually execute its function. Note: clicking can be modified to execute with a single-click (see *Control Panel, Folder Options*), but this is not recommended.

20. **Drag** – dragging refers to holding the left mouse button down while moving the mouse. Dragging is most often used to move highlighted files, text, etc. from one place to another, but it is also used to highlight groups of icons, ranges of text in word processing documents, and groups of cells in spreadsheet programs.

21. **Double-click** – clicking the left mouse button twice in rapid succession causes the icon to execute. If the icon is not executable, it will cause the program associated with the file to execute with that file.

22. **Right-click** – PC-compatible mice generally have two buttons: one on the left, typically under the index finger, and one on the right, typically under the middle finger. Click the right mouse button, or "right-click" for short, to see a custom short cut menu based on the object that you click (even the desktop itself).

23. **Shortcut Menu** – sometimes called context menu because it changes based on the context of the object you right-click.

24. **Properties** – although shortcut menus are customized to the item you click, virtually all shortcut menus contain a "properties" menu item. Properties are typically modifiable elements of an object, and they vary by object. Consider the properties of an object to be all the adjectives you can use to define how the object appears or behaves. There are so many variances from object to object, the best advice is simply to check them out: right-click and select properties on a variety of objects, and see what options are available to you.

25. **Taskbar** – the taskbar is normally at the bottom of the screen, and contains a button for each active program. Although it can be relocated to any of the four corners of the desktop, moving the taskbar is not recommended – remember the importance of maintaining predictability.

26. **Buttons** – buttons contain a raised, shadow-embossed appearance to make them look 3-dimensional (like a push-button). Clicking a button generally makes the button appear pressed – and activates some function until the button is clicked again and returned to the unpressed position. For example, pressing a taskbar button gives focus to its window. Clicking the button again minimizes it.

27. **Quick Launch Button** – the left side of the taskbar contains the "quick launch" buttons, which activate programs with a single click. Again, these buttons can be relocated anywhere on the taskbar, but it is not recommended. To see text defining these buttons, simply hover the mouse pointer over the button.

28. **Notification Area** – the right side of the taskbar is an area commonly known as the "system tray", now called the Notification Area in XP, consisting of applications which run "in the background", meaning the programs run but do not necessarily manifest themselves in separate windows. Also, this area usually contains the system clock. More icons in the system tray may indicate that the system is consuming too many resources.

29. **Start Menu** – the Start Menu refers to the menu of items that appears when you click the "start" button, located in the far left of the taskbar. The Start Menu in Windows XP is self-customizing, so it can appear very different at different installations. The Start Menu is the starting point for running any programs installed on the system, particularly those which have no icons on the desktop for them. The Start Menu also contains the Shut Down button, which some in the industry find amusing; you have to click *start* to *stop* the computer.

30. **Programs /All Programs** – from within the Start Menu, click "Programs" or "All Programs" to view a menu of all the applications installed.

31. **Title bar** – the title bar is the bar at the top of a window which contains the title of the application (e.g., "Microsoft Word") and some information about the file opened by the application (e.g., "LA Trip.doc"). You can click and drag the title bar to move the entire window around the screen, or double-click the title bar to toggle between maximized and non-maximized window appearance. The title bar appears blue by default when the window has the *focus* and gray when the window does not. Note that the title bar doesn't have to be blue, but again, for standardization, leave this setting alone.

32. **Focus** – when referring to a window, focus is its activation, bringing it to the foreground. A window has to have focus if you want to perform any operation in it. Objects within a window can have the focus within that window. A text box, for example, has to have the focus for you to type in it. By the way, when referring to focus, one usually says that the object "has the focus" rather than being "in focus."

The next four definitions refer to the three buttons on the far right side of the title bar.

33. **Restore** – for a window, restore is the process of returning a maximized or minimized window to its previous size. The windows in the diagram have not been maximized or minimized, but supposing they were, the restore button would return them to the original sizes and locations shown.

34. **Maximize** – maximizing a window causes it to get the focus, fill the entire desktop, and be the foreground program running. Since restore and maximize are exclusive of one another, they share the same middle button space on the title bar.

35. **Minimize** – minimizing a window causes it to disappear, but continue running. Minimizing a window causes an animation of the window disappearing into its corresponding taskbar button and that button returning to the unpressed position.

36. **Exit** – the exit function is on the third and final button on the right side of the title bar. If you want to close a window and exit, just click this button (or "X" it).

37. **Scroll Bars** – windows with content greater than the screen size have scrollbars to allow you to move around within the window to see the additional content. A window with additional vertical content has a vertical scrollbar which can be dragged up and down. A window with additional horizontal content has a horizontal scrollbar, which can be dragged side to side on the bottom of the pane.

38. **Pane / Panel** – some windows, especially many on Web sites, are split into multiple sections, called panes or panels. Often, clicking an object in the left or top pane affects the content shown in the right pane.

39. **Menu Bar** – a menu bar is usually at the top of the window, just below the title bar. It contains words (like a menu, as opposed to buttons) which can be clicked to display a menu. The most common menu items are File, Edit, and View, but many more can appear. Menu items are arguably the most common controls you will click within a window, so familiarize yourself with them in whatever application you will be using. If you ever consider programming for Windows, you will create these menu items yourself, so pay attention to how they are organized and try to stick with the standards.

40. **Keyboard Shortcuts** – keyboard shortcuts provide an alternative to using the mouse and once you are accustomed to them, you use them more than the mouse because you don't have to take your hands off the keyboard. Keyboard shortcuts are indicated by an underlined letter in the menu item (e.g., File, Edit, etc.), and can be activated by pressing the Alt key plus the underlined letter.

41. **Alt Key** – the Alt key provides an alternative use for keys when used in conjunction with it. Alt plus an underlined character in the menu bar opens the dropdown menu for that menu selection. Alt + F, for example, usually invokes the File menu.

    a. **Alt + Spacebar** invokes the title bar menu, which contains a text menu of the main window functions: maximize, minimize, restore, etc.

    b. **Alt + Tab** moves through the active windows and allows you to select the window to receive the focus without using the mouse. Since Shift + Tab invokes the backward tab function, Alt + Shift + Tab moves backward through the active windows.

    c. **Alt + PrtSc** copies only the window in focus to the clipboard so it can be pasted into another Windows application.

42. **Ctrl Key** – the control key plus a character key invokes various functions without having to use the menu bar at all. The control key functions vary from application to application, but can generally be seen by viewing the dropdowns from the menu bar selections.

43. **Function Key** – function keys are along the top of most keyboards. Similar to the Ctrl + *character* functions, many of the function key capabilities can be found by reading the menu bar dropdowns. Many of these functions are standardized across applications, but are not as rigidly standardized from application to application.

44. **Address Bar** – the address bar, most often found in Explorer and Internet Explorer windows, shows the path to the file in use.

45. **Tool Bars** – toolbars vary widely from application to application, and consist mainly of graphic buttons that can invoke various functions. Some toolbar buttons contain text to tell you what they represent, but if not, simply hover the mouse pointer over the button to see its purpose.

46. **Status Bar** – the status bar appears at the bottom of the window and provides useful information about the window. For example, in Internet Explorer, the status bar shows the destination of a link when you hover the mouse pointer over that link, shows whether a Web site is secure (employing encryption to safeguard information sent to and from it via the browser) using a padlock indicator, and shows a status bar with an analog representation of the amount of data that has been loaded into a page prior to its completion. In Windows Explorer, the status bar shows the number of objects in a window and the total number of objects selected with their aggregate byte size.

47. **Dialog Box** – a dialog box, as shown in the diagram, is an informational form which is filled out to adjust settings. A dialog (for short) is not a separate application, but rather is used to provide information to an application which is running. In the diagram, the dialog box is displayed from Microsoft Word by selecting Tools / Options. This particular example is a multi-part dialog which encompasses examples of the next three definitions.

48. **Tabs** – tabs look like file folder tabs and allow one window or dialog box to toggle among different pages. In the diagram, the dialog box from MS-Word contains eleven sections of options, selectable by their tabs.

49. **Checkbox** – a checkbox is an indicator which can be filled in with an "x" by clicking with the mouse (or using the keyboard shortcut, if available). Checkboxes in the diagram are used to modify properties of the MS-Word window.

50. **Dropdown** – a dropdown is a box with multiple options which can be displayed by clicking the dropdown arrow (). These are very common in Windows applications, and if you are involved in helping others with Windows at any time, you will grow accustomed to saying "click the dropdown".

51. **Cut & Paste / Copy & Paste** – cut & paste is perhaps the most useful function in Windows (and in other applications which emulate Windows). The more you use this function, the more you will appreciate and rely on it. For example, you can take a range of cells from Microsoft Excel and paste them into a document. You can also clip graphics and put them into documents (as was done in the "dropdown" definition).

52. **Clipboard** – the clipboard refers to the memory of the items which have been cut or copied. The clipboard generally contains the last item cut or copied, although a number of applications allow for *multiple* clipboards, since cut & paste is so widely used. If some item of data you pasted is not in the right location or doesn't appeal to you, just remember that the data is still "on the clipboard", so you can paste it somewhere else or even into some other application altogether.

Getting Started

With only a brief introduction, you should be able to begin using a Windows computer. A program may be selected from the Start menu to be executed, such as a default text editor Notepad (Start > Programs > Accessories > Notepad). Often when files are to be copied or deleted, Windows Explorer is opened first (right-click Start Menu, choose Explore). It is usually a good idea to create a shortcut to Explorer and place it somewhere easily accessible, like on the desktop (see the *Odds and Ends* section).

File System

The Windows file system is based on drives, folders (directories), and files. Programs, documents, images, sounds, and everything that makes a computer run is a type of file. These files are organized in folders, and then often those folders are organized within more folders, and ultimately the hierarchy converges at a drive. A drive is a memory location that is named with a single letter followed by a colon. The default Windows structure defines C: as the main storage drive (this can be altered using Administration Tools, see the *Control Panel* section).

The A drive is typically the name given to the floppy disk drive, while the D drive is often the name given to the CD-ROM drive. Some Windows computers will have more named drives than this, but by default, a typical PC will have the A, C, and D drives. Windows XP machines will start with a few default file folders in the C drive (or other drive if not C), including Program Files, Documents and Settings, and WINNT.

Naming

Windows files and folders can be named fairly flexibly. A name may be any combination of letters, numbers, and underscores, and may not contain any of the characters: / \ * | < > ? ". The names are not case sensitive and they may contain spaces, as well as zero or many periods. File names end with a period followed by a three letter extension that is a signal to the OS as to the type of data the file contains, and therefore what program to launch if that file is opened. The extensions (such as .txt, .exe or .doc) are often hidden when viewed in Windows Explorer, and can be displayed by unchecking the 'Hide Extensions' checkbox after selecting Tools > Folder Options.

Windows Explorer

Nearly every action that is performed on a file can be managed through a tool named Windows Explorer. Windows Explorer allows you to cut, copy, paste, rename, move, and map drives. It is a physical representation of the computer's entire file system, and oftentimes the contents of remote file systems as well. A networked computer file system provides views to drives and folders located on other computers throughout the network. This is done by 'mapping' a logical drive letter on the local computer to a physical drive of a remote computer, allowing the contents of the remote drive to be traversed as if it were local.

The Explorer program is named explorer.exe and is located in the system root directory (often C:\winnt). It can always be started by right-clicking on the Start button, and choosing Explore from the pop-up menu.

The Explorer GUI has a list of the drives down the left side of the window. Expanding a drive on the left side will cause the folders of that drive to be displayed down the left side. Selecting a folder on the left side causes the contents of that folder to be displayed on the right side. The GUI layout and display properties can be edited by selecting Tools > Folder Options from the upper window pane.

Using Explorer

Programs are run from the Explorer simply by using the point-and-click method. A program can be executed either by double clicking on the program name in the right panel of the Explorer, or by single clicking the name so it becomes highlighted and pressing the Enter key. Double-clicking a file opens the associated program (see *#16. File Association*, above). Using Windows XP, it is possible to change that association by right-clicking the file name and choosing Properties > Change on the General tab.

A file can be moved from one directory to another simply by selecting the file name and dragging it to the new location. Note that if the new location is on another drive, the file is copied and not moved. The typical way of copying a file is by right-clicking on the file name and selecting Copy from the pop-up menu. This will put the file onto the clipboard. The file is then pasted to the new location by right-clicking there and selecting Paste from the pop-up menu.

A file is deleted by right-clicking and choosing Delete, and a file can be renamed by right-clicking and choosing Rename.

Odds and Ends

This section provides some useful, and in some cases undocumented, tips for getting the most out of Windows.

The cutting, pasting, deleting, and renaming methods described above for files also hold true for file folders in Windows Explorer. Additionally, Ctrl-C, Ctrl-V, and Ctrl-X shortcuts can be used in the Explorer to copy, paste, and delete. In order to select more than one file or folder to perform an operation upon, hold down the Ctrl key while clicking each of the selections, or hold down the Shift key while choosing a range of selections.

Drives and folders existing on other computers in the network can be ‘mapped’ to, creating a virtual drive on a remote computer. A drive is mapped by choosing Tools > Map Network Drive, choosing a drive letter, and entering the name and location of the remote drive or folder. This new virtual drive can be navigated through as if the files existed on the local computer.

You can also hold down the Ctrl key as you click and drag a file (and in most cases, highlighted text in documents or on Web pages) to copy the object without placing it on the Clipboard. You can drag and drop the object on another window or onto a folder in the left panel.

While Windows Explorer is designed to do all of the things mentioned in this section (and more), most of the same exercises can be performed by a default tool called *My Computer* on the desktop which, if double-clicked, opens up to display a GUI much like the Explorer interface. Some prefer to use this method for file navigation and manipulation.

In many windows which contain column headings (especially Windows Explorer), you can click the column heading to sort the results in column order, as shown. If you click the Name heading, then sort in alphabetical order, folders will display first and then the files. Click Name again, and they're in descending order. Click Date Modified, and the sort order becomes Date, ascending:

Figure 14-2. Windows Explorer Using the 'Details' View

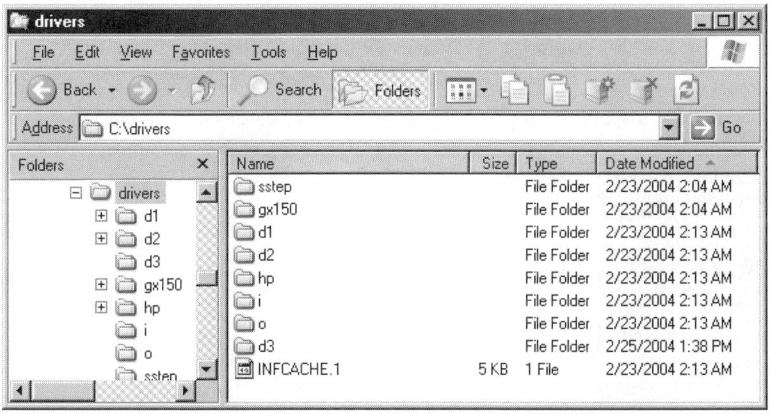

Notice that folders are sorted separately from files, thus "INFCACHE.1" appears at the bottom of the list even though it is newer than the folder preceding it.

Try this technique whenever you see column headings. Any application which conforms to the general standards of Windows should have these features built in.

Alt + Tab toggles forward among the open windows (as reflected on the taskbar). Alt + Shift + Tab toggles backward.

Finally, though it has already been mentioned, "Help and Support" is available. Just click it from the Start Menu. It may sound obvious, but it's probably one of the most underused functions in Windows because people are accustomed to figuring out Windows intuitively.

Permissions

Windows allows permissions to be set on files and folders. This is accomplished through the use of Windows Explorer (right-click > Properties > Security) or the cacls command line utility (see *NT Shell Commands* later, or type 'help cacls'). The permissions can apply to groups as well as individual users. When a user is a member of more than one group, the least restrictive permission is adhered to, unless any of those permissions is 'no access', in which case, no access is allowed. The permission types are described below:

- Read (R) - can view contents, attributes and permissions.
- Write (W) - can create files and folders, and modify file contents and file attributes.
- Read (R) and Execute (E) - can Read, change subfolders, and execute files.
- List Folder Contents - can Read and Execute, and view folder contents and permissions.
- Modify - can Read, Write, Execute, and Delete.
- Full Control - can Modify, take ownership, and change permissions.

The security capabilities of Windows 98 or ME machines do not provide as much flexibility as provided by Windows NT, 2000, or XP machines. It is also important to note that file level permissions are only possible on NTFS disk volumes, and cannot be set on FAT volumes.

System

The Windows OS is an ideal example of multitasking. Multiple windows can be opened at the same time, each running a different program, and each sharing the same computer resources. A tool named the Task Manager can be used to view all of the programs that are running at any given time, and to see the percentage of processor time being used by each. The Task Manager can be started by pressing Ctrl + Alt + Del. Using Windows NT, 2000, or XP, the Task Manager can also be invoked by right-clicking in an empty space of the taskbar at the bottom of the desktop or by pressing Ctrl + Shift + Esc.

The Task Manager displays all of the applications currently running on one tab, displays all of the processes running on the next tab, and provides vital statistics about the CPU and memory usage on the third tab. On the Processes tab, notice that background processes are listed here. Most processes may be abruptly killed by highlighting the process and clicking the End Process button.

The Application Tab is useful when a program locks up, as will sometimes occur, using all of the system resources unsuccessfully, while disallowing the use of other programs. When this happens, the Task Manager should be used to kill the application, which will display Not Responding in the Status column. The application will be abruptly killed, but control of the computer will be granted back to the user.

Often programs can be configured to run automatically as soon as the computer has started. These types of programs are called services, and are controlled using the Services folder of the Control Panel. The Services folder is reached by selecting Start > Control Panel > Administrative Tools > Services. From here, services can be stopped and started, and their properties can be modified. The Control Panel is discussed in the following section.

Control Panel

Below are some of the system administration settings and controls set through the Control Panel (Start > Control Panel). In Windows XP, the Administrative Tools folder contains many of the important administration programs. This is not an all-inclusive list, so explore Control Panel to see many additional functions available.

Computer Management - used to manage system tools, storage, and services. Groups, users, and permissions can be viewed and modified, event logs can be monitored, and devices can be managed. In addition, a hard disk can be defragmented or repartitioned, and services can be modified again through a shortcut to the Services panel.

Data Sources (ODBC) - Open Database Connectivity Data Source Administrator. This setting allows the creation and modification of data sources. The data sources can then be used by programs to connect to databases of certain types and execute SQL statements.

Event Viewer - used to manage and view the three Windows Event logs: System, Application, and Security.

Local Security Policy - used to configure and manage security settings for the local machine. Policies include password restrictions, account lockout rules, audit policies, and security options. If the computer is in a domain, domain settings may override these policies.

Services - used to manage services on the local machine. Services can be stopped and started, and set to run manually or automatically.

Other files in the Control Panel that are fairly common are listed below:

Add Hardware - used to add, remove, and troubleshoot hardware. This works in conjunction with the automatic Plug and Play tool.

Add or Remove Programs - used to manage programs on the local machine. Updates to Windows and software not included in the original install can be added here. The remove option removes an existing program cleanly using its installer/uninstaller. Use this menu instead of trying to delete programs using Explorer.

Folder Options - used to manage the appearance of the desktop and Windows Explorer. Default views can be set, as well as other settings like switching between double-clicking and single-clicking to open files.

Network Connections - used to configure settings for connecting to a network, another computer, or to the Internet. Connections can be made using a LAN, dial-up, or high-speed modems. There is also a shortcut to this tool under the Start menu.

Printers and Faxes- used to create and manage connections to printers for the local machine's access. The printers may be anywhere on the network. Once a printer connection has been created, any Windows application can print to any of the configured printers.

System - used to view and configure information about a network connection or a user profile, and about hardware and hardware configurations. System is also used to set environment variables for both system and users, and to set memory usage values.

Command Shell

Instead of the point and click functionality of the GUI, Windows features an alternative way to do many of its operations through the *command shell.* The command shell in Windows is a console application, one that interacts with the user through the console rather than the GUI. The command shell is always in *interactive* mode, waiting for input, unless it is executing a script, and then it is considered to be in *script* mode (see the next section for more about scripts).

A command shell is automatically started when a .bat or .cmd file is double-clicked in the Windows Explorer. The shell can be manually started by either selecting the command prompt from the Start Menu, or by typing 'cmd' in the dialogue box sprouted by selecting Run... from the Start Menu. Either way, the shell opens, displaying a command prompt with the current drive / directory and waiting for a command.

Any command entered at the command prompt will be executed upon pressing Enter. Parameters passed to a command are usually separated by spaces, and if a single argument contains a space, it must be enclosed in double quotes. There are a number of special characters that can be used at command prompts (see Table 14-6), and any reserved character not in double quotes must be escaped using the carat. Reserved characters include: & | ( ) < > ^ .

```
C:\>echo apples ^& pears
```

The previous line would print 'apples & pears'. Quotes and double quotes are considered part of the string:

```
C:\>echo "apples ^& pears"
```

The entry above would print '"apples & pears"'.

Commands

The cd and dir commands are probably the most widely used commands from the command prompt; they are used to change directories and list the contents of the directory. The cd command changes the current directory to the directory specified. This new directory can be relative to the current directory or an absolute path, including the drive. Calling the command as cd .. will make the parent directory the current directory. To change to a different drive, simply type the drive letter followed by a colon at the command prompt (no cd command).

The dir command lists files in the named directory, or if no directory is named, the files in the current directory will be listed. Table 14-1 contains a list of switches for the dir command.

Files and directories may be copied, renamed, and deleted from the command line. Permissions may be set, services may be stopped and started, and a host of other operations may be performed from the command line. A listing of major shell commands is included in the *NT Shell Commands* section at the end of this chapter.

The question remains, "If these things can be done by pointing and clicking in the GUI, why use the command line?" The answer, aside from personal preference, can be found in shell programs. Shell, or batch, programs can relieve repetitive tasks, such as assigning permissions to hundreds of users, or can run either of two programs based on conditions. Batch programs can be very useful in Windows.

Table 14-1. Switches for dir Command

/p	Pause after each page of listings.
/w	Wide format.
/b	Bare format, no summary information.
/n	Include summary information (default).
/a:*att*	Filter by attribute, ***att*** is D (directories), R (read-only), H (hidden), S (system).
/o:*srt*	Sort by *srt, srt* is N (names), S (size), D (date), - (invert order).
/t:*ti*	Select time field to display.
/l	Use lowercase characters in display.
/x	Include ms-dos compatible names.

PATH

The way Windows knows where to find programs that are called from the command line is through the use of the PATH environment variable. The PATH variable defines the Windows search path, which is a list of directories separated by semicolons. When a program is called, Windows first searches the current directory for a command with a matching name, and if nothing is found, begins searching the search path. The listed directories are searched in listed order until a match is found, or an error is reported (when no match is found).

The variable can be set in the Environment tab of the Control Panel > System selection, or can be set in the current window by using the path command or the set command. The following line appends a new path to the end of the existing value:

```
C:\> set PATH=%PATH%;c:\temp\dev
```

The PATHTEXT variable contains a list of semicolon separated file extensions that Windows considers executable files. When a command is called and before it is searched for, Windows looks here for the possible file extensions, and then it begins its search for the command name with one of the attached extensions. While PATHTEXT can be edited like any other environment variable, it has a default value of .com; exe; .bat; .cmd.

Shell Programming

A shell script is nothing more than a series of simple commands grouped together in a single text file, such that when the text file executes, the commands in the file execute. Part of the strength of a shell script is that the commands need not execute in the order that they appear, utilizing loops and goto statements. A shell script is often called a batch file because of its .bat extension. Any simple text file (edited in Notepad or any text editor) can be saved with a .bat extension and it will become a batch file.

A batch file is executed by either calling its name from the command prompt (or from another batch file) or by simply double clicking the file name in Windows Explorer. A script should be ended simply by executing to the end of the file, or by using a 'goto :EOF'. The exit command can be used, but be aware that this ends the script and immediately closes the shell window. A typical Windows batch file may look like this:

```
@echo off
rem This is a test script
set PATH=%PATH%;c:\temp\dev
echo %PATH%
if %1 == 1 echo You entered 1
goto :EOF
```

The echo command followed by text will display the text to the console, while the echo command followed by 'on' or 'off' toggles the echo option for the entire window. The command alone will display the current status of the feature, while any line beginning with '@' will not be displayed to the console, regardless of the toggle setting:

```
C:\> echo This will be printed
```

The rem command indicates that a comment, or remark, is listed to the right of it. The set command is used to set the values of environment variables. Parameters passed into the script are accessed using the percent sign ahead of the numbers 1 - 9. The goto command causes execution to jump to the label defined, and the :EOF is an automatic label that Windows recognizes as the end of the file.

Variables

Each Windows process is given its own environment, complete with a set of variables, both system and user defined. While these variables are permanently set using the Environment tab of the Control Panel > System, each command shell session can create and modify variables for that session only. Once that command shell is closed, the changes made to the environment variables are erased, and the variable values resort back to the values set in Control Panel > System. Each process initially inherits the environment of its parent process.

The set command is the key to variables in shell scripts, with a no argument set returning the current environment variables and values. Set followed by a few letters will return only those variable names that match that string pattern. To create a variable, use the following format:

set *variable_name=variable_value*

Note that everything to the right of the equal sign is saved as the *variable_value*, including spaces. A variable is deleted by using the above set format with a null *variable_value*, and a specific *variable_value* is displayed with this command:

set *variable_name*

When the set command is used on an existing variable, the old value of the variable is lost. This can be avoided by using environment variable substitution, initiated by surrounding a variable by percent signs. The following line appends one more directory path to the existing value of the PATH variable:

```
set PATH=%PATH%;c:\bin\myUser
```

Parameters are passed into a shell script from the command line by listing the parameters separated by spaces following the command name. These parameters, the first through the ninth, are handled in the script using a percent sign and the numbers 1 through 9, accordingly. The special variable %* returns all of the parameters, even those greater than 9. Otherwise, the shift command can be used to reach variables after the 9th.

The two parameters param_one and “param two”, passed into the command call below are referenced using the variables %1 and %2:

```
C:\>theTestScript param_one "param two"
```

Flow

Windows provides a number of commands that are used to cause batch files to perform activities that one might not suspect possible with such a simple language using only flow statements such as if, for, goto, and labels.

If

The if command executes a command *conditionally*, using the format:

```
if condition (true_commands) else (false_commands)
```

The parentheses, as well as the else segment, are not required to create a valid if statement. The command list, if surrounded by parentheses, may span multiple lines (though no comments can be inserted between the lines). Multiple if commands may be nested within one another. The most common condition in an if statement is probably a string comparison, achieved using two equal signs. Though not technically necessary, the strings should always be enclosed in double quotes. Trailing and leading spaces are noticed if enclosed in quotes:

```
if "%MYVAR%" == "hello there" echo It is hello there
```

The if defined command tests for the existence of the named variable; if errorlevel checks the exit code of the command that most recently executed; if exist tests for the existence of the named file or directory. The not keyword can be used in if statements to test for opposite conditions.

For

The for command proves to be very powerful in shell scripts, creating a loop, repeating a command, often for an unknown number of times:

```
for iterator do command
```

The *iterator* is comprised of an iteration variable, the keyword in, and a set of objects to iterate through. The iteration variable is a variable that exists only within the loop, represented by a single letter preceded by two percent signs (iteration variables in interactive mode, or called from the command line, require only a single percent sign). The *command* can be a single command or a number of commands on multiple lines surrounded by parentheses:

```
C:\> for %N in (c:\temp\bin\*.exe) do echo %N
```

The above example iterates through all of the files with a .exe extension in the directory c:\temp\bin and prints their names to the screen. The for command can be used to iterate directories by adding the /d switch to the command. The following command lists the names of all of the files in the c:\temp directory:

```
C:\> for /d %N in (c:\temp\*) do echo %N
```

The for command called with the /L switch is most similar to for loops in other programming languages. It loops as specified by a starting integer, stepping value, and ending integer specified in that order, separated by commas. The following batch program uses a for loop to call a procedure named :myProc ten times, passing it a new parameter each time. Notice that it uses two percent signs since it is called from a script body. The procedure :myproc then uses %1 to refer to the argument that is passed to it:

```
@echo off
for /l %%N in (1,1,10) do call :myProc %%N
  goto :EOF
:myproc
  echo Hello %1
  goto :EOF
```

Goto and Labels

A label is a character string prefixed with a colon that must be on its own line. It is not case sensitive, but labels are usually in caps so they stand out. Labels can contain letters, numbers, and underscores, and while spaces are allowed before and after the colon, they are not allowed in the label itself. Every script is provided with one automatic label, the :EOF. This label signifies the end of a file, and is used with the goto command as other programming languages use a return statement. Labels are used in call statements as the name of the procedure to execute and in goto statements indicating the line to jump to.

The goto command, when executed, immediately transfers execution to the line following the specified label. The command name is followed by the label name. Although it is not required to add the colon before the label name in a goto statement, it is good practice because the colon is required when executing a call statement:

```
:START_OF_BLOCK
rem Add conditional command here
goto :START_OF_BLOCK
```

Call and Labels

The call command is used to execute either a separate shell script or a procedure inside its own script. Calling another script is as simple as naming the script to call, followed by any arguments to pass to the script. The second script executes in its own command shell, and when finished, returns control back to the line following the original call command:

```
call myScript
```

Calling procedures is a little more interesting, as it involves first creating a procedure with the use of a label. The label indicates the start of the procedure, and the end of file indicates the end. A procedure is a block of commands which, when called using the call command, executes and once it is finished, returns to the statement immediately following the call command. It is often a useful way to code a commonly called group of commands because you can write it once and call it when needed.

Procedures begin with the label name, and usually end with a goto :EOF statement. In this manner, multiple procedures can be created in the same script file. The goto :EOF command acts much like a return statement does in other programming languages:

```
@echo off
rem Body of script here
call :Proc1
rem More script here
call MyExternalScriptFile
rem More script here
call :Proc2 param1
goto :EOF

rem Start Proc1
:Proc1
  rem Body of Proc1 here
  echo In Proc1
  goto :EOF

rem Start Proc2
:Proc2
  rem Body of Proc2 here
  echo In Proc2, parameter: %1
  goto :EOF
```

Special Commands

Windows provides a few characters with special powers in script programming. A few of the most used characters are described in Table 14-2.

Table 14-2. Script Programming Special Characters

Character	Description
command > *file*	The greater than sign is used to send the output of the *command* to the specified *file*. If the *file* already exists, it is overwritten.
command >> *file*	Appends the output of the *command* to the file if it already exists.
command < *file*	The *command* takes its input from the *file* specified rather than from user input.
cmd1 | *cmd2*	The pipe between two commands takes the output from *cmd1* and pipes into *cmd2* as input. Multiple pipes can be used together.
cmd1 & *cmd2*	The ampersand is used to create compound commands, executing *cmd1* and then *cmd2* when the first is finished. Multiple ampersands can be used together.
cmd1 && *cmd2*	Double ampersands executes conditionally, only executing *cmd2* if *cmd1* finished successfully.
cmd1 || *cmd2*	Executes *cmd2* only if *cmd1* did not execute successfully.
( )	Parentheses are used to group multi-line IF...ELSE commands or to group nested command sequences.

Windows Script Host

Windows Script Host (WSH) is a scripting environment that can be used with compatible scripting engines to run scripts from the command prompt. It is best used for non-interactive administration tasks and is often used to map network drives, connect to network printers, and modify environment variables. It is built into all versions of Windows, and the latest version may be downloaded from the Microsoft Web site.

A WSH file is a text file that ends with a .vbs, .js, or .wsh_extension, indicating that it contains either VBScript, JScript, or XML-encoded scripting code. The file can be executed by double-clicking the file icon or by entering the file name from the command prompt. WSH files are often scheduled or are designed to run automatically each time a PC boots.

The WSH environment includes a hierarchical object model of 14 objects that aid in administrative PC tasks. The WScript object provides access to system objects (including the commands), the WshEnvironment object provides access to system environment variables, and the WshShortcut object allows you to create a shortcut.

The following lines of VBScript create a WshNetwork object using the WScript object (the root of the hierarchy), and then adds a printer connection to the PC's printers:

```
Set MyNetwork = WScript.CreateObject("WScript.Network")
MyNetwork.AddPrinterConnection "LP1", "\\PrintServers\Print1"
```

WSH 1.0 came with Windows 95, 98, and NT 4.0. WSH 2.0 came with Windows 2000 and ME. The latest version is WSH 5.6, included with Windows XP, and is available for upgrade at http://www.msdn.Microsoft.com. The numbers were skipped to put WSH in sync with the Microsoft Windows Script 5.6 download package, which also includes VBScript, JScript, and the Windows Script Components and Runtime.

NT Shell Commands

The following is a brief description of NT shell commands. A full usage description is available by typing help followed by the command name at any command prompt. Commands followed by an asterisk are available with the Windows NT Resource Kit, a free download from http://www.msdn.microsoft.com. Characters, &, |, (,), ^, are reserved in shells.

Table 14-3. Application Control Commands

Command	Description	Command	Description
assoc	Displays and edits current mappings between file extensions and file types.	logoff*	Ends the current Windows session, logging out user.
associate*	Displays and edits current mappings between file extensions and applications.	pulist*	Lists active process on named computer along with associated user.
at	Schedules commands to run at certain times and dates, same as winat.	reg*	Edits registry on named computer or local computer by default.
attrib	Sets attributes of named files, such as read-only (R), system (S), and hidden (H).	sclist*	Lists the services on named computer or local computer by default.
cmd	Starts a command shell.	shutdown*	Begins shutting down Windows, often with a delay.
command	Starts an MS-DOS shell.	sleep*	Pauses execution of a script for a specified number of seconds.
exit	Exits the current window.	soon*	Schedules a command for a time relative to current time, uses AT command.
ftype	Displays and edits file type commands in the registry.	start	Starts a new command window and runs the named command there.
kill*	Kills the named process.	winat	Schedules commands to run at certain times and dates, like AT.
local*	Lists members of the named local group.		

Table 14-4. File and Directory Commands

Command	Description	Command	Description
attrib	Displays or alters attributes of named files.	move	Moves named files to named directory.
cacls	Displays or alters ACL (access control list).	net file	Manages server files.
Cd	Displays current directory or changes to named directory.	ntbackup	Used for automatic volume backup.
chdir	Displays current directory or changes to named directory.	rd	Deletes named directories, as well as their contents.
copy	Copies named files.	ren	Renames files or directories.
del	Deletes named files.	rename	Renames files or directories.
dir	Lists contents of named directory, or current directory if no directory is named.	replace	Replaces a file with a new version.
diruse*	Displays file and directory space usage.	rmdir	Deletes named directories as well as their contents.
diskuse*	Displays file usage by user.	robocopy*	Copies named directory trees.
erase	Deletes named files.	scopy*	Copies files and carries over security information.
fc	Compares named files.	sort	Sorts lines of text.
find	Searches specified text for named character lines.	subst	Creates virtual drive mappings.
findstr	Searches specified text for named strings	type	Displays named text file in console.
md	Creates named directory.	xcacls	Displays or alters ACL (access control list).
mkdir	Creates named directory.	copy	Copies named files or directories.
more	Displays text one page at a time.		

Table 14-5. Scripting Language Commands

Command	Description	Command	Description
call	Initiates a script file or a script label as a procedure.	if	Creates conditional execution of a command.
choice*	Retrieves input entered from keyboard.	path	Sets the PATH variable with paths that are searched when a command is called.
clip*	Puts the named command onto the clipboard.	pause	Pauses a script until a key is pressed by the user.
cls	Clear the console window.	popd	Restores a directory that was saved using pushd.
cmd	Starts a command shell.	prompt	Sets the shell prompt to the listed characters, often special characters (see list).
color	Used to set background and foreground color of console.	pushd	Saves a directory to be restored by popd.
command	Starts a MS-DOS shell.	rem	Indicates a comment to the right of rem (remark).
doskey	Manages command history and macro buffers.	set	Sets environment variables using the form, set VAR=value.
echo	Sends output to the console when on.	setlocal	Signifies the beginning of a scope for a local variable.
endlocal	Signifies end of a local scope for a variable.	shift	Accesses command arguments beyond the first nine.
exit	Closes the current command shell.	start	Starts a new command window and runs the named command there.
for	Creates a loop, repeating a command for a variable number of iterations.	title	Sets the title bar of the console window.
goto	Jumps to the named label in a script.	ver	Returns the Windows version.

Table 14-6. Special Shell Prompt Characters

$a	Ampersand	$p	current drive with directory path
$b	Pipe	$q	equal sign
$c	left parenthesis	$s	Space
$d	current date	$t	current time
$e	escape code	$v	windows version number
$f	right parenthesis	$_	new line
$g	greater than	$$	dollar sign
$h	Backspace	$+	'+' signs, used in pushd command
$l	less than	$m	remote name of current drive
$n	current drive letter		

Looking Forward

There is no disputing the popularity of Microsoft's Windows OS. It is the OS on which hundreds of millions have been introduced to PCs and the Internet, and most of those users are going to stay with Windows for a long time to come.

Microsoft has been producing three lines of its operating systems for some time now. There is the home PC version (Windows 95, Windows 98, and Windows ME), the business version (Windows NT and Windows 2000), and the server version (Windows NT Server, Windows 2000 Server, and Windows 2003 Server). The latest version at time of press is named Windows XP, for Windows Experience, and currently includes Service Pack 2 to address multiple security threats and other issues.

Updates to Windows are as close as http://www.windowsupdate.com, which will automatically evaluate your system Information for Windows XP. Of course, general Windows information, updates, or downloads can be found at http://www.microsoft.com or http://www.msdn.microsoft.com.

Much of Microsoft Windows is "caught" rather than "taught", meaning you will learn many new techniques just by using the product. One final note: if you want to look like a genius, use Windows Help. You won't believe how many people overlook the built-in help. Above all, Windows is based on intuition; once you are comfortable using a mouse to activate tasks, navigate, and so forth, you will figure out many tips and techniques of your own. Don't forget to share them.

Chapter 15

Linux/GNU

The Linux kernel started as a personal project by Linus Torvalds. His motivation for writing Linux was displeasure with the operating system (OS) that came with the computer he purchased in 1990. Another contributing reason was that gaining access to a UNIX system required going to school, usually in the blistering cold. Instead, he wanted a UNIX system he could use on his Intel-based system at home.

He started the daunting task of writing a complete OS from scratch only one year after taking his first C programming language class. He worked at a feverish pace in 1991 on the kernel itself and ported the GNU bash shell and the GNU compiler. By August 1991, he had enough to present to the open source community. He did this with this famous Usenet post:

> From: torvalds@klaava.Helsinki.FI (Linus Benedict Torvalds)
>
> Subject: What would you like to see most in minix?
>
> Date: 25 Aug 91 20:57:08 GMT
>
> Hello everybody out there using minix -
>
> I'm doing a (free) operating system (just a hobby, won't be big and professional like gnu) for 386(486) AT clones. This has been brewing since april, and is starting to get ready. I'd like any feedback on things people like/dislike in minix, as my OS resembles it somewhat (same physical layout of the file-system (due to practical reasons) among other things)...
>
> Linus (torvalds@kruuna.helsinki.fi)
>
> PS. Yes - it's free of any minix code, and it has a multi-threaded fs. It is NOT protable (uses 386 task switching etc), and it probably never will support anything other than AT-harddisks, as that's all I have :-(.

All of Torvald's exposure to OS design up to this point was Minix, an operating system written by Andrew Tanenbaum, a college professor. While Minix and Linux had a lot in common in terms of platform, they differed in their design approach and license. Torvald's disagreement with Tanenbaum was the fact that Minix wasn't free--it didn't allow developers to openly collaborate.

Fast Facts

- List the files in a directory: ls [*path*].
- Change from one directory to another: cd <*directory*>.
- Edit a file: vi <*file name*>.
- Make a new directory: mkdir <*directory name*>.
- At the shell prompt, whitespace doesn't matter, but case does.
- Execute a script or program: <*program name*>.
- Execute a script or program in the current directory: ./<*program name*>.
- Use output of one program to another by 'piping': <*output program*> | <*input program*>.
- Log in to another UNIX or Linux host: telnet <*hostname*> or slogin <*host name*>. Note that slogin (ssh) is much more secure as telnet sends all content, including user and passwords, as clear text over the network.
- Schedule a command (event) to occur on a scheduled basis: crontab -e.
- Schedule a command (event) to occur a single time: echo '<*command*>' | at <date/time or 'now + time'>.
- Determine who you are logged in as and what groups you are in: id.
- Reboot the system (*must* be logged in as root): shutdown -r now.
- Switch to a different user without logging back in: su - [*user account id*].
- Look for text in all the files in the current directory: grep <*text*> *.
- Search for a file by name recursively: find . -name '<*filename*>'.
- Find a process ID: ps -eaf | grep <*process name*>.
- Kill a process: kill [-9] <*process ID*>, where the -9 does an unclean force quit.

Basics of Linux

This section contains basic information on navigating the file system, making and removing directories, and editing files.

Documentation

Linux documentation ranges from extremely well-documented, easily readable and searchable, to non-existent. While the Linux kernel is extremely well-documented and comes with the kernel source code, many packages that come with the system might not be. There is typically a good deal of online documentation available for these packages. This can be in the form of a project site or online discussion forums (Usenet or message board). For either, Google Web and group searches will yield good results, depending on how large the user/install base of the package is.

Man Pages

The first thing to learn with using either UNIX or Linux/GNU is how to read man pages. Man pages document a particular aspect—usually a command, but at times a sub-system (i.e. NFS). For commands, man pages detail what the command does, the options that are provided, what is expected as input, and what the output should be. For example, to read the man page for the ls command, use:

```
$ man ls
```

The Linux Documentation Project (TLDP)

The Linux Documentation Project (http://tldp.net) is the largest known resource for documentation for both the OS and tools/applications.

The majority of the documentation is in the form of HOWTOs or MINI-HOWTOs. HOWTOs are large documents that usually include not only step-by-step procedures to get something working under Linux/GNU, but also introductions to the technology it covers. MINI-HOWTOs are exactly what they sound like: small versions of HOWTOs, sometimes overlapping, sometimes not.

File System

From a user perspective, the Linux/GNU file system is no different than a UNIX file system. The file system is often called a tree because it has a root and branches (directories) and leaves (files).

Anyone familiar with Microsoft Windows will find everything but the path separator, which is a forward slash in Linux (/) instead of a backward slash (\). In fact, it is simpler because it has only one root, where Windows can have as many as 24 (one for each drive letter).

Listing Files

The historical name for selecting more than one file is 'glob'. A glob is a special syntax used to select more than one file. Globs have some of the capabilities and analogous purpose to regular expressions and are pretty straight forward. Globs select 0 or more file names with a particular syntax.

The asterisk (*) is used as a wildcard that matches any characters in a file or directory name. For example, if you invoked ls, you would get a print out of every file and directory name in the current working directory. If you invoked ls foo*, you would get files and directories that started with foo, like foobar, foo, foobaz. Directories that matched the pattern are printed, not the directories themselves. To list directory names, use the -d option.

Most commands can take multiple parameters, each indicating a file in the above example. In this case, the shell itself expands the glob from the syntax (the asterisk) and then passes all matching files as arguments to ls. The ls command iterates through each argument and prints file names. If you add the -l option, you'll get a more detailed listing, including permissions and sizes.

Directory Commands

You can navigate the file system with the shell's cd command. For example, if the directory foo existed and you wanted to go (change) to it, use cd foo. To go up to the parent directory, use cd...

Command Line Interface

The command line interface refers to a textual user interface where commands are entered and the system replies with any output and results in the same text window under the command issued.

Shell

A shell is a program that enables a user to easily start programs and other typical end user tasks. Microsoft Windows users might be familiar with the MS-DOS "command.exe" shell. Both have the concept of a working directory, which is the directory the shell is currently 'in'. Once in a directory, it becomes easier to access and manipulate files and execute programs in the respective directory.

The default shell under Linux/GNU is the GNU bash shell (/bin/bash). This is an extended rewrite of the Bourne shell (its name stands for 'Bourne again shell').

Prompt

Again, the shell is the program that connects the user to the system via the OS. The *shell window* is a terminal or screen of text that contains user input and the output of commands. The shell prints a prompt whenever it expects user input. It usually looks something like <*hostname*>$, or [*hostname@user*]$.

Usage

When you type something at the shell prompt and hit enter, the shell interprets the first word (also called a token; delimited by whitespace) as the command, and the remaining tokens as arguments to that program. Once it has done this parsing, it invokes the command and passes the arguments to the program. Note that there are some exceptions to this rule for more advanced usages like command groups and temporary environment variables.

After the invoked command starts, the shell stops and waits for the command to finish. Any output from the command is displayed in the terminal shell window. There are cases where the command expects input interactively. In these cases, the command won't usually proceed until the input is given. Most commands that use this feature will run in a 'batch' mode or non-interactive mode by providing command line switches or redirecting standard input.

Environment Variables

Environment variables are a set of key-value text pairs that are used by the shell and programs invoked from the shell.

For example, when invoking the command man, how text is printed on the screen is defined by the PAGER environment variable. If you have a terminal that is capable of ASCII escape sequences, you could set this to 'less', which is an enhanced version of the command 'more', which does rudimentary text representation.

There are two kinds of shell variables: environment variables (exported) and non-exported local variables. If a shell variable is exported, it is copied and 'shows up' in a child program invoked by the shell (or any other program). For this reason, you must export the aforementioned PAGER environment variable for man (the subordinate program) to get your setting.

To define a local shell variable, separate the variable name on the left and the value on the right with an equal sign (=) *with no space between* variable name and value. For example:

```
PATH=${PATH}:/home/john/bin
export PATH
```

In this example, we first set the PATH variable to the current path (${PATH}) and add :/home/john/bin to it. The next line exports the variable making it an environment variable.

Invoking Commands and Scripts

To invoke any command from a shell, type the command and hit enter. For example, typing ls at a shell prompt runs the ls program, which prints out the contents of the current working directory.

For the sake of simplicity, the terms executable, script, and program in the context to command-line and shells refer to the same thing for this chapter. In short, scripts are programs that are interpreted by a program like a shell (i.e. bash or ksh) or an interpreter meant solely to execute scripts like PERL. An executable is a program that is compiled into a low level binary form, and while typically takes more effort to write and maintain, is usually faster and more efficient than a script.

As mentioned, the shell parses each token (word) of the user input as a list of tokens separated by whitespace. The first token is the executable and all subsequent tokens are arguments passed to the executable being executed.

One type of argument is a program switch or option. These are usually a dash (-) or two (--) following a letter with no whitespace in the middle. The GNU convention is to use one dash followed by one or more letters. Each letter after a single dash usually expands as if there were several options given with their own respective dashes. For example, '-elf' would expand out to '-e -l -f', each turning on or off a specific functionality in the executable.

Two dashes are usually indicative of a 'long option' meaning that the entire token following the dashes (again no whitespace) will turn on one particular feature of the program (i.e.--sort-time). Long options exist because they are easier to remember or to force the user to explicitly turn a feature or communicate something. For example, --delete-all might do something destructive, where as -d is too easy to mistakenly type. Most GNU commands have both a long and short form.

One subtle thing to note is that if you want to invoke an executable in the current directory, you must put a './' first. Otherwise, you might be invoking a command somewhere else in the file system or you might not be able to invoke anything in the current directory, depending on the PATH environment variable.

PATH Variable and Command Searching

This is an environment variable that controls where the shell looks for a command to execute. Its value is a list of directories separated by a colon (:) where each directory contains executable programs and scripts to be searched. For example, the command:

```
$ export PATH=${HOME}/bin:$PATH
```

This adds the bin directory found in your home directory to the existing PATH. The PATH variable is almost always already exported, but putting export at the beginning assures that it is.

Also, note that while our curly braces are around HOME, they are not around PATH. This is partly historical, but it is also for parsing purposes, as well as in cases where additional alphanumeric text right after the PATH would be interpreted as part of the variable name (if there were text afterward).

The vi Editor

The vi editor is useful to know since it is ubiquitous and prevalent not only in Linux, but any distribution. It is fairly robust in capability, although advanced use of the editor is beyond the scope of this chapter.

Many are critical of vi because it can be awkward to new users, but in the hands of a master, it is one of the fastest editors available. Subsequently, vim, a graphical user interface version of vi, became popular and is still used today. However, vi remains the de facto bare bones Linux install editor, if for no other reason, its binary size, prevalence, and history.

It's hard not to mention the very powerful Emacs editor in the context of vi. However, because of the power of Emacs, it is very complicated and altogether outside the scope of this chapter. However, it is highly recommended to anyone (there are ports to almost all operating systems) since the long term rewards are huge.

Modes

In vi, functionality is determined on the current mode the editor is in. For the purposes of this text, there are basically two modes to be concerned with: command and editing (insert) modes.

The editor starts in command mode, meaning all input is interpreted as a command (i.e. navigation) or to put the editor in a different mode. For instance, after starting vi, you can move around the document using the navigation keys (see *Navigating in vi* below), but you cannot insert text. To insert text, enter insert mode (see *Editing Text*).

To put the editor in the command mode, you can always press the Escape key (ESC) no matter where you are or what mode you are in. Note that it never hurts to press the escape key twice, although depending on what mode you are in, it might beep indicating that the key has no effect. That said, it is better to not get into this habit since it is important to know what mode you are in.

Navigating in vi

In most cases, the arrow keys will work to go up and down lines and forward and backward though characters. However, if the terminal settings aren't correct, you might be forced to use the more primitive navigation keys. They are listed in the following table.

Table 15-1. Navigation Commands in vi

Command	Description
j	Move down a line.
k	Move up a line.
h	Move back (left) a character in the same line.
l	Move forward (right) a character in the same line.
$	Go to the end of the line.
0	Go to the beginning of the line.
<*number*> G	Go to the line number <*number*>.
G	Go to the last line.
ESC	The escape key puts the editor back in the command mode, regardless of the current mode.

Inserting Text

For all insertion commands, it is assumed you are already in command mode (the mode vi starts in or a mode close enough in functionality for these insert commands to work). To insert text, you must first type `i` to put the editor into insert mode. If you want to move around again after inserting text, you must press the Escape key to put the editor back into the command mode.

To insert text after the current character, use '`a`', and '`A`' to insert at the end. As with insertion, Escape puts you back in command mode. To insert text at the beginning of the line, use '`I`'.

To break a line, type '`i`' and then Enter. At this point, you are still in insert mode, so either insert more text or press Escape to return to command mode. When in command (or similar) mode, you can also type '`o`' to put first add a new line and then jump into an insertion mode.

Use '`J`' in command mode to join two lines together.

Deleting Text

You must be in command mode to delete text. The deletion commands follow:

Table 15-2. Deletion Commands in vi

Command	Description
x	Delete a single character.
dd	Delete an entire line.
dw	Delete a word.
D	Delete the rest of the line.

Undoing

Most commands can be undone by using 'u' in command mode.

Searching

To search for text in vi, you must be in command mode. To search for a text string, press '/', type the string to search for, and hit Enter. This search is case sensitive. To search for the same string, press '/' followed by Enter. This searches the entire file. If it doesn't find the text from the current cursor position forward, but finds it earlier instead, this will be indicated by 'search hit BOTTOM, continuing at the TOP' or 'search wrapped', depending on the version of vi or nvi.

Note that this command is used for regular expressions (see the PERL chapter for explanation of regular expressions) as well. Typing '/foo.*bar', then Enter will find occurrences of 'foo bar', 'foo bar baz', 'foobar', etc.

Replacing Text

All text replacing is done with regular expressions. If you don't know regular expressions, you can easily get by with simple text replacements.

To replace text on a single line, use ':s/*<find expression>*/*<replace expression>*', then Enter. This will replace only the first occurrence. If you want to find/replace all occurrences on the current line, add a '/g' at the end of the same command. To search and replace throughout the entire document:

':%/*<find expression>*/*<replace expression>*/'

This finds and replaces only the first occurrence of the *find expression* on each line. To replace all occurrences, add '/g' to the end of the command.

Command Prefix

Most editing commands (i.e. deleting a line) can be done multiple times by typing the number of times you want the command done, then the command itself. For example, to delete 5 lines, type '5dd'.

Line Numbers

To add line numbers, use : and then type 'set nu', then Enter. To turn line numbers off, use ':set nonu', then Enter. Other editing features include 'set autoindent', which indents lines of source code files upon hitting Enter, and 'set showmode', which as the name suggests, shows what mode you are in at the bottom of the window.

Saving and Quitting

Quitting in vi is a command executed in command mode. To quit, first enter command mode by pressing the Escape key. Then type one of the following to quit:

Table 15-3. Saving and Quitting Commands in vi

Command	Description
:q	Quit.
:w	Write the current file, but don't exit.
:wq	Write and quit.
:q!	Quit without saving or prompting - useful if file being edited is read-only.
ZZ	Save (if the file needs to be saved) and quit.

Organization

This section explains system architecture and organization. This includes some theory, but is utilitarian in nature.

Roots in UNIX

While Linux/GNU looks, feels, and otherwise behaves like UNIX, it technically isn't, as "UNIX" is a trademarked name. It is also different in that most, if not all the tools, programs, and applications come from the GNU organization, the Free Software Foundation, whereas UNIX tools, etc. are written by the company producing the complete system.

That said, it appears more or less the same and is derived from UNIX. The majority of Linux/GNU comes from System V release 4 (i.e. start up mechanism) and is successfully, for the most part, POSIX compliant. However, it takes from Berkeley Software Distribution (BSD) as well.

Architecture

This section explains the overarching design of Linux and GNU tools. The vast majority of the core OS user commands and tools come from the GNU organization, which is why most refer to a Linux installation as GNU/Linux.

Platforms

The Linux kernel runs on everything from PDAs and embedded systems to mainframes (zOS). However, its largest install base is on Intel based architecture platforms.

Distributions (Distros)

A distribution is a set of software containing the Linux kernel, tools, applications, and installer programs needed to create a working Linux/GNU system.

Table 15-4. Linux Distributions

Distro	Description
Red Hat	This is the corporate de-facto distribution. It is the distribution that started the package system, RedHat Package Management (RPM).
SUSE	This started as a German distribution. It was 'acquired' by Novell in 2004.
Slackware	The first usable distribution and the distribution the author started with. This was one of the first distributions available in the early days of Linux/GNU. The only other way to obtain it was to download the kernel and system software and build it yourself.
Gentoo	This distribution ships with just source code (with some exception). The complete system (OS and applications) is built from source code. The system is easier to modify, assuming you have the expertise to do so. For this reason, this is considered a hacker's OS. It is also considered by some, including Richard Stallman (GNU/Free Software Foundation founder), the only real 'free' (as in freedom) distribution.
Yellow Dog	An Apple Macintosh distribution.

Layers

As with any OS, Linux/GNU sits between the hardware layer and the user interface. The end user controls the system through an interface, either graphical or command line.

As with UNIX, Linux/GNU has historically been a command line operating system. However, this is slowly evolving into a more graphical user interface.

Components

"Linux" refers to just the kernel. The kernel is the part of the OS that interacts with hardware devices at a very low level. All of the user commands (i.e. 'ls') are also part of the system, but separate from the kernel.

Kernel vs. User Space

Kernel space refers to memory and execution control owned and held by the kernel. User programs cannot touch or access memory held by the kernel or interrupt or manipulate kernel execution.

User space programs are the area of memory and typical execution processes of the system. While there is a pretty definite line, sometimes kernel tasks are deliberately put in user space and the program interfaces with the kernel by executing system functions.

Graphical User Interface

A third part of Linux/GNU is a graphical user interface. However, not all consider this a part of an OS, particularly one that is traditionally command line driven.

The X Window System

The X Window System is a package that controls the screen and provides a framework for a Windows Manager to interact with graphical windows. The X Window System originated at MIT.

Window Manager

A window manager interacts with the X server to size and position graphical windows.

Graphical Desktop Environment

A graphical desktop environment refers to any system that works in conjunction with X to add value by providing icons, panels, task bars, and other graphically rich artifacts.

The idea of having a richer graphical environment that models a real life desktop is a new development for UNIX, considering it originated during the 70's. As an extension of UNIX, Linux has been a breeding ground for this development, with some exception to UNIX implementations like Solaris CDE.

GNU Network Object Model Environment (GNOME)

The philosophy of the GNOME system is to create a "user-friendly desktop". A GNU project, all software associated with this project is free. GNOME uses a Common Object Request Broker Architecture (CORBA) through which all applications communicate. What sets GNOME apart is that it uses the GTK+, which is a graphical drawing API. The latest distributions ship with Metacity as the default window manager.

K Desktop Environment (KDE)

KDE has the same purpose as GNOME. It differs from GNOME in that it is mostly associated with open source (and thus considered more "business friendly") than the GNU organization. It promotes a consistent look and feel, whereas GNOME applications differ more in this regard. KDE uses Qt and is written (mostly) in C++, whereas GNOME is written mostly in C.

Kernel Version

Kernel versions use a three numbered decimal system. Even numbered kernels (i.e. 2.2, 2.4, and 2.6) are "stable" versions, where odd numbered kernels (i.e. 2.1, 2.3, 2.5, and 2.7) are "development" or experimental kernels. You'll probably want to use the stable versions, because the others are for testers, kernel hackers (kernel developers), or those that want a new untested feature.

Open Source

Technically, open source is a more general license concept than the GNU General Public License, which is what both the Linux kernel and GNU tools are under. However, most people refer to Linux/GNU and as an 'open system', deriving its name from open source software.

License

GNU General Public License (GPL) can be found in its full entirety at http://www.gnu.org/copyleft/gpl.html. In summary, it mandates that any code under the license may be re-distributed in any form and for any price, which makes for profit distributions like RedHat possible. However, any distribution must offer the source code, along with the distribution or indicate where the source can be obtained.

In addition, all authors of the source code must be cited. Any modification of the source can also be made and distributed, as long as it is distributed with the source, or a reference to the source is available, and all previous authors are cited and given credit, as well as any new authors making modifications.

Some distributions of Linux/GNU include software that is not under the GNU public license or any open source license. This is perfectly legal, but it isn't considered completely open source and its implications, like intellectual property issues, differ from that of typical Linux/GNU software.

Community

The term 'open source community' refers to any group of developers, quality control/testers, documenters, or anyone else contributing to an open source or free software package.

Trademark/Copyright

The kernel code is copyrighted by Torvalds and the name 'Linux' is a registered trademark by Torvalds as well. The code continues to be free and must continue to do so legally under the GNU Public License.

Advanced

This section covers more advanced topics like processes, users/groups, Inter Process Communication, File I/O and scheduling.

Processes

Processes are running programs under Linux/GNU. Each process has a numerical identifier associated with it, called the process ID (PID). One of the most powerful features of UNIX and Linux/GNU is the ability to access and manipulate running processes with the PID.

Parent/Child

When a program wants to start another program, such as a shell process that wants to run ls to show the contents of the current directory, it 'forks' a process, meaning it runs the program as a new process. This process has a separate memory (static and heap), along with separate kernel space resources as well. The forked process is called the *child* process and the process that forked the child is called the *parent* process.

Each process under Linux/GNU has this child/parent relationship since all processes fork all others with one exception, which is the process that creates all other processes. This is known as the 'init' process and is invoked by the kernel at the beginning of startup process. The primary responsibility of this process is to enable logons and start the /etc/rc.d script start sequence, which in turns starts programs called 'daemons' that do very OS-specific things like allow logins via telnet or FTP.

Each process has both its own process id (PID) and a parent process ID (PPID) except for the aforementioned 'init' process, which has a process ID of 1 and a parent process ID of 0. The entire 'heritage' of a process can be traced by traversing up through each parent process ID until the init process ID of 1 is reached. The only exception is when a parent process dies, the init process inherits the parent's children processes.

Process Ownership

One of the many aspects associated with a process is who started it. This is represented by two things: the numerical user and group IDs.

Once a process is started, it will always be associated with a user, group, and process ID. It is usually associated with a parent process, but the exception to this rule, as mentioned, happens when the parent process dies and child process doesn't. This creates processes known as *orphans*. When this happens, the orphan's parent process ID changes to that of the init process.

Ownership of a process is important because of how it allows or disallows users to do certain things with running processes. For example, no user except for the root user can stop system processes like daemon (i.e. ftp server). Without this permission, anyone could bring down system services and render the host useless or worse.

ps

The ps command is the primary command to view running processes in the system. In addition, it has the capability of showing process statistics like memory and CPU consumption. For example, the following command gives information about the processes running for the currently logged in user:

```
$ ps
```

In the output, the PID is the process ID, TTY is what terminal is connected to this process, time is the amount of CPU time the process is taking, and CMD is the command executed.

The following command gives all process ids, parent process ids, command name and arguments, and other detailed information like process size. This command shows all processes for the entire system as well:

```
$ ps –eaf
```

top

The top command is used to, among other things, monitor the system health and determine what might be slowing the system down. This is a (text) graphical application, so just invoke:

```
$ top
```

Use this command to track down run away processes, obtain the offending process by id, and use kill to get rid of it.

Users and Groups

Like UNIX, Linux/GNU categorizes resource ownership in two dimensions: users and groups.

Users

The primary way of identifying who is doing what on a Linux/GNU system is with users and groups. The term 'user name' refers to a (historically) 8 or less character string. Each user name is associated with a numerical user ID. This user ID is used to denote ownership of all resources on the system like files and running programs (processes).

Groups

Group representation is analogous to each user and even has its own name and numerical ID, but marks ownership but at a different level. The difference is that a user can be associated or 'in' many groups at once. Each kernel resource is associated with a group ID as well.

Files

The /etc/passwd and /etc/shadow files contain user information and passwords. The /etc/passwd file contains information about the user like user ID, user name, primary group ID, etc. The /etc/shadow file contains the user's encrypted passwords.

The content of these two files used to be in the /etc/passwd file, but for various reasons, the /etc/passwd file has to be readable by everyone and brute force dictionary attacks can be used to find out a user's password. After the /etc/shadow file surfaced, things became more secure because it is readable only by the root (super) user. The /etc/group indicates which group users are members of.

Interprocess Communication (IPC)

IPC refers to the basic mechanism by which running processes communicate with each other. All IPC messaging happens through the kernel. There are two kinds of IPC: messaging and shared memory.

Messaging

Messaging IPC is a simple sender/receiver paradigm. The sender writes data to the IPC (i.e. a pipe) and the receiver, waiting (blocking) until there is data available. All data that is transferred from one process to another is buffered in the kernel's memory space.

Pipes

The basic and most prevalent types of messaging IPC are pipes. Pipes are simply represented as integers in a user space program. These integers are returned from and passed to function that in turn are called in the kernel and map to kernel space data structures representing the data flow.

FIFOs

First in, first out pipes (FIFOs) are simply named pipes, meaning they are represented as special files in the file system. Since pipes can only be created and used between parent and child processes, FIFOs provide a way to communicate between any two processes, regardless of process creation hierarchy.

Typical usage of a FIFO, like any other file, is to open it for writing on one side, and open for reading on the other. Like many other usages under Linux/GNU and UNIX, the fact that it isn't a real file is abstracted from the user.

Sockets

These are traditionally known as 'BSD Sockets' since the BSD implementation became the convention. There are two kinds of sockets: UNIX domain and the Internet (IP) socket. TCP or UDP are protocol abstractions that exist on top of the socket (IP layer).

Just like other messaging IPC, all buffering is done through the kernel. In this case, the messaging is done through the network and to a particular process instead of one process to another.

Shared Memory

Shared memory is a section of RAM that is literally shared between a number of processes. Another IPC mechanism, 'semaphores', is used to synchronize read/write access to the shared memory area.

Think of shared memory as memory shared by threads and semaphores as a mutex or a Java monitor. In this analogy, the processes are the threads and the shared memory is the heap.

File I/O

File input and output is one of the strongest aspects of Linux/GNU and UNIX. It enables the user to stream input and output together from one process to another in a seamless way.

File Descriptors

As mentioned, the term 'file descriptor' refers to a simple integer in a user space program that maps to a kernel space data structure, which is associated with a messaging IPC.

Standard Descriptors

There are three *standard* descriptors in every process: standard in, standard out, and standard error, each with their respective descriptors 0, 1, 2. If a program chooses to read from standard in, it opens standard in using 0 as the descriptor and reads input from it with the standard IO functions like read.

Standard input is the input that is given to the process from another. Standard output (i.e. ANSI C getchar()) is the default place where output goes (i.e. ANSI C printf()). Standard error is just like standard out, but is only used for reporting errors from a program.

This is discussed further in the *Advanced Shell* section.

Shell

The shell is a program that provides an interface to the OS for administration and daily tasks. It is also a programming language that allows for a rich set of syntax and functionality to do anything that can be done interactively, as well as non-interactively.

Piping Commands

The philosophy of UNIX and subsequently Linux/GNU is to write tools and programs with a specific purpose that perform their tasks well. Adding the ability to string these commands together proves to be one of the strongest features of the UNIX and Linux/GNU systems.

The act of taking the output of one command and feeding it another command as input is known as 'piping,' not to be confused with IPC pipes.

In a shell, this is denoted with the pipe (|) symbol and is placed between each command. For instance, to obtain the process ID of all Mozilla Web browser IDs, you would invoke 'ps -eaf | grep mozilla'. In this example, the output of the ps command is all of the processes in the system detailing, among other things, the process name and ID. The grep command only prints lines of text that match a string, in this case the Mozilla process name.

Redirection

Redirection is the file analog of piping commands. Instead of taking input or output from a process, redirection does so with files.

In shell notation, a less than (<) or greater than (>) symbol is used to forward data using IPC from one process to another via the standard descriptors (see File IO). In the Bourne-derived shells (i.e. sh, bash, ksh), you can specify the descriptor you want to redirect with the notation N>FILE where N is the standard descriptor (see *IPC Standard Descriptors* section) and FILE is the file name to redirect the output.

For example, the find command outputs to standard out files with a certain file name pattern. However, if it encounters directories that it doesn't have permissions to traverse into, it prints an error. If you want to find all files that have the '.txt' extension, but don't care if you can't descend recursively in a directory because of permission issues, you could use this:

```
$ find . -name '*.txt' 2>/dev/null
```

The file /dev/null is a special file that takes any standard input and doesn't do anything with it.

Automation and Scheduling

Like UNIX, one of the many virtues of Linux/GNU is the flexibility and options available for automating tasks (scheduling programs to run at a later time).

cron

Cron is the system by which you can schedule tasks to occur. A 'task' in this context is just a command that runs at specific time intervals. These time intervals can be anything from minutes to months.

The crontab file tells cron what to run and when, using the following format:

```
<minute> <hour> <day of month> <month> <day of week> <command>
```

All but the last field use glob syntax (whitespace delimited). They are integers, integer ranges, comma-separated integers, or asterisks. The asterisk, analogous to files, expands to every possible instance. For example, for the case of minute, * is semantically equal to 0-59 (integer range). The following command will run every five minutes after midnight, every day:

```
5 0 * * *     $HOME/bin/daily.job
```

The following command executes at 4:20 am for the first 7 days of the month, and then only the 14th and 21st for the remainder of the month.

```
20 4 1-7,14,21 * * root /usr/local/bin/backupall –full
```

at

An at command executes a command at a particular time, like cron, but executes it only once. The name takes the English verb usage. For example, to send an email to someone at midnight, use:

```
$ echo 'hi john | /bin/mail john@doe.com' | at 12:00am
```

The first part of the echo command feeds a mail program that takes the text of the message as standard in. It will be executed 'at' 12:00am tonight, or the next time midnight occurs.

The Linux Kernel

The Linux kernel is the primary OS program that runs for the duration of the up- time of the system. The kernel is the part of the OS that interacts directly with the hardware. It bridges hardware and user space software programs by providing a system call API (i.e. open(), read()).

You can both legally and technically modify the Linux kernel code, but it is discouraged as it is usually very complex, esoteric, and mutually dependent. Modifying something might inadvertently add new bugs somewhere else. The consequences of an OS not doing its task correctly can be anything from losing data to lack of stability.

Recompiling

While modifying the kernel code is not suggested, recompiling the kernel, and thus giving a smaller and more efficient kernel by disabling or leaving out some functionality is recommended.

The reason you might want or need to recompile the kernel can be anything from making the system more responsive or efficient by removing certain unneeded features, to adding drivers or using software, which has a kernel space component.

This overview is given as a means to proceed quickly, but it is very risky without previous experience, as you can render you machine useless if the boot up kernel gets defuncted. For more information, read the /usr/src/linux/README file (to be extracted if not already present on the system).

The basic process for recompiling a new Linux kernel and using it is:

1. Download and extract the kernel source code.
2. Configure the options and all other kernel configuration.
3. Compile the kernel image.
4. Compile kernel modules.
5. Install the modules and new kernel image.
6. Modify your boot loader to include this image *and* keep the current image in case something goes wrong with the new image.
7. Run the boot loader software to put the recently edited configuration in the boot sector(s)/boot record.
8. Reboot and select the new kernel to reboot inside the Linux loader software.

1. Download and Extract

The Linus Torvald's tree, which is considered the official 'vanilla' distribution is at http://kernel.org. Under the GPL, others can modify it to their heart's content and re-distribute it. One example of this is the RedHat distribution. In this case, each kernel release is roughly the same in functionality, but it does differ quiet significantly from the Torvald's distribution.

In general, it is better to stay in the major kernel version that came with the distribution. For example, Fedora core comes with 2.6.5 so you can download the latest version of 2.6.x (x being the greatest number available). You can tell what version of the kernel you are currently running by invoking `uname -r`.

Technically, the source code can exist anywhere on the file system, but it is best to make it accessible from /usr/src/linux, since many programs that need to compile against the kernel source code expect it there. These programs will almost always allow you to specify the location.

Since a new kernel release (at least Torvald's distribution) can come out weekly and you might need to revert to a previous kernel in case something goes wrong with the new kernel, you should put kernel source trees in different directories and create a symbolic link to them.

For example, if you want to install a [new] 2.6.9 version, extract the source into /usr/src/linux-2.6.9 and make a symbolic link to /usr/src/linux from it.

If you've downloaded the source ~/linux-2.6.9.tar.gz, execute the following as root:

```
$ su - root
# cd /usr/src
# # only rename 'linux' to something else if a directory
# [ -d linux ] && mv linux linux.old
# rm -f linux
# gzip -cd ~<user name su'ed from>/linux-2.6.9.tar.gz | tar xfv - > untar.log
# ln -s linux-2.6.9 linux
```

This extracts the source and lists what was extracted in untar.log. It is always good to know what you extract as root to make sure things don't go where you don't want, by accident or otherwise. After looking at the untar.log, you can delete. There is no reason to have this but documentation.

2. Configure

All work at this point happens in /usr/src/linux. Before doing anything else at this point, it is suggested that you read the README in this directory. It covers how to configure, compile, and install the code. If you don't have time, proceed with a lot of caution.

There are several ways to configure the kernel, but the most user-friendly is by typing 'make xconfig'. This invokes GNU make to first compile code needed to update the '.config' configuration tool, then it runs that graphical configuration tool.

If for some reason this fails (i.e. [software] packages are not installed on the system), you can use 'make menuconfig' instead, which provides an ASCII menu driven configuration. While primitive, this is actually a very nice interface once you get accustomed to the navigation system.

You can use make config as a last resort if you don't have ASCII capability (i.e. you're on a primitive terminal), but it is a painful setup.

3. Compile the Kernel Image

After the dependencies are set up, invoke 'make clean' to get rid of any stale object files or any derived files from a previous kernel compile. This is only necessary after a compile so you don't need to do this if you just extracted the source tar ball.

This depends on your circumstances as to how to compile the image, but most want make bzImage. With the 2.6 kernel (current at the time of this writing), you will get a series of well-formatted lines indicating the source file being compiled. In the 2.4, you get the GNU gcc compilation command line and other make spawned commands.

Occasionally, you might get warnings complaining about something like a potentially dangerous casting, but otherwise, it should complete successfully. If it does not, you'll have to learn a lot more about kernel compilation to fix it, as it won't be trivial to understand what went wrong.

In that case, try a different kernel version, usually a previous version to start with is better. You might need to go down a 'major' version like from 2.6 to 2.4 since in some cases, the distribution is setup for a major kernel.

4. Compile the Kernel Modules

If you select certain features as modules, you'll need to have these available with the new image once you reboot. To compile the modules, use 'make modules_install'.

5. Install the Modules and New Kernel Image

To install the recently built modules, use 'make modules_install'. The command 'make install' actually does the same thing, but it doesn't hurt to do it twice and installing the modules first allows you to see any potential problems with setup before hand. Installing the modules creates a directory /lib/modules/<*kernel version*> where <*kernel version*> is the output of uname -r.

If the directory doesn't exist, this process creates one. If there were modules there beforehand, they are blown away so you can configure, make, install, reboot, test, configure, etc. without having to worry about details like this. In fact, the process was designed to allow folks like kernel hackers (those that actually write the kernel) to easily test as they develop.

Important: before installing the kernel image, make sure to back up files like /etc/lilo.conf and /etc/grub.conf, as they will be modified. It is also a good idea to back up the entire /boot directory.

The image refers to the kernel binary that is loaded and then transferred control to from the OS loader. It is usually created in /usr/src/linux/arch/i386/boot/bzImage for Intel platforms, but using 'make install' copies this file in the right place, along with other things needed to reboot off of the new kernel.

6. Modify the Boot Loader

Invoking 'make install' not only installs the image and the modules, it also edits the /etc/lilo.conf and/or the /etc/grub.conf files. This might add duplicate entries once recompiling a second time. Just make sure the configuration file has both the new and old kernel entries so you can select the older kernel in case you forgot to add hard disk support and now can't boot off of the root file system.

7. Run the Boot Loader Software

Invoking 'make install' also runs the boot loader program to install this new configuration into the boot sector or master boot record. It's important to watch this step and look at the output of these configuration files and know exactly what is going on in this step.

8. Reboot

Once you have compiled, installed, and rebooted, watch the messages that come up after you reboot and make note of anything that fails. Once booted up, you can also look at /var/log/messages to see any error messages that might have occurred or something that scrolled by too fast to see.

You can also look at the output of the dmesg command, which shows just kernel output.

If you fail to boot up into the kernel for any reason (including kernel panics), you'll need to reboot, select your previous kernel that you kept for situations like this, boot into the old kernel, and do the whole cycle again until you have a kernel that works.

This is usually a very time consuming process, but fortunately doesn't need to be done frequently. Most distributions come with a kernel that has almost every piece of functionality turned on for the majority that don't need to recompile their kernel.

After testing and settling on a kernel, you can save a little space by cleaning up the install directory:

```
# cd /usr/src/linux
# make clean
```

Looking Forward

Secure Linux (SeLinux) is a project to increase the level of security for the Linux/GNU OS and is provided by the United States National Security Agency (NSA). It can be found at http://www.nsa.gov/selinux/.

The objective is to displace some of the assumed correctness of security from user space applications to the kernel space. Traditionally, security is associated with files and then into the process by the way running processes inherit ownership security criteria from the user logged in. In some cases, like set user or group IDs, security is inherited from the file being executed. SeLinux instead associates security policies at the kernel level so that risk is mitigated by isolating access to an application or daemon.

As of the writing of this chapter, the 2.6 kernel is the latest kernel version and will be for the foreseeable future given the rate of kernel development.

IBM has been and continues to expand its support for Linux both on the mainframe (zOS LPARs) and Intel platforms. One research project currently involves a huge machine of 64 processors running Linux/GNU as a beowulf cluster.

Chapter 16

UNIX

Bell Labs initially developed the UNIX operating system (OS) in 1969. Its main attraction was the ability to time-share the computer's resources. This allows the system to effectively distribute its resources amongst multiple users and processes at the same time. Along with this multitasking and multi-user environment capability, the ability to port to different computer types without major code changes made UNIX one of the most powerful and popular operating systems in the world.

For the first part of the 1970's, UNIX was used solely at Bell Labs. But as the technology developed, they wisely distributed the OS freely to universities for experimentation. The first commercial implementation of UNIX, Interactive System One (IS/1) occurred in 1978. The C-coded System V was released in 1984. Today, there are multiple vendors with their own versions of UNIX, the most notable being Sun Solaris, HP-UX, and IBM AIX.

Fast Facts

- UNIX is case sensitive.
- Use the ls -l command to list the files of a directory along with their types.
- Use the pwd command to find the current directory, and the cd to change directories.
- The root directory is the top of the file system hierarchy, and it is usually represented as a slash (/).
- When navigating directories, use the period (.) to write a relative path and the tilde (~) as a shorthand symbol for your home directory.
- Use cp to copy a file, mv to move a file, and rm to delete a file.
- UNIX supports the single character wildcard ?, the zero or many character wildcard *, and the range of values wildcard [...].
- Use the echo command to print text to the standard out.
- A UNIX filename is not required to have an extension like in DOS, but it provides information about the file. UNIX filenames may contain zero or many periods.
- The greater than and less than signs direct data to and from files. The *command > filename* sends to the file, and *command < filename* reads input from the file.
- The pipe sends output from *command1* as input for *command2* when used in this format: *command1 | command2*.
- The permissions, or mode, follows this order, left to right: owner: read, write, exe, group: read, write, exe, world: read, write, exe.
- Adding & to the end of a command line will run the command in the background.
- The Bourne shell is started by typing sh, the Bourne again shell by typing bash, the C shell by typing csh, the TC shell by tcsh, and the Korn shell by typing ksh.

UNIX Basics

To access a UNIX system, enter the user name and password when prompted. Once logged on, notice that there isn't much to notice. UNIX is a command line OS, with no Graphical User Interface. Commands are run, programs are executed, and directories are navigated from that same command prompt.

UNIX can be thought of as three separate pieces - the kernel, the shell, and the tools. When logging in, you are logging into the kernel. The core of the OS, the kernel schedules multitasking, handles load balancing, and organizes the processing. The kernel gets its orders from the shell. The shell serves as a buffer between the user and the kernel. There are a number of shells that can be used and hot-swapped in and out of a user session. Each shell has its own set of commands that only it recognizes, though most commands are similar. Some of the more common shells include the Bourne shell (sh), the Korn shell (ksh), the C shell (csh), and the Expanded C shell (tcsh). A shell is really just another process that executes, which means a shell can be started by typing its name as a command (assuming that particular shell is present on that machine). The name of the current shell can be found by typing:

```
> echo $SHELL
```

A group of commands can be saved together in a file and executed together as a program. This program is called a shell script, and is very common in UNIX. Unfortunately, the programming commands vary slightly from shell to shell, making portability between shells challenging. Shells and shell programming is covered more thoroughly in the sections toward the end of the chapter.

Advanced scripting tools like PERL can expand the capabilities of an administrative minded developer quite nicely. Keep in mind that UNIX is case sensitive. Putting a capital letter at the front of a command makes it a new command.

The third part of the UNIX OS is composed of the many programs and tools that can be executed. Programs that search, compare files, edit text, and network tools are just some of the different aspects that make UNIX such a complete package. Some tools are standard with the OS, but others are add-ons to make everyday UNIX life a little easier. The easiest way to find out about UNIX commands is to use the man pages.

man *topic* Gives you a general description of the *topic* from man pages. If you want to learn more about functionality, this is an excellent source of information that represents one of the first online documentation packages in the computer industry.

passwd Changes your password in the system. Usually it is a good idea to change this from the default assigned to you soon after you get started.

File System

A user saves data in UNIX by creating a file and putting it into a directory, like putting a paper into a file folder. The UNIX file system is a sum of all of the directories and all of the files that are stored within them. Directories then have directories within them, called subdirectories, and even the subdirectories can have subdirectories. This hierarchical structure, which begins at the top with the root directory, is not mirrored onto the physical storage devices. The OS actually stores data in a manner of no concern to the user.

The top of the hierarchical structure of the file system is the root directory, usually represented by a slash (/). After that, there is no limit to the number of directories that can be present. There are a number of typical directories that remain pretty standard across UNIX systems (though any administrator can change this at any time).

Table 16-1. Standard UNIX Directories

Directory	Purpose
bin	Holds standard UNIX programs and utilities.
dev	Holds device files.
etc	Holds configuration and other system files.
include	Holds header or include files for programs (sometimes inc).
lib	Holds programming libraries.
local	Holds user created files, different from those that come with UNIX.
man	Holds online manual pages (you can usually add your own here as well).
src	Holds source code for programs.
share	Holds files that may be shared between systems.
tmp	Holds working files temporarily.
usr	Holds commands, user specific.
var	Holds files that vary over time, such as log files.

When a user logs onto a UNIX system, they begin in the directory called the *home directory*. Each user gets a home directory, usually called the same name as their login name, and it is dedicated purely to that user. The home directory is usually referenced by the character tilde (~).

cd *path* Changes your current working directory to the *path* given. If the *path* starts with a "/", then it assumes you are typing in an absolute path. If the *path* starts with a "~/", then it assumes you want to start from your home directory. Note that `cd` with no arguments defaults to your home directory. Moving up to a parent is done by calling the dot-dot directory. *cd ..*

pwd Displays the entire absolute path.

Run pwd from your home directory and you will probably use something like /usr/dave/ as a home path. The first slash represents the root, the text 'usr' represents the first directory. The second slash is a way to delimit (let the system know they are different directories) the directories. The text 'dave' represents a subdirectory that happens to be my id. This whole process is known as a path. It is the definition of where you are in the tree. The PATH variable tells the commands what parts of the tree to use when you try to run a command.

Files

Unlike in DOS, a period is a regular character in UNIX, so there can be zero or numerous periods in a UNIX filename. A filename can contain letters, numbers, periods, underscores, but no spaces. While filename extensions are not required in UNIX like in DOS, they are a useful way of indicating the type of data stored in the file. File names that begin with a period are hidden files, typically used for OS housekeeping. Files like .profile and other hidden files are not listed using a normal ls command (see below). Wildcards are expanded by the system to mean any single character (?), number of characters (*), or range of characters [...]. They increase the power of commands like copy and move.

Many UNIX commands support optional values. In most cases, these can be combined or separated. The command 'rm –rf *.txt' does the same thing the 'rm –r –f *.txt' command does. When there are options, they almost always come before the other parameters. For example, the command 'rm *.txt –f' doesn't work.

Files are defined by something called an *inode*. The inode points to a block of data representing the contents of a file. This could be through a link or the original creation of the file. The inode has three date-times. One is the access date, which represents the last time the file was opened. A second time stamp is the modified time, which indicates the last time the file was changed. A third is the last time the inode was changed.

ls This command shows you all of the files and directories that exist in the current working directory.

- -a All files, shows the files starting with a '.'
- -d Lists only the directory name (not the contents).
- -l Long list, shows more file details in a single column.
- -p Puts a slash after directory names.
- -r Reverses the order of the list.
- -t Sorts by the Modification time.
- -R Recursively lists all subdirectories found.
- -1 Lists files in a single column.

mkdir ***dir***	Creates a directory called *dir* in the current directory.
-p	Creates intermediate directories if needed.
ln ***tgt name***	Creates a link to a file or directory designated by *tgt*. It acts like a constantly updated copy of the file or directory it is linked to.
-s	Creates a symbolic link, locally it is just a name pointing to the target location.
cp ***file file2***	Makes a copy of the *file* at *file2*. If *file2* is a directory, cp places a copy using the same name *file* in that directory. Wildcards can be used in this command for the first parameter *file* only. If *file* is actually a directory, the contents will be copied to *file2*. Entering 'cp –f *.c src/' copies all the files ending in .c to the local src directory:
-i	Prompts before overwriting existing files.
-f	Forces replacement if there is already a file by that name.
-r	Recursive call to copy all the directories found.
mv ***file file2***	Allows you to change the directory location of the file to be *file2*. If *file2* is a filename instead of a path, this simply acts to rename the file.
-i	Prompts before overwriting existing files.
-f	Forces replacement if there is already a file by that name.
rm ***file***	Removes a *file*. If the *file* is linked by a hard link, the *file* is simply removed from the current directory, but is still accessible from the other hard links. This is not true of symbolic links. Wildcards can be used here to indicate a group of files.
-f	Forces the *files* to be deleted without prompting.
-i	Prompts before removing each *file*.
-R or r	Recursively follows all subtrees. This command allows the rm command to act as a rmdir command. This is a dangerous command in combination with –f.

rmdir *dir* Deletes an empty directory. It cannot delete files.

-f Forces the directories to be deleted without prompting.

-i Prompts before removing each directory.

-p Path removal deletes empty parents as well.

Permissions

People who have access to the system are called users. In large organizations, handling hundreds of users became a daunting task, so administrators developed the group concept. All the users in a group can be affected at the same time by running commands targeting that group, while setting the group security on files can control file sharing. There is also one user that is not part of a group; that is the superuser. The superuser has the power to do anything, regardless of permissions. It is usually best not to work as the superuser though, as that much power often magnifies mistakes. Imagine running 'rm -rf' from root with the ability to affect any file.

One way security is handled in UNIX is through the use of permissions on files and directories. The permissions are part of the inode discussed earlier. Permissions come in three types. Read permission on a file means it can be read and on a directory means that the contents of the directory can be listed. Write permission on a file means it can be saved to, and on a directory means that files or subdirectories can be created or deleted there. Execute permission on a file means that it can be run as a program.

For each file or directory, there are nine possible permissions. Those permissions include read, write, and execute permission for each of the owner, the group, and the world. The first three permissions refer to those rights of the owner of the file, the second three are the rights of the group that the owner belongs to, and the third three permissions are the rights of the rest of the system users.

chmod Change the permissions of a file. The three accesses are read/write/execute. They are represented by binary values 4, 2, and 1. In order to grant more than one, you give the value of the two combined. For example, this command grants read and execute to the world and group, but read, write, and execute to the owner:

```
chmod 755 filename
```

There is an alternative approach, which uses a combination of characters:

Who: User (u), Group (g), Others (o), All three (a)

Action: Add (+), Remove (-), Replace (=)

Permission: Read (r), Write (w), Execute (x)

For example, the same command as above if the file were read only to all three:

```
chmod u=rwx, g+x, o+x filename
```

chown Changes the owner of a file. You must have write permissions to the file to use this command.

-h Changes the owner of a symbolic link.

-R Recursively changes the owner of all files and directories under the directories indicated.

chgrp Changes the group that the file is associated to. The group does not have to be a group that the owner belongs to.

-h Changes the group of a symbolic link.

-R Recursively changes the group of all files and directories under the directories indicated.

newgrp ***grp*** If you are a member of *grp,* you can execute this command. It changes the group you are currently associated with and thus your access to files that are attached to that group.

File Manipulation

These are some of the common editors that exist in the UNIX environment. These tools are what you will usually use to create files. This is also a good time to cover a related topic; redirection. UNIX allows the commands to have their inputs and/or outputs redirected from or to a file or other location. The vertical bar (shift-backslash) is called a pipe. It takes the output of one command and sends it to another command. For example 'ls –la | more' gets the listing of the current directory and sends the result to the command more. The characters greater-than (>) and less-than (<) allow data to be put to a file or pulled from a file respectively. For example, the following command will append the second file to the first and save the result as file3:

```
cat file1 file2 > file3
```

To execute part of a complex command before the rest of the command, the subshell indicator is useful. Surrounding the command with parentheses '( )' will execute that call before the rest of the command line is evaluated.

cat ***file***	Shows the contents of *file.*
-n	Numbers the lines sequentially.
-v	Shows normally hidden characters to be shown with "^" representing control characters.

more ***file***	Shows the contents of a *file* one page at a time. Uses spacebar to page forward. It only loads the data it needs to display, so this is an excellent tool for very large files. Quits with the letter 'q'.

less ***file***	Shows the contents of a file like 'more' does, however 'less' allows search and navigation keys just like vi.

head ***file***	Shows the first 10 lines of a *file*.
-n#	Shows the first # lines instead of 10.

tail ***file***	Shows the last 10 lines of a *file*.
-n#	Shows the last # lines instead of 10.
-f	Continues to update as the *file* is written. This is very useful for following log files as they are being created.

pg ***file***	Outputs the contents of a *file* one page at a time. Like 'more' it progresses by pressing the spacebar, however this command can control direction better.
*n*l	Moves to *n* lines down.
*n*d	Moves to *n* half pages down.
/*string*	Searches for *string* in the *file* text.

page ***file***	Outputs the contents of a *file* one page at a time. It progresses a page by pressing the Return key.
n	Moves to the line *n*.
*n*d	Moves *n* lines down.
*n*u	Moves *n* lines up.
/*string*	Searches for *string* in the *file* text.

vi *filename*	A text based editor. Described later in the section *Editor vi*.
emacs	A graphical editor. Described later in the section *Editor emacs*.
sort *files*	Changes the lines in a *file* to be alphabetically sorted. If multiple *files* are listed, the command merges the *files* and outputs the sorted result. Typically used on data files.
-o *file2*	Outputs to *file2* which may not be the same as the target *file*.
spell *files*	Outputs a list of words that are not found in the dictionary.
-v	Suggested derivations are provided.
tee	Copies the data flow to standard output and to a file: `ls –la |&tee filelist.txt`
awk	The awk command parses lines that match patterns specified in program or from a file. Each pattern can be associated to an action, then a match occurs. The input line is parsed as a list of words divided by whitespace of the regular expression FS. Each of the fields is designated by $1, $2, $3, etc. The entire line of data is designated by '$0'.
-F *fs*	Specifies regular expression to separate words on an input line.
-f *file*	Declares the awk program file named *file* to be used for pattern matching. Up to 100 files can be declared. Order is based on declaration order.
sed	Copies text files to the standard output, edited according to a script of up to 100 commands. Only complete lines are executable, so a new-line is required on the last line.
-f *file*	Takes the script from the *file* given.
-e *script*	Edits according to the script.
-n	Suppresses the default output.

uniq *in out* Reports repeated lines in a file *in* to a file *out*. If no *out* is provided, it will print to the standard output.

- -u Prints only the lines that are not repeated.
- -d Prints once only the lines that are repeated.
- -c Generates the output, but precedes the line with the count of repeats.

Environment Variables

UNIX also allows you to save information for use at later times or by jobs during their execution. This information is stored within the system as environment variables. The variables typically control things like paths, default parameters, or definitions (like versions or sizes). To use the value of a variable, the $ is used as an indicator. The command 'echo $HOME' prints out the absolute path of the user's home directory. UNIX also provides a way to create "commands" of your own that represent commands that you use most often.

env Displays all of the environment variables defined in the current environment.

setenv *var df* Creates a variable called *var* and is defined as *df* in the cshell. If the variable already exists, it overwrites the value. In the Korn shell, you simply write 'HARPER="Test data"' at the command prompt.

echo Prints the data to standard output. Entering 'echo $PATH' will print out the system path variable.

alias Lists all of the aliases currently defined. An alias is a way of defining a shortcut. For complex actions that you repeat many times, this is an excellent way to speed up the process. You can have an alias execute several commands in a row by using a semicolon to divide the commands.

ll=ls –l	ksh version of setting an alias value.
ll ls –l	csh version of setting an alias value.

export ***var*** The export command makes the variable global so that other programs can use it. It is used extensively in ksh to give global access to variables.

Searching

These are powerful commands that can greatly improve your ability to find things on a large or complicated file structure. One feature of UNIX that developers often use is buffered input. If a command is still running and another command is entered, the second command will run right after the first is completed. This is useful if you want to know how long something runs, but don't want to sit and watch. After entering the command to run a long process, type in date <Rtn>. When the job ends, the time and date will be printed, telling you exactly when the job completed.

find A file searching tool that finds files based on inode information. The find command can be used with grep to provide a way to follow subtree, which grep doesn't allow you to do. However, we want to use the result of the find as a file list instead of data, so we need to use the xargs command. Using xargs is similar to using –exec, except that it allows several files at a time.

```
find . –name "*"txt –print | xargs fgrep 'some data'.
```

-name *d* This is the data *d* to look for. Puts quotes around wildcard.

-print Outputs the result to standard output.

-follow Normally, find does not follow symbolic links, this allows those links to be followed.

-print This is one operator that many developers forget to use. It tells the find command to actually print out the results of the query. Because it is so commonly forgotten, some systems have their commands altered to assume the user wants it added onto the end.

-newer *f* This compares the modified times of the file *f* given to those found by the command. Using the touch file to set an access time to a file will allow you to find files newer than any date you choose.

-exec This is the operator to use if you wish to perform an action on the results. For example, you might want to copy a group of files to an archive directory. This could be accomplished using the following command:

```
find . –name "*".c –exec cp {} ~/archive/ \;
```

grep *tx path* A very powerful text search utility that allows you to look for a text string *tx* in files described by *path*. The *path* can include wildcard characters to allow searching through a large number of files. The following command will find the characters *some data* in the local inc directory only looking at files that end in '.h'. Note the quotes are needed because we want the space to be used in the search not as a separator for the command parameters.

```
grep "some data" inc/*.h
```

-i Ignores case.

-c Shows a count of the matches per file.

-l Shows only the filenames that have a match.

egrep *tx path* The same functionality as grep, but it allows you to use extended regular expressions. In many cases, it is also faster than the baseline grep. This example allows you to find a_in_t and a_out_t in all the files ending in '.h'.

```
egrep "a_(in|out)_t" *.h
```

fgrep *tx path* The same functionality as grep, however it is limited to only use plain text for the search.

comm *f1 f2* Compares file *f1* to file *f2*, showing the results in three columns; lines only in *f1*, lines only in *f2*, and lines in both.

-1(2,3) Suppresses the column given.

diff *f1 f2* Shows the differences between two files *f1* and *f2*.

-w Ignores whitespace.

-i Ignores letter case.

wc *file* Provides a word count of a *file*. If multiple *files* are provided, a total count is also given.

-l Counts the number of lines.

-m Counts the number of characters.

-w Counts the number of words.

who Displays names and information for current users.

whoami Displays the username to which you are logged in.

hostname Displays the name of the host machine you are currently logged onto.

which *exe* Follows the PATH variable and tells you where the executable *exe* you designate is being run from. Since executables are run from the first place they are found in the PATH order, it may not be the one you expect.

date Shows or modifies the date and time.

-u Displays time in GMT.

sleep *n* Pauses operation for *n* seconds:

```
(sleep 60; echo "Complete!")&
```

touch *date f* Changes the modification date of the file *f*. If no *date* is provided, it defaults to system date. If the file *f* does not exist, it creates an empty file.

-a Changes the access time.

-m Changes the modification time.

-c Prevents creation of the file.

-t *time* Uses *time* rather than the current time as a decimal [YYYYMMDDhhmm.ss].

Jobs

If you have a long running job, you can have it run in the background. A job in the background still continues to process unless it needs user input. This frees up the command prompt to do other activities.

& When used at the end of a command, runs job in background.

bg ***job*** Puts the specified job into the background. The current job is put into the background if *job* is not specified.

fg Foreground. This brings a process from the background to run in the foreground. This is particularly useful if you accidentally put an & at the end of a command.

nohup When used with a process being run in the background, this allows the process to continue to run even if the terminal window is closed.

ps Prints information about processes:

- -e Selects all processes.
- -l Long version prints all of the parameters.

kill ***sig pid*** Sends a command *sig* to the kernel in reference to the process id *pid.* The default is signal –15, this allows the process the chance to clean up first.

- -9 Kills the process with no chance of the signal being trapped or ignored. Use this if the original kill doesn't do the job. It does not allow the process to clean up.

nice This command changes the priority level of a job. It is probably not a good idea to run on a job in the foreground.

- -n *prty* The difference from normal priority *prty* with a higher number being lower priority. Negative numbers require superuser permissions. The modified number cannot go lower than 0 or higher than 39.

Recurring Tasks

The following commands control running jobs at regular times. While this can be a powerful tool, it can also be a dangerous tool if the jobs unexpectedly use up resources. On most projects, it is best to consult with the local systems administrators to determine who is managing cron and when you should run large jobs. This functionality is sometimes disabled to avoid problems.

cron Runs the commands submitted by crontab or at. Once started, this never stops executing, so it should only be executed once.

at *time cmd* Schedules jobs to be run by the cron:

- -l Lists jobs to be invoked.
- -r Removes listed job (*cmd* being the job_id).

crontab Submits a list of jobs to be run by cron.

Changing Hosts, Terminals, IDs

Often, the host that a user logs into isn't the one where the tasks need to be performed. Sometimes there are files that need to be transferred from one system to another and there are also times that it is useful to operate on another system or perhaps as another user. This kind of functionality can be done with the following commands.

Most of these commands have a large number of complex activities that they can accomplish. The options presented below cover the most common actions developers need. Explore the various help options in these tools to learn more about specific tasks you may need to accomplish.

xterm This is a terminal emulator for the X Windows System. It provides a window in a X Windows compatible environment. This applies to UNIX graphical interfaces and Windows X Windows emulators:

```
xterm –T title –sb –sl 1000 –ls –display $DISPLAY
```

ftp *host* Stands for file transfer protocol. Allows the transfer of files from one system to another. The following are not options, but commands to use within the ftp tool.

Table 16-2. FTP Commands

Command	Description
open *host*	Opens a connection to a remote server if it isn't open already.
ls	Does a directory listing on the remote host.
cd	Changes the directory on the remote host.
delete *file*	Deletes the *file* on the remote host.
get *file*	Transfers the *file* from the remote host to the local host.
put *file*	Transfers the *file* from the local host to the remote host.
help	Lists all the ftp commands available.
close	Closes the connection, but do not exit ftp.
bye	Closes the connection to the remote host and exit ftp.

rcp

Remote copy does the same thing as cp, but can do so across systems. It follows a slightly different format to allow for the system designation:

```
rcp user@host:path user2@host2:path2
```

rlogin *host* This allows you to open a virtual terminal on another *host*.

-l *user* Allows you to specify a user other than the current *user*.

telnet *host* Uses the TELNET protocol to communicate with a host. If the host is specified, it immediately tries to open the connection.

Table 16-3. Telnet Commands

Command	Description
open *host*	Opens a connection to the *host*.
close	Closes the TELNET session.
quit	Closes any open sessions and exits.
?	Displays the help summary.

su Sets user command and allows one user to become another user without logging out.

System Definitions

There are more advanced tools that can tell you more about the environment than the simple path or hostname. However, when there is a problem these tools are valuable for determining the cause of the problem.

file ***filename*** Tries to classify a file according to the data the file contains. The command only looks at the first 512 bytes in the file to make the determination.

-h Doesn't follow symbolic links.

bdf ***location*** Displays the amount of free space on the file system containing the *location* in kilobytes.

df ***path*** This command reports on the amount of free 512byte blocks and inode values available on the filesystem described by the *path*.

-b Reports free kilobytes.

-e Reports the numbers of files free.

-v Reports the percentages used.

du Displays amount of used disk space in blocks (512 or 1024 bytes/block).

-a Displays all information.

-r Reports files and directories that cannot be opened.

-s Displays only totals.

stty Sets the terminal options.

-a Displays the current settings.

Tools

There are a number of commands that allow you to do everyday tasks. Each of these commands fills a particular role that you will need at various times.

lp (lpr) *files* The print command for UNIX. This will queue the *files* for printing.

-c Copies into the spool directory.

-d *prntr* Designates the printer *prntr* to which to send the data.

-m Sends mail to the user after the request has printed.

-n# Prints # copies of the *files*.

mail Displays the contents of the mailbox one by one.

Table 16-4. Common Mail Commands

Command	**Description**
<Rtn>	Goes to the next message (+ and n do the same thing).
-	Goes to the previous message.
s file	Saves the message into *file*.
q	Puts unread mail back in the mailfile and stop.
?	Lists command summary.

tar *files* Puts the *files* into a compressed file. Not as sophisticated as some of the later compression schemes like zip, but a commonly used and understood format. Originally designed for making tape archives.

c Creates a new archive.

f *file* Uses *file* as the archive name instead of /dev/rmt/0m.

r Adds the *file* to the end of the archive.

t Lists all the *files* in the archive.

x Extracts the *file* from the archive and restores it to the directory.

v Verbose, displays activities, shows more data when listing *files*.

cc *file*.c This is the C compiler that comes with the UNIX system. UNIX is actually compiled from C code, so it is quite familiar with this compiler. Running the command can be as simple as: 'cc file.c a.out'. However, it can also become a very complicated combination of libraries and headers that are typically controlled by make files.

make Creating make files is a bit of an art. Used in the compile process, a make file can make complex compilation processes simple to use. Make files can be comprised of four different kinds of lines.

Target Lines These are lists of targets separated by spaces. These are followed by a colon (:) or double colon (::), followed by a list of dependents. Pattern matching is supported for the dependents.

Shell Commands A semicolon (;) followed by text and all the following lines that start with a tab are shell commands to be executed to update the target. The next line that does not start with a tab or # (used for comments) defines the beginning of a new target.

Macros These are substitutions that the compiler makes prior to compilation. This makes the code easier to maintain and manipulate.

Includes These are the header files that are used by the system during compilation to define the format of the functions and public structures.

expr This command evaluates the parameters and outputs the result.

Table 16-5. Example expr Parameters

<table>
<tr><th>Parameters</th><th>Action</th></tr>
<tr><td>v1 | v2</td><td>Returns v1 if neither is NULL nor 0, otherwise v2 is returned.</td></tr>
<tr><td>v1 & v2</td><td>Returns v1 if neither is NULL nor 0, otherwise 0 is returned.</td></tr>
<tr><td>v1 [=,>,<,!=] v2</td><td>Returns 1 if the comparison is true and both are integers, otherwise 0 is returned.</td></tr>
<tr><td>v1 [+,-] v2</td><td>Simple addition or subtraction is performed.</td></tr>
<tr><td>v1 [*,/,%] v2</td><td>Multiplication, division, or remainder performed on integer values.</td></tr>
<tr><td>v1:v2</td><td>Matching of v1 and v2 regular expressions.</td></tr>
<tr><td>length v1</td><td>Returns the length of v1.</td></tr>
<tr><td>substr v1 c len</td><td>Substring of v1 starting at character c containing len characters.</td></tr>
<tr><td>index v1 c</td><td>Position in v1 of first occurrence of character c.</td></tr>
<tr><td>(…)</td><td>Expressions within the parentheses will generate a result before being used by operators outside of the parentheses.</td></tr>
</table>

Messages

UNIX supports ways to communicate with other users across terminals. These are similar to simple instant messengers ubiquitous on the Internet today.

write Copies lines from your terminal to another user. To instigate communications, the recipient must type: 'write *yourusername*'.

mesg This stops messages via write. It removes write permission to users without appropriate privileges.

Editor vi

Nearly every UNIX system ships with a text editor called vi, which stands for VIsual editor. While it may seem primitive to PC users today, it is fast and efficient and users who are accustomed to its quirks swear by it. It does not support text formatting, nor does it have any spell checking function or document templates, but vi proves very useful for everyday tasks such as shell script programming and system file editing.

Starting vi is as simple as typing vi filename to open the file in the editor. You also have the option of opening the file at a particular location. You can do this by typing 'vi +# *filename*' or if you are looking for *something* you can start it with 'vi +/*something filename*' to open the file for editing on that particular line.

Once you open the file, you cannot simply start typing in your text. The different key possibilities are handled by vi using various modes. The *edit* mode allows you to type characters into your document exactly as you would like to see them. *Command* mode allows you to use those same keys to perform various actions for you. The commands are done by lower-case and upper-case characters, as well as using the control key along with the characters. If the system is not responding as you might expect, check your Caps-lock key! There is also a command line mode in vi, where you can do activities that are more related to the application or the file as a whole rather than to the text in the document. The command mode is the default mode, and you can get back to it using the Escape key. From the command mode, you can then execute various commands to perform related actions as described below.

There is also an additional feature that can be used as a form of combining. You can use numbers before the command to indicate that you would like to repeat a command multiple times. For example, 4x will delete 4 characters. 20j will move down 20 lines. The following basic commands will get you started with vi:

Table 16-6. Basic vi Commands

Command	**Description**
:w	Overwrites your original version with your current edits.
:w filename	Writes the information to the file given instead of the file that was opened. The new file now becomes the open document for vi.
:q	Quits, but will not allow you to quit if there are unsaved changes.
:q!	Quits and throws away any unsaved changes.
:wq	Combining the commands causes the system to save and quit.
h	Moves Left.
j	Moves Down.
k	Moves Up.
l	Moves Right (also the space bar).
<Rtn>	Jumps to the first character of the next line.
i	Inserts before the cursor.
x	Deletes a character from command mode.

You now know enough to be able to make vi function for you. Everything else is just an extension of these capabilities.

Table 16-7. Additional vi Move Commands

Additional Move Commands			
Ctrl-f	Move forward one page.	[[	To the last start of a section.
Ctrl-b	Move back one page.	]]	To the next start of a section.
Ctrl-d	Move down half a page.	H	Move cursor to top of screen.
Ctrl-u	Move up half a page.	*n*H	Move to *n* lines below top.
w	Beginning of next word.	M	Move cursor to middle of screen.
e	End of current word.	L	Move to bottom of screen.
b	Beginning of current word.	*n*L	Move to n lines from bottom.
0	Start of the line.	G	Move to the end of the file.
$	End of the line.	*n*G	Move cursor to the *n*th line.
(	To last start of a sentence.	:*n*	Move cursor to the *n*th line.
)	To the next sentence start.	z Rtn	Put current line at the screen top.
}	To the next paragraph start.	z.	Put the line in the screen center.
{	To the last paragraph start.	z-	Scroll the page so that current line is at the bottom of screen.
^	Back to the start of line.		

Table 16-8. Additional vi Commands

Searching

/text	Search for the *text* forward.	f*char*	Find next *char* on same line.
?*text*	Search for the *text* backward.	F*char*	Find last *char* on same line.
n	Find the next instance of search in the same direction.	;	Repeat the "f" or "F" command.
N	Find the previous instance, in reverse direction of search.	Ctrl-g	Tells you the file name, current line number and total lines.
%	Match the current brace, parentheses, square bracket.		

Insert Mode Options

I	Insert at beginning of the line.	R	Overwrite characters as you type
a	Append after the cursor.	s	Substitute a character.
A	Append at end of the line.	S	Substitute the line.
C	Replace text until end of line.	~	Replace letter with opposite case
o	Open a new line for editing below the current line.	r	Overwrite one character, then exit back to command mode.
O	Open a new line for editing above the current line.		

Advanced Editing

p	Paste buffer before the cursor.	:j!	Join, but preserve spaces at the start of the second line.
P	Paste buffer after the cursor.	M*a*	Mark the location with the character you enter in place of *a*.
d	Delete.	‘a	Return to the line you marked.
x	Delete a character before the cursor.	‘’	Return to line you were on before moving (any Move cmd).
dd	Delete line and save in buffer.	J	Join current line with next line.
y	Yank (copy).	u	Undo the last edit.
yy	Copy the whole line into the buffer.	Dw	Delete to the end of the current word (same as de).
c	Change (basically a delete and edit).	dG	Delete to the end of the file.
cc	Change the whole line.	d^	Delete back to start of the line.

Advanced Options

From the vi command line, you can issue a set command. This command allows you to change the default settings of the editor. We have included a couple of the more commonly used options to give you an idea of how they work. Putting a ‘no’ in front of the option usually sets the setting to the opposite condition.

:set all — This shows all of the options that set understands.

:set noai — Turns off the automatic indenting, often useful for source code.

:set nu — Turns on line numbering through the file.

To insert stored information, this command will handle those activities.

:r *file* — Inserts the data from the *file* filename after the cursor.

:r !*command* Runs the UNIX *command* and paste the results after the cursor.

An interesting feature of the editor allows you to save into a named buffer:

"ayy — Copies current line to buffer a.

"ad — Cuts to buffer a.

"ap — Pastes from buffer a.

You can also open a second file:

:e file — Opens the file for editing.

:n *filename* — Switches to a file called *filename.*

:e# — Switches between two loaded files (vi can keep two in its buffer).

:e! — Opens the same file, removes all changes since the last save.

Editor emacs

Windows users might have a slightly easier time using the emacs editor, as it has a menu bar with drop down lists of commands. However, many UNIX systems do not support a mouse, so the commands are all entered using keystrokes. Unlike vi, there is only one mode of operation in emacs. But like vi, the emacs editor is started by typing 'emacs' from a command prompt either alone to open up a new file, or followed by the file name to open.

Commands in emacs use the Control key and the Meta key, which is usually the Escape key, in combination with typical characters (it is not necessary to keep the Escape key pressed down like it is with the Control key). Useful commands are listed here, illustrating Control as '^' and Meta as 'M'.

Table 16-9. Essential Emacs Commands

^h	Enters online help.	^b	Moves backward one char.
^x ^s	Saves the file.	^v	Moves forward one screen.
^x ^c	Exits emacs editor.	Mv	Moves backward one screen.
^x u	Undo the last edit - repeatable.	^s	Searches forward for chars.
^g	Breaks out of the command.	^r	Searches in reverse.
^p	Moves to up to previous line.	^d	Deletes the next character.
^n	Moves down to next line.	<Del>	Deletes previous character.
^f	Moves forward one character.		

Shells

A shell is a program that sits between the user and UNIX to mediate. The shell reads in the text from the user, and then passes it on to the OS kernel. There are a number of shells that are freely available, and some common shells come standard with UNIX. A shell is typically stored in the \usr\bin directory, and each one has its own features and pitfalls. The name of the current shell can be obtained by checking the SHELL environment variable:

```
% echo $SHELL
```

Some of the more common shells include the C shell (csh), the Bourne shell (sh), and the Korn shell (ksh). To start a shell other than the default shell that has started automatically, simply type that shell's name (such as csh or sh) at a command prompt. Typing exit will then exit that shell and return you to the default shell. To change the default shell, use the chsh command, with the format 'chsh username new_shell':

```
chsh paul /bin/bash
```

Each shell has a file that runs when a user logs into the shell, called a login file. Some shells also have a file that runs when a shell window is started (called a startup file) and one that runs when the user logs out. These files contain settings and variables that are specific to that shell. The following table lists some of the common shells and the name of their config files:

Table 16-10. Shells and their Configuration Files

Shell	Login file	Startup file	Logout file
csh	.login	.cshrc	.logout
ksh	.profile	$ENV	none
tcsh	.login	.tcshrc/.cshrc	.logout
sh	.profile	None	none

Because csh supported job control, it was typically the shell of choice for basic user interactivity purposes before ksh became available. Today, however, the ksh is generally available combining the sh programming language and the interactive capabilities of ksh, making it a good shell choice.

Bourne shell

The Bourne shell, sh, is one of, if not the original shell. It first shipped with the original UNIX System V release, and is named after its creator, Stephen Bourne. The Bourne shell is noted for its strength in its programming language. It is often chosen while programming shell scripts.

C shell

The C shell, csh, is a powerful, highly configurable shell developed with the Berkeley UNIX System. At the time, it was developed for C programmers. The .login and .cschrc files contain many configuration toggle values including noclobber, autologout, and filec. The noclobber feature prevents writing over an existing file, the autologout feature can be set to expire a session after a period of inactivity, and the filec feature turns on the filename completion. The filename completion feature automatically completes a filename once enough characters are entered to uniquely distinguish it from the other filenames and the Escape key (Esc) is pressed.

The C shell can be set to operate in either vi or emacs mode. To enter emacs editing mode, type 'bindkey -e', and to enter vi editing mode type 'bindkey -v'. In either mode, the C shell supports editing and recalling of previous commands by typing Ctrl-P, and then recalling the next command by typing Ctrl-N.

The C shell supports the history command, which keeps track of the most recent commands entered. By setting the history value to a number other than its default '1' in the .cshrc file, that number of commands are remembered and recalled by their assigned number.

```
set history = 20
```

The line below will execute the sixth command in the history list, while typing ! re-executes the previous command.

```
!6
```

A variant of C shell is the TC shell, or tcsh. Though the TC shell is a bit more powerful than the C shell, most commands are identical for the two systems. One slight difference is that the tcsh uses the Tab key to complete its filenames using the filename completion feature, rather than the Escape key for the csh.

Korn shell

The Korn shell, ksh, was developed by AT&T based on advances in both the C shell and the original Bourne shell, sh. It contains a .profile file that is run when a user logs onto the system, and a $ENV that contains environment variables. The Korn shell, with its addition of command line editing, is one of the most popular shells on commercial versions of UNIX.

The Korn shell can also operate in either vi or emacs mode. Toggling between these modes involves setting the VISUAL variable to either 'vi' or 'emacs', or else by entering the commands set '-o vi' and set '-o emacs' into the environment variable file.

The Korn shell uses the history command as well. The HISTSIZE environment variable must be set to the number of commands to remember. Then the r command is used to execute the commands, as the r by itself executes the last command entered. Entering r -6 executes the command that was six commands ago. The Korn shell also has an fc command, much like the history command in the C shell. Typing 'fc -l' lists the previous commands.

Shell Programming

A shell script is nothing more than a series of simple commands grouped into a single text file so all of the commands in the file execute with one call. Since each shell is a little different from the next, there are different sets of commands that are acceptable in shell scripts run on the different shells.

A shell script can be created in any of the UNIX text editors. It should be saved, and using the chmod command, ensure that execute privileges are granted to whomever will run the script. Then, from any of the shell prompts, simply typing the file name will execute it. The first line of a shell script is often something like this:

```
#!/bin/sh
```

This is a command to whatever shell that is currently running, telling it to run this shell script using the Bourne shell. This keeps errors from occurring when a command is valid using one shell but not valid using another. Variables can be used in shell scripts to temporarily store data. A variable using sh or ksh is set like this:

```
variable_name=variable_value
```

There cannot be spaces before or after the equal sign, and the variable name must begin with a letter. The rest of the variable name can be any combination of letters, numbers, and underscores(_). Remember that UNIX is case sensitive. To set a variable using the csh, use the set keyword. Here, spaces are allowed around the equal sign:

```
set variable_name = variable_value
```

Variable naming rules remain the same between shells, as does the retrieval method. To retrieve the value of a variable, list the variable name preceded by a dollar sign ($):

```
myVar="Hello There!"
echo "I just said $myVar"
```

The above lines first set the value of myVar, and then retrieve the value using a '$'. Notice that a text string must be surrounded by quotes in UNIX.

Parameters may be passed into a shell script from the command line (or another shell script) simply by calling the script name followed by the parameters, with a space separating each one. Using those parameters in the sh or ksh involves a set of special variables, $1-$9. The first parameter is $1, the second is $2, and so on up to $9, and any after that are silently ignored. This means that there can only be nine parameters, however the special variable $* holds all of the command line parameters together, no matter how many there are. The variable $# returns the total number of parameters.

When using the csh, the parameters are stored in a special array named $argv. The first parameter is $argv[1], the second is $argv[2], and so on. The total number of parameters can be obtained using $#argv.

Following is a description of a few built-in shell commands that are similar, if not the same, between the most commonly used shells. Later, the control statements are listed, displaying the syntax for the sh, ksh, and csh.

Table 16-11. Shell Commands Consistent Across Shells

<table>
<tr><td>#!shell</td><td>When used as the first line of a shell script, invokes the named shell.</td><td>\</td><td>Escape character, indicating the next character is to be quoted.</td></tr>
<tr><td>></td><td>Redirects output, often to a file.</td><td>break</td><td>Breaks from the current loop statement.</td></tr>
<tr><td>>></td><td>Redirects output to the file and append to the file.</td><td>continue</td><td>Stops current loop iteration and continue with next one.</td></tr>
<tr><td><</td><td>Redirects input.</td><td>bg</td><td>Background execution.</td></tr>
<tr><td><<</td><td>Redirects input - ‘here’ document.</td><td>fg</td><td>Foreground execution.</td></tr>
<tr><td>|</td><td>Pipe output - sends output from left command as input to right command.</td><td>cd</td><td>Change directory - makes the named directory the new current directory.</td></tr>
<tr><td>&</td><td>Runs process in background.</td><td>echo</td><td>Sends output to standard out</td></tr>
<tr><td>;</td><td>Separates multiple commands on the same line.</td><td>eval</td><td>Evaluates arguments.</td></tr>
<tr><td>*</td><td>Wild card for any characters and any number of characters.</td><td>exec</td><td>Executes a new shell or another program.</td></tr>
<tr><td>?</td><td>Wild card, single character.</td><td>jobs</td><td>Lists all running jobs.</td></tr>
<tr><td>[...]</td><td>Wild card for a number of characters, matching any characters enclosed.</td><td>kill</td><td>Terminates the job with the named Process ID.</td></tr>
<tr><td>( )</td><td>Commands inside are to be executed in a subshell.</td><td>shift</td><td>Shifts positional parameters.</td></tr>
<tr><td>‘ ‘</td><td>Output of surrounded command is substituted.</td><td>umask</td><td>Sets default permissions for new files.</td></tr>
<tr><td>“ “</td><td>Partial quote - allows variable and command expansion.</td><td>time</td><td>Lists amount of time that a command took to execute.</td></tr>
<tr><td>$*</td><td>Accesses all arguments.</td><td>suspend</td><td>Suspends a foreground job.</td></tr>
<tr><td>$var</td><td>Obtains the value of a</td><td>stop</td><td>Suspends a background job.</td></tr>
<tr><td>$$</td><td>Processes ID.</td><td>unset</td><td>Clears variable assignment.</td></tr>
<tr><td>$0</td><td>Command name.</td><td>#</td><td>Indicates comment to right.</td></tr>
<tr><td>$n</td><td>Obtains the nth argument, between 0 – 9.</td><td>wait</td><td>Pauses until a background job has completed.</td></tr>
</table>

The following statements vary between shells, sometimes more than others.

if *statement* Executes different commands based on the outcome of a condition evaluation. Statements can be nested within each other using 'elsif' or 'else if' statements.

sh and ksh	**csh**
if *condition1* then	if *condition1* then
command1	*command1*
elif *condition2* then	else if *condition2* then
command2	*command2*
else	else
command3	*command3*
fi	endif

case/switch Used instead of if/else statement when there are more than two conditions. When pattern matches the tested value, the related set of commands are executed, and only those commands.

sh and ksh	**csh**
case *value* in	switch (*string*)
pattern1)commands1;;	case *pattern1*:
pattern2)commands2;;	*commands1*
pattern3)commands3;;	breaksw
esac	case *pattern2*:
	commands2
	breaksw
	default:
	commands3
	breaksw
	endsw

while loop The commands will execute while the listed condition evaluates to true. Condition is tested before beginning each loop. Used when total number of iterations is not known.

sh and ksh	**csh**
while *condition*	while (*expression*)
do	*commands*
commands	end
done	

for/foreach The first for loop listed for sh and ksh below is used to execute commands when the number of loop iterations is known. The other two loops execute the body of the loop once for every variable value in the *list_of_values*.

sh and ksh	**csh**
for ((*init*; *cond*; *incr*))	foreach *variable* (*list_of_values*)
do	*commands*
commands	end
done	
for *variable* [in *list_of_values*]	
do	
commands	
done	

Looking Forward

Because of its speed and reliability, UNIX systems are often the machine of choice for servers - application servers, print servers, email servers, file servers, database servers, etc. Microsoft holds a part of the server market share, but high performance servers are almost always a variant of UNIX. The bottom line is that UNIX isn't going anywhere but up.

The IBM AIX OS runs on IBM RS/6000, IBM Power, and PowerPc platforms with a promised Intel version on the way. At the time of this writing, the latest release is AIX 5L. Hewlett-Packard's HP-UX is a very reliable OS that gives Sun and IBM a run for their money with its latest HP-UX 11i release. The OS runs on HP 9000 servers. At the head of the class is the Sun Solaris OS running on the Sun Spark machines, as well as Intel workstations and servers. Solaris has the broadest application support of any UNIX based system, and with its ownership of Java and iPlanet involvement, Sun will always be a safe bet.

Chapter 17

Mac OS X

The fact that Apple's market share is less than 5% of computers leaves most users unfamiliar with the operating system that Apple CEO Steve Jobs describes as "The most technically advanced operating system in the world." However, upon use of an Apple computer, most users will be pleasantly surprised to discover that Mac OS X - despite being built on some of the most powerful technologies in computing - is intuitive, user-friendly, and above all, one of the most stable and secure operating systems available.

Historically, the Mac OS family began with Apple's release of the first graphical user interface in 1984, and every version through OS 9.2 was based on that original. However, OS X is independent of the previous operating systems. When Steve Jobs left Apple due to a power struggle with then CEO John Sculley, he created a company called NeXT. NeXT's BSD-based operating system was built to utilize concepts in computer science, such as object-oriented programming, in order to create the most advanced operating system ever conceived. On Jobs's return to Apple as CEO in 2000, Apple acquired NeXT and used their operating system as the foundation for OS X. Now, after its fourth major revision (10.4/Tiger), OS X continues to outperform the competition and remains arguably the most advanced operating system in the world.

Fast Facts

- The Mac OS X is a robust, completely rebuilt operating system with a UNIX-based kernel beneath the Apple look and feel.
- OS X can be installed with or without a copy of OS 9 to run independently of that installation.
- If installed, a virtual Classic environment (Mac OS 9) is automatically invoked when programs requiring the old environment are launched.
- Macs use a single button mouse. Holding the Control key (Ctrl) down while clicking launches a context sensitive menu. It is the same as right-clicking on a two-button mouse, which OS X can also utilize if one from a third party is connected.
- Macs use the Command (□) key for menu mnemonics. A number of shortcuts are invoked by pressing it in combination with other keys.
- Add an application to the Dock by dragging and dropping the icon there.
- Changing from one active application to another can be done using the □ + Tab shortcut. Changing windows within an application can be done using □ + `. Holding the shift button reverses the order.
- In a Finder window, drag a file into another location to move it. If that location is on another drive, it results in a copy rather than a move. Holding the option key will reverse this behavior and additionally, holding option and command (□) results in creating a symbolic link.
- While working in Finder, File -> Get Info or □-I gives extended information on whatever is selected, including size and date modified.
- Option + Command + Esc brings up the Force Quit dialog. This dialog, similar to "End Task" in Windows or "kill" on BSD/*nix platforms, ends a process immediately.
- The Activity Monitor provides detailed information about which processes are running, including the background processes that don't appear in the Dock. It also provides information on CPU usage, memory usage, disk activity, disk usage, and network activity.
- Complete system information for both hardware and software can be viewed by opening the System Profiler.
- By pressing F9, Exposé temporarily moves and resizes every window so that a user can find it. F10 performs the same action, but only for the windows that belong to the current application. F11 provides quick access to the desktop.

Basics of OS X

OS X has a multi-layered architecture built upon a core that handles basic processing and file system operations. The next level is a collection of services and frameworks that are responsible for higher level processing, such as graphics, but still remain transparent to the user. On the highest level, the user interface engine interacts with the user and provides the graphical user interface that is renowned for its functionality and usability. OS X Server provides additional server-specific services that are among the most popular and powerful in computing. The following sections will provide a brief, non-technical overview of each of the eight basic components, as well as the additional server components. Further information for these technologies can be found at http://developer.apple.com.

Darwin

Darwin is the processing core of OS X. Built on the open source Mach 3.0 kernel and a version of free BSD 5, this component of the operating system is similar to the BSD/*nix operating systems available in other distributions. In fact, it is so similar that there is an option to install an X11 environment. Furthermore, projects such as OpenDarwin, Fink, and Gentoo have compiled large port collections of popular open source applications and libraries, allowing OS X to run a substantial portion of the popular BSD/*nix applications. This has been made possible, in part, by the fact that Darwin is open source. For a variety of reasons, Apple decided to utilize not only the products of the open source community, but also the community itself, to further the development of the core of OS X. By combining the expertise of Apple staff with the manpower and enthusiasm of the open source community, Darwin has become a great success. However, one shortcoming of Darwin seems to be that it does not support kernel space threads, but rather user space ones. This causes it to perform poorly in benchmarks of applications such as Apache and MySQL because the threads themselves are slower.

Cocoa, Carbon, and Java

Cocoa, Carbon, and Java represent the three environments in which OS X applications can be developed. Each environment caters to a specific type of developer. The following provides an overview of the characteristics of each and the situations in which they are typically encountered.

Cocoa

Cocoa is a high level API for developing OS X applications quickly and easily. It is based on frameworks, or functional pieces of code, that are extended to include the functionality desired by the developer. The framework concept was adopted by NeXT in its original form because the majority of Cocoa is rooted in NeXT APIs. This is evidenced by a large number of classes being prefixed with NextStep (NS). Because the Cocoa API does not require the developer to implement much low-level functionality, and because the framework concept makes it easy to rapidly develop applications, it is often the preferred application environment for developing OS X native applications, including iPhoto, Safari and Mail. Cocoa applications are either written in Objective-C or Java and are only deployable in OS X.

Carbon

Carbon is a lower level API than Cocoa. It utilizes lower-level functionality because it is most typically used for porting older applications to OS X. Keeping the functionality of the API at a low level allows the flexibility to replace the functionality of other APIs and provides for an easy transition from other operating systems to OS X and vice versa in the case of iTunes. Carbon is usually the ideal environment for porting OS 9 and earlier applications because much of the API is rooted in APIs from earlier versions of the Mac OS that have been updated for OS X. Additionally, applications from other operating systems such as the Microsoft Office suite have been ported using Carbon. Carbon applications are written in C/C++ and are only deployable in OS X. Also, it should be noted that much of Cocoa is implemented using Carbon.

Java

In addition to being a programming language, Java is an application environment because it too provides an API for developing on OS X. The version of Java running on OS X is essentially the same as that distributed by Sun for various other operating systems, but is unique to OS X because it is controlled by Apple via Software Updates and resides in a somewhat atypical directory structure. Other than those subtle differences, Java on OS X is identical to any other Java SDK. Java applications are, obviously, written in Java and unlike the other application environments, they are deployable on any operating system with a compatible Java virtual machine.

Quartz, OpenGL, and QuickTime

This level of OS X provides for the technological foundations or the user interface. Specifically, these technologies provide the foundation for audio and graphics.

Quartz

Quartz is the operating system's 2D rendering engine. This is the component responsible for the high performance graphics that allow for the effects that make OS X extraordinary, like magnification of the Dock, the "genie effect" when windows are minimized, and the user favorite, exposé. By utilizing the power of PDF (portable document format), Quartz delivers outstanding performance.

Figure 17-1. The Genie Effect for Minimizing Windows

OpenGL

OpenGL is an open graphics library that is widely used for high performance 3D graphics. OS X utilizes an implementation of this graphics library that has been optimized for the operating system to provide powerful 3D graphics.

QuickTime

QuickTime is Apple's system for handling audio, video, and images. It is responsible for creation, delivery, and playback of content on OS X machines, as well as Windows machines. The visual representation of this technology is the QuickTime player, which is the application in which the content is displayed.

Aqua

Aqua is the portion of the operating system responsible for the graphical user interface. By utilizing the aforementioned technologies, Aqua provides a visually stunning user interface that continues to receive recognition for being powerful, intuitive, and well designed. The specifics of navigating Aqua will be covered later.

Other Components

In addition to the technologies that have been listed, OS X utilizes many others that Apple has developed to enhance the functionality of the operating system. Tools like Bonjour for automatically configured networking, Core Audio and Image for enhanced multimedia processing, and Universal Access for alternative I/O methods are just a few examples of the aspects of the operating system that aren't necessarily essential, but combine to make OS X a robust and versatile solution. A complete list of technologies in OS X can be found at http://www.apple.com/macosx/techspecs/.

OS X Server

Beyond the capabilities of the standard operating system, OS X Server provides various server technologies for use with OS X. Each of these services is configurable via a suite of graphical administration tools, which will be discussed later in the chapter.

Please note that personal versions of afp, samba, http, ssh, ftp, print, firewall, dhcp, and nat services are also included in the standard version, but are not as readily configurable as those found on OS X Server.

AFP

Apple's proprietary Apple Filesharing Protocol (AFP) is the main mechanism for file sharing on OS X. Fully integrated with the other services available on OS X, it is the most robust filesharing protocol for homogeneous Apple networks. It integrates fully with Finder to provide a user experience that is virtually identical to that of the local file system. Regarding security, AFP is particularly useful in the fact that, by default, file transfers are not encrypted, but the login procedure is. Therefore, performance isn't lost through encrypting files, but passwords are still secure. Also, AFP is configurable to be used through an SSH tunnel if data security is a concern.

Application Server

Apple refers to its various J2EE containers as an Application Server. OS X Server is currently bundled with Tomcat 4.1.29 and a distribution of JBoss 3.2.3 that utilizes Tomcat. This service can be configured to use both JBoss and Tomcat or just JBoss, depending on the functionality desired from the application server.

DHCP, DNS, FTP, Firewall, NAT, NFS, VPN, Print Server

Each of these services on OS X is based on its Free BSD Counterparts. As such, they are essentially the same as their BSD/*nix counterparts. The DNS server is BIND, the FTP server is a modified wu-FTPd, the firewall is ipfw, the VPN is implemented so that it supports L2TP and PPTP, and the print server supports AppleTalk, LPR and USB printers, and AppleTalk, SMB, and LPR clients.

Mail

The mail delivery agent distributed with OS X Server is the widely used Postfix mail server. Combined with Cyrus for POP3 and IMAP support, OS X Server is an enterprise grade mail server. Additionally, it is configured to use Mailman to handle mailing lists (if desired) and SquirrelMail for Web-based email access. Each of these components is integrated with the Directory Service for user authentication and OpenSSL for security.

OS X Server 10.4 provides two very important extensions for mail security and usability. It is now bundled with SpamAssassin for spam filtering and ClamAV for virus scanning. These two applications and the standards for their respective functionalities provide services that are essential today and give a standard implementation of a setup that was chosen by many OS X Server system administrators before 10.4.

NetBoot

The NetBoot service allows for network-based installation or booting. By utilizing DHCP and a file sharing service (nfs, www, or afp), disk images created by Apple's Network Image Utility can be distributed from the server to various client computers by booting the client to the network volume. This is convenient for a variety of applications from diskless workstations to computer cloning.

Open Directory

Open Directory is possibly the most vital of all the services OS X Server provides. Open Directory handles all user information and authentication for every other service. Essentially, Open Directory is the synthesis of various other services including Apple's Lookup server and NetInfo server, an LDAP server, and Kerberos. Apple provides a uniform service for accessing information that is specific to OS X's directory system through Lookup and NetInfo, as well as information that is not OS X specific through the LDAP server. All of this information is kept secure in part by the standard Kerberos service. OS X Server utilizes Open Directory in almost all of its other services, including the Windows compliant samba service. This allows OS X server to integrate with Microsoft's Active Directory as Master, Slave, or Replica with virtual transparency.

QuickTime Streaming

As the creator of QuickTime, it is only fitting that Apple has included a streaming server for QuickTime media. This server, as a default, is configured for a maximum of 1,000 users at 100 Mbps, and leaves the user limited only to the available bandwidth. The QuickTime Streaming sever should provide ample functionality for any multimedia need.

Web

OS X Server utilizes Apache httpd 1.3 as its default provider of Web services. This server is the world's most popular Web server and is regarded as the most secure and reliable available. Much like the installation of the Java Runtime Environment, the Apache server lies in an atypical directory structure, but is easily accessible for novice and veteran users. Built with an extensive list of modules, this distribution most notably includes: all of the standard apache modules, ssl support, proxy support, php support, WebDAV support, a connector for Apple's WebObjects, a connector for Tomcat, and integrated authentication with Open Directory and Apple's Sherlock searching engine.

Also, with OS X Server 10.4, an independent version of tomcat can be run to provide a container for a weblog server. Apache 2.0 is also installed on OS X, but it is not enabled by default.

Windows

Despite long standing animosity between Apple and Microsoft, OS X server includes full support for Windows networking through the open source SAMBA project. In fact, Apple is so confident in their implementation of Windows compliant networking that OS X Server is advertised to behave "just like a Windows server" to a Windows client.

Software Update

The software update server is nothing more than a mirroring service for the software updates that are available from Apple. By selecting which updates are available on the local mirror, administrators can test updates before distributing them to local workstations.

WebObjects

OS X comes with a deployment license of WebObjects, their web-based application development environment. WebObjects is a technology that predates many of the technologies commonly used today and is the technology behind many of Apple's services, such as the Apple Store and .Mac.

Xgrid

OS X Server 10.4 now includes Xgrid as one of its services. Xgrid is the technology that has enabled collections of computers such as Virginia Tech's System X to perform distributed computing so efficiently that it has become the third most powerful supercomputer in the world. By enabling this with OS X Server, any collection of Macs can become a cluster for distributed computing.

iChat

The new iChat service is a Jabber server that utilizes XMPP to provide private instant messaging services to users. Combined with the iChat client, users on a local network can chat in a private environment that is more suitable for business-related interaction.

Additional Apple Server Solutions

Apple offers a few other additions to OS X Server that are not part of the operating system, but are powerful, important additions. The first, Apple Remote Desktop, is a server for providing workstation management from a centralized source. Both the server and client utilize a variety of technologies, including versions of VNC, to provide live interaction between users and administrators and grant administrators control over virtually every aspect of the client workstations.

Another addition is Xsan. This technology allows storage devices to be pooled into a storage area network (SAN). By creating one volume across the entire network, wasted space is minimized and storage becomes uniform. Xsan is implemented with performance in mind, and with the appropriate hardware can become an ideal solution for anything from high performance computing to HD editing.

The User Experience

As mentioned earlier, the graphical portion of OS X is referred to as Aqua. This unique look and feel is what defines the user experience and is the means by which most of the power of OS X is accessed.

When first using a new machine running OS X, a setup wizard walks you through a step-by-step process for setting the basic preferences such as user information, network settings, etc. This wizard is extremely easy to navigate and you should have no trouble following its instructions. Also, any functionality available through the setup wizard is available by logging in as an administrator.

Upon starting the machine under any other circumstances, you will be confronted with the login window. This window lists the available accounts in the directory search path. This path may include network users, local users, or a combination of the two, depending on how the machine was configured. A spot for "Other" users may be listed as well, which allows users not listed to log in by typing their user name manually. By selecting a user (or manually entering a user name) and entering the correct password, the login process will begin and the desktop will appear.

The Landscape

The background of the screen is a desktop analogous to desktops in most other GUI operating systems. On it are icons for all of the mounted disks, as well as any files or folders that may have been placed there. The menu bar is located at the top and will display the menus for the application that is currently in the foreground. The name of the application that is currently active is in bold next to the apple in the upper left corner. The default application is Finder, which is responsible for the items on the desktop. The unique rectangle filled with icons is referred to as the Dock. These three components - the menu bar, Finder, and the Dock - are the methods for navigating OS X.

The Menu Bar

As mentioned, the menu bar is dynamic. As the active application changes, much of its content will change. However, some content will remain static, regardless of which program is active.

The first static item is the apple icon. Users familiar with the apple icon from earlier versions of the Mac OS will find this one to be much different. This menu holds items that are system-wide commands, such as "About this Mac" for viewing system information, "Software Update…" for updating Apple branded software, "System Preferences…" for accessing various preferences, and the "Shutdown," "Restart," and "Sleep" commands.

The remainder of the static items is found on the rightmost portion of the menu bar. These icons are indicators that reflect various application and system statuses. Icons for display preferences, wireless connectivity, Bluetooth connectivity, battery life (on portable computers), a clock, and many others are available as preferences to be enabled for each service.

Some of the typical dynamic items found in the menu bar are menus for file, edit, and help. These menus are analogous to those in most other operating systems and have little, if any, functional difference.

Finally, the name of the application is a menu itself. It will often contain an "about" item to give information about the application, and some application-wide commands. This includes access to the applications preferences, a design feature that is useful because it provides a common location for an often hard-to-locate item. Although convenient, this feature may not be obvious to users of other operating systems that are accustomed to finding it in an edit or window menu.

The Dock

The Dock is a collection of icons that gives direct access to whatever the icons represent, including executables, files and folders, trash, running applications, and minimized windows. The meaning of each icon is differentiated by its location, graphic, and whether or not an arrow underscores it.

Items found in the left portion of the Dock or to the left of the vertical separator, are applications. Clicking an icon will launch it or bring it to the foreground if it is already running. The one application that is always present is the Finder, which can be identified as the two-tone blue smiling face. This application is always in the Dock, because all running applications are added to the Dock temporarily. It can also be observed that a black arrow underscores the icon for the Finder, which indicates that the application is running.

To the right of the vertical separator is the area for files, folders, and minimized windows. Clicking on a file or folder icon will open it with the default application for that item. Clicking on a minimized window will restore it to its original state.

The difference between a minimized window and a file will be that the icon for the window has a small version of the icon for its parent application in the lower right corner. The item that is always present in this portion of the Dock is the trash. This trash is analogous to trash/recycling in other operating systems and can be emptied from the Finder menu or by Crtl-clicking that icon and selecting "empty trash". For the security-conscious, the Finder menu offers a Secure Empty Trash option that overwrites deleted files to prevent recovery by another party.

Figure 17-2. Example Dock

Finally, if the Dock seems to have disappeared, it is probably because it has done just that. The Dock is very customizable and as such can be repositioned, resized, and even reshaped. From the apple menu, system preferences, or accessing the contextual menu on the vertical separator on the Dock, users can set Dock preferences. They include options such as the side of the screen on which the Dock is anchored, the ability to hide the Dock unless the mouse is over it, and the magnification of icons when they are under the cursor. Tracing the perimeter of the screen with the cursor will usually find a missing Dock.

Finder

Finder is where the majority of the user's interaction with the file system takes place. Like other GUIs, icons are representative of files and windows where most user interaction takes place within a window. Therefore, the normative concepts will not be discussed but rather, the unique portions will be highlighted.

The first of the unique aspects of Finder is its method for navigation. Clicking on the Finder icon in the Dock or double-clicking on a folder/drive icon on the desktop brings up a Finder window. This window, like many windows in OS X applications, is separated into three portions. The area to the left is the sidebar in which shortcuts to common locations are stored, and can be modified by dragging folders in and out of this area as desired.

The area at the top of the window is the toolbar. This area contains shortcuts to common tasks and commands, and can be customized by Ctrl-clicking the toolbar and selecting "customize toolbar."

The final, main portion of the window is the area in which the window's contents are displayed. For Finder, this can be done in one of three ways as selected in the view menu. The Icon view is the same view as that of the desktop. The List view displays the contents as a list and allows folders to be expanded in a tree format. Finally, the column view displays the contents in a view unique to OS X. As a folder is selected, its contents are displayed in a new column to the right of the previous. This allows for a view of the entire directory structure that contains the user's current location. If a file is selected, a preview of that file is displayed in the new column along with some essential information about the file.

Figure 17-3. Finder Window Using the Column View

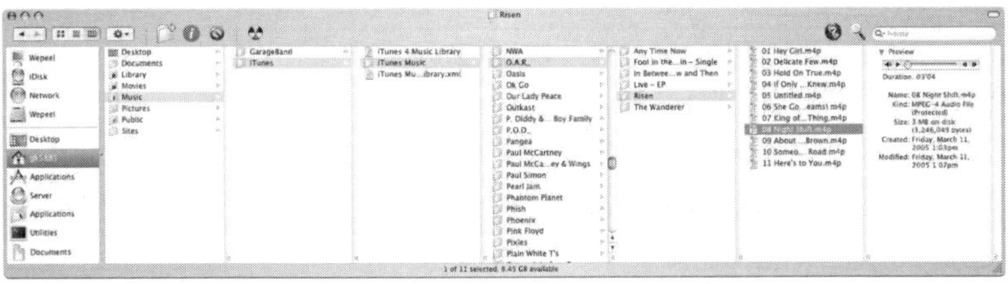

Another element that is unique to Finder is the use of labels. Any file or folder can be organized by giving it one of seven different colored labels. By giving common files the same label via the File menu, users have a visual way of identifying files based on whatever organizational scheme they define in the Finder preferences.

Spotlight

As of OS 10.4, there has been a new addition to the operating system that changes the landscape entirely. Spotlight, the searching engine that has been integrated into the core of the operating system, gives users the ability to instantaneously access data and functionality regardless of location. Based on both meta-data and content, it provides for results that are more complete than any previous search. To clarify, Spotlight indexes every file based on meta-data such as the file name, date modified, user comments, etc., as well as the content of the file itself so that any possible reference to a user's search is found almost instantaneously.

For example, in the search of my local drive for "bluetooth," I received the following results in Figure 17-4.

Figure 17-4. Spotlight Search for "bluetooth"

As you can see, files such as "PowerBook G4 17-inch Getting Started.pdf" were included in the results, but do not have the word "bluetooth" in the title. That is because, as found by opening the document from the Spotlight window, the word Bluetooth first appears on page two and Spotlight automatically navigates to it and highlights it.

Another thing to note is that system preferences are included in the search results. This is because they are also indexed so that settings can be found and changed without having to know their precise location. This behavior has a useful graphical effect that highlights the location of the results if the search is performed within the System Preferences application.

Figure 17-5. Search for "bluetooth" in the System Preferences Application

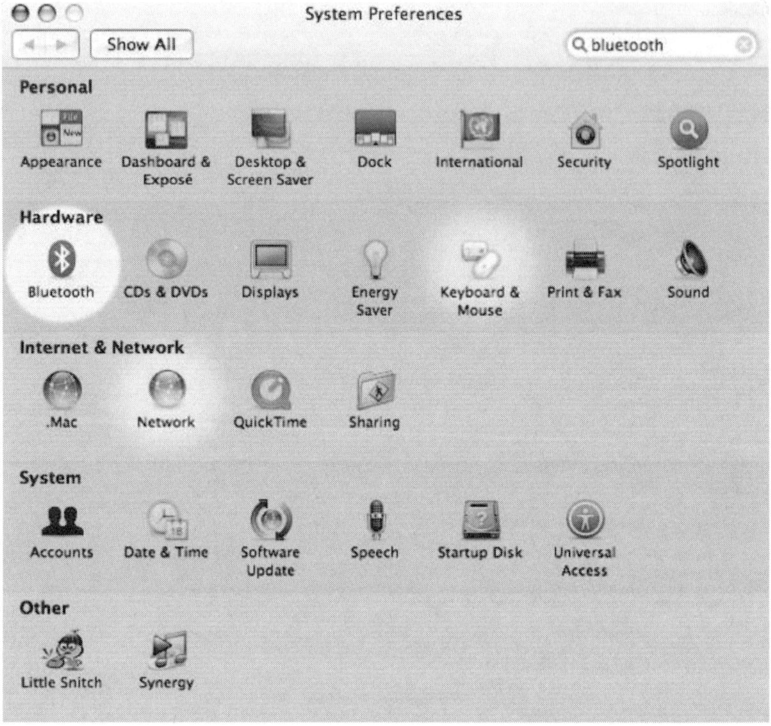

However, eye candy is not the reason that Spotlight has become so renowned so quickly. The sheer amount of previously untapped meta-data is what has allowed it to become so powerful. Things like the subject in an email, the caption on a picture, the composer on an audio file, the screenname of a friend in an AIM chat, and the copyright on a PDF are all pieces of meta-data that Spotlight indexes so that the result of a search ensures that what a user is looking for is present. And it doesn't stop there. Through a plug-in based interface, Spotlight is extensible to any type of document that has a plug-in to interpret it.

The File System

The first key to understanding the OS X file system is to understand that what is seen in Finder is not the whole truth. Referring back to the discussion of Darwin, OS X is actually built on a BSD file system. Apple understood from the beginning that BSD was not nearly intuitive enough for the common user, and thus OS X was built to bridge that gap. Therefore, it is important to differentiate what is seen from what is actually occurring.

The first difference is in the location of the root of the file system. Finder would lead the user to believe that the computer as a whole is the root of the file system, but since the file system resides within the hard drive, it is impossible for it to reside outside of it. Therefore, the root of the file system is actually the BSD root directory "/", which represents the directory encompassing all other directories on the hard drive. This is the same directory as the computer's local hard drive, typically named "Macintosh HD." All of the items listed under the computer directory are either links to connected servers or items in the local hard drive.

Within this root directory lie several important folders. The Applications folder contains OS X applications. Within that folder is the Utilities folder, which contains smaller utilities for OS X. There is also an Applications folder for OS 9 applications, if the classic environment is installed. The Developer folder, if present, contains applications, documentation, source code, libraries and frameworks for developing on OS X. The Documents folder contains documents for use by all of the system's users. The Library folder contains support files for OS X that are typically not related to the operation of the operating system. The System folder, however, contains a Library folder whose contents are related to the operating system, and also contains support files for OS 9 or classic. Finally, the Users folder contains personal files for each account on the machine, as well as a folder called Shared in which every user can store files. The personal files are contained in a folder for each user called the Home folder, which has the name of each user's account.

Each Home folder contains a set of folders that are common to each user, many of which are user-specific versions of the folders in the root directory. Folders that are unique to the home folder are the Desktop, Movies, Music, Pictures, Public, and Sites folders. The Desktop folder holds all of the items that are on that user's desktop. Since they are two different representations of the same folder, changes in one will affect the other. The Movies, Music, and Pictures folders are simply folders to hold those types of items. The Public folder is a location in which the user who owns the home folder can place items for others to access. Within this folder there is a Drop Box folder for other users to leave files for the owner. Finally, the Sites folder is for personal Web sites to be hosted via the personal Web sharing service. This service will be covered later in the chapter.

Another difference is that Finder hides a large portion of the file system from the user. Since OS X utilizes the BSD file system, one would expect to see the typical BSD directories such as /etc, /usr, etc. However, according to Finder, these directories do not exist. They can be accessed by using the "Go to Folder" command in Finder's Go menu or via the terminal, which will be discussed later.

Mac names for files, folders, and aliases can be composed of any characters except colon (:), including commas, spaces, and slashes. There can be a maximum of 31 characters, and there need not be an extension at the end (like in Windows). However, to maintain consistency and the ability to share files with Windows machines, the Windows rules should be kept in mind.

The latest versions of Windows allow blank spaces and extra periods, but special characters such as slashes, question marks, and commas should be avoided. Each file typically ends with a period and a three letter extension, though this is not required, that is read by the operating system to determine which program to invoke when opening the particular file.

Mac does not need the extensions to determine which program to invoke because Mac files contain meta-data, as well as the file content. Each Mac file is made of three components - a header, a data fork, and a resource fork. The header contains information such as the date the file was created and the application that was used. The data fork contains information that is readable by other applications, such as text, while the resource fork contains information readable by the native application only. When a file is invoked, the header is the first part sent to the Finder, and the information there is used to decide which application to open.

System Preferences

The majority of the System Preferences are self-explanatory, so this section will provide a cursory glance at some of the more important and less obvious preferences.

Dashboard & Exposé

This preference pane concerns two features that have not yet been mentioned. Exposé is a user interface tool that provides a quick and easy method for navigating through open windows. By pressing certain keys, windows will resize and tile in order to help you find the window you are looking for. Exposé can also be used to clear all of the windows for easy access to the desktop. The keys to activate these features can be set in this preference pane.

Dashboard is an application that behaves in a similar way to hide and display utility applications called Widgets. These applications, in truth, are really just Web pages with a small amount of added functionality and enhanced graphics, but like typical Web pages, they can perform extremely useful functions on short notice. Apple provides widgets for checking the weather, controlling iTunes, checking stocks, and accessing the Address Book, but by basing the Widget architecture on HTML, CSS, and JavaScript, impressive new widgets are constantly being created by third-party developers.

Figure 17-6. Dashboard With a Collection of Widgets

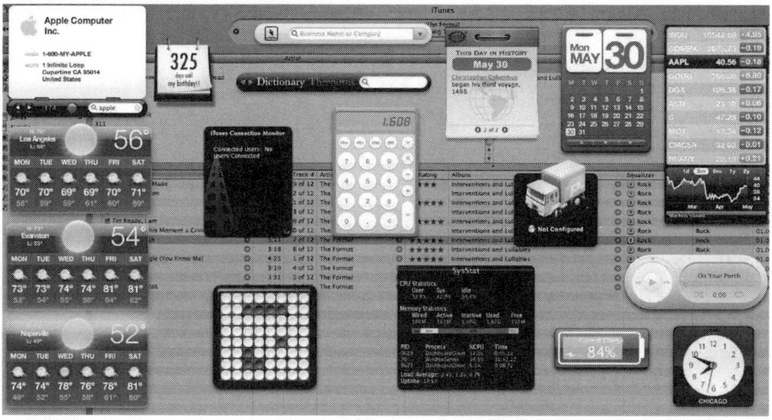

.Mac

This preference pane manages Apple's subscription service, .Mac. Users that subscribe to this service receive an email address at http://www.mac.com and have access to various Web-based features such as preference synchronization and Web site hosting. .Mac also integrates with Finder to give users an online storage area called an iDisk. Various settings related to .Mac can be set in this preference pane.

Network

The network preference pane is responsible for virtually everything having to do with networking in OS X. It manages every network interface and its settings, including interfaces for VPNs. It is also the location for proxy settings.

Sharing

This preference pane is one of the most powerful. Within, personal versions of the server technologies previously discussed can be enabled. Since these are personal versions of the servers, most of the configurations for these servers are limited and thus this preference pane only allows for turning the services on and off. However, it is quite remarkable that advanced services such as SSH, AFP, SMB, VNC (via Apple Remote Desktop), and even distributed computing can be enabled on every machine.

The second portion of this preference pane controls the firewall. Again, the details of configuration are hidden from the user, but the firewall itself remains effective and powerful.

The final portion enables network address translation for sharing an Internet connection. Users are allowed to select a connection to share and an interface on which to share. By clicking the start button, dhcp and nat are started and are ready to serve.

Accounts

This is where user accounts are added and deleted. Each user has a variety of settings available, the most important of which is found in the security portion. Here, a user can be declared as an administrator by checking the box at the bottom of the pane. Administrators have the ability to access directories and preferences that have system-wide effects. Administrators should be chosen extremely carefully as the damage that can be done to the system by an administrator is limitless.

Also, a new addition to OS 10.4 is the Parental Controls portion. This provides control over Applications that can be accessed by a particular user, as well as how he or she is able to interact on the Internet. It even allows administrators to block profanity from being accessed in the dictionary. Despite the fact that this is obviously geared towards children, limiting access to applications and within applications can be a legitimate policy option and is especially useful for guest accounts.

The other portion of the accounts pane is login options section. This controls the behavior of the login window. The most crucial option is the one to allow automatic login. This can pose a major security risk and choosing to do so should be done with extreme caution.

Applications

Despite everything that OS X brings to the user experience, it is not nearly the whole story. The applications Apple has developed to run within that environment are some of the most innovative and useful ever created and are essential to being able to work with OS X effectively. The following gives descriptions of some of the most useful.

Automator

This application is a coordinator for all of the tasks that programs in OS X can perform. Any program that exposes actions that Automator can utilize can be manipulated by stringing those actions together, as long as the input and output types match. For example, Safari's Download URLs action has an input of URLs and an output of Files/Folders. Any action that has Files/Folders as an input can then be chained to that action to create unlimitedly complex and powerful actions. These chains are referred to as workflows.

Those familiar with AppleScript will notice that Automator provides much of the same functionality, but is accessible through an intuitive graphical user interface instead of a scripting language. This gives the power of automation to any user at any level of technical proficiency.

Dictionary

Dictionary is a useful application that is nothing more than an electronic version of the Oxford American Dictionaries and Thesaurus. As a standalone application, it is useful, but Dictionary is most convenient everywhere else. You can access the dictionary and thesaurus from dashboard and by Ctrl-clicking on text in applications designed for OS X 10.4.

Font Book

For those familiar with OS 9, this application is Apple's version of Type Manager Light, which it purchased from Adobe. Font Book allows users to add and organize fonts based on user-defined collections and dynamically enable or disable them. Additionally, Font Book provides previews of each font, whether or not it is enabled.

iCal & Address Book

These programs combine to provide convenient methods for managing personal information. iCal provides calendars and to do lists and Address Book provides contact and other personal information. Both of them integrate with other applications, including Mail, to make all of this information available automatically.

Mail

Mail is a complete solution for all types of mail services, including Microsoft Exchange. By providing OS X specific extensions to the standard functionality that is expected from a mail client, Mail is a showcase of the usefulness of Apple frameworks in common applications. It is laid out in typical Aqua fashion and boasts a plethora of features, including junk mail filtering that is very accurate with minimal setup. Also, it is one of the best examples of the power of Spotlight. Using the pre-existing meta-data from mail headers combined with full content searching, Mail allows users to quickly find messages and easily sort mail using smart mailboxes.

Figure 17-7. Example Smart Mailbox Configuration

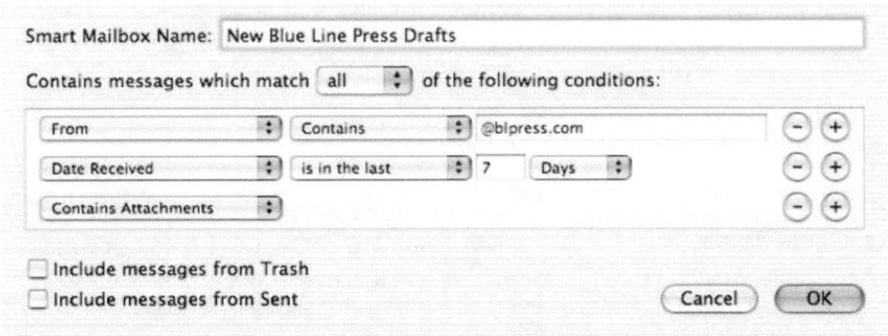

Preview

Preview is Apple's lightweight application for viewing images and pdfs. Designed to be a small utility application, Preview lacks the features of larger competitors, but is excellent for viewing documents. It is the default handler of large number of file formats that are commonly encountered.

iChat

iChat, OS X's instant messaging software, is much more than the typical text-based software. It connects to AIM, Jabber, and directly to other clients via Bonjour. However, versatility is not the selling point. iChat has integrated audio and video conferencing so that it supports voice conferences of up to 10 people and video conferences of up to four. The quality of iChat's multimedia is what truly sets it apart. By utilizing the new H.264 codec, iChat provides real-time video with quality that surpasses any previous video chat. Combined with Apple's iSight camera, iChat is a complete solution for social or business collaboration.

Utilities

The various applications in the Utilities folder are small technical applications. All applications have specific purposes described by their titles, and are generally single function applications. In fact, many are graphical representations of BSD commands. Activity Monitor is much like ps; the Network Utility is a graphical representation of ping, traceroute, netstat, and others; and Console is a display utility for log files. Terminal is especially tied to the BSD subsystem because it provides direct shell access.

Similarly, the X11 application provides a graphical interface for that same BSD subsystem. The remainder of the applications allow for management of various entities, including Bluetooth, hard drives, directory access, and NetInfo.

Table 17-1. Useful Shortcuts

Shortcut	Description
□+A	Select all.
□+K	Connect to a server.
□+C	Copy.
□+D	Duplicate.
□+F	Find.
□+G	Find again.
□+I	Get info.
□+L	Make alias.
□+N	Create a new folder or document.
□+O	Open.
□+P	Print.
□+R	Show original file.
□+S	Save.
□+V	Paste.
□+W	Close window.
□+X	Cut.
□+Z	Undo.
□+M	Minimize window.
□+H	Hide an application.
□+Q	Quit an application.
□+□+esc	Force quit an application.
□+□+3	Capture screen to file.
□+□+^+3	Capture screen to clipboard.
□+□+4	Capture selection to file (press the spacebar to select a window).
□+□+^+4	Capture selection to clipboard (press the spacebar to select a window).
F9	Use Exposé on all windows.
F10	Use Exposé on application windows.
F11	Use Exposé to view the desktop.
F12	View Dashboard.

Odds and Ends

Moreso than other graphical environments, Aqua implements the drag and drop concept to its fullest. More often than not, if there is a task that seems as though it could make sense to drag and drop an item, it will work. For example, dragging a picture from a Web page to the desktop will save that image on the desktop.

Also, OS X is full of features that are undocumented. For example, holding the shift key while performing animated actions such as minimizing a window will cause them to happen in slow motion. Additionally, the option key will often modify actions. One example is that in Finder, the option key will change "Get Info" to "Show Inspector," which is a permanent info window that changes its contents depending on what is selected. There are many other features that won't be found in any manual, so always try new things. Table 17-1 lists some of the useful keyboard shortcuts.

Looking Forward

Something that has always been a characteristic of Apple is its determination to be the most advanced. From the original Macintosh computer, to the decision to remove floppy drives from its machines, to the adoption of FireWire to the iPod, to the iTunes Music Store, Apple is constantly making products that utilize the latest technologies in the most creative ways. Now, with the release of Tiger, Apple has shown that that pattern will not end any time soon.

By incorporating technologies that Microsoft doesn't plan to have in its operating system until at least 2006, Apple has again set the standard for personal computing, but the future seems to be much broader for Apple. Having already seeded development in commercial music (iPod/iTunes), personal music (GarageBand, Logic), commercial video (iTunes' video playback), personal video (iMovie, FinalCut), mobile phones (Apple/Motorola), and other areas, OS X can almost certainly be expected become the center of a digital media universe that Apple will create.

Chapter 18

Oracle and PL/SQL

A relational database is one that uses table structures to store data and logical links between tables to represent relationships between the data. The physical location of the data is transparent to the user of the database. Structured Query Language (SQL), an industry standard query language, is used to access the data stored in a Relational Database Management System (RDBMS). Most popular databases including Oracle, DB2, and SQL Server use the standard SQL language to retrieve data.

Oracle Corporation developed their first relational database management system (RDBMS) in 1977, written in Assembly language. They released new versions over the next few years that were able to run on VAX machines and mainframes. In 1985, Oracle V5 was released, featuring a true client/server operability and the first RDBMS to tout distributed capabilities. Oracle 8 was released in 1997, capable of supporting more users and more data. Oracle 8i and 9i added a great number a features for data warehousing, as well as improvements across the board. Oracle 9i also ushered in Real Application Clusters, the successor to Parallel Server. The latest release, Oracle 10G, boasts enhanced manageability, better cluster support, and other significant enhancements.

Oracle databases run on almost any operating system, and are now often tightly integrated with an Oracle Applications suite. This chapter focuses on the needs of a developer using an Oracle database, including reference for the SQL language, the procedural language PL/SQL and the SQL*Plus tool.

Fast Facts

- SQL and PL/SQL commands are not case sensitive, but character data stored in a table is case sensitive. Use single quotes for string literals.
- A comment is anything on the same line and to the right of a double hyphen (--) or between /* and */, spanning multiple lines.
- The DUAL table is a dummy table in the SYS schema, useful in SELECT statements for returning expressions or pseudocolumns.
  ```
  SELECT SYSDATE FROM DUAL;
  ```
- A row of a column that has no value is said to have NULL value.
- Every user account in an Oracle database is given a *schema*. Every object that user creates is created in that user's schema.
- A WHERE clause can use the LIKE comparison operator to find character strings that match a partial string using the wildcard character, %.
- The basic SQL select statement is SELECT *columnname* FROM *tablename* WHERE *clause*.
- The basic SQL insert statement is INSERT INTO *tablename*(*columnlist*) VALUES(*col1_value*, *col2_value*).
- The basic SQL update statement is UPDATE tablename SET *col1* = *val1* WHERE *clause*.
- The basic SQL delete statement is DELETE FROM *tablename* WHERE *clause*.
- Using SQL*Plus, the EDIT command (ED for short) is used to view and edit the contents of the buffer, which contains the last statement executed.
- Using SQL*Plus, typing a slash (/) executes the statement in the buffer. The RUN command also does this.
- Using SQL*Plus, the DESCRIBE (DESC for short) can be used to list the column names and types in the named table: DESC *tablename*.
- Using SQL*Plus, you can execute the statements in a SQL file using the format @*scriptname.sql*.
- Using SQL*Plus, typing SHOW ERRORS will display any errors that occurred during the execution of the previous statement.
- PL/SQL variables must be declared before they are used.
- PL/SQL variables are set using the := operator.
- PL/SQL and SQL use the semicolon (;) as a statement terminator.

Oracle Basics

An Oracle database is the foundation of a client/server application. The actual database that contains all of the data is located on a central computer called a server. Users who want to work with the data use a separate piece of software that resides on a remote computer, the client. The database engine manages the different client connections and ensures that only one client is modifying the data at a time.

To access an Oracle database, you must have a username and a password created in that particular database. That username is created by a database administrator (DBA), and with every username that is created, a corresponding *schema* is created. A schema is a collection of objects, including tables, constraints, triggers, synonyms, packages, and views. Every object in a database is owned by one schema. Objects in a user's own schema can be referred to by simply stating the object name, but the schema name must prefix an object in another schema.

```
external_schema.object
```

Data is protected in a database by assigning each user certain privileges. If a user is to create a table, that user must have CREATE TABLE privileges. If a user is to create a trigger, that user must have CREATE TRIGGER permissions. These privileges are granted by DBAs and keep users from accidentally damaging important data.

There are a number of proprietary tools available that make use of the database client software. Many of them provide a user-friendly Graphical User Interface (GUI) and useful templates and wizards. Often, the SQL*Plus development tool (discussed at the end of this chapter) is used to execute database queries and procedure writing. Regardless of the tool or application being used, anything that is accessing data in an Oracle database is using the SQL language to do it.

This chapter is broken into three main parts. The first part describes the SQL language and how Oracle uses SQL. The next part covers the PL/SQL programming language, and the last part provides reference for using the SQL*Plus tool to perform operations on an Oracle database.

SQL

Structured Query Language, or SQL, is the standard language used to work with data in a relational database. Everything that is done on an Oracle database, even if it is done using a GUI, is at some level performing the SQL command calls. Creating tables, selecting values, inserting values, and modifying a trigger are all done using SQL. The SQL language used on an Oracle database is usually the same as the SQL used on any major RDBMS.

There are three categories of SQL statements: Data Manipulation Language (DML), Data Definition Language (DDL), and Data Control Language (DCL). Oracle actually does not categorize the most common statement, SELECT, into any of these three. Below is an example of a basic SQL statement:

```
SELECT * FROM my_table WHERE col1 = 4
```

The above statement tests for equality using an equal sign. Oracle uses a number of equality operators, as well as condition statements. A list of these operators is shown in Table 18-1.

Table 18-1. Oracle Operators

Operator	**Description**
=, !=, <>, <, >, <=, >=	Comparison operators for equal, not equal, less than, etc.
IS [NOT] NULL	Checks if the expression on the left is NULL.
LIKE	Performs a partial string comparison, uses % for wildcard.
[NOT] BETWEEN	Checks for existence of left expression in between limits on right.
[NOT] IN	Checks for existence of left expression in group on right.
EXISTS	Checks if expression on left exists or not.
IS OF type	Returns TRUE if expression on left is of the type on right.
NOT	Returns TRUE if condition is FALSE.
AND	Returns TRUE if conditions on left and right are both true.
OR	Returns TRUE if left or right condition is true.

The following sections discuss the SELECT, INSERT, UPDATE, and DELETE statements. The examples in these sections refer to the following tables.

```
CREATE TABLE location (
  loc_id NUMBER(6) PRIMARY KEY,
  city VARCHAR2(30),
  state VARCHAR2(30));
```

```
CREATE TABLE employee (
emp_id VARCHAR2(16) PRIMARY KEY,
  name VARCHAR2(30),
  salary NUMBER,
  start_date DATE,
  location_id NUMBER,
 FOREIGN KEY (location_id)
   REFERENCES location(loc_id));
```

Select Statement

The SELECT statement is the most commonly used SQL statement. It is used to retrieve data from tables and views in the database:

```
[ subquery_factoring_class ] SELECT [ hint ] [ { DISTINCT | UNIQUE | ALL
  select_list
  FROM table_ref [ , table_ref...]
  [ WHERE condition ] [ { hierarchical_query_clause | group_by_clause }... ]
  [ { UNION [ ALL] | INTERSECT | MINUS } ( subquery ) ] [ order_by_clause ]
```

The following SELECT statement uses a WHERE clause to retrieve all columns (using the * shortcut) for all employees who earn more than 35,000:

```
SELECT * FROM employee where salary > 35000
```

The following SELECT statement retrieves only the employee name and salary from the employee table. It uses the LIKE operator and the % wildcard to select all names that end in 'SMITH', and it also uses an ORDER BY clause to list the names with the highest salaries first:

```
SELECT name, salary FROM employee
  WHERE name like '%SMITH'
  ORDER BY salary DESC
```

The following SELECT uses an inner join with the location table on the loc_id column:

```
SELECT emp.name, emp.salary, loc.city FROM employee emp, location loc
  WHERE loc.city= 'Memphis'
  AND emp.location_id = loc.loc_id
```

Data Manipulation Language

DML, as it is most commonly called, is used for altering the data. There are three basic types of commands. INSERT statements add new data to the table, UPDATE statements change data already loaded in the table, and DELETE statements remove data from the table.

Insert Statement

The INSERT statement is used to append new records to an existing table:

```
INSERT [hint] {insert_into_clause {values_clause[ returning_clause] | subquery } |
{conditional_insert_clause | ALL insert_into_clause [values_clause]... } subquery };
```

The first example below inserts into the location table, where the names of the columns that are being inserted are specified because a value is not being specified for every column in the table. The second example below inserts a row into the employee table, specifying a value for every column:

```
INSERT INTO location ( loc_id, city)
  VALUES (100, 'Memphis');

INSERT INTO employee
  VALUES (1, 'John Smith', 30000, SYSDATE, 100);
```

The following example uses a subquery to select values from the employee_europe table for European employees that have started in the last 7 days, and inserts them into the employee table after appending a 'EUR' string to their emp_id. Assume the employee_europe table has the same structure as the employee table:

```
INSERT INTO employee
  (SELECT emp_id||'EUR', name, salary, start_date, location_id
    FROM employee_europe
      WHERE start_date > SYSDATE-7);
```

Update Statement

The UPDATE statement is used to make changes to an existing record in a table. The columns that are being modified are listed in the *set_clause*, each column/value pair separated by a comma:

UPDATE [*hint*] { *dml_table_ clause* | ONLY (*dml_table _clause*) } *tab_alias*
  SET *set_clause* [*where_clause*] [*returning_clause*] ;

The following statement gives raises to all employees at location_id = 2, updating the salary and resetting their start_date to the current date:

```
UPDATE employee
  SET salary = 1.05 * salary,
  start_date = SYSDATE
  WHERE location_id = 2 ;
```

Delete Statement

The DELETE statement is used to remove rows from a table. If the delete was executed by mistake, it can be 'undone' by issuing a ROLLBACK statement before issuing a COMMIT statement:

DELETE [*hint*] [FROM] { *dml_tbl_clause* | ONLY (*dml_tbl_clause*) } *tbl_alias*
  [*where_clause*] [*returning_clause*] ;

The following example statement deletes records from the employee table based on the SALARY value:

```
DELETE FROM employee WHERE salary > 100000;
```

Data Definition Language

The most common data definition statements are CREATE, ALTER, and DROP. They vary greatly with the type of object affected. Each one will be covered in a respective section with the objects. All DDL statements terminate the active transaction with an implicit commit, except a ROLLBACK statement, which reverses the transaction.

Truncate

The TRUNCATE statement is used to remove rows from a table, like a DELETE statement. However, a TRUNCATE cannot be qualified, as all rows are removed in a TRUNCATE statement. Also, a TRUNCATE statement cannot be rolled back:

```
TRUNCATE
{ TABLE [ schema .] table [ { PRESERVE | PURGE } MATERIALIZED VIEW LOG
| CLUSTER [ schema . ] cluster }
[ { DROP | REUSE } STORAGE ]
```

Commit

The COMMIT statement is used to submit changes to a database. Until a COMMIT statement is issued, every change since the previous COMMIT was issued can be rolled back using the ROLLBACK statement:

```
COMMIT [ WORK ] [ { COMMENT  ' text ' | FORCE ' text ' [ , integer ] } ] ;
```

Rollback

The ROLLBACK statement can be used to return a database to the state it was in when the last COMMIT statement was issued. All changes made since then are 'undone':

```
ROLLBACK [ WORK ] [ { TO [ SAVEPOINT ] savepoint | FORCE ' text ' } ] ;
```

Data Types

Every value in Oracle has a data type. Each data type has a certain amount of physical storage space allotted to it, stores a certain kind of data, and has certain characteristics because of that data. Oracle supports a number of built-in data types, described in Table 18-2. User-defined types can also be created.

Table 18-2. SQL Data Types

Data Type	Description
	Character Data Types
CHAR	Basic alphanumeric characters.
NCHAR	Same as char, but with characterset support.
VARCHAR	Basic alphanumeric characters. Server automatically trims the stored value to the exact length of the value.
VARCHAR2	Basic alphanumeric characters. Server automatically trims the stored value to the exact length of the value.
NVARCHAR2	Same as varchar2, but with special characterset support.
	Numeric Data Types
NUMBER	Basic numeric characters.
FLOAT	Basic numeric characters with decimal support.
	Time/Date Data Types
DATE	Date with time down to seconds of precision.
TIMESTAMP	Date with fractional second accuracy.
TIMESTAMP WITH TIME ZONE	Same as timestamp, but with storage of the time zone.
TIMESTAMP WITH LOCAL TIME ZONE	Same as timestamp, but uses the local time zone of the database.
INTERVAL YEAR TO MONTH	Time length in years and months.
INTERVAL DAY TO SECOND	Time length in days, hours, minutes, and seconds.
	Large Object Data Types
LONG	Similar to varchar2, but can store up to 2 GB for data.
BLOB	Large binary objects.
CLOB	Large character objects.
NCLOB	CLOB, but with multibyte character support.
RAW	Variable length binary data.
LONG RAW	Similar to RAW, but with support for up to 2 GB of data.
	Miscellaneous Data Types
BFILE	Pointer to binary file on server file system.

Data types that are prefixed with "N" designate special support for Unicode character sets. The length of a data type is specified between parentheses. CHAR (Character) data types will pad whatever value stored in the row with spaces. VARCHAR (Variable Character) data types will only store the value of the text inserted with no padding. They should be used instead of CHAR data types unless one has a specific reason.

Built-In Functions

Oracle provides a number of built-in functions that can be used when creating SQL statements or PL/SQL blocks. Some of the more useful functions are listed in Table 18-3. A brief description is followed by either the function syntax, or an example of that function being used.

Database Objects

There are several types of objects that can be created in an Oracle database. Objects such as tables are simply containers for data. Other objects like views do not contain any data, yet they present a customized "view" of the data.

Tables

A relational table is the basic storage mechanism in a relational database. Upon creation, a table has no data in it. A user must have CREATE TABLE permission to create a table in their schema:

```
CREATE [ GLOBAL TEMPORARY ] TABLE [ schema . ] table
  [ ({ column datatype [ DEFAULT expr ] [ col_ref_constraint ] [ col_constraint ]... |
  table_constraint | table_ref_constraint | supp_logging_props } ) ]
  [ ON COMMIT { DELETE | PRESERVE } ROWS ]
  [ physical_props ]  [ table_props ] ;
```

The first statement below creates a table named hourly_employee, traditionally listing the column names and types. The second line creates a table contractor by selecting from the hourly_employee table, so both tables have the same columns (and data, if any existed):

```
CREATE TABLE  hourly_employee (name VARCHAR2(50), phone
  VARCHAR2(14), hire_date DATE);

CREATE TABLE contractor  AS (SELECT * FROM hourly_employee);
```

Table 18-3. Oracle Built-In Functions

Function	Description
	Date Functions
ADD_MONTHS	Adds x months to date given.
CURRENT_DATE	Represents the current date.
CURRENT_TIMESTAMP	Represents the current timestamp.
MONTHS_BETWEEN	Calculates months between two dates.
NEXT_DAY	Returns the date of the next given weekday from the provided date.
TO_DATE	Converts character to a date.
	Character Functions
CONCAT	Concatenates two fields.
RTRIM	Trims the right side of the variable by the given characters.
LTRIM	Trims the left side of the variable by the given characters.
SUBSTR	Returns the string of characters between the given position and the length provided.
LENGTH	Returns length of given string.
TO_CHAR	Converts date to a character string of given format.
TRIM	Removes provided string from variable provided.
	Numeric Functions
SUM	Summation of given numbers.
COUNT	Count of given numbers.
FIRST_VALUE	First numeric value returned from a list.
LAST_VALUE	Last numeric value returned from a list.
MIN	Minimum value of list.
MAX	Maximum value of list.
ROUND	Rounds numeric value to provided precision.
	Conditional Functions
DECODE	Basic conditional statement.
NVL	Returns second value provided if the first is null.
NVL2	Returns second value provided if the first is null and the third, otherwise.
CASE	Conditional statement optimized for several tests.

Alter and Drop

A table can be removed from a database using the DROP TABLE command. It can also be modified in a few ways once it is created using the ALTER TABLE statement. If the ALTER TABLE command does not allow the change that needs to be made, the table must be dropped and recreated:

```
ALTER TABLE [ schema . ] table { alter_table_clauses | alter_table_partitioning |
  alter_column_clauses | alter_constraint_clauses | alter_column_properties |
  alter_external_table_clause | move_table_clause }
  [{{ ENABLE | DISABLE }{ TABLE LOCK | ALL TRIGGERS } |
  enable_disable_clause }]... ;

DROP TABLE [ schema . ] table [ CASCADE CONSTRAINTS ] ;
```

The first example below adds the column emp_no to the table hourly_employee, and the following line adds a primary key constraint to that column:

```
ALTER TABLE hourly_employee ADD (emp_no NUMBER);
ALTER TABLE hourly_employee
  ADD CONSTRAINT emp_pk PRIMARY KEY (emp_no);
```

Views

A view is an object that provides a filtered view of a table. It is most often used to limit what you may see or to hide the complexity of an underlying design:

```
CREATE VIEW AS [ schema . ] view  (<query>);

DROP VIEW [ schema . ] view
```

The following lines create a view called new_hires. It contains only the name for records that have a hire_date in the last week:

```
CREATE VIEW new_hires AS
  (SELECT name FROM hourly_employee WHERE hire_date > SYSDATE-7);
```

Triggers

A trigger is comprised of a PL/SQL block that is executed automatically when certain specified conditions are met:

```
CREATE [ OR REPLACE ] TRIGGER [ schema . ] trigger
{ BEFORE | AFTER | INSTEAD OF }
{ [ OR ] INSERT | [ OR ] DELETE | [ OR ] UPDATE [ OF column [,...] ]
  ON [ schema . ] table [ referencing_clause ] [ FOR EACH ROW ] |
{ [ OR ] ddl_event | [OR] database_event }
  ON { schema . SCHEMA | DATABASE }}}
[ WHEN ( condition ) ]
{ pl/sql_block | call_procedure_statement } ;
```

The following example creates a trigger on the hourly_employee table. When a new row is inserted into the table, the values of that row are also inserted into the contractor table. The example uses ':new' to refer to the row that initiated the trigger; in this case, an inserted row:

```
CREATE OR REPLACE TRIGGER emp_trigger
AFTER INSERT ON  hourly_employee
FOR EACH ROW
BEGIN
  INSERT INTO contractor VALUES(:new.name, :new.phone, sysdate);
END;
```

Alter and Drop

To remove a trigger that is no longer desired, use the DROP TRIGGER statement. If the trigger needs to be modified, the ALTER TRIGGER statement allows changes to be made without dropping the trigger and recreating it:

```
ALTER TRIGGER [ schema . ] trigger
  { ENABLE | DISABLE | RENAME TO new_name |
  COMPILE [ DEBUG ] [ REUSE SETTINGS ] } ;

DROP TRIGGER [ schema . ] trigger ;
```

Enable and Disable

The following ALTER TRIGGER statement disables the emp_trigger without dropping it:

```
ALTER TRIGGER emp_trigger DISABLE;
```

Synonyms

A synonym is a symbolic link for a database object such as a table, view, or package. Synonyms are often created to simplify object referencing by creating a synonym in *schemaB* for an object that exists in *schemaA*:

```
CREATE [ PUBLIC ] SYNONYM [ schema . ] synonym
  FOR [ schema . ] object [ @ dblink ] ;
```

The following example creates a synonym in the current schema for the table hourly_employee, which exists in the 'scott' schema. Now a user in the current schema can reference the table specifying emp_synonym instead of scott.hourly_employee:

```
CREATE SYNONYM emp_synonym FOR scott.hourly_employee;
```

The DROP SYNONYM statement is used to remove the synonym from the database:

```
DROP SYNONYM emp_synonym;
```

Sequences

A sequence is a numeric variable that increments when selected from. It is commonly used to generate a unique identifier to represent a primary key. The following example creates a sequence named empno_seq and uses the sequence to generate values for the emp_no column of the hourly_employee table. It uses '.nextval' to retrieve the next value in the sequence:

```
CREATE SEQUENCE empno_seq;
INSERT INTO hourly_employee (emp_no, name)
  VALUES (empno_seq.nextval, 'Bob Smith');
```

Packages and Procedures

Packages and Procedures are very common database objects, and they are discussed in full detail in the following *PL/SQL* section.

PL/SQL

PL/SQL is a programming language that uses the power of SQL commands, combined with the flexibility of a procedural format. This allows you to take advantage of programming constructs such as variables, subprograms, and error-trapping, thereby greatly expanding the capabilities of the SQL language.

The PL/SQL language is block structured, which means that logical blocks of code comprise the basic units of a program. While a block is divided into a declaration section, an executable section, and an exception handling section, only the executable section is required. A block may have sub-blocks within it, and typical blocks include procedures and functions.

PL/SQL is used to write subprograms, functions, and procedures, often encompassing a related group of these subprograms into a package. If the function or procedure is created individually, that subprogram is stored in the database and any user with the proper privileges can execute that procedure. If the subprograms are created as part of a package, than they are stored together and must be referenced using the package name and the subprogram name.

Oracle provides you with built-in packages that can be used to assist in PL/SQL programming.

Table 18-4. Built-In Packages

DBMS_OUTPUT	A very useful debugging tool, this package allows output to be displayed to the console. The PUT_LINE procedure is often used to print an entire line. Ensure that the serveroutput variable is set to 'ON' to view the output in SQL*Plus ('set serveroutput on').
DBMS_ALERT	Allows you to use database triggers to send alerts to applications asynchronously upon the activation of the trigger.

Data Types

A PL/SQL program enables the usage of any SQL data type and expands on that selection with some of its own data types. While the SQL data types can be found in the *SQL* section, the PL/SQL types are shown in Table 18-5.

Variables

Variables in PL/SQL must be declared before they are used. Variables in PL/SQL may be SQL types or PL/SQL types. Sample declarations are:

```
my_counter NUMBER (10);
my_switch BOOLEAN;
```

Table 18-5. PL/SQL Data Types

Data Type	Description
Record	Stores a record.
Table	Collection type. Stores a nested table, no max. size.
Varray	Collection type. Stores collection data, has max.size.
Ref cursor	Stores a reference to a cursor.
Ref object_type	Stores a reference to an object.
Boolean	Stores values TRUE, FALSE, and NULL (missing, unknown value).
binary_integer	Stores signed integers. Require less storage than NUMBERS.
Natural	Subtype of Binary_integer. Stores non-negative values only.
Naturaln	Subtype of Binary_integer. Stores non-negative values only, no nulls.
Positive	Subtype of Binary_integer. Stores positive values only.
Positiven	Subtype of Binary_integer. Stores positive values only, no nulls.
Signtype	Subtype of binary_integer. Stores only values -1, 0, and 1.
Dec	Subtype of number. Stores fixed point number, 38 decimal digit max.
Decimal	Subtype of number. Stores fixed point number, 38 decimal digit max.
Double precision	Subtype of number. Stores float number, 38 decimal digit max (appx.).
Int	Subtype of number. Stores integer, 38 decimal digit max.
Integer	Subtype of number. Stores integer, 38 decimal digit max.
Numeric	Subtype of number. Stores fixed point number, 38 decimal digit max.
Real	Subtype of number. Stores float number, 18 decimal digit max (appx.).
Smallint	Subtype of number. Stores integer, 38 decimal digit max.
Pls_integer	Stores signed integers. Requires less storage than NUMBER, and faster.
Character	Subtype of VARCHAR2. Same as CHAR.
String	Subtype of VARCHAR2. Same as CHAR.

Note that names are not case sensitive, and cannot include spaces, hyphens (-), ampersands (&), or slashes (/). Variables, or any identifier for that matter, cannot exceed 30 characters in length. Variables are declared in the DECLARE section of a function or procedure. A value is then assigned to a variable using the assignment operator (:=). The following line sets our variables above to the values shown:

```
my_counter := 25;
my_switch := TRUE;
```

The value of a variable can be set while declaring it, as shown in the first line below. If a value being assigned during initialization is a typical value, it can be assigned using the DEFAULT keyword. This is shown in the second line below:

```
your_name VARCHAR2(12) := 'Sam';
your_counter NUMBER (9) DEFAULT 0;
```

Similarly, during the declaration of a variable, a constraint can be imposed on a variable which prevents the value of NULL from being assigned to it. This is the NOT NULL constraint, and an example of this is shown below. Note that the NOT NULL clause must be followed by an initialization clause:

```
day_of_birth INTEGER(2) NOT NULL := 1;
```

A constant can be defined in PL/SQL simply by adding the word CONSTANT in the variable declaration. The value of a constant cannot be changed during a program:

```
my_constant_number CONSTANT REAL := 999.00;
```

PL/SQL variables and database columns have special properties, or attributes, that prove to be very useful when writing programs. The %TYPE attribute is used to retrieve the data type of a variable or database column. The %ROWTYPE attribute can be used to create a record type representing a row in a table. The following variable declaration lines illustrate these attributes:

```
var_name employee. name%TYPE;
emp_rec employee%ROWTYPE;
```

Cursors

A cursor (CURrent Selection Of Rows) in Oracle represents a 'work area', storing information and allowing you to easily view and manipulate the data. Cursors are used to temporarily store the result of a SQL statement, known as the *result set*, usually when the result set contains more than one row.

Implicit and Explicit Cursors

Oracle uses two types of cursors, explicit and implicit. An implicit cursor is used each time Oracle processes an SQL statement, and the attributes of the cursor for the most recent statement may be retrieved.

Explicit cursors are programmable and need to be declared like a PL/SQL procedure or function. The declaration of a cursor follows the format below:

CURSOR *name* [(*parameter* [IN] *datatype* [{ := | DEFALUT } *expression*]) ...]
[RETURN *return_type*] IS *select_statement*;

Notice that the cursor may take one or many input parameters, and they may be initialized to default values. Any parameter used in a cursor is local to that cursor. Once a cursor has been declared, it is used to retrieve data by executing the OPEN, FETCH and CLOSE statements. The *select_statement* in a cursor is executed only when the cursor is opened. Likewise, once the data has been retrieved, the cursor should be closed using the CLOSE statement.

Once the *select_statement* has been executed, the result set is retrieved using the FETCH statement. The FETCH statement retrieves one row of the result set and uses the INTO keyword to temporarily store the values of the returned columns in local variables. The number and type of variables specified with the INTO keyword must correspond to the number and type of columns that are returned in the SELECT statement.

The FETCH statement will return the first row the first time it is called, the second row the next time, and so on. FETCH statements are usually put inside of a loop, testing for the end of the record set using the %NOTFOUND attribute. The following example illustrates a basic cursor that prints a statement for each row returned:

```
DECLARE
  c_name VARCHAR2(16);
  c_phone VARCHAR2(16);
  CURSOR emp_cur IS SELECT name, phone FROM hourly_employee
    WHERE emp_no < 100;
BEGIN
  OPEN emp_cur;
  LOOP
    FETCH emp_cur INTO c_name, c_phone;
    EXIT WHEN emp_cur%NOTFOUND;
    DBMS_OUTPUT.PUT_LINE('Name: ' || c_name || ' Number: ' || 'c_phone');
  END LOOP;
  CLOSE emp_cur;
END;
```

Control Flow

The idea behind PL/SQL is to combine the flexibility of a procedural programming language with the strength of the SQL language. Like any procedural programming language, PL/SQL features a number of statements that control the execution flow. This includes looping statements and conditional decision statement and jumping statements. This section describes the flow constructs of PL/SQL.

IF

A condition is a variable or expression that evaluates to a BOOLEAN value, either TRUE or FALSE. The IF statement is used to execute a statement or statements based on the results of a condition. An IF statement can include an ELSE clause, which is executed if nothing else has, and an ELSIF statement that is used to test multiple conditions:

```
IF condition1 THEN
  statements1;
[ ELSIF condition2 THEN
  statements2; ]
[ ELSE
  statements3; ]
END IF;
```

CASE

A CASE statement is used like an IF statement to test conditions when there are more than two conditions to test. The *selector* is the variable whose value is tested, and if its value is equal to *expression1*, *statements1* are executed. *Expression1* is often a quoted literal. The *statements3* will execute if no other statements have:

```
[ << label_name >> ]
CASE selector
  WHEN expression1 THEN statements1;
  WHEN expression2 THEN statements2;
  ...
  [ ELSE statements3; ]
END CASE [ label_name ] ;
```

LOOP

The LOOP construct enables one set of statements to be executed a number of times. The body of the loop contains a conditional statement that is tested during each iteration, and exits the loop when that condition is met using an EXIT statement. Alternatively, an EXIT WHEN statement can be used combining the EXIT and conditional statements into one. Note that some sort of EXIT statement must be included or an infinite loop is created:

```
LOOP
  statements1;
  --conditional EXIT;
END LOOP;
```

WHILE

The WHILE loop is another version of the LOOP described above, but with the EXIT condition built into the statement itself. Before each iteration of the loop, the condition is tested, and when the condition is met, the loop body does not execute and operations proceed after the END LOOP statement:

```
WHILE condition LOOP
  statements;
END LOOP;
```

FOR

The FOR loop is used when the number of iterations to perform is known. This loop iterates over a specified range of integers, with the range indicated by a value *lower* through to a value *higher*. Three dots indicate the span between the numbers, and the *counter* takes the value of each number in that range, one per iteration:

```
FOR counter IN [REVERSE] lower...higher LOOP
  statements;
END LOOP;
```

GOTO

The GOTO branches unconditionally to the place in the code where the specified label is found. A label is a group of characters in a program that is surrounded by << and >>:

```
<< label_name >>
```

The GOTO statement consists of the keyword followed by the label name (without the brackets). The label must directly precede an executable statement or a PL/SQL block. Often, the NULL statement can be inserted into a PL/SQL program, and the label put directly in front of the NULL statement. This causes execution to jump to the label even though no execution actually takes place:

```
GOTO label_name;
  ...
<< label_name >>
NULL;
```

Subprograms

A subprogram in Oracle is a block of code that works together to perform one task. The subprogram may take input parameters and may return a value back to the part of the program that invoked it. Oracle subprograms come in two different types, procedures and functions. A subprogram has three main components including a declaration section for variable declarations, an executable section that contains the statements that perform the work, and an optional exception-handling section for catching and handling errors.

Procedures

A procedure has the following formation:

```
[CREATE [OR REPLACE]]
PROCEDURE procedure_name[(parameter[, parameter]...)]
[AUTHID {DEFINER | CURRENT_USER}] {IS | AS}
[PRAGMA AUTONOMOUS_TRANSACTION;]
[local declarations]
BEGIN
executable statements
[EXCEPTION
exception handlers]
END [procedure_name];
```

A procedure can be removed from a database using the following DROP statement:

```
DROP PROCEDURE [ schema . ] procedure ;
```

Parameters may be passed into the procedure by minimally specifying the parameter name and data type. It is also possible to declare a default value, and the parameters may optionally be used as output values. A parameter is specified using this syntax:

```
parameter_name [IN | OUT [NOCOPY] | IN OUT [NOCOPY]] datatype
[{:= |DEFAULT} expression]
```

Notice that the DECLARE keyword is not used in subprograms, as declarations occur between the IS/AS keyword and the BEGIN keyword. Once defined, a procedure can be invoked by stating the procedure name with any parameter values included in parentheses.

The following procedure finds the average number of days that employees in the hourly_employee table are employed. It then prints a message based on the outcome:

```
CREATE or REPLACE PROCEDURE avg_days_employed
IS
BEGIN
DECLARE
  v_num number := 0;
BEGIN
SELECT AVG(sysdate-hire_date) INTO v_num FROM hourly_employee;
IF v_num > 365 THEN
  DBMS_OUTPUT.PUT_LINE('Long Term. Average time on the job is ' || v_num);
ELSE
  DBMS_OUTPUT.PUT_LINE('Short Term. Average time on the job is ' || v_num);
END IF;
END;
END;
```

Functions

Functions are very similar to procedures, with the added benefit of a RETURN statement, so they are used to compute a value and then return it to the caller. The function construction is as follows:

```
[CREATE [OR REPLACE]]
FUNCTION function_name[( parameter[, parameter]...)] RETURN datatype}
[AUTHID {DEFINER | CURRENT_USER}] PARALLEL_ENABLE
[{[CLUSTER parameter BY ( column_name [, column_name]...])|
[ORDER parameter BY ( column_name [, column_name]...])
[(PARTITION parameter BY{[ {RANGE|HASH} ( column_name [,
column_name]...)]| ANY } ) ]
]
[DETERMINISTIC] {IS | AS}  [PIPELINED [USING implementation_type]]
[AGGREGATE [UPDATE VALUE] {WITH EXTERNAL CONTEXT]
USINGimplementation_type] [PRAGMA AUTONOMOUS_TRANSACTION;]
[ local declarations]
BEGIN
executable statements
[EXCEPTION
exception handlers]
END [function_name];
```

The following function computes the number of days that an employee is employed. It takes a DATE input and returns a NUMBER that is the difference between the input date and today:

```
CREATE OR REPLACE FUNCTION days_employed(hire_date DATE)
RETURN NUMBER
IS
BEGIN
DECLARE
  v_num number := 0;
BEGIN
  SELECT ROUND(SYSDATE-hire_date) INTO v_num FROM DUAL;
  return v_num;
END;
END;

DROP FUNCTION [ schema . ] function ;
```

The RETURN statement in a function specifies the value to be returned. Any data type may be returned, and multiple RETURN statements are allowed throughout a function. The return value must be of the same type listed in the return clause in the function specification. The parameters in a function follow the same format as procedure parameters described above.

Packages

Related types, items, and subprograms can be grouped into a single schema object called a *package*. A package typically has two parts, a specification (spec) and a body, though the body is not always required. The spec contains all of the subprogram and cursor specifications, while the body contains the implementation of the cursors and the programs. Only declarations made in the spec are accessible outside of the package. A package spec uses the following syntax:

```
CREATE [OR REPLACE] PACKAGE package_name
[AUTHID {CURRENT_USER | DEFINER}]
{IS | AS}
[PRAGMA SERIALLY_REUSABLE;]
[collection_type_definition ...] [record_type_definition ...] [subtype_definition ...]
[collection_declaration ...] [constant_declaration ...] [exception_declaration ...]
[object_declaration ...] [record_declaration ...] [variable_declaration ...]
[cursor_spec ...] [function_spec ...] [procedure_spec ...] [call_spec ...]
[PRAGMA RESTRICT_REFERENCES(assertions) ...]
END [package_name];
```

A cursor spec that would be included in the package spec looks as follows:

CURSOR *cursor_name* [(*parameter*[, *parameter*]...)] RETURN *return_type*;

A function spec that would be included in the package spec looks as follows:

FUNCTION *funct_name* [(*parameter*[, *parameter*]...)] RETURN *return_type*;

A procedure spec that would be included in the package spec looks as follows:

PROCEDURE *proc_name* [(*parameter*[, *parameter*]...)];

Package Body

A package body contains the implementation of the specification. The words in a spec of the package header must exactly match the spec in a package body. The package body is allowed to contain local declarations that are private to the package:

```
[CREATE [OR REPLACE] PACKAGE BODY package_name
{IS | AS}
[PRAGMA SERIALLY_REUSABLE;]
[collection_type_definition ...] [record_type_definition ...] [subtype_definition ...]
[collection_declaration ...] [constant_declaration ...] [exception_declaration ...]
[object_declaration ...] [record_declaration ...] [variable_declaration ...]
[cursor_body ...] [function_spec ...]  [procedure_spec ...] [call_spec ...]
[BEGIN
sequence_of_statements]
END [package_name];]
```

A package can be removed from a database using the DROP PACKAGE statement:

DROP PACKAGE [BODY] [*schema* .] *package* ;

A function or procedure can be called from outside a package by listing the package name followed by the subprogram name, separated by a dot modifier (.). Typically, packages containing related procedures and functions are created and stored in the database, and then those subprograms are invoked using this syntax:

```
package_name.subprogram_name ( params ) ;
```

The following example creates a package emp_tools, which contains the procedure and function defined in the preceding sections. It starts by creating the package specification, and follows with the package body:

```
CREATE OR REPLACE PACKAGE emp_tools
IS
FUNCTION days_employed(hire_date in date) RETURN NUMBER;
PROCEDURE avg_days_employed;
END emp_tools;
/
CREATE OR REPLACE  PACKAGE BODY emp_tools
IS
FUNCTION days_employed(hire_date DATE)
RETURN NUMBER
IS
BEGIN
DECLARE
  v_num number := 0;
BEGIN
  SELECT ROUND(sysdate-hire_date) INTO v_num FROM DUAL;
  RETURN v_num;
END;
END days_employed;

PROCEDURE avg_days_employed
IS
BEGIN
DECLARE
v_num number := 0;
BEGIN
  SELECT NVL(AVG(SYSDATE-hire_date),0) INTO v_num
  FROM hourly_employee;
IF v_num > 365 THEN
  DBMS_OUTPUT.PUT_LINE ('Long term. Average time on the job is ' || v_num);
ELSE
  DBMS_OUTPUT.PUT_LINE ('Short term. Average time on the job is ' || v_num);
END IF;
END;
END avg_days_employed;
END emp_tools;
/
```

PL/SQL Error Handling

Errors, or exceptions, in PL/SQL programs are generated when something goes wrong in a program. There are a number of system-defined errors that Oracle will raise, and additional user-defined errors may be declared and raised under certain circumstances. Oracle provides a convenient error handling mechanism that follows this format:

```
EXCEPTION
WHEN error_type THEN...;
WHEN error_type2 THEN ...;
...
WHEN OTHERS THEN...;
END;
```

The action to perform upon occurrence of the named error is listed after the THEN keyword. If the raised exception does not match any of the listed *error_types*, the WHEN OTHERS catcher can be used to handle any other exception types. Use of the WHEN OTHERS clause guarantees that no exception will go unhandled.

The exception handler section comes at the end of a PL/SQL program. If there was no handler, the exception would bubble up from the subprogram in which it originated into the subprogram that called the subprogram. This bubble up process continues until the error is handled or until it reaches the main program, at which time execution stops.

SQL*Plus

Oracle SQL*Plus is a tool used to access the objects stored in the Oracle database, enabling you to execute SQL commands and PL/SQL blocks, in addition to a number of SQL*Plus specific operations.

To use SQL*Plus, the Oracle client software must be installed on the computer, as well as the SQL*Plus software. To begin using SQL*Plus, a user will need a username and password created on the database instance that is to be accessed. The user will be prompted for these values, along with the name of the Oracle instance, or the Oracle Net service name. If starting SQL*Plus from a command line, the following line is typical of one used to logon:

```
SQLPLUS scott/tiger@test1
```

The line above starts SQL*Plus, logging onto the 'test1' database instance as user scott with tiger as its password. A file named TNSNAMES.ora is created in <*oracle_home*>\<*version*>\network\admin with an Oracle client installation. The TNSNAMES file must contain an entry for each database instance that a particular Oracle client is to access. To connect to an instance on the network that does not appear in TNSNAMES, an entry must be created. This can be done using the Network Configuration Assistant.

Once logged into an instance using SQL*Plus, the SQL*Plus CONNECT command can be used to connect as a different user or to connect to a different database. From the SQL*Plus command prompt, a user can enter SQL commands that are then sent to the Oracle database and executed. PL/SQL command blocks are also supported from SQL*Plus, and SQL*Plus itself contains a number of useful commands that can be called from the prompt (a description of the SQL*Plus commands follows).

SQL*Plus offers a convenient method of help for SQL*Plus specific commands (not SQL and not PL/SQL). Typing HELP followed by the command name will display descriptions of the questioned command. HELP INDEX or HELP TOPICS will list the SQL*Plus commands for which SQL*Plus provides help. To end a SQL*Plus session, type the EXIT command.

Commands

Following is a list of SQL*Plus commands with a brief description, and many include either the usage blueprint or an example of the command being used. Most commands have an abbreviated shortcut version, which is the command name without including the part in brackets.

Table 18-6. Useful SQL*Plus Commands

Command	Description
@	Executes the statements in the named file. If full path is not included, it searches the current working directory. Example: @c:/temp/myPackage.sql ;
@@	Executes the statements in the named file. If full path is not included, it searches the same path of the program that called it. Example: @@c:/temp/myPackage.sql
/	Executes the SQL currently in the SQL buffer. Similar to RUN.
ACC[EPT]	Accepts a line of input and stores it as the named user variable. Example: ACC passwd PROMPT 'Enter password: ' HIDE
A[PPEND]	Appends the following line of text to the end of the text in the SQL buffer. Example: A WHERE f_name LIKE 'P%'
ARCHIVE LOG	Starts, stops, lists, and directs the online redo log files. ARCHIVE LOG {LIST|STOP}|{START|NEXT|ALL|*integer*}[TO *dest.*]
ATTRIBUTE	Sets and lists the display characteristics for a named object type. Example: ATTRIBUTE OFC_TYPE.location FORMAT a16
BRE[AK]	Specifies display and control formatting options reporting. Example: BRE ON location_id SKIP 2 BTI[TLE]
C[HANGE]	Edits the first occurrence of the named text in the SQL buffer. CHANGE sep_char old_char [sep_char [new [sep_char]]] Example: C /mycat/myhat

Command	Description
CL[EAR]	Resets the value specified. CLEAR {BREAKS | BUFFER | COLUMNS | COMPUTES | SCREEN | SQL | TIMING }
COL[UMN]	Lists and configures column attributes and format. Example: COL canonical_id FORMAT a32
COMP[UTE]	Performs standard computations on selected rows. Example: COM SUM OF ot_hours on emp_num;
CON[NECT]	Connects the user to the specified SID. CONN [username [/password][@conn_id][AS {SYSOPER|SYSDBA}]]
COPY	Copies data from a query into a table, local, or remote. COPY FROM scott/tiger@ora TO scott/tiger@ora2 INSERT employee_list USING SELECT * FROM employee_old
DEF[INE]	Lists the value of a variable, or assigns a value to it. DEFINE [*variable_name*] | [*variable_name* = *text_value*]
DEL	Deletes line(s) from the SQL buffer, often by specifying the line number.
DESC[RIBE]	Displays the column definitions of the table, view, or synonym.
DISC[ONNECT]	Logs the current user out of instance, committing pending changes.
ED[IT]	Opens local text editor. If named file does not exist in current directory, file is created. If no filename is given, contents of buffer are displayed. User variable _EDITOR contains name of text editor.
EXEC[UTE]	Executes a single PL/SQL statement. EXEC *statement*
EXIT	Quits SQL*Plus. Can specify return code for OS. Default = Success. Example: EXIT FAILURE
GET	Puts the contents of the named OS file into the SQL buffer. Example: GET mySql.txt
HELP	Initiates the SQL*Plus help for named topic. HELP INDEX lists topics. Example: HELP execute
HO[ST]	Sends the named command to the local OS to be executed. Example: HO ls –l *.exe
I[NPUT]	Appends listed lines of text after current line in the SQL buffer. Example: I ORDER BY emp_id
L[IST]	Lists the numbered line(s) or the last line(s) in the buffer. L LAST
PASSW[ORD]	Changes password for named user. PASSWORD *username*
PAU[SE]	Waits for the user to press Return, displaying an editable text message.
PRI[NT]	Displays the named bind variables and their values. Example: PRINT [*variable…*]
PRO[MPT]	Displays the listed text message, or a blank line if no text is included. PROMPT [*text*]
RECOVER	Executes a recovery on tablespaces, datafiles, or the entire database. RECOVER DATABASE

Command	Description
REM[ARK]	Indicates a comment follows on that particular line.
REPF[OOTER]	Controls report footer messages, either setting or listing the current. REPFOOTER CENTER 'Worldwide Office'
REPH[EADER]	Controls report header messages, either setting or listing current. REPHEADER CENTER 'World Office'
RUN	Executes the SQL currently in the buffer. Similar to Slash (/).
SAV[E]	Saves current SQL buffer contents as a command file of the OS. SAV mySQL.sql
SET	Sets the values of the named system variable. SET *variable_name variable_value*
SHO[W]	Displays the value of the named variable or named environment setting. Example: SHO ERRORS
SHUTDOWN	Stops an Oracle instance. By default, allows users to disconnect. SHUTDOWN [ABORT | IMMEDIATE | NORMAL | TRANSACTIONAL [LOCAL]]
SPO[OL]	Sends query output to a named file. Can also print the output. Example: SPO mySQLOutput.sql
STA[RT]	Executes the SQL statements in the named command file. Similar to @. Example: STA mySqlFile.sql
STARTUP	Starts an Oracle instance. No parameters uses default parameter file. STARTUP
STORE	Captures current environment settings into named command file. STORE SET file_name[.ext] [CREATE | REPLACE | APPEND]
TIMI[NG]	Configures timing data recordings. Can start, stop, or list. TIMING [START *text* | SHOW | STOP]
TTI[TLE]	Configures title options at the bottom of reporting pages. Example: TTI RIGHT 'World Headquarters'
UNDEF[INE]	Deletes the named user variables. UNDEF myVarA myVarB
VAR[IABLE]	Declares a bind variable. VAR myCountVar NUMBER
WHENEVER OSERROR	Causes SQL*Plus to exit in the event of a system error. WHENEVER OSERROR EXIT
WHENEVER SQLERROR	Causes SQL*Plus to exit in the event of a SQL or PL/SQL error. WHENEVER SQLERROR EXIT

Looking Forward

The current trend of the industry is towards clustered computing. Oracle has embraced this with the RAC 9.2 and now, RAC 10G. The features added in these releases move the database into the realm of utility computing. The feature list of 10G is extensive, including a flashback query, which allows the quick recovery of dropped objects. Service groups in 10G Rac allow for finer control over how applications utilize nodes of the cluster. Regular Expressions can now be used in a query, and there has been a complete revamp of the Oracle scheduler.

Oracle will continue to move to a landscape of cheaper, more plentiful servers. We have only seen the beginning of grid and utility computing. A great place to download and get started with Oracle is http://otn.oracle.com. You can even use two laptops with Linux and Firewire to simulate an RAC cluster. Ultimately, the best way to learn about any software product is to install it and work through the issues.

Chapter 19

Microsoft SQL Server & T-SQL

In 1988, Microsoft released its first version of SQL Server for the OS/2 platform, developed in cooperation with Sybase. Joint development with Sybase continued until 1994 when the partnership officially ended and Microsoft shifted focus to its Windows NT platform. Microsoft released SQL Server 6.0 in 1995, and then a more stable version 6.5 the following year. A new and completely revised product was distributed in 1999 as Microsoft SQL Server 7.0, featuring OnLine Analytical Processing and a faster database engine, among other things.

With the release of Windows 2000, Microsoft also released SQL Server 2000. The new SQL Server 2005 continues to extend functionality of the traditional database and improve performance and reliability.

SQL Server 2005 introduces Service Broker for message queuing and upgrades Notification Services platform for notifying database users, as well as the Reporting Services platform for report generation and formatting. Data Transformation Services (DTS) has been rewritten and is being shipped with SQL Server 2005 as Integration Services. The tool set introduces several new tools, some with brand new functionality and some that combine the functionality of other preexisting tools.

SQL Server 2005 integrates the Microsoft .NET framework by allowing programmable database objects to be written in .NET programming languages such as C#. This allows development and debugging to be done in the Visual Studio environment. It also adds try/catch blocks for T-SQL error handling and continues Microsoft's focus on XML by adding an XML data type and a language for querying data stored in the data type, called XQuery.

While the product is constantly evolving, the basics remain the same. A `SELECT` statement still returns records from a table, and that's not likely to change any time soon. This chapter looks at using Microsoft's Transact SQL language (T-SQL) to explore and develop in a SQL Server 2005 environment.

Fast Facts

- Single quotes should be used around string values in T-SQL statements.
- SQL Server and T-SQL are not case sensitive by default. A query for 'Smith' would return 'smith'.
- The USE keyword followed by a database name specifies the database to execute against. For example, 'USE mydb' will send commands to a database named mydb.
- Comments are ignored by the database engine. A comment is anything on the same line and to the right of a double hyphen (--) or between /* and */ spanning multiple lines.
- The PRINT statement displays a user-defined message to the client. For example, PRINT 'Hello ' + @myfirstname.
- The basic T-SQL select statement is SELECT *column1*, *column2* FROM *tablename*.
- The number of rows in a table can be found using SELECT count(*) FROM *tablename*.
- A WHERE clause can be included in common SQL such as a SELECT or UPDATE statement to limit the number of rows affected. For example, SELECT *column1* FROM *tablename* WHERE *column1=value*.
- A WHERE clause can use the LIKE comparison operator to find character strings that match a partial string using the wildcard character (%). You can also use underscore (_) to match a single character, or match a list or range of characters within the square brackets ([]).
- The basic T-SQL insert statement is INSERT INTO *tablename* (*column1*, *column2*)VALUES(*value1*, *value2*).
- The basic T-SQL update statement is UPDATE *tablename* SET *column1* = *value* WHERE *condition*.
- The basic T-SQL delete statement is DELETE FROM *tablename* WHERE *condition*.
- T-SQL variable names must begin with @, and must be declared before using them.
- @@ERROR is a system-defined function that contains the error number for the last statement executed. A zero value indicates no error.
- A batch is a set of T-SQL commands that are sent as a group from a client to the SQL Server, and are parsed and executed together at one time.

SQL Server Basics

A Microsoft SQL Server 2005 database is a component of a client/server application. The actual database that contains all of the data is typically located on a powerful central computer called a server. A user who wants access to the data uses a database client application, which is a separate piece of software that often resides on a remote computer. The database management system (DBMS) manages the different client connections using separate threads for each connection and either record or table level locking to ensure that only one user can modify a record at a time.

The actual database is a storage mechanism for data. In addition to the data, the database contains a number of objects that are used to manage and manipulate the data. The most basic database object is the table, and it is used to store the data as records (rows in the table) with attributes (columns in the table). Other database objects include triggers, views, stored procedures, and functions.

To connect to SQL Server 2005, you must be authenticated in one of two ways. One is Windows Authentication, which validates your Windows network account or Windows local machine account without requiring an additional SQL Server ID. The second way is SQL Server Authentication, which requires a login ID and password created within the SQL Server instance you would like to access. That ID or account is granted certain database privileges by an administrator, and those privileges determine what you can and cannot do in a database (can select from this table, cannot insert to that table, etc). In addition, that ID is assigned a role, which also carries certain privileges (cannot create triggers, can perform db backups, etc). Privileges are specifically required to do anything and everything in a database, including creating database tables, viewing data, and adding data to tables. There are eight fixed server roles for administrators. Custom roles are usually created and defined by the DBA.

To get started in a SQL Server database, use either the SQL Server Management Studio or the sqlcmd command line tool. Using the sqlcmd tool, at a Windows Command Prompt (assuming you're using a Windows Operating System), type:

```
sqlcmd -U userId -S ServerName –d database
```

If the *database* name is not specified, you'll be connected to the database that was defined as your default database when your user ID was created. To confirm the database you have connected to and the user ID you are using:

```
SELECT db_name(), system_user
GO
```

Now that you have access, read on for more about the T-SQL development tools.

Tools

A SQL Server installation comes with a number of tools for managing and manipulating data and databases, but you will mostly be concerned with the SQL Server Management Studio and sqlcmd utility.

Also the main tool for DBAs, the Management Studio combines the Enterprise Manager, Query Analyzer, and Analysis Manager from SQL Server 2000. It is a GUI tool that presents administrators with a hierarchical representation of all database objects on all servers, and provides point-and-click functionality for any task, from creating databases and tables to setting or changing permissions.

You will be interested in the tab-separated query windows. Here, you can list T-SQL statements up and down the window, executing only those statements you want by highlighting them and clicking the Execute button. You can then save your list of T-SQL statements as a .sql file and load it again in the future. When a query is executed through the query window, the results are displayed conveniently in the window at the bottom of the screen.

The sqlcmd utility is a very basic command line tool that uses OLE DB to communicate with the server. This new utility replaces the osql and isql from SQL Server 2000. Once you are logged in, you will see a 1> prompt waiting for your T-SQL commands. The statements you enter will be sent to the server as a batch once you type GO.

To quit the utility, type quit or exit. The best way to review all of the sqlcmd switches is by typing sqlcmd -? at a standard command prompt.

Database Organization

SQL Server 2005 supports multiple databases within a single database instance or installation. A database is a *container* for related database objects, and depending on the application(s) using it and the size of the company, a different database may be designated for each application. By default, a database instance comes with four system databases that are used in the operation of SQL Server 2005 to store information such as stored procedures and logon information, and are named *master*, *model*, *tempdb*, and *msdb*.

Within each database are schemas, or logical organizational structures used for grouping objects in a database. If you think of a database as a city, the schema is a neighborhood within that city, and instead of containing houses and other buildings, the schema contains tables and other database objects (triggers, procedures, etc.). Every database object is contained in or owned by a schema – and there are multiple schemas in a database.

Every user has a default schema that is set up when the user is created, but it may or may not be the same as the user name. When a database object is specified without a schema name, the default schema is searched for the object. To access an object in another schema, the schema_name.object_name must be specified.

Before SQL Server 2005, schemas and users were synonymous. That created problems because the user could not be dropped if the user had objects existing in their schema, and only that user could grant or revoke permissions within their schema. To drop a user, those objects would have to be dropped first. Now permissions can be more easily managed and the schema can exist without the user.

T-SQL

Structured Query Language, or SQL, is the standard query language used to work with data in a relational database. Everything that is done with data in a SQL Server database, even if it is done using a proprietary tool, is at some level performing SQL command calls. Creating tables, selecting values, inserting values, and modifying triggers are all done using SQL. The SQL language used on a SQL Server database is in general the same as the SQL used on most major RDBMS, and they are based on the latest SQL standard. SQL Server uses an adaptation of SQL called Transact-SQL, or T-SQL. The rest of this chapter discusses using T-SQL to access and store data in a database.

T-SQL is made up of words like CREATE, INSERT, and DELETE. While the commands are often capitalized for easy readability, case is not important in T-SQL. Tabs, extra spaces, carriage returns, and comments are all acceptable within a command. A comment, which is ignored by the SQL engine, is anything on the same line and to the right of a double hyphen (--). A comment that spans multiple lines starts with /* and ends with a */.

When accessing database objects, the fully qualified name of a database object should be used. If the databasename or schemaName are omitted, the current database and schema are assumed. The object name is always required:

```
databaseName.schemaName.object
```

Condition Operators

When reviewing the T-SQL statements through the rest of this chapter, you will notice the use of clauses such as WHERE and HAVING to restrict the data returned to a specific subset meeting the criteria. An example of this is:

```
SELECT * FROM my_table WHERE column1 = 4
```

In the above statement, we tested for equality using an equal sign. SQL Server uses a number of equality operators, as well as condition statements. A list of the operators that can be used in a search condition are shown here:

Table 19-1. Search Condition Operators

Operator	Description
=, !=, <, >, <=, >=, <>, !<, !>	Comparison operators for equal, not equal, less than, etc.
ALL, ANY, SOME	Returns TRUE if the scalar predicate matches ALL or ANY of the results of a subquery result set.
AND	Returns TRUE if conditions on left and right are both true.
[NOT] BETWEEN	Checks for existence of left expression in between limits on right.
CONTAINS	Checks for the search string specified in the column specified.
[NOT] EXISTS	Checks for the existence of the condition specified in the subquery, returns TRUE if the query returns any rows. Example: SELECT XYZ FROM tablename WHERE EXISTS (SELECT *something* FROM *tablename* WHERE *condition*).
[NOT] IN	Checks if the required value is in a list. Example: SELECT customerId FROM Customer WHERE customerID IN (1,2,4,5,6,).
IS [NOT] NULL	Returns TRUE if the expression is NULL.
[NOT] LIKE	Performs a partial string comparison, uses % for wildcard.
OR	Returns TRUE if either Boolean expression is TRUE.

Built-In Functions

SQL Server 2005 provides a number of built-in functions that can be used when creating SQL statements or T-SQL stored procedures blocks. Some of the more common built-in functions are listed in Table 17-2 with a brief description. A number of system functions begin with @@. These functions used to be referred to as global variables, but are simply system functions with no parameters.

Table 19-2. Commonly Used Built-In Functions

Function	Description
@@error	Returns error number for last T-SQL statement, 0 if successful.
@@rowcount	Returns the number of rows that were affected by the last statement.
@@servername	Returns the string name of the local SQL Server.
@@FETCH_STATUS	Returns the status of the last cursor FETCH statement issued. Returns 0 if successful, -1 if the FETCH failed, or -2 if the fetched row is missing.
cast(*expression* AS *datatype* [(*length*)])	Converts the *expression* from its current data type to the *datatype* specified, optionally specifying its *length.*
convert(*datatype*, [(*length*)], *expression*, [*style*])	Similar to cast above, but also accepting the *style* of format used when converting to character data from datetime, smalldatetime, float, real, money, or smallmoney.
count(*expression*)	Returns the number of non-NULL values in a column for the result set.
count(*)	Returns number of rows that match the search criteria specified for the query.
current_timestamp	Returns the system date and time - same as GETDATE().
dateadd(*datepart*, *number*, *date*)	Returns a datetime value after adding the *number* to the specified *datepart* (year, day, minute, etc) of the *date* specified.
datediff(*datepart*, *startdate*, *enddate*)	Returns the difference between the *startdate* and *enddate* calculated on the part of the date specified by *datepart* (year, day, min, etc.).
getdate()	Returns the current system date and time.
isnull (*check_exp*, *replacement_value*)	Returns *replacement_value* if *check_exp* is NULL, else returns *check_exp.*
left(*char_expression*, *num_char*)	Returns the *num_char* characters from the left of *char_expression.*
len(*string_expression*)	Returns the number of characters in the expression, excluding blank spaces.
nullif(*exp1*, *exp2*)	Returns NULL if the two expressions are equivalent, else returns *exp1.*
replace(*'expr1'*, *'expr2'*, *'expr3'*)	Returns *expr1*, replacing all occurrences of *expr2* with *expr3.*
right(*char_expression*, *num_char*)	Returns the *num_char* characters from the right of *char_expression.*
substring(*expression*, *start*, *length*)	Returns *length* number of characters, beginning with *start* character.
system_user	Returns current Windows NT or SQL Server login name.

Data Manipulation Language

Data Manipulation Language (DML) is the subsection of SQL that is used to view and manipulate data in a database. This includes querying the existing data, inserting new data, and deleting or modifying the data. The examples in this section use the following tables:

```
CREATE TABLE dealers (
  locationId INT
  CONSTRAINT deal_pk PRIMARY KEY,
  city VARCHAR(16),
  state VARCHAR (16))
```

```
CREATE TABLE cars (
  carId INT NOT NULL
  CONSTRAINT car_pk PRIMARY KEY,
  color VARCHAR(16),
  price DECIMAL,
  locationId INT CONSTRAINT loc_fk
  FOREIGN KEY REFERENCES
  dealers (locationId),
  lastUpdateDate DATETIME)
```

Select Statement

The SELECT statement is the most commonly used T-SQL statement, as it queries tables and returns rows of data. The rows and columns returned depend on the list of columns and any search criteria specified. The SELECT statement is very flexible and thus very powerful, and cannot be completely explored here. For more on the SELECT syntax and usage, see the SQL Server Books Online:

```
SELECT [ ALL | DISTINCT ] [ TOP n [ PERCENT ] [ WITH TIES ]
  { * | { column_name | expression | IDENTITYCOL | ROWGUIDCOL }
  [ [ AS ] col_alias ] | col_alias = expression } [ ,...n ] [ INTO new_table ]
  FROM table_name
  [ WHERE condition ] [ GROUP BY expression ] [ HAVING condition ]
  [ ORDER BY expr ]
```

The following example uses the * shortcut to select all columns from a table named cars where the value of the color column is equal to 'red'. It uses an optional ORDER BY clause so that the results are listed in ascending order of the carId value:

```
SELECT * FROM cars WHERE color = 'red'
  ORDER BY carId;
GO
```

The following statement joins tables cars and dealers and selects the value of color and price from the cars table, and city from the dealers table. This join matches on the locationId column in each of these tables:

```
SELECT c.color, c.price, d.city
  FROM cars c INNER JOIN dealers d
  ON c.locationId = d.locationId
GO
```

The following example uses a subquery in the WHERE clause. The subquery selects locationId of the states that begin with 'I' in the dealers table. The outer query then returns color and price from records with a locationId in the result of the subquery. Note also that the subquery uses the LIKE comparison and wildcard %:

```
SELECT color, price
FROM cars WHERE locationId IN
  (SELECT locationId FROM dealers
  WHERE state LIKE 'I%')
GO
```

Insert Statement

The INSERT statement is used to add a row of data to a table or view in a database. The statement uses the VALUES keyword to list the values that are to be inserted. If a value is not specified for every column, the affected column names must be included in parentheses following the table name (*column_list*). Single quotes must surround string values. There are many variations of the INSERT statement. For more on this topic, see the SQL Server Books Online help feature:

```
INSERT [INTO] table_name
  { [ column_list ] { VALUES ( { DEFAULT | NULL | expression } [ ,...n ] )
  | derived_table | execute_statement } }
  | DEFAULT VALUES
```

The following statement inserts string and numeric values into the columns of the dealers table. A value is specified for each column of the table. String values are quoted, while numeric values are entered directly:

```
INSERT INTO  dealers VALUES (1, 'Chicago', 'Illinois')
GO
```

The following statement inserts a new row into the table cars, but only specifies values for four columns, carId, color, locationId, and lastUpdateDate. The remaining column, price, receives NULL, and therefore must be able to contain

NULL values. Note the use of the CURRENT_TIMESTAMP function, which returns the current date and time:

```
INSERT INTO cars (carId, color, locationId, lastUpdateDate)
  VALUES (1, 'red', 1, CURRENT_TIMESTAMP)
GO
```

The following statement inserts values into dealers based on the results of a SELECT statement using the dealers_east table (assume the same table structure as the dealers table). It also adds 100 to each locationId to avoid unique constraint problems:

```
INSERT INTO dealers
  SELECT locationId + 100, city, state
  FROM dealers_east;
GO
```

Update Statement

The UPDATE statement is used to alter existing data in a database table. The statement uses the SET keyword before a comma separated list of columns and column values that are to be updated. This description has been simplified, but to learn more about it,view the SQL Server Books Online help feature.

```
UPDATE  table_name
  SET {column_name = {expression | DEFAULT | NULL}  [,...n]
  [FROM {<table_source>} [,...n] ] [WHERE condition]
```

The following example updates every record in the table cars where the locationId column is 2. The values of two fields in the cars table are updated (color and price):

```
UPDATE cars SET
  color = 'black',
  price = 14000
  WHERE locationId = 1;
GO
```

Delete Statement

The DELETE statement removes rows from a database table that match the search criteria specified in the WHERE clause. If no search criteria is specified, all rows are removed from the table. If a DELETE statement tries to remove a row referenced by a FOREIGN KEY in another table, the DELETE operation fails and no rows are removed. However, if the FOREIGN KEY constraint was defined using the ON DELETE CASCADE option, the row will be removed along with the referencing child row in the other table:

```
DELETE [ FROM ] { table_name | view_name | rowset_function }
  [ FROM {<table>} [ ,...n ] ]
  [WHERE  <condition> ]
```

The following example statement deletes every row from the cars table that is priced below 10000:

```
DELETE FROM cars
  WHERE price < 10000;
GO
```

Truncate Table

The TRUNCATE TABLE command is very similar to a DELETE command, as they both remove rows of a table. A TRUNCATE TABLE statement cannot include a WHERE clause, and therefore must remove all rows. TRUNCATE TABLE deallocates the data page to remove the data, and its actions are not logged:

```
TRUNCATE TABLE table_name
```

Begin Transaction

The default behavior in SQL Server 2005 is that data modifications are committed automatically and become permanent once they complete successfully. To group multiple statements together as a single transaction, use the BEGIN TRANSACTION statement at the start of the group:

```
BEGIN TRAN [ SACTION ] [ [ transaction_name | @tran_name_variable ]
```

By issuing the SET IMPLICIT_TRANSACTIONS ON statement, any data retrieval or modification statement will automatically begin a transaction. The transaction will remain open until an explicit COMMIT or ROLLBACK statement is issued. The connection will remain in this mode until a SET IMPLICIT TRANSACTIONS OFF statement is issued, or until the connection is closed. If a connection is closed before a transaction is committed, it will be automatically rolled back.

Commit Transaction

The COMMIT TRANSACTION statement makes all modifications that have occurred in that particular transaction become part of the database. All statements that have executed since the previous transaction ended will be made permanent. The statement marks the end of a transaction, and resources held by a database connection are released:

COMMIT [TRAN[SACTION] [*transaction_name* | *@tran_name_var*]]

Rollback Transaction

The ROLLBACK TRANSACTION is used to reset the state of the database to the beginning of the transaction or to the last save point. Once a COMMIT TRANSACTION is executed, a transaction cannot be rolled back:

ROLLBACK [TRAN[SACTION] [*trans_name* | *@tran_var* | *savepoint* | *@savepoint_var*]]

Save Transaction

Within a transaction, a savepoint can be set using the SAVE TRANSACTION statement. A ROLLBACK that specifies a *savepoint_name* will roll back only the changes since the specified checkpoint, but the transaction will remain open. From the savepoint, the transaction can proceed to completion (COMMIT TRANSACTION) or be rolled back completely (ROLLBACK TRANSACTION):

SAVE TRAN [SACTION] { *savepoint_name* | *@savepoint_variable* }

Data Definition Language

Data Definition Language (DDL) is the subsection of SQL that is used to create and modify database objects. A SQL Server database is made of the data that is stored and the objects that are used to organize and manipulate the data. The objects that store the data are called tables and are the main database objects. Other objects can be defined that typically reference tables, including views, stored procedures, functions, and triggers. These objects are discussed in this section, beginning with the types of data that can be stored in tables.

Data Types

Every value in a SQL Server database has a certain data type. Each data type has a certain amount of physical storage space allotted to it, stores a certain kind of data, and has certain characteristics because of that data. SQL Server supports a number of built-in data types, described below. Additionally, user-defined data types can be created.

Table 19-3. SQL Server Data Types

Numeric Data Types

BIGINT	Stores integer. Ranges from 2^63 through 2^63-1.
BIT	Stores integer. Values of either 0, 1, or NULL.
DECIMAL	Stores exact decimal numbers. Max = 38 digits.
FLOAT	Stores approx. floating point numbers, 15 digit precision.
INT	Stores integer. Ranges from -2^31 to 2^31-1.
MONEY	Stores currency data (-922 trillion to 922 trillion).
NUMERIC	Same as DECIMAL.
REAL	Stores approx. floating point numbers, 7 digit precision.
SMALLINT	Stores integer. Ranges from -2^15 to 2^15-1.
SMALLMONEY	Stores currency data (-214,748.3648 to 214,748.3647).
TINYINT	Stores integer. Ranges from 0 to 255.

Date and Time Data Types

DATETIME	Stores date and time data (Jan. 1, 1753 to Dec. 31, 9999).
SMALLDATETIME	Stores data and time data (Jan. 1, 1900 to Jun. 6, 2079).

Character String Data Types

CHAR	Fixed length character data. Max = 8000 characters.
NCHAR	Fixed length Unicode data. Max = 4000 characters.
NTEXT	Variable length Unicode data. Max=1,073,741,832 bytes.
NVARCHAR	Variable length Unicode data. Max = 4000 characters.
VARCHAR	Variable length character data. Max = 8000 bytes.
TEXT	Variable length non-Unicode. Max=2,147,483,647 bytes.

Miscellaneous Data Types

BINARY	Fixed length binary data. Max = 8000 bytes.
CURSOR	Contains reference to a cursor.
IMAGE	Variable length binary data. Max = 2,147,483,647 bytes.
SQL_VARIANT	Any type but TEXT, NTEXT, IMAGE, TIMESTAMP.
TABLE	Stores a result set as a temporary table.
TIMESTAMP	Stores an automatically generated unique binary number.
UNIQUEIDENTIFIER	Stores 16-byte (GUID) globally unique identifier.
VARBINARY	Variable length binary data. Max = 8000 bytes.
XML	Stores XML documents and fragments, 2GB maximum.

Tables

A table is the basic storage mechanism in a relational database. A table represents a single entity, and attributes of that entity are contained in the table columns. Records are the rows of data that make up the table. Upon creation, a table has no data in it. You must have the proper permissions to create a table or to query a table.

```
CREATE TABLE
  [ database_name . [ schema_name ] . ] table_name
  ( { column_name  data_type [ NULL | NOT NULL ]
  [ CONSTRAINT constraint_name { DEFAULT constant_expression | PRIMARY
  KEY | FOREIGN KEY |
  UNIQUE | CHECK } ]
  [ ,...n ]
)
```

A database column should be set to NULL to allow null values or NOT NULL if explicit data values are required. In addition, other database objects can be created 'on' a table, including constraints and indexes. A constraint is a rule defined on the type of data allowed in a column used to maintain data integrity in a database. The types of constraints include PRIMARY KEY, FOREIGN KEY, UNIQUE, and CHECK. When a PRIMARY KEY or UNIQUE CONSTRAINT is created, an index is automatically created on a table. An index is a collection of column key values and pointers to the associated data rows that allows data to be retrieved faster.

The following statement creates a table named mytable that includes a column named guid, of type UNIQUEIDENTIFIER, which uses a DEFAULT constraint. It calls built-in function NEWID() to create a unique value for each record. It also builds PRIMARY KEY and NOT NULL constraints on the last_name column. Additionally, it includes a VARCHAR first_name column, a cube_num column of type INT, and a salary column of type MONEY:

```
CREATE TABLE mytable (
  guid UNIQUEIDENTIFIER CONSTRAINT guid_def DEFAULT NEWID(),
  first_name VARCHAR(16),
  last_name VARCHAR(16)   CONSTRAINT my_pk PRIMARY KEY NOT NULL,
  cube_num INT,
  salary MONEY
)
```

Alter and Drop

A table can be removed from a database using the DROP TABLE command. It can also be modified once it is created using the ALTER TABLE statement. If the ALTER TABLE command does not allow the change that needs to be made, the table must be dropped and recreated:

```
ALTER TABLE table_name {
  [ALTER COLUMN column_name { new_data_type [ (precision[, scale] ) ]
  [ NULL | NOT NULL ] | {ADD | DROP} ROWGUIDCOL } ]
  | [ADD { column_name datatype | CONSTRAINT constraint_name } ]  [,...n]
  | [WITH CHECK | WITH NOCHECK] ADD { <table_constraint> } [,...n]
  | DROP { COLUMN column_name | [CONSTRAINT] constraint_name } [,...n]
  | [ {CHECK | NOCHECK} CONSTRAINT {ALL | constraint_name [,...n]}
  | [ {ENABLE | DISABLE} TRIGGER {ALL | trigger_name [,...n]} ]
}

DROP TABLE [ db . ] [ owner. ]table_name
```

The following three statements alter a table without dropping it. The first statement sets the NOT NULL property on the guid column, while the next statement adds a CHECK CONSTRAINT. This restricts the values you can enter into a column, requiring the salary value be less than 50,000. The third statement drops the column cube_num, while the last statement adds a new column named building:

```
ALTER TABLE mytable ALTER COLUMN guid UNIQUEIDENTIFIER NOT NULL
GO
ALTER TABLE mytable ADD CONSTRAINT sal_chk CHECK (salary < 50000 )
GO
ALTER TABLE mytable DROP COLUMN cube_num
GO
ALTER TABLE mytable ADD building VARCHAR (12) NULL
GO
```

Views

A view is a virtual table that is actually the result of a query. That query can collect data from one or more tables or from other views and present the data in one place. The data in a view continues to exist only in the base tables, but is produced by the view dynamically when the view is referenced:

```
CREATE VIEW [ schema_name . ] view_name [ (column [ ,...n ] ) ]
  [ WITH <view_attribute> [ ,...n ] ]
  AS
  select_statement
  [ WITH CHECK OPTION ]
```

A view is useful by simplifying access to data when a combination of columns from multiple tables is queried often. It can also provide security by limiting the columns that a user has access to. It is possible to modify data in a view's underlying base table through a view, provided that the modification affects only a single base table. The following view contains car information for a car buyer with the color, price, city and state information in one place:

```
CREATE VIEW for_buyers_v
  AS
  SELECT c.color, c.price, d.city, d.state
  FROM cars c JOIN dealers d on c.locationId = d.locationId
GO
```

Triggers

A trigger is like a stored procedure that is executed automatically when a particular action for which the trigger is defined is performed. A trigger gets attached to a table, and can execute when a table is modified with an INSERT, UPDATE, or DELETE statement. A trigger can be used to check other tables when enforcing business rules, archiving deleted data, and even sending emails of notification. If a trigger on one table performs an operation on a second table, the owner of the trigger must have the necessary permissions on the second table or the trigger will not execute. A trigger is created using the CREATE TRIGGER statement, and is removed from a database using the DROP TRIGGER statement:

```
CREATE TRIGGER trigger_name ON ( table | view ) {
  { FOR | AFTER | INSTEAD OF }
  { [ DELETE ] [ , ] [ INSERT ] [ , ] [ UPDATE ] }
  AS
  sql_statement [ ...n ] }

DROP TRIGGER [ owner . ] trigger_name ;
```

SQL Server automatically keeps track of new records inserted into a table in a server-managed table named inserted. It also keeps track of deleted records in a table named deleted, and keeps track of updates in both the deleted and inserted tables. These temporary tables exist only in memory and are only visible from inside of a trigger to test the effects of certain data modifications.

This example creates a delete trigger on the table mytable. When a record is removed from mytable, the first_name and last_name values are added as a new record in a table mytable_archive. The values are first selected from the deleted table, then a separate INSERT statement is used:

```
CREATE TRIGGER mytable_trigger ON mytable
  AFTER DELETE
  AS
  INSERT  INTO mytable_archive(first_name, last_name)
  SELECT first_name, last_name FROM deleted
GO
```

With the introduction of SQL Server 2005, Microsoft introduced DDL triggers, which are invoked as a result of a Data Definition Language (DDL) action. The traditional DML trigger described in this section executes when records are modified using INSERT, UPDATE, and DELETE statements. The DDL trigger will execute when CREATE, ALTER, and DELETE statements are invoked by users of the database. While probably most useful to a DBA, the syntax of a DDL trigger is very similar to that of the DML trigger defined here.

Procedures

A procedure, or stored procedure, is a group of precompiled T-SQL statements that works to perform a particular task. It is stored in the database and can be executed at any time. A procedure can take parameters passed into it as well as return a value, a result set, or both, back to the caller. SQL Server provides many built-in stored procedures for administrative tasks. These are stored in the master database and start with sp_. To avoid confusion, be sure to name yours differently. More on stored procedures can be found in the section titled *Procedural Programming*.

```
CREATE PROC[EDURE] procedure_name [ ;number ]
  [ {@parameter data_type} [VARYING] [ = default_value ] [ OUT [ PUT ] ] ] [ ,...n ]
  [ WITH { RECOMPILE | ENCRYPTION | RECOMPILE, ENCRYPTION } ]
  [ FOR REPLICATION ]
  AS sql_statement [ ...n ]

DROP PROCEDURE [ owner. ] procedure_name
```

Functions

A function is a group of T-SQL statements just like a stored procedure, but a function has a return value or table result set. SQL Server 2005 allows functions to be defined using T-SQL or any .NET programming language. A function can be invoked through a query or by using the EXECUTE statement, and dropped using the DROP FUNCTION statement. See the *Procedural Programming* section for more on functions.

```
CREATE  FUNCTION [ schema. ] function_name
  ( [ { @parameter_name [AS] data_type [ = default ] } [ ,...n ] ] )
  RETURNS data_type  [ AS ]
  BEGIN
  function_body
  RETURN scalar_expression
END
```

```
DROP FUNCTION { [ owner_name . ] function_name } [ ,...n ]
```

Procedural Programming

T-SQL is a language that uses the power of SQL commands combined with the flexibility of a procedural language. This allows you to take advantage of programming constructs such as variables, procedures and functions, and error-trapping, thereby greatly expanding the capabilities of the SQL language.

The procedural qualities of T-SQL are useful when creating stored procedures, batches, and scripts. A stored procedure is a group of T-SQL statements that work together to perform a task and is stored in the database. In addition to promoting code reusability, the statements of a stored procedure are combined to form one execution plan, which improves performance.

Similar to a stored procedure, a batch is simply a group of one or more T-SQL statements that is executed as a group. The GO statement is the last command in a batch and can be used to separate groups of commands into batches. Some of the CREATE commands such as CREATE TRIGGER and CREATE PROCEDURE cannot share a batch with any other commands, so they must be separated from other commands using GO statements.

A group of batches separated by GO statements is known as a script. Scripts can contain the statements that create all of the objects in the database.

Variables

T-SQL batches and stored procedures can use local variables to temporarily store data. A local variable must begin with the at sign (@), and must be declared before they are used. Variables are declared in the body of a batch or procedure using the DECLARE keyword followed by the variable name and the data type. Multiple variables may be declared in the same line separated by commas. Declaring a variable initializes it to NULL automatically, and the variable may not be initialized to anything else during declaration:

```
DECLARE @var_one VARCHAR(16), @var_two DATETIME
```

Once created, a variable is very useful in a T-SQL block. A value is assigned to the variable by using either the SET keyword or a SELECT statement. The following statement illustrates the use of the SET keyword:

```
SET @var_one = 'Hello Mom'
```

Using the SELECT statement to set a variable is done by adding the variable and an equal sign before the SELECT expression, as shown below. Note that if the SELECT statement returns multiple rows, the @varTwo variable will retain the first_name value from the last row returned:

```
SELECT @varTwo = first_name
FROM employee  WHERE last_name = 'SMITH'
```

Cursors

SQL is designed as a set-oriented processing language. Occasionally, there may be a need to process result sets on a row-by-row basis. Cursors provide a mechanism to define a result set and to retrieve and process the rows of the result set individually. A cursor must be declared and then opened using the DECLARE and OPEN keywords. The OPEN statement populates the result set, and data is retrieved from it using the FETCH statement. The CLOSE statement is then used to release the result set and to free any cursor locks, while the DEALOCATE statement releases the resources used by the cursor.

Declare and Open

The DECLARE ...CURSOR statement is used to define characteristics of the cursor and the result set to be processed. A cursor can be specified as FORWARD_ONLY, in which rows can only be scrolled from the first row to the last. Alternatively, they can be declared as SCROLL, in which rows can be navigated forwards and backwards. The READ_ONLY attribute does not allow updates to be made through the cursor. The FAST_FORWARD attribute provides performance optimization, but requires a FORWARD_ONLY and READ_ONLY cursor. The T-SQL extended syntax is shown below:

```
DECLARE cursor_name CURSOR
  [LOCAL | GLOBAL] [FORWARD_ONLY | SCROLL]
  [STATIC | KEYSET | DYNAMIC | FAST_FORWARD]
  [READ_ONLY | SCROLL_LOCKS | OPTIMISTIC] [TYPE_WARNING]
  FOR select_statement
  [FOR UPDATE [OF column_name [,...n]]]
```

Once the cursor has been declared, the OPEN command needs to be called. It is here that the *select_statement* is executed. This statement positions the cursor just before the beginning of the first row of the result set:

```
OPEN { { [GLOBAL] cursor_name } | cursor_variable_name}
```

Fetch and Close

The FETCH command is used to retrieve a row from the cursor. It typically is used in conjunction with local variables to store the data temporarily. The FETCH FIRST or FETCH LAST commands are used to retrieve the first and last rows in the result set. The FETCH NEXT command returns the row after the last one that was fetched, and FETCH PRIOR returns the row before the last one that was fetched. The FETCH ABSOLUTE *n* command is used to fetch the nth row from the beginning, while the FETCH RELATIVE *n* command will fetch the nth row relative to the last row fetched. These RELATIVE and ABSOLUTE fetches can be negative numbers, but only cursors declared with the SCROLL attribute can fetch backwards using these attributes:

```
FETCH [[ NEXT | PRIOR | FIRST | LAST | ABSOLUTE
  {n | @nvar} | RELATIVE {n | @nvar} ] FROM ]
  { { [GLOBAL] cursor_name } | @cursor_variable_name}
  [INTO @variable_name [,...n] ]
```

The CLOSE statement should be called once the cursor is no longer needed to release the result set. The DEALLOCATE statement will release the resources used by the cursor:

```
CLOSE { { [GLOBAL] cursor_name } | cursor_variable_name }
DEALLOCATE { { [GLOBAL] cursor_name } | @cursor_variable_name}
```

Example

The @@FETCH_STATUS built-in function is often used when working with cursors. It returns the integer value representing the status of the last FETCH made by any cursor on the connection. A return value of 0 indicates that the FETCH was successful, while a -1 indicates a failed statement. A value of -2 is returned when the fetched row is missing.

The following example declares a cursor named my_cur and uses the @@FETCH_STATUS to monitor cursor status in conjunction with a WHILE loop (see the section below for more about loops). It prints a line for each record in the table mytable:

```
DECLARE @lname VARCHAR(12), @fname VARCHAR(12)
DECLARE my_cur CURSOR FOR
  SELECT last_name, first_name FROM mytable
  OPEN my_cur
  FETCH NEXT FROM my_cur INTO @lname, @fname
  WHILE @@FETCH_STATUS = 0
  BEGIN
    PRINT 'The lucky winner is ' + @fname + ' ' + @lname
    FETCH NEXT FROM my_cur INTO @lname, @fname
  END
CLOSE my_cur
DEALLOCATE my_cur
GO
```

Control Flow

Transact-SQL provides a number of statements and keywords that can be used to add procedural logic to the basic SQL commands. Included in these procedural keywords are control-of-flow constructs such as loops and conditional branching.

BEGIN...END

The BEGIN statement denotes the beginning of a block, while its matching END statement marks the end of the block. The statements between them are then executed as a group. Use BEGIN...END to create a *statement_block* for use in the control-of-flow expressions here.

IF...ELSE

An IF statement uses a BOOLEAN expression that evaluates to either TRUE or FALSE. The statements of the IF block are executed if the expression evaluates to TRUE. An IF statement can optionally include an ELSE clause, the statements of which are executed if the IF block *boolean_expression* is FALSE. The *statement_block* may be multiple statements surrounded by the BEGIN...END keywords:

```
IF boolean_expression
  statement_block
[ELSE
  statement_block]
```

The example here will print two lines if the records exist in mytable. Otherwise, it will print one line indicating no records were found:

```
IF ((SELECT COUNT(*) FROM mytable) >0)
  BEGIN
    PRINT 'There ARE records in the table'
    PRINT 'This line is also executed since it is in a block'
  END
ELSE
  PRINT 'There are no records in the table'
GO
```

CASE

A CASE expression is used within a SELECT statement, and is used like an IF...ELSE statement when there are more than two possible outcomes. The simple CASE expression evaluates the *input_expression*, and then evaluates each *when_expression*, in order. The *result_expression* of the first *when_expression* that equals the *input_expression* is executed. If there is no match and an ELSE clause is present, the *else_expression* is executed:

```
CASE input_expression
  WHEN when_expression THEN result_expression [..n]
  [ ELSE else_expression ]
END
```

There is also a searched CASE expression, which evaluates a series of BOOLEAN statements. The *result_expression* of the first *boolean_expression* that evaluates to TRUE is returned:

```
CASE
  WHEN boolean_expression THEN result_expression [..n]
  [ELSE else_expression]
END
```

WHILE

The WHILE statement creates a loop that will execute a *statement_block* as long as a BOOLEAN condition is satisfied. The *statement_block* will continue to execute as long as the *boolean_expression* is TRUE. Multiple statements can be packaged as the *statement_block* using the BEGIN...END statements.

The BREAK and CONTINUE statements can be used to escape immediately from a WHILE loop:

```
WHILE boolean_expression
  statement_block
```

BREAK, CONTINUE

The BREAK statement can be used from within a WHILE loop to exit the loop immediately. The BREAK statement is typically used with an IF statement to test a condition and exit depending on the result. If multiple WHILE loops are nested, the BREAK statement will exit the innermost loop. The CONTINUE statement can also be used in WHILE loops and cause execution to jump immediately to the beginning of the loop, where the condition is tested once again:

```
WHILE (SELECT AVG(price) FROM cars) > 14000
BEGIN
  UPDATE cars
    SET price = price * .99
    WHERE price > 14000
  IF (SELECT SUM(price) FROM cars) < 100000
    BREAK
  ELSE
    CONTINUE
END
PRINT 'Just enough to pay our bills'
```

This sample code reduces by 1% prices of cars at a dealer that are priced higher than $14,000, as long as the average price is above $14,000. The WHILE loop continues and the UPDATE statement continues to reduce the prices by 1% until the total sum of all cars is less than $100,000. At this point, the BREAK statement causes execution to jump to the END and then execute the PRINT statement. It also uses the built-in SUM and AVG functions.

RETURN

The RETURN keyword is used to exit immediately from the procedure, batch, or block in which it is placed. If used in a block, it also exits from the procedure or batch it is in. RETURN can optionally return an integer value, the *return_value*:

```
RETURN [return_value]
```

GOTO

The GOTO statement is used with a label and causes execution to jump from the GOTO statement to the statement immediately following the label. The label is simply a string followed by a colon (:). The GOTO statement can jump to a label defined before or after the GOTO statement. Use of the GOTO statement is not recommended because code can become difficult to maintain:

```
GOTO label
```

Procedures

A stored procedure is a block of T-SQL code that works together to perform one or more tasks that can be invoked with a single stored procedure call. A procedure is created using the CREATE PROCEDURE statement and it is stored in the database. The procedure is invoked using the EXECUTE keyword, and the T-SQL statements of the procedure are executed. A simple procedure named give_raises is created here (see the DML section for more detailed syntax):

```
CREATE PROCEDURE give_raises @percent INT = 2, @raises_given INT
OUTPUT
AS
BEGIN
  UPDATE mytable SET salary = salary * (1 + (@percent * .01))
  SET @raises_given = @@ROWCOUNT
END
```

This procedure has two parameters and updates the salary values in mytable. Parameters may be defined in a procedure by specifying the parameter name preceded by an at symbol (@) and the variable type. Multiple parameters are separated by commas, and if a parameter is defined, it must be specified when the function is invoked. The exception to this rule is when a default value has been defined in the procedure. A default value can be added using an equal sign and specifying the default value after the data type. The example above specifies a default value of 2 for the @percent parameter.

Additionally, a value may be passed out of a procedure using the OUTPUT keyword in a CREATE PROCEDURE statement. Then, the OUTPUT parameter can be set to a value in the procedure body, and that value can be retrieved by the caller of the procedure. The procedure above uses an OUTPUT parameter named @raises_given to return the number of rows that have been updated. A stored procedure can also return one or more result sets. For instance, a stored procedure that contains a SELECT statement will return the result set of the SELECT.

Invoking

A procedure is invoked using the EXECUTE keyword (EXEC for short) followed by the procedure name and all parameters that are defined in the CREATE PROCEDURE statement and do not have a default value specified. The parameters with default values defined may be omitted, so invoking the procedure may be as simple as EXEC *proc_name*.

When using an output value, the procedure is invoked with the keyword OUTPUT following the output parameter. The following example invokes the give_raises procedure created above, storing the value returned in a variable named @myout:

```
DECLARE @myout INT
EXEC give_raises  7, @myout OUTPUT
PRINT 'You gave ' + CAST(@myout AS VARCHAR) + ' raises!'
```

Functions

Functions are very similar to procedures, except that functions can be used within SQL statements and can return data of any type (except text, ntext, image and timesamp). Functions cannot modify data, and must include parentheses following the function name, whether there are parameters defined or not. Procedures do not use parentheses. A basic function named get_meters converts feet to meters:

```
CREATE FUNCTION get_meters (@feet INT)
RETURNS DECIMAL
AS
BEGIN
  DECLARE @meters DECIMAL
  SET @meters = @feet / 3.28
  RETURN(@meters)
END;
```

This function takes a number of feet as INT input, and returns a DECIMAL value of meters to the caller. The RETURN statement of a function specifies the value to be returned, and the return value can be of any scalar data type.

In addition, a function can be designed to return a temporary table full of data in the form of a TABLE data type. In this case, the RETURN statement is a SELECT statement rather than a scalar value. Notice that since the function body consists of only the RETURN statement, the BEGIN and END statements are omitted.

This example returns rows from mytable that match the input criteria for first_name:

```
CREATE FUNCTION mytablefunction (@fname VARCHAR(12))
  RETURNS TABLE
  AS
  RETURN (SELECT * FROM mytable
  WHERE first_name = @fname)
```

Parameters may be defined in a function by specifying the parameter name preceded by an at symbol (@) and the variable type. The example here uses a VARCHAR variable named @fname. Multiple parameters are separated by commas, and if a parameter is defined, it must be specified when the function is invoked. A default value can be specified by using an equal sign and specifying the value to default to after the data type. To use the default value in a function, the word 'default' needs to be passed specifically. This is different from stored procedures, where the DEFAULT keyword is not required.

Invoking

All of the parameters defined in a CREATE FUNCTION statement must be passed to the function when invoking, and they must be passed in the sequence they were defined. The exception to this rule is when a default value used, the word default must be passed instead. Use the fully qualified function name when possible, and the *schema.function_name* at minimum. The statement that follows invokes the get_meters function created above:

```
DECLARE @temp DECIMAL
SET @temp=dbo.get_meters(13)
PRINT CAST(@temp AS VARCHAR) + ' meters!'
```

An advantage of functions is that while they can be invoked using an EXECUTE statement like a stored procedure, they can also be called from a DML statement, like SELECT. The following example uses the temporary table returned by the mytablefunction defined above:

```
SELECT * FROM dbo.mytablefunction ('Bill')
```

Error Handling

SQL Server 2005 presents a number of options for handling errors that occur in a batch, procedure, or function, including new TRY...CATCH statements, described later. Traditionally, the built-in system function @@ERROR was the main method for error monitoring. It is automatically loaded with the error number of the last statement executed.

The following example checks for an error number 547, which corresponds to a constraint violation:

```
UPDATE mytable SET salary = $60000
  WHERE first_name = 'Tom';
IF @@ERROR = 547
  PRINT 'Constraint Violation - salary too large'
GO
```

If the return value of @@ERROR is zero, there was no error. Notice that the PRINT statement is useful in handling errors, as it allows a specific message to be returned back to the user if something fails.

RAISERROR

The RAISERROR statement can be used within a procedure, user-defined function, or batch to explicitly generate an error message. The RAISERROR statement has the following syntax:

```
RAISERROR ( { msg_id | msg_str } { , severity , state }
  [ , argument [ ,...n ] ] ) [ WITH option [ ,...n ] ]
```

The *msg_id* represents an error number as represented in the *sys.messages* view, and the *msg_str* value is for ad hoc error messages. The *severity* value is an integer value that represents the user-defined level of severity of the error, between 0-25. Levels 0-19 can be used by any user, while 20-25 are considered fatal errors and can be used only by members of the sysadmin group. The *state* is an arbitrary value between 1-127, used to keep unique the same error used in different places:

```
RAISERROR ('This value is too large', 16,1)
```

The values set in RAISERROR are made available to the @@ERROR function, as well as the ERROR_MESSAGE, ERROR_SEVERITY, ERROR_NUMBER, and ERROR_STATE functions that are used inside a catch block.

Try...Catch

New to SQL Server 2005 is the Try/Catch method of handling errors, which is similar to the way Java and C# manage errors. Statements that are to be *monitored* are inserted between a BEGIN TRY and END TRY statement. If an error is generated in this block, execution jumps immediately into the catch block to be handled.

The catch block is a group of T-SQL statements that is bordered by a BEGIN CATCH and END CATCH statement:

```
BEGIN TRY
  UPDATE mytable SET salary = $60000
  WHERE first_name = 'Tom'
END TRY
BEGIN CATCH
  SELECT ERROR_NUMBER() AS ErrorNumber,
  ERROR_SEVERITY() AS ErrorSeverity,
  ERROR_STATE() as ErrorState,
  ERROR_MESSAGE() as ErrorMessage;
END CATCH
```

The example above shows an UPDATE statement inside a try block. When the UPDATE fails because of a check constraint, the catch block handles the error. The catch block uses four built-in functions that can be used only within a catch block to obtain information about the error. ERROR_NUMBER() returns the error number, ERROR_SEVERITY() returns the severity, ERROR_STATE() returns the error state number, and ERROR_MESSAGE() returns the complete error message.

It is also important to note that the BEGIN CATCH statement must immediately follow the END TRY statement, or a syntax error is generated.

Looking Forward

SQL Server 2005 began the integration of the .NET CLR (Common Language Runtime) with the database, allowing stored procedures, functions, and triggers to be coded using the .NET languages such as C#. Look for this marriage to get stronger as Microsoft continues to promote Web services with a common runtime and libraries between programming languages.

The SQL Server 2005 product home page is http://www.microsoft.com/sql/. There you can find press releases about current SQL Server activities, industry articles about SQL Server, and links to documentation for older releases. The Microsoft developer's Web site for SQL Server is http://msdn.microsoft.com/sql/default.aspx. It contains recent articles, links to documentation, links to user communities, and product announcements. This Web site should be the first stop for SQL Server developers looking for information.

Chapter 20

DB2

DB2 (Database 2), is a Relational Data Base Management System (RDBMS) that uses table structures to store the data and links between the tables in order to show the relationships between the data. The physical location of the data is transparent to the database users. Structured Query Language (SQL) is used to access the data that is stored in the tables. SQL is an industry standard query language which is used across today's more common relational databases including DB2, Oracle, and SQL Server.

Dr. Ted Codd, an IBM researcher, first developed a set of rules for a RDBMS in 1970. Honeywell Information Systems Inc. implemented these rules in the first commercial RDBMS in 1976, and IBM released its first commercial product, named 'System R', in 1978. This product was improved and in 1982 was released as SQL/DS and later named DB2. At the time of this writing, IBM has released DB2 Universal Database 8. Dr. Codd's relational database rules are currently implemented as today's industry standard.

DB2 databases are now supported on most major platforms, and can be used with a large variety of administration and development tools. This chapter focuses on the needs of a developer using a DB2 database, including the SQL language, the SQL Procedures Language, and common SQL commands.

Fast Facts

- DB2 Server can run on 22 platforms including OS/390, AIX, Linux, OS/2, Numa-Q, HP-UX, Sun, and Windows.
- DB2 uses schemas to organize objects logically. Every object belongs to a schema, and the full name of the object is schema.object.
- DB2 and SQL are not case sensitive, except when dealing with quoted strings.
- Comments are ignored by the SQL database engine. A comment is anything on the same line and to the right of a double hyphen (--).
- A row of a column that has no value is said to have NULL value.
- A double-pipe (||) symbol is used to concatenate two strings.
- Single quotes should be used around a string literal value.
- Query Management Facility (QMF) is a useful utility for adhoc reporting.
- The CURRENT DATE special register is a storage area that is automatically populated with the current date.
- A WHERE clause can use the LIKE comparison operator to find character strings that match a partial string using the underscore wildcard character (_) to represent a single character, or the percent sign (%) to represent more than one character.
- The basic SQL select statement is SELECT *columnname* FROM *tablename* WHERE *clause*.
- The basic SQL insert statement is INSERT INTO *tablename* VALUES (*col1_value*, *col2_value*).
- The basic SQL update statement is UPDATE *tablename* SET *col1* = *val1* WHERE *clause*.
- The basic SQL delete statement is DELETE FROM *tablename* WHERE *clause*.
- Deleting all the rows in a table by using a DELETE statement may not be very efficient. Using DELETE in this manner can consume a lot of log space when your tables are large.
- The DESCRIBE command can be used to list the column names and data types in the named table: DESCRIBE *tablename*.
- The special variables SQLCODE and SQLSTATE are set automatically after each SQL statement and can be used to track errors.

Basics of DB2

A database is made up of database objects, as well as the data being stored. Some of the database objects include triggers, tables, views, stored procedures, and indexes.

A schema is a logical collection of database objects. Every object in a database belongs to a schema, and the full name of an object is *schema_name.object_name*. When the schema is not included in an object reference, the schema of the current user is assumed.

To access a DB2 database, you must have a username and password. That username is created by a DBA (database administrator), and that user connects using the CONNECT string:

```
CONNECT TO databasename USER username USING password
```

In addition to a username and password, you must have certain privileges in order to access the data. In most IT shops, the privileges vary between the different versions of the database. For example, if you are performing development work in a development database, the DBA may grant you full privileges in order for you to have the ability to create and drop tables, add or delete columns, and read, modify, or delete existing data. In a production version of the database, the permissions granted to you by the DBA will most likely be read only permissions so you can only query the production data.

The privileges that are granted by the DBA may be granted either implicitly or explicitly. An explicit privilege is granted directly to the user, while an implicit privilege is granted to a group.

Data Types

Every value in DB2 has a certain data type. Each data type has a certain amount of physical storage space allotted to it, stores a certain kind of data, and has certain characteristics because of that data. DB2 supports a number of built-in data types, described below. Additionally, user-defined data types can be created. Table 20-1 lists the commonly used built-in SQL data types.

Table 20-1. Built-in SQL Data Types

Data Type	Description
SMALLINT	Two byte integer with 5 digit precision. Support values ranging from -32768 to 32767.
INTEGER	Four byte integer with 10 digit precision. Support values ranging from −2,147,483,648 to 2,147,483,647.
BIGINT	Eight byte integer with 19 digit precision. Support values ranging from -9,223,372,036,854,775,808 to 9,223,372,036,854,775,807.
DOUBLE or FLOAT	64 bit approximation of a floating point number with double precision.
DECIMAL (*digits*, *precision*)	A packed decimal number with up to 31 digits including precision (digits right of decimal). If *digits* and *precision* are omitted, 0 and 5 are assumed. Same as DEC, NUMERIC, and NUM.
DATE	Year (from 0001 to 9999), month (from 1 to 12) and day (range varies by month). Represented internally using the first two byes for the year, third byte for month, fourth byte for days.
TIME	Hour (from 0 to 24), minute (from 0 to 59), and second (from 0 to 59). Represented internally using the first byte for the hour, the second for the minute, and the third for the second.
TIMESTAMP	Year, month, day, hour, minute, second, microsecond. Represented internally using the first four bytes for the date, the second three bytes for the time, and the last three for the microseconds. Range is from 0001.01.01.00.00.000000 to 9999-12-31-00.00.00.000000.
CHAR[ACTER] (*length*)	Fixed length character string of specified length, between 1 and 254. If *length* is omitted, 1 is assumed.
VARCHAR (*length*)	Variable length character string, up to *length* bytes.
GRAPHIC (*length*)	Fixed length graphic string, or sequence of bytes representing double-byte character data. *Length* can range from 1 to 128. If omitted, 1 is assumed.
VARGRAPHIC (*length*)	Variable length string of double-byte characters. If *length* is omitted, 1 is assumed.
REAL	Four byte approximation of a floating point number with single precision.

Built-In Functions

DB2 provides a number of built-in functions that can be used when creating SQL statements. This is helpful because it eliminates unnecessary coding for a number of common functions.

Scalar functions perform some type of operation on a value in order to return another value. Column functions operate on a set of values in a column to derive a result value. You can nest scalar functions within scalar functions, scalar functions within column functions, or column functions within scalar functions, but you will receive a -112 SQLCODE if you attempt to nest column functions within column functions.

Table 20-2. Common DB2 Built-In Functions

Function	Type	Description
MONTH(*expression*)	Scalar time/date	Returns the month part of a date, timestamp, or character representation of a date or timestamp value.
DATE(*expression*)	Scalar time/date	Returns a date when passed a string, date, number, or timestamp value.
DAY(*expression*)	Scalar time/date	Returns the day part of a date, timestamp, or character representation of a date or timestamp value.
DAYOFYEAR(*expression*)	Scalar time/date	Returns the numeric day (1-366) of the date, timestamp, or string.
HOUR(*expression*)	Scalar time/date	Returns the hour part of a date, timestamp, or character representation of a date or timestamp value.
YEAR(*expression*)	Scalar time/date	Returns the year part of a date, timestamp, or character representation of a date or timestamp value.
TIMESTAMP(*expression1*, *expression2*)	Scalar time/date	Returns a timestamp value from time/date value or character representation of a time or date value - *expression2* may be included (for specifying date and time).
INSERT(*expression1*, *expression2*, *expression3*, *expression4*)	Scalar string	Returns a string after replacing the bytes of *expression1* with *expression4*, beginning with *expression2* and going until *expression3*.
LEFT(*expression1*, *expression2*)	Scalar string	Returns the leftmost *expression2* number of bytes of *expression1*.
LENGTH(*string*)	Scalar string	Returns the length of the string in number of characters.
LTRIM(*expression*)	Scalar string	Removes leading whitespace from the string *expression*.

<table>
<tr><th>Function</th><th>Type</th><th>Description</th></tr>
<tr><td>CONCAT(str1, str2)</td><td>Scalar string</td><td>Concatenates str1 and str2, equivalent to || operator.</td></tr>
<tr><td>RIGHT(expression1, expression2)</td><td>Scalar string</td><td>Returns the rightmost expression2 number of bytes of expression1.</td></tr>
<tr><td>RTRIM(expression)</td><td>Scalar string</td><td>Removes leading whitespace from the string expression.</td></tr>
<tr><td>SPACE(expression)</td><td>Scalar string</td><td>Returns a string of blanks, the length specified by the expression.</td></tr>
<tr><td>SUBSTR(string1, position1 [, length1])</td><td>Scalar string</td><td>Returns portion of string1, beginning at position1 (continuing for length1).</td></tr>
<tr><td>LOCATE(search-string, source-string [,start-position])</td><td>Scalar string</td><td>Returns the starting position of the first occurrence of the search-string.</td></tr>
<tr><td>LCASE (expression)
LOWER (expression)</td><td>Scalar string</td><td>Converts a character string into all lowercase characters.</td></tr>
<tr><td>UCASE (expression)
UPPER (expression)</td><td>Scalar string</td><td>Converts a character string into all uppercase characters.</td></tr>
<tr><td>ROUND(expression1, expression2)</td><td>Scalar numeric</td><td>Returns expression1 rounded to expression2 decimal places.</td></tr>
<tr><td>FLOOR(expression)</td><td>Scalar numeric</td><td>Returns the smallest value less than or equal to the expression.</td></tr>
<tr><td>CEIL[ING] (expression)</td><td>Scalar numeric</td><td>Returns the smallest integer value greater than or equal to the expression.</td></tr>
<tr><td>COUNT({ * | [DISTINCT] expression })</td><td>Column</td><td>Returns number of rows that match the query (* is often used to mean 'All').</td></tr>
<tr><td>MAX({ALL|DISTINCT} expression)</td><td>Column</td><td>Returns the largest value specified in the column or expression.</td></tr>
<tr><td>MIN({ALL|DISTINCT} expression)</td><td>Column</td><td>Returns the smallest value specified in the column or expression.</td></tr>
<tr><td>SUM({ALL|DISTINCT} expression)</td><td>Column</td><td>Returns the accumulated total of all the values specified in the column or expression.</td></tr>
<tr><td>AVG({ALL|DISTINCT} expression)</td><td>Column</td><td>Computes the average of the values specified in the column or expression.</td></tr>
</table>

Special Registers

A special register is a global variable-like storage area that can be used in SQL statements. DB2 defines a number of special registers that can be used. The values of some special registers are managed automatically by the database management system, and some must be manually set.

Table 20-3. Commonly Used Special Registers in DB2

Register	Description
CLIENT ACCTNG	Contains the value of accounting string for the connection. Default is empty string. Set value using the sqleseti API.
CLIENT APPLNAME	Contains the client application name for the connection. Default is empty string. Set value using the sqleseti API.
CLIENT USERID	Contains the user ID for the connection. Default is empty string. Set value using the sqleseti API.
CLIENT WRKSTNNAME	Contains the client workstation name. Default is empty string. Set value using the sqleseti API.
CURRENT DATE	Contains the current date. Value managed by the DBMS.
CURRENT NODE	Contains an integer value representing the coordination node number. Set value using the CONNECT statement.
CURRENT PATH	Contains a list of comma-separated schema names representing the SQL path used to resolve function and data type references in dynamic SQL Statements. Default value is "FERMAT", "XGRAPHIC", <USER>. Set values using the SET CURRENT FUNCTION PATH.
CURRENT QUERY OPTIMIZATION	Contains an integer value (between 0 and 9) representing the query optimization done when binding dynamic SQL statements. Set value using the SET CURRENT QUERY OPTIMIZATION statement.
CURRENT SCHEMA	Contains the value of the schema name used to qualify object references not already qualified. Default value is the current session authorization ID. Set value using SET SCHEMA statement.
CURRENT SERVER	Contains the name of the current application server. Set value using CONNECT statement.
CURRENT TIME	Contains the current time. Managed by the DBMS.
CURRENT TIMESTAMP	Contains the current timestamp. Managed by the DBMS.
CURRENT TIMEZONE	Contains a decimal value representing the difference between the local time and Coordinated Universal Time (UTC). Managed by the DBMS.
USER	Contains the primary authorization ID used to start the process.

SQL

SQL is the industry standard for querying & manipulating data and objects in a relational database. The statements used to perform these operations make up the Data Manipulation Language (DML) and Data Definition Language (DDL). Each database has its own *flavor* of SQL, but in general, once you learn the basics of SQL, you can transfer your knowledge to any other common relational database. All database actions are done using SQL, whether the SQL is done behind the scenes or is used directly to access the database. The SQL commands are not case sensitive, although you will often see the SQL commands capitalized for easy readability.

Data Manipulation Language SQL

DML statements are used to query or update the data in the database and typically need to be committed specifically using the COMMIT command.

Tabs, extra spaces, carriage returns, and comments are interpreted as whitespace and are acceptable within a command. A comment, which is ignored by the SQL engine, is anything on the same line as and to the right of a double hyphen.

SELECT

The SELECT statement is the most commonly used DML statement. It is used to retrieve data from tables and views in the database:

SELECT [{ ALL | DISTINCT }] { *select_list* | * }
FROM *table_name* [, *table_name*...]
[WHERE *clause*] [*group_by_clause*].[*having_clause*]
[{ UNION [ALL] | EXCEPT [ALL] | INTERSECT [ALL] } (*subquery*) }]
[*order_by_clause*] [*fetch_first_clause*] [{*read_only_clause* | *update_clause* }]
[*optimize_for_statement*] [WITH {RR | RS | CR | CS}]

DISTINCT is used to eliminate duplicate rows. Since using DISTINCT creates more overhead for DB2, make sure you really need this option before coding it in your program.

The isolation level is set using the WITH keyword and one of the following values: Repeatable Read (RR), Read Stability (RS), Cursor Stability (CS), Uncommitted Read (UR).

The following SELECT statements specify WHERE clauses to limit the number of rows that are returned. The * symbol can be used to return all columns in the table. The ORDER BY clause will return the result set ordered by the office_code values:

```
SELECT * FROM office_tbl
  WHERE city = 'CHICAGO'
  ORDER BY office_code
```

This example uses a sub query in its WHERE clause. The result of the sub query is used to specify the criteria for the main query. It returns the last_name and salary of employees who work in an office which was opened before today.

```
SELECT last_name, salary
  FROM emp_tbl
  WHERE office_code IN
    (SELECT office_code FROM office_tbl
    WHERE open_date < CURRENT DATE)
```

SELECT INTO

The SELECT statement can be combined with the INTO keyword to store values of a result set into one or more host variables. This statement can only be run if embedded into a program. For SQL embedded in your program, the statement must start with EXEC SQL and end with END-EXEC:

SELECT *select_values* INTO *variable* [,...] FROM *from_clause*
  [WHERE *where_clause*] [*group_by_clause*][*having_clause*]
  [WITH {RR | RS | CS | UR}]

The following embedded statement selects the number of rows in table office_tbl and puts that value into a previously declared variable named num_offices:

```
EXEC SQL
SELECT COUNT(*) INTO num_offices
  FROM office_tbl
END-EXEC.
```

Refer to the *Cursor* section for information on the SELECT INTO statement.

INSERT

The INSERT statement is used to insert new records to an existing table:

INSERT INTO {*table_name* | *view_name* } [*column_name* [,...]]
{VALUES ({*expression* | NULL | DEFAULT} [,...]) | *full_select_clause* }
[WITH {RR | RS | CS | UR}]

DB2 will automatically try to insert the values in the order of the table or view columns, unless you specify the columns you are trying to add the data to. While it is not required, it is good practice to list each column in the table you are trying to update. This practice can prevent future problems. The following example inserts data into four columns of a new row in the table emp_tbl:

```
INSERT INTO emp_tbl (ssn, last_name, first_name, office_code)
  VALUES (123456789, 'SMITH', 'THERESA', 71)
```

UPDATE

The UPDATE statement is used to make changes to an existing record in a table. The columns that are being modified are listed in the *assignment_clause*, and each column/value pair is separated by a comma:

```
UPDATE {table_name | view_name | ONLY ( {table_name | view_name} ) }
[AS [ correlation_name]]
SET assignment_clause [WHERE clause] [WITH {RR | RS | CS | UR} ]
```

The following statement updates the address in table office_tbl on all records where the office_code is equal to 71:

```
UPDATE office_tbl
  SET street_address = '123 EASY STREET',
  city = 'CHICAGO'
  WHERE office_code = 71
```

DELETE

The DELETE statement is used to remove rows from a table or a view. If used on a view, the DELETE statement removes rows from the table upon which the view is based. If the DELETE was executed by mistake (and the auto commit was not turned on), it can be "undone" by issuing a ROLLBACK statement before issuing a COMMIT statement:

```
DELETE FROM {table_name | view_name | ONLY ( {table_name | view_name} ) }
[[AS] correlation_name]
[WHERE clause] [WITH {RR | RS | CS | UR} ]
```

The following statement removes an employee record from the table emp_tbl where the ssn = 123456789:

```
DELETE  FROM emp_tbl
  WHERE ssn = 123456789
```

COMMIT and ROLLBACK

The COMMIT statement is used to submit changes to a database. Until a COMMIT statement is issued, every change since the previous COMMIT was issued can be rolled back using the ROLLBACK statement (assuming auto commit was not enabled). You will not be able to see the database changes which were applied until the COMMIT is performed.

```
COMMIT [ WORK ]
```

The ROLLBACK statement can be used to return a database to the state it was in when the last COMMIT statement was issued. It can also be used to roll back changes to the last SAVEPOINT, or arbitrary point in a transaction, indicated using a SAVEPOINT statement. All changes made since then are ignored when a ROLLBACK is invoked:

```
ROLLBACK [ WORK ] [ TO SAVEPOINT [ savepoint_name ] ]
```

Operators

A statement often has many optional branches and modifiers, which can lead to the inclusion of clauses, such as WHERE or HAVING. An example of this is:

```
SELECT * FROM emp_tbl WHERE salary = 40000
```

Notice in the above statement we tested for equality using an equal sign. DB2 uses a number of equality operators, as well as condition statements. A list of these operators is shown here:

Table 20-4. DB2 Operators

Operator	Description
=, !=, <, >, <=, >=	Comparison operators for equal, not equal, less than, greater than, less than or equal to, greater than or equal to.
IS [NOT] NULL	Checks if the expression on the left is NULL.
LIKE	Performs a partial string comparison, uses % for wildcard.
[NOT] BETWEEN	Checks for existence of left expression in between limits on right.
[NOT] IN	Checks for existence of left expression in group on right.
[NOT] EXISTS	Checks if expression on left exists or not.
NOT	Returns TRUE if condition is FALSE.
AND	Returns TRUE if both conditions are true.
OR	Returns TRUE if condition on left or condition on right is true.

SPUFI and QMF

SQL Processor Using File Input (SPUFI) is available through the DB2 Interactive (DB2I) utility. It allows you to interactively create and submit SQL for execution and see your results on your terminal. This is helpful if you want to execute SQL statements quickly without coding and compiling a program.

The Query Management Facility (QMF) is another utility that can be used to execute SQL through interactive screens and display the results on your monitor. QMF gives you the option to enter and execute SQL directly or through a set of prompts. You do not need to know SQL to use the prompted query option.

QMF also offers formatting capabilities, which is helpful for adhoc reporting.

Data Definition Language SQL

Data Definition Language (DDL) is a subset of SQL that is used to create or manipulate objects within the database. DDL statements are more commonly written and executed by the DBA, although there are situations where you may need to use DDL (such as executing DDL to set up a test environment). DDL statements can be executed interactively or within program execution.

If you need to write DDL SQL, your DBA probably has some samples you can use to start as a base. In this section, we will look at DDL in more detail, including creating a sample table, view, alias, index, trigger, procedure, and function.

CREATE TABLE

The CREATE TABLE SQL will create a table that has no data in it. A user with SYSADM or DBADM authority can create a table. Alternatively, a user can have CREATETAB authority on the database, USE privilege on the tablespace, and IMPLICIT_SCHEMA authority on the database if the schema does not yet exist and CREATEIN authority on the schema if it exists:

CREATE [SUMMARY] TABLE *table_name*

{*element_list* | OF *type* [*options*] | *summary_def*

| LIKE {*table_name* | *view_name* | *nickname*}}

[DATA CAPTURE NONE | DATA CAPTURE CHANGES]

[IN *table_space* [*table_space_options*]]

[{PARTIOINING KEY (*column* [,...] [USING HASHING] | REPLICATED}]

[NOT LOGGED INITIALLY]

The following statement creates a table named emp_tbl in the myspace tablespace. There are five columns in the table. The INTEGER field ssn is the primary key. There is a CHECK constraint named chk_sal on the salary column specifying that it must contain a value greater than 35000:

```
CREATE TABLE emp_tbl (
  first_name    VARCHAR(16),
  last_name VARCHAR(16),
  ssn    INTEGER NOT NULL,
  salary DECIMAL(7,2),
  office_code  INTEGER,
  PRIMARY KEY (ssn),
  CONSTRAINT chk_sal CHECK (salary > 35000))
IN myspace
```

Note that a unique index must be created on the primary key column ssn before the table can be used. The following statement creates a table named executive_tbl with the same structure as emp_tbl:

```
CREATE TABLE executive_tbl
  LIKE emp_tbl
  IN myspace
```

ALTER TABLE

The ALTER TABLE statement is used to make an adjustment to a table structure without deleting its contents:

```
ALTER TABLE tablename
{ADD column-name data-type [NOT NULL WITH DEFAULT]}
{ADD PRIMARY KEY...} {ADD FOREIGN KEY...}
{ON DELETE [RESTRICT/CASCADE/SET NULL]}
```

The following statement adds a new column job_code into emp_tbl:

```
ALTER TABLE emp_tbl
  ADD job_code CHAR(5)
```

This example adds a FOREIGN KEY to emp_tbl based on the matching primary key, office_code from office_tbl. The ON DELETE SET NULL option will put nulls in the office_code field of the emp_tbl if office_code is deleted from office_tbl.

```
ALTER TABLE emp_tbl
  ADD FOREIGN KEY (office_code)
  REFERENCES office_tbl
  ON DELETE SET NULL
```

Views

A view is used when you only want to see or work with a subset of data. It can be used in lieu of coding a SELECT statement within your program and can combine data from more than one table:

```
CREATE VIEW view-name [column1, [column2]] AS subselect
```

A horizontal view is one which limits the rows that can be selected from the base table. The following statement creates a horizontal view named CHICAGO based on the office_tbl table, which allows a user to view only details on offices located in Chicago:

```
CREATE VIEW  CHICAGO
AS SELECT *
  FROM office_tbl
  WHERE city = 'CHICAGO'
```

A vertical view is one which limits the columns that can be selected from the base table. The following statement creates a vertical view named NAME_ADDR based on the emp_tbl table, which allows a user to view only the name and office code of other staff members in the company. This can be used to restrict access to more personal information such as Social Security Number or salary:

```
CREATE VIEW name_addr
AS SELECT first_name, last_name, office_code
  FROM emp_tbl
```

A view can be removed from a database using the DROP statement:

```
DROP VIEW  view_name
```

Aliases

An alias, or synonym, is an alternate name for a database object such as a table, view, package, and others. Aliases are often created to simplify user rights by creating an alias in one schema for an object that exists in a different schema:

```
CREATE {ALIAS | SYNONYM} name
  FOR {table_name | view_name | nickname | alias2_name}
```

The following SQL statement creates an alias named night_shift in the current working schema for a table of the same name in the yourschema schema:

```
CREATE ALIAS night_shift
  FOR yourschema.night_shift
```

The DROP ALIAS statement is used to remove an alias from the database:

```
DROP ALIAS aliasname
```

Indexes

An index provides faster access to data by providing DB2 with a more direct route to a subset of the data. If an index is not used, DB2 is forced to read all data in the table until it finds the appropriate match. This is referred to as a table space scan. For example, if someone were to query the emp_tbl using only last_name in the where clause, the fact that last_name is not indexed would force a table space scan, which in turn could have a significant impact on performance.

A non-unique index will allow rows into the table that contains duplicate data on the index columns. A unique index will not allow duplicate data on the index columns and will trigger an error (-803) if an attempt is made to insert duplicate data.

A unique index must be created on a primary key column before that column can be populated or referenced as a foreign key of another table. The CREATE INDEX statement is used to create an index within a table:

```
CREATE [UNIQUE] INDEX index-name
  ON tablename (index_col1[, index_col2...])
```

The following statement adds a new unique index, emp_tbl_pki, on the column ssn of table emp_tbl:

```
CREATE UNIQUE INDEX emp_tbl_pki
  ON emp_tbl (ssn)
```

Triggers

A trigger is an event driven SQL block that is stored and managed by the RDBMS. If a trigger performs operations on other database objects, the owner of the trigger must have the necessary permissions or the trigger will not execute. Triggers can be used to manage data integrity when data is changed in the database:

```
CREATE TRIGGER trigger_name {NO CASCADING BEFORE | AFTER }
{INSERT | DELETE | UPDATE [OF col_name [,...]]} ON table_name
[REFERENCING {OLD | NEW | OLD_TABLE | NEW_TABLE} name ]
FOR EACH {ROW | STATEMENT} MODE DB2SQL
[WHEN (condition)] action_sql
```

The following statement creates a trigger named sal_upd. The trigger executes if the salary field is updated more than 25% in a record on the table emp_tbl. If this condition occurs, an error is raised before the update occurs:

```
CREATE TRIGGER sal_upd
  AFTER UPDATE OF salary
  ON emp_tbl
  REFERENCING OLD AS A NEW AS B
  FOR EACH ROW MODE DB2SQL
WHEN (B.salary > (A.salary * 1.25))
  BEGIN ATOMIC
    SIGNAL SQLSTATE '98765' ('Raise exceeds 25%');
END
```

The DROP TRIGGER statement is used to remove a trigger from a database:

```
DROP TRIGGER trigger_name
```

Procedures

A stored procedure is a block of code that works to perform a particular task. It is stored in the database and can be executed at any time. A procedure is called by listing the name of the procedure along with the parameters that are required by it:

```
procedure_name(parameter1[, param2])
```

In DB2, a procedure can be created using Java, C, Cobol, OLE, or SQL. When the language is something other than SQL, the procedure should be contained in an external file, and that file name should be referenced in the CREATE statement:

```
CREATE PROCEDURE procedure_name ( [ {[IN] | OUT | INOUT} param_name
  datatype] [,...] )
[SPECIFIC name] {[DYNAMIC RESULT SETS 0] | DYNAMIC RESULT SETS
  integer}
{[MODIFIES SQL DATA] | NO SQL | CONTAINS SQL | READS SQL DATA}
{[NOT DETERMINISTIC] | DETERMINISTIC} [CALLED ON NULL INPUT]
LANGUAGE {C | JAVA | COBOL | OLE | SQL} procedure
```

The following procedure updates the employee salary based on their rating. It uses rating and Social Security Number as input to the procedure:

```
CREATE PROCEDURE upd_salary
(IN ssn_in INT, IN rating_in INT)
LANGUAGE SQL
BEGIN
  SELECT salary INTO cur_sal FROM emp_tbl WHERE ssn = ssn_in;
  IF rating_in > 0 THEN
    UPDATE emp_tbl
    SET salary = cur_sal * 1.05
    WHERE ssn = ssn_in;
  END IF;
END @
```

A procedure can be removed from a database using the DROP statement:

```
DROP PROCEDURE procedure_name
```

Refer to the *SQL Procedure Language* section of this chapter for more detailed information on this topic.

Functions

A function is a block of code that works to perform a particular task. It is stored in the database as SQL and can be executed at any time. A function is similar to a procedure with the addition of being able to return a value back to the caller. DB2 allows for five different types of functions to be created. The syntax of a function written in SQL is given here:

```
CREATE FUNCTION function_name ( [param_name datatype] [,...] )
RETURNS {datatype | ROW col_list | TABLE col_list} [SPECIFIC name]
[LANGUAGE SQL] {[NOT DETERMINISTIC] | DETERMINISTIC}
{[EXTERNAL ACTION] | NO EXTERNAL ACTION}
{[READS SQL DATA] | CONTAINS SQL}
[CALLED ON NULL INPUT] [PREDICATES ( [predicate spec] )]
sql_function body
```

The following statement creates a function named get_last_name. This function takes a VARCHAR parameter named first_name_in and returns a VARCHAR value. The body of the function executes a SELECT statement:

```
CREATE FUNCTION get_last_name ( first_name_in VARCHAR(16) )
  RETURN VARCHAR
  LANGUAGE SQL
  READS SQL DATA
  NO EXTERNAL ACTION
  DETERMINISTIC
  RETURN
  SELECT last_name
    FROM emp_tbl
    WHERE first_name = first_name_in
```

A function can be removed from a database using the DROP statement:

```
DROP FUNCTION function_name
```

Cursors

A cursor in DB2 represents a work area, storing information and allowing you to easily view and manipulate the data. Cursors are used to temporarily store the result of a SQL statement, known as the result set. The cursor points to one row of the result set at a time, and the rows can be read sequentially until the NOT FOUND condition occurs (SQLCODE +100, SQLSTATE 02000). Cursors can only be used within in a program.

Each cursor that is created must be declared using a DECLARE CURSOR statement. An OPEN statement executes the SQL query and loads the cursor, and FETCH statements retrieve one row at a time from the cursor. The CLOSE statement ends the cursor.

The DECLARE statement defines the name of the cursor and includes the SELECT INTO statement that queries the data (refer to the *Data Manipulation Language SQL* section of this chapter for the SELECT INTO syntax). Note that the query is not executed during the DECLARE statement, only defined. The WITH HOLD clause, if included, indicates that the cursor is to remain open if a unit of work issues a COMMIT statement. All other cursors are closed automatically by the database manager:

```
DECLARE cur_name CURSOR [WITH HOLD] [WITH RETURN {TO CALLER |
  TO CLIENT }]  FOR select_statement
```

The OPEN statement is used to execute the SQL statement and load the cursor with the result set. The command OPEN followed by the cursor name will execute the query, and only after it is opened can rows from a cursor be retrieved:

```
OPEN cur_name {USING [host_var]}
```

The FETCH statement is issued to assign the values of the current row to the specified host variables, and position the cursor on the next row of the result set:

FETCH [FROM] *cur_name* {INTO *host_var* [,...] | USING DESCRIPTOR *name*}

When using a cursor for data modification, the WHERE CURRENT OF statement must be included to specify for DB2 which row to perform the operation on:

DELETE from [*table1*|*view1*] WHERE CURRENT OF *cur_name*

UPDATE [*table1*|*view1*] SET *conditions* WHERE CURRENT OF *cur_name*

A CLOSE statement should be used for each opened cursor, specifying the CLOSE command, followed by the cursor name:

CLOSE *cur_name*

Bind

The BIND command compiles SQL statements within a program. It also uses the DB2 optimizer to determine the most efficient access path to the DB2 tables. The BIND information is stored in the DB2 system tables at BIND time and is referenced at runtime.

There are two types of BINDS: BIND PLAN and BIND PACKAGE. BIND PLAN accepts other DB2 compiled programs as input. BIND PACKAGE creates a single package based on your program. If you use the BIND PACKAGE option, the package must then be bound to the plan before you can run the executable.

You need to re-bind your program each time you make changes to it. If a program is not bound or the BIND errors out, you will get a -805 SQLCODE at runtime.

SQL Procedure Language

The SQL Procedure Language (SPL) is a programming language designed for writing DB2 stored procedures, which allows certain control statements to be used with SQL to manage the flow of a group of statements.

Prior to DB2 7.1, stored procedures could be written in languages such as C, Java, or Cobol, but not SQL. SPL enables you to take advantage of programming constructs such as variables, subprograms, and error trapping without using an external programming language. There are a number of programming constructs that can be used in SPL. This section focuses on a subset of the constructs including IF, CASE, LOOP, WHILE, FOR, LEAVE, and GOTO.

The procedure is created using a CREATE PROCEDURE statement and is sent to the UDB DB2 engine. In the background, it converts the logic to a C program, which is then compiled and stored. For this reason, a C or C++ compiler must be on the DB2 server in order to utilize SPL procedures.

One of the biggest benefits to using SPL is the ability to perform operations on data within a set of code. The capability does introduce SQL limitations which a developer would not need to worry about if they were to use straight SQL.

Two DB2 system tables required to support SPL are SYSIBM.SYSPSM, which holds the source code for the SQL procedures, and SYSIBM.SYSPSMOPTS, which contains the procedure options for SQL stored procedures.

Stored Procedure Builder

The SPL stored procedures can be written directly by the developer or created using the Stored Procedure Builder (SPB) tool.

SPB is a new feature within DB2 that provides a user friendly environment for building stored procedures. It can be used to develop stored procedures for mainframe, as well as distributed environments, and can be used as a standalone utility or in conjunction with a development tool such as Microsoft Visual Basic or Microsoft Visual Studio. It supports both SPL and Java as stored procedure host languages.

IF

A condition is a variable or expression that evaluates to either TRUE or FALSE. The IF statement is used to execute a statement or statements based on the results of a condition. An IF statement can include an ELSE clause, which is executed if nothing else is, and an ELSIF statement that is used to test multiple conditions:

```
IF condition1 THEN
  statements1;
[ ELSIF condition2 THEN
  statements2; ]
[ ELSE
  statements3; ]
END IF;
```

CASE

A CASE statement is used like an IF statement to test conditions, but it is used when there are more than two conditions to test. The *selector* is the variable whose value is tested, and if its value is equal to *expression1*, *statements1* are executed. *expression1* is often a quoted literal. The *statements3* will execute if no other statements have:

```
CASE selector
  WHEN expression1 THEN statements1;
  WHEN expression2 THEN statements2;
 ...
  [ ELSE statements3; ]
END CASE
```

LOOP

The LOOP construct enables one set of statements to be executed a number of times. The body of the loop will contain a conditional statement that is tested during each iteration, and exits the loop when that condition is met using an LEAVE statement. The LEAVE statement transfers control out of any of the loops or a compound statement. Note that without including a LEAVE statement, an infinite loop is created. If an ending label is used, a matching beginning label must also be used:

```
[label:]
LOOP
  statements1;
  --conditional LEAVE
END LOOP [label]
```

WHILE

The WHILE loop is like the LOOP described above, but with the exit condition built into the statement itself. Before each iteration of the loop, the condition is tested, and when the condition is met, the loop body does not execute and operations proceed after the END WHILE statement. If an ending label is used, a matching beginning label must also be used:

```
[label:]
WHILE condition DO
  statements;
END WHILE [label]
```

FOR

The FOR loop is used to execute each row of a table or result set. For each row returned by the *select statement*, the statements of the loop are executed. The loop uses a cursor to access the result set, and if a cursor is not named, DB2 will generate a unique cursor name automatically. If an ending label is used, a matching beginning label must also be used:

```
[label:]
FOR loop_name AS [cursor_name CURSOR FOR] select_statement DO
  statements;
END FOR [label]
```

LEAVE

The LEAVE statement transfers control out of any of the loops or a compound statement. The statement may be followed by a label, indicating that execution will jump to the named label. This is often useful when loops are nested. A label is required at the start of the loop to use this statement:

```
LEAVE label
```

GOTO

The GOTO branches unconditionally to the place in the code where the specified label is found. A label is a legal group of characters in a program that is followed by a colon.

Use of the GOTO statement is not recommended because it makes code difficult to read and maintain.

Error Handling

DB2 provides a few mechanisms for handling errors that occur during a stored procedure. The values of SQLCODE and SQLSTATE are set automatically by the DBMS after the execution of each statement. The values of these registers can be checked immediately following the execution of a suspect statement. The error, should it occur, can then be handled appropriately. In order to check one of these two values in a stored procedure, declare a variable of the same name in the declarations section of the procedure. An SQLCODE is feedback provided by DB2 regarding the status of your SQL command. SQL codes are provided after the execution of any SQL statement, regardless if the statement is submitted using SPUFI or executed as an embedded SQL statement in a batch or online program.

There are many SQL codes within DB2. For a complete list, you can refer to an IBM Database 2 Messages and Codes manual. Table 20-6 lists some commonly encountered SQL codes.

Table 20-5. SQLCODE Guidelines

SQLCODE	**DESCRIPTION**
SQLCODE = 0, SQLWARN() is blank	Successful statement.
SQLCODE > 0 (but not 100)	Successful with warnings.
SQLCODE = 0, SQLWARN() = 'W'	Successful with warnings.
SQLCODE < 0	Statement Failed.

Table 20-6. Common SQLCODES

SQLCODE	**DESCRIPTION**
000	Successful Execution within your DB2 program.
+100 (SQL State 02000)	Row not found for FETCH, UPDATE or DELETE, or the result of a query is an empty table – Within Program Execution.
+100	Successful SELECT within QMF/SPUFI.
-112	The operand of a column function is another column function.
-501	The cursor identified in a FETCH or CLOSE statement is not open.
-502	The cursor identified in an OPEN statement is already open.
-803	One or more INSERT or UPDATE values are invalid because the object columns are constrained such that no rows of the table can be duplicates with respect to the values of those columns.
-805	DBRM OR PACKAGE NAME location-name.collection-id.dbrm-name.consistency-token NOT FOUND IN PLAN plan-name. REASON reason. Check that the bind of your DB2 program was successful.
-904	Unsuccessful execution caused by an unavailable resource. (This is common in a development environment after loading a table with test data. To correct this issue, a repair job usually needs to be run after the load job is finished.)
-911	The current unit of work has been rolled back due to a deadlock or timeout.

WHENEVER is another keyword that can be used for error handling. It is recommended that this be avoided whenever possible. It is usually safer to code SQLCODE checks and avoid GOTO statements. Here is an example using WHENEVER & GOTO:

```
EXEC SQL
  WHENEVER SQLERROR GOTO sql-error-routine
END-EXEC.
```

Here is another example using specific SQLCODE error checking right after a DELETE statement was attempted:

```
EXEC SQL
IF SQLCODE = +100
  --do something
ELSE
  IF SQLCODE < 0
    --do something else
END-EXEC.
```

Looking Forward

DB2 remains one of the world's most popular and powerful databases. Its smooth interaction with the rest of IBM's products will only help maintain its popularity. At the time of this writing, DB2 UDB V8 has been released, and can run on over 22 platforms including AIX, Linux, OS/2, Numa-Q, HP-UX, Sun, and Windows. Web Services is the emerging architecture for making it easier to integrate Web applications.

A few of the Version 8 enhancements include enhanced SQL and row level security, as well as enlarged limitations on database objects and virtual storage. These enhancements lead to improved scalability, productivity, and portability. All of these factors are essential to withstand the competition in today's market.

Index